Working
towards
the Führer

MANCHESTER
UNIVERSITY PRESS

Working towards the Führer

Essays in honour of
Sir Ian Kershaw

edited by
Anthony McElligott and
Tim Kirk

Manchester University Press
Manchester and New York
distributed exclusively in the USA by Palgrave

Copyright © Manchester University Press 2003

While copyright in the volume as a whole is vested in Manchester University Press, copyright in individual chapters belongs to their respective authors, and no chapter may be reproduced wholly or in part without the express permission in writing of both author and publisher.

Published by Manchester University Press
Oxford Road, Manchester M13 9NR, UK
and Room 400, 175 Fifth Avenue, New York, NY 10010, USA
www.manchesteruniversitypress.co.uk

Distributed exclusively in the USA by
Palgrave, 175 Fifth Avenue, New York,
NY 10010, USA

Distributed exclusively in Canada by
UBC Press, University of British Columbia, 2029 West Mall,
Vancouver, BC, Canada V6T 1Z2

British Library Cataloguing-in-Publication Data
A catalogue record for this book is available from the British Library

Library of Congress Cataloging-in-Publication Data applied for

ISBN 0 7190 6732 4 *hardback*
     0 7190 6733 2 *paperback*

First published 2003

12 11 10 09 08 07 06 05 04 03   10 9 8 7 6 5 4 3 2 1

Typeset in Minion
by Northern Phototypesetting Co. Ltd, Bolton
Printed in Great Britain
by Biddles Ltd, King's Lynn

Contents

List of figures and tables

Figures

Tables

Notes on contributors

Richard Bessel is professor of twentieth-century history at the University of York. He is co-editor of the journal *German History* and a member of the editorial board of *History Today*. Having researched extensively on the social history of Nazism and on the Weimar Republic, he now works on the Soviet occupation zone, the early history of the former German Democratic Republic and, more generally, the emergence of the German people from the violence and trauma of Nazism and war. He is the author of *Germany After the First World War* (Oxford, 1993); and editor of *Fascist Italy and Nazi Germany: Comparisons and Contrasts* (Cambridge, 1996). *Life After Death: Approaches to a Social and Cultural History of Europe During the 1940s*, co-edited with Dirk Schumann, will be published shortly.

Helen Boak is the associate dean (learning and teaching) in the Faculty of Humanities and associate head of the Department of Humanities at Hertfordshire University. She is the author of several seminal essays on women under the Weimar Republic, including: '"Our Last Hope": Women's Votes for Hitler – A Reappraisal', *German Studies Review*, 12 (1989); 'Women in Weimar Politics', *European History Quarterly*, 20 (1990); 'The State as an Employer of Women in the Weimar Republic', in W. R. Lee and E. Rosenhaft (eds), *The State and Social Change in Germany 1880–1980* (1990); and 'National Socialism and Working-Class Women before 1933', in Conan Fischer (ed.), *The Rise of National Socialism and the Working Classes in Weimar Germany* (1996).

John Breuilly, a former chairman of the German History Society, is professor of modern history at the University of Birmingham. Widely recognised as a leading authority on nineteenth-century Germany, he has held a visiting professorship at the University of Hamburg. Recent publications include *Nationalismus und moderner Staat: Deutschland und Europa* (1999) and *Austria, Prussia and Germany 1806–1871* (2002). His current interests are modernisation theory and German history, and a comparative cultural history of urban elites in mid-nineteenth-century Hamburg, Lyon and Manchester.

Pauline Elkes is a senior lecturer in European history at Staffordshire University. She is the founder and co-editor of the *British International History Group Newsletter*. Among her publications are 'Die Political Warfare Executive: Zur geheimdienstlichen Aufklärung des deutschen Widerstandes 1943–1944', in Klaus Müller and David Dilkes (eds), *Grossbritannien und der deutsche Widerstand 1933–1944* (1994) and 'British Planning for Occupational Rule', in *The Proceedings of a Symposium on 'The Cultural Legacy of the British Occupation of Germany'* (1997). More recently she has been working on film documentaries on the Jewish community in north Staffordshire and on the Saharawi humanitarian convoy to the Sahara Desert. She is currently writing a book on the PWE and 'human intelligence'.

Elke Fröhlich is a senior research fellow at the *Institut für Zeitgeschichte*, Munich, where she is co-editor of the *Biographical Sources on Contemporary History* series. She is the world's foremost expert on the diaries of Joseph Goebbels and heads the monumental project *The Diaries of Joseph Goebbels* which has to date published 17 volumes from a planned 33: *Die Tagebücher von Joseph Goebbels. Sämtliche Fragmente* (1987); *Die Tagebücher von Joseph Goebbels*, part 1:*Aufzeichnungen 1923–1941* (1998–); *Die Tagebücher von Joseph Goebbels*, part 2: *Diktate 1941–1945* (1993–). She co-edited six volumes (published over 1977–83) with Martin Broszat and Falk Wiesemann, *Bayern in der NS-Zeit*, and is the author of the seminal study 'Die Herausforderung des Einzelnen: Geschichten über Widerstand und Verfolgung', in Martin Broszat and Elke Fröhlich (eds), *Bayern im Nationalsozialismus* (1987).

Tim Kirk is lecturer in modern history at the University of Newcastle. Among his recent publications are: *Nazism and the Working Class in Austria* (1996 and 2002); and *Opposing Fascism: Community, Authority and Resistance in Europe*, co-edited with Anthony McElligott (1999). He is a founding member of the Research Group in European Urban Culture and has co-edited a number of collections on this subject, including *The City in Central Europe: Culture and Society from 1800 to the Present*, with Malcolm Gee and Jill Steward (1999); and, with Malcolm Gee, *Printed Matters: Printing, Publishing and Urban Culture in Europe in the Modern Period* (2002). He is currently working on a study of the Nazi new order in Europe.

Anthony McElligott holds the Chair of History at the University of Limerick and has been a visiting professor at the universities of Michigan and Hamburg. His publications include: *Contested City: Municipal Politics and the Rise of Nazism in Altona, 1917–1937* (1998); *The German Urban Experience 1900–1945, Modernity and Crisis* (2001); and, as co-editor with Tim Kirk, *Opposing Fascism: Community, Authority and Resistance in Europe* (1999), and with Jordan Goodman and Lara Marks, *Useful Bodies: Humans in the Service of Medical Science in the Twentieth Century* (2003). His *Rethinking the Weimar Republic, State and Society 1916–1936* will be published in 2004. He is co-editor of the journal *Cultural and Social History*.

Hans Mommsen held the chair of modern European history at the Ruhr University of Bochum from 1968 until his retirement in 1996. His distinguished career has included visiting professorships at Harvard University, the University of California at Berkeley, the Hebrew University of Jerusalem and at Georgetown University, Washington; visiting fellowships at the Institute for Advanced Study in Princeton, the *Wissenschaftskolleg*, Berlin, and at St Antony's College, Oxford. In 1999–2000 he was senior Shapiro scholar-in-residence at the Holocaust Memorial Museum in Washington, DC. In numerous articles and essays he has contributed to the scholarly debates on the legacy of National Socialism and on the Holocaust. His most recent publications are: *The Rise and Fall of Weimar Democracy*, (with Manfred Grieger) *Die Geschichte des Volkswagenwerks und seiner Arbeiter im Dritten Reich*; *Von Weimar to Auschwitz: Zur Geschichte Deutschlands in der Weltkriegsepoche* (1999); and *Alternative zu Hitler: Studien zur Geschichte des deutschen Widerstandes* (2000).

Bob Moore is reader in modern history at the University of Sheffield. He has published widely on the Netherlands under the Occupation, and is the author of, *inter alia*, *Refugees from Nazi Germany in the Netherlands 1933–1940* (1986); *Victims and Survivors: The Nazi Persecution of the Jews in the Netherlands 1940–1945* (1997) and the editor of *Resistance in Western Europe* (2000). An internationally acclaimed scholar of the Netherlands during the Second World War, he has held a fellowship in the Department of War Studies, King's College London and is a member of the *Koninklijk Nederlands Historisch Genootschap*. His doctoral thesis was supervised by Ian Kershaw, and, like his supervisor, he is a long-time supporter of Oldham Rugby League Club.

Jeremy Noakes is emeritus professor of history at the University of Exeter and has published extensively on the Weimar Republic, the Nazi Party and Nazi Germany. Among his many distinguished publications are the classic regional study of the organisation, spread and rise to power of Nazism, *The Nazi Party in Lower Saxony, 1921–1933: A Study of National Socialist Organisation* (1971); and a number of edited volumes: *Government, Party and People in Nazi Germany* (1980); with Christopher Andrew, *Intelligence and International Relations 1900–1945* (1987); *The Civilian in War: The Home Front in Europe, Japan and the USA in World War II* (1992) and, with Peter Wende and Jonathan Wright, *Britain and Germany in Europe 1949–1990* (2002), and *Nazism 1919–1945*, vol 4: *The German Home Front in the World War II: A Documentary Reader* (1998). He edited, with Geoffrey Pridham, the three earlier volumes in the series *Nazism 1919–1945: A Documentary Reader* (1983–97).

Nadine Rossol graduated with a first-class degree in modern history and Italian from St Andrews University and is now a government of Ireland scholar and postgraduate student in history at the University of Limerick working on the *Reichskunstwart* and cultural policy during the Weimar Republic. Her essay 'Ordinary Police Work? The Anti-Semitic Policy of Cologne's City and Administrative Police in the Nazi Period' appeared in Gerard Oram (ed.), *Conflict and Legality: Policing Mid-Twentieth Century Europe* (2003).

David Welch is professor of modern European history at the University of Kent, Canterbury, and the director of the Centre for the Study of Propaganda. He has published numerous books on the Third Reich and on propaganda. Among his most notable scholarly works are: *Nazi Propaganda, the Power and the Limitations* (1983); *Propaganda and the German Cinema 1933–1945* (1985, 2001); *The Third Reich: Politics and Propaganda* (1995 and 2002); *Hitler: Profile of a Dictator* (2001) (1998); and *Germany, Propaganda and Total War 1914–1918: The Sins of Ommission* (2000). He is the general editor of Routledge's Sources in History series.

Editors' introduction

Over half a century after the end of the Second World War perspectives on modern European history – and not least popular perceptions of it – are dominated more than ever by the Third Reich. Hitler himself remains the yardstick for all modern dictators, and the Nazis a constant reference-point in public discussion by journalists and politicians of present-day threats to democracy and security. Popular histories of the Third Reich are matched and even exceeded in number by scholarly analyses of all aspects of Nazism, the Second World War and the Holocaust. Immediately after the end of the war, on the other hand, it was in some ways much more difficult to talk and write about these subjects, to disengage from the direct experience of the Nazi regime and the enormity of its crimes. Attempts to explain Nazism in terms of the real politics of a real state were effectively disabled. The instinct to write in terms of moral condemnation and focus on the responsibility of Hitler and the other leading Nazi war criminals for the conspiracy to wage a war of aggression and commit genocide was also convenient for those who wanted to set Nazism apart from normal historical development.[1] The political imperatives of the Cold War further inhibited a proper understanding of the origins and nature of the dictatorship on both sides of the Iron Curtain. Thus the Third Reich was understood as a monolithic system of *totalitarian* rule dominated by Hitler's personal will. In this model of interpretation the Nazi leader and his paladins had hijacked Germany, and the traditional ruling class was displaced and dispossessed of its political birthright.[2] The richer and complex interface between society and regime was ignored entirely, and even those individuals located within the structures of the regime itself had merely decorative parts rather than being agents in their own right.

This rather static perception of the Third Reich remained hardly challenged until the later 1960s. For Martin Broszat and his contemporary Hans Mommsen, it would no longer do to leave the political machinery unexamined. They looked more closely at what exactly Hitler did, how the implementation of policy worked in practice and how the minority of Nazis in the cabinet in 1933 worked with a governing class dominated by conservatives, not only in national, regional and local governments, but in the bureaucracies that supported them. Their path-breaking studies of the civil service and the nature of the 'Hitler State' constituted a challenge to the prevailing theoretical and ideological consensus.[3] Ian Kershaw's intellectual engagement with Hitler and Nazism thus came at a critical turning-point for the historiography of the period, just as the 'totalitarian' model was finally giving way to a more complex understanding of the way dictatorships worked.

Kershaw's first contribution to this changing perspective on Hitler's Germany was a study of the Führer himself. This was to go to the heart of the matter. The study was appropriately named *Der Hitler-Mythos*, and although the figure referred to in the title was the mythologised Hitler of German popular opinion in the 1930s, it was a book that also demythologised the all-powerful demonic, rabble-rousing, Hitler of conventional biographies.[4] The instrumentalist understanding of Hitler as the all-powerful dictator who commanded and was obeyed was replaced by an analysis of 'Hitler'– as distinct from the chancellorship – as a functioning element of the machinery of state. This approach required a rethinking of explanations of the Nazi regime; it also had more general implications for understanding dictatorship as a system of government. Dictatorships do not function by coercion alone, but require a recognition of the importance of some measure of consensus. The starting-point for the construction of Hitler's *Führer* persona was the utopian yearning on the *völkisch* Right for a strong authoritarian leader, who would then become the symbol and figurehead of a regenerated German nation. It was the function of 'Hitler' within the Nazi system to fill this symbolic role, to invite acclamation, mobilise and maintain political support, and thereby assist in the manufacture of popular consensus. If the Nazi Party claimed to be a '*Volkspartei*' transcending the *selfish* sectional interests of the other parties in the Weimar political system, then Hitler – or the Hitler myth – was the fulcrum of the entire project to integrate the various segments of German society into a single *Volksgemeinschaft*. As Kershaw's study showed, Germans who were otherwise sceptical, if not downright hostile, were prepared to suspend their disbelief when making judgements about the Führer himself.

The popularity that set Hitler apart from the other Nazi leaders was founded on a kind of leadership that was defined as 'charismatic' – in the technical sense of the term as it was used by Max Weber. In analysing Hitler's role in the Third Reich in these terms, Kershaw created a space for taking into account popular responses to dictatorship. The guarantee of Hitler's charismatic authority was the widespread acceptance of the 'Hitler myth' as a stable focus amid the shifting, unstable contours of popular opinion in the Third Reich. Hitler's stage managers were alert to this aspect of the relationship between the Führer and his public, and as a result the archives of the Third Reich came to be stuffed with detailed reports on the public mood (*Stimmungsberichte*) from the party and the SD, among others; in addition, the regime's opponents in the social-democratic underground had been compiling their own secret reports since 1934, and publishing them in Prague.[5] It was on the basis of such reports that Kershaw went on to complement his study of popular acclaim in the Third Reich with an incisive analysis of oppositional opinion and dissent in Bavaria.[6] This work, like *The Hitler Myth*, arose out of Kershaw's connection with a larger project on the social history of the Third Reich in Bavaria directed by Martin Broszat at the Institut für Zeitgeschichte in Munich during the 1970s and early 1980s. The nominal remit of the project was 'resistance and persecution in Bavaria from 1933 to 1945', but it also embraced a diverse range of studies by a new generation of historians (among them Elke Fröhlich), employing new methods and perspectives, and in particular the then-innovative approach of 'history from below'.[7]

What the project revealed was a far more complicated and nuanced relationship between regime and people in Bavaria than was suggested by its title. Support and opposition alike were partial, limited and often temporary. Particular social groups in German society, such as industrial workers or even shopkeepers, might one day approve of the Government, in so far as they welcomed full employment or were impressed by the regime's foreign policy triumphs; but the next day they might decry food shortages and rising prices, or express their anxieties about the possibility of another war. Broszat himself pioneered the notion that certain large groups already bound together by shared experience, values, beliefs or aspirations – such as the industrial working class or the Roman Catholic population – were particularly immune (*resistent*) to Nazi ideological penetration.[8] And indeed the regime's own internal sources on popular opinion and morale revealed that the authorities were well aware of the limitations of Nazism's appeal to these latently oppositional sections of society. Moreover, as Kershaw showed in a study of popular responses to the economic problems of 1935, even those groups associated with support for the regime – such as the lower-middle class – were given to 'grumbling' at particular times of crisis.[9] Kershaw thus distinguished between the mundane sphere of everyday life, which was characterised by latent conflict, and the 'consensual sphere' of the extraordinary charismatic politics of Nazism. He attributed the unstable dynamic of the Nazi regime to the relationship between the two, thus opening up an entirely new dimension to understanding the functioning of Nazism in power.[10]

Crises such as that of 1935 provide one focus for examining the role of public opinion on a contentious question. The regime's anti-Semitism was a relatively insignificant issue with the wider German public in 1933, but was increasingly deployed in a targeted fashion by the regime in order to manipulate opinion. A boycott of Jewish businesses instigated in the summer of 1935 was, as Kershaw shows, a way of overcoming social unrest among the urban *Mittelstand*.[11] Lawless attacks on Jews by party members were prompted and manipulated by the *Gauleiters* and local party leaders. Ever mindful of public opinion (both international and domestic), the party leadership was prompted by such actions to intervene in order to regulate the behaviour of the rank and file, so that the undisciplined violence of 1935 was followed by Hitler's announcement of the Law for the Protection of German Blood and Honour at the Nuremberg Party Congress in September of that year. It was a measure that both appeased the restless anti-Semitic foot soldiers of the party and, at the same time, reassured a public that was increasingly alarmed by the disorder.[12]

The anti-Semitic activity of 1935 was still sporadic and regionalised. The initiative had been taken by the Gauleiters, whose action was condoned by the leadership, until it had got out of hand. The *pogrom* of 9 November 1938, however, broke this pattern. It was organised from the centre by Goebbels, and it was nationwide. It was also the first time since the 'national revolution' that the leadership was prepared to involve itself directly in an outburst of open violence. The German public was shocked by the 'night of broken glass' (*Kristallnacht*), but more by the disorder and damage to property than by the overtly violent racism of the Nazis. For by then the Jews had been marginalised and impoverished – effectively depersonalised – by the various supplementary decrees to the Nuremberg laws, and their exclusion from the public consciousness reinforced the indifference to their fate. Public opinion ceased to be an important factor shaping the regime's actions.[13] But that did not mean that radical anti-Semitic initiatives now simply came from above as a consequence of the leadership's euphoria in the wake of some political and, later, military triumph.[14] Kershaw's seminal study of anti-Semitic policies in the Warthegau, published in 1992 (and based on material recently made more easily accessible in the Polish archives), reflects a consistent explanation of the genesis of the Holocaust in terms of responses to crisis from below: the abrasive rivalry between Gauleiter Arthur Greiser and Hans Frank, who ran the *Generalgouvernement*, Kershaw argued, forced a radicalising of measures against the Jews in the absence of a clear policy from above. Both men justified their actions in terms of 'working towards the Führer's will'.[15]

The instability and 'systemlessness' of the regime are central to one of the most important controversies about the nature of the Third Reich and the role of Hitler, and is the one explored in Kershaw's historiographical overview *The Nazi Dictatorship*. For at least a generation of students, the interpretations of the regime were crystallised around the opposing camps of 'intentionalists' and 'structuralists'. As Tim Mason noted, the debate began as a dispute between two schools of 'liberal' historians.[16] On the one hand, conservative historians in the main clung to a Hitler-centric interpretation of the Third Reich, in which the long-formulated plans of the Führer were eventually implemented one way or another. Progressive historians, on the other hand, focused on the uncharted territory of its chaotic political structure, developing a functionalist interpretation of the implementation of policy. The debate became a vehicle for a more extensive exploration of problems of interpretation, not least the definition of the essence of *Nazism*, the primacy of ideology over economics, and explanations of the Holocaust. At the centre, of course, stood the question of whether or not Hitler was 'master in the Third Reich' or a 'weak dictator', formulations derived from the opposing perspectives of Norman Rich and Hans Mommsen.[17] When *The Nazi Dictatorship* first appeared in 1985 this question had been for some years the most acrimonious disagreement between historians of Nazi Germany. As the book was updated students were introduced to new and more topical controversies and perspectives, notably a review of the so-called historians' debate (*Historikerstreit*), which raged in the 1980s, but has since lapsed from public attention and no longer appears in the present edition. Although the treatment of divergent interpretive positions is even-handed, that is not to say that Kershaw has been a bystander in these debates. In fact, the influence of the structuralist school on his own approach is clear from his own work and has been noted by reviewers. While he presents the two cases even-handedly, he also evaluates their relative merits, making clear his own preference as a practising historian.

Alongside Kershaw's research interest in the relationship between regime and society, and in particular between the Führer and the German people, a broader engagement with the history and the historiography of twentieth-century Germany developed, arising from his role as teacher and professional historian. The Modern German History Seminar, organised by Ian Kershaw and John Breuilly in collaboration with the Goethe Institute, attracted a succession of distinguished historians to Manchester University during the early 1980s. The seminar brought together historians with distinctive and often divergent perspectives, and extended the range of historiographical issues with which all its participants engaged. This broader engagement with issues of interpretation has also been reflected in Kershaw's publishing collaborations. Two particular problems that bear on all attempts to understand Nazism are its immediate origins in the 'failure' of the Weimar Republic, and the extent of its similarity to Stalinism.[18] In the case of the former, Kershaw and his collaborators focused on one particular controversy – that of the 'sick' nature of the republic's economy – and the subsidiary questions related to it. Although the controversy continues unresolved, it nevertheless remains a useful starting-point for exploring some of the issues arising from the pre-history of Nazism. The latter project reflects a persistent instinct on the part of historians and their readers alike to liken the Hitler regime to that of Stalin. The originality of Kershaw's collaboration with Moshe Lewin is that, rather than reiterate the familiar 'totalitarian' perspective of the Cold War, it brings together the new perspectives in social history that had characterised work on Nazi Germany since the time of the Bavaria project with similar approaches to the history of Stalinism among historians of the Soviet Union since the 1980s, when the totalitarian thesis had re-emerged, albeit in modified form.[19] Although it was certainly legitimate to compare the two regimes, they 'were *in essence* more unlike than like each other', and it made more sense to see Nazism as a variant of fascism with unique features. In any case, 'totalitarianism' is inadequate as an explanatory model, the argument continued, because it is a descriptive notion, and a shallow one at that, limited to the apparatus of rule.[20]

It was in the context of this comparison of Nazism with Stalinism that Kershaw first explicitly developed the thesis of 'working towards the Führer'. Hitler's leadership style, he argued, was fundamentally different from that of Stalin. The focus of his comparison was the role and nature of leadership in the two dictatorships and the difference between the two leaders in the way they worked (or functioned) within their respective systems of rule: Stalin's insistence on control of every detail of government, which reflected the way he attained and consolidated his power within the system, is contrasted with Hitler's neglect of routine administration. Nor was this neglect deliberate. It was not, as is often supposed, an intentional experiment in 'social Darwinism', designed to ensure the self-selection of the best policies and the strongest leaders: he simply could not afford to be drawn into disputes which would lead to him openly taking sides. Hitler was not merely instinctively *un*-bureaucratic: he was in a very concrete sense *anti*-bureaucratic. The polycratic chaos of the Third Reich was a functional – or rather dysfunctional – consequence of the unrestrained personal authority ('Führer power') on which Hitler insisted, and which undermined the impersonal authority of the legal State.

Hitler's apparently lackadaisical leadership style, Kershaw argued, created a space for those wishing to ingratiate themselves with the Führer by anticipating his wishes and 'working towards' him, in that they were aware of the general objectives of the regime and were able to take their own radical initiatives with those aims broadly in mind. Hitler's persona, his mythical function, acted as a bond which brought together the fissiparous factions within party and regime, and at the same time both prompted and enabled the initiatives of countless individuals whose actions were sanctioned so long as they were within the framework of the leader's redemptive vision for Germany. This stimulated a 'cumulative radicalisation' of policy, generated as often as not from below rather than by the leadership or by Hitler, as functionaries at all levels and in all spheres of activity competed for the Führer's favour, and thereby asserted their own position within the regime.[21]

On one level, then, the notion of 'working towards the Führer' is intended as a literal description of the behaviour of individuals and groups working towards goals set out by Hitler in only the vaguest terms. This is the sense in which it was used by a minor official in 1934: 'anyone who really works towards the Führer along his lines and towards his goal will certainly both now and in the future one day have the finest reward in the form of the sudden legal confirmation of his work'.[22] This applied not only to civil servants in the government administration and to party functionaries, but to public servants and institutions, particularly in welfare and medicine, and to universities and research institutes, whose endeavours and interests had been hitherto constrained or frustrated and which could now be pursued.[23] It included also those who unwittingly worked towards the Führer, Kershaw argues, by taking advantage of the political conditions in the Third Reich and occupied Europe to denounce their neighbours, for example, or to profit from the war and the Nazi new order. It was by 'working towards the Führer' that German doctors moved from sterilisation to euthanasia and experimentation on human subjects, and it was within the logic of this system-less system that conflicts were fought out between individuals and institutions, between – for example – Arthur Greiser and Hans Frank.[24]

The notion of 'working towards the Führer', then, is a metaphor with considerable explanatory force. On a micro-historical level it describes the ways in which initiatives based on a variety of social motivations are located within the dynamic of politics in the Third Reich, as a number of the contributions to this *festschrift* show. On a more general level it serves to explain how the Nazi dictatorship worked, and was one of the principal organising ideas behind Kershaw's approach to the political biography of Hitler.[25] The two-volume work that appeared between 1998 and 2000 represents the culmination of three decades of intellectual engagement with the history of the Third Reich. In almost 2,000 pages Kershaw applied the ideas developed in his earlier writings within the narrative framework of Hitler's life. Yet the biography constitutes much more than a life of Hitler. Martin Broszat commented of his earlier study, *Der Hitler-Mythos*: 'Adolf Hitler stands at the centre of this book. It is nevertheless not a continuation of the long series of new Hitler biographies.'[26] Similarly, the distinctiveness of Kershaw's more recent biography is that in it the Führer's life is the vehicle for explaining the political system of the Third Reich, for demonstrating that there was more to Nazism than Hitler's will. It is a neat trick to colonise the natural territory of the intentionalists with a structuralist biography of Hitler. In this context the concept of 'working towards the Führer' has the virtue of rendering accessible the otherwise very complicated corpus of ideas associated with structuralist approaches to Nazism. This was also demonstrated by the popular success of the television series *The Nazis: A Warning from History*, for which he was the principal historical advisor. Where Kershaw's approach to the history of Nazism and the Third Reich once challenged the prevailing orthodoxy, it now very much sets the agenda, on both a scholarly and a popular level.

Each of the contributions to this volume honouring Ian Kershaw's scholarly career engages, in one way or another, with the themes that have preoccupied him over three decades. They are written by his former postgraduate students (Boak, Elkes, Kirk, McElligott, Moore) and close friends and collaborators (Bessel, Breuilly, Fröhlich, Mommsen, Noakes, Welch), and represent their current interests as scholars whose work has been, in some measure, influenced by Kershaw's contribution to the field of modern German history. Inevitably, the collection covers a wide range of themes, but it makes no claim to be a comprehensive 'history of the Third Reich'. Nevertheless, what unites each of the essays intellectually is concern with the personal, professional and political strategies of those in government and the party 'working towards the Führer', and with popular perception of and responses to Hitler's particular charismatic authority.

Richard Bessel, whose early work on Nazi stormtroopers in eastern Germany during the Weimar Republic, followed by a study of demobilisation after the First World War,[27] established him as one of the leading historians of the period, was a contributor to *Weimar: Why Did Germany Democracy Fail?* His opening contribution to this volume raises again the 'German question' within the framework of a comparison of the defeats of Germany in 1918 and 1945. In this general chapter, Bessel argues that, in contrast to 1945, Germany's acceptance of defeat in 1918 had been ambivalent, creating a climate in which the charismatic appeal of the 'strong leader' could find a resonance. One of the key figures in constructing Hitler as charismatic leader was, of course, Joseph Goebbels. Elke Fröhlich examines a critical moment in the career of Goebbels, and in his relationship with Hitler. Fröhlich, who is the world's foremost historian of Joseph Goebbels and edited the multi-volume diary of Goebbels, was an early collaborator with Kershaw on the Bavaria project.[28] Here, she draws on hitherto little-known sources to document a conflict between Goebbels and Gregor Strasser. The personal rivalry and factional strife that came to be characteristic of the Third Reich is clear even in this early incident; the pattern of 'working towards the Führer' was already established in the senior party hierarchy as early as 1927. Goebbels went on to become the propaganda chief of the Third Reich, and was able to claim in 1941 that he had created the Führer myth, and this is the starting-point for David Welch's discussion of charismatic leadership. Welch, also an early colleague and collaborator of Kershaw and a pioneer in the history of propaganda in the Third Reich,[29] analyses the mythologising of Hitler's public image, and in particular the role that appeals to Germanic mysticism played in binding Führer and people. Welch draws our attention to the irony that by the end of his life Hitler had come to believe in his own propaganda image, and as a consequence found his people wanting. The foundation of Hitler's charismatic authority was laid prior to 1933, when Nazi propaganda still had to compete with that of other political parties. Helen

Boak, Kershaw's first doctoral student at Manchester University and one of the first British historians to work seriously on the Weimar female electorate,[30] examines the relative success of propaganda from a range of political parties in its appeal to women voters. Her contribution examines the nature of Nazi appeals to women as voters within a comparative framework by looking also at Weimar's other political parties and their electoral strategies. Boak concludes that all political parties drew on a common iconography of womanhood and a shared vocabulary of symbols, and that a distinctive approach by the NSDAP was very limited prior to the crisis years of the republic. It was only in 1932, she argues, that the Nazi Party realised the significant role of women as voters in its electoral fortunes and thus made specific appeals to them.

The development of the early Nazi Party (NSDAP) in the 1920s required both propaganda and organisation. Jeremy Noakes, internationally recognised as a foremost historian of Nazism, has engaged in an intellectual dialogue with Ian Kershaw for some three decades. His study of the Gauleiter builds on his earlier work on the history of the NSDAP[31], and shifts the focus of the collection from the construction of image to the political machinery of the party and the regime. Noakes argues that while we know a great deal about a number of Nazi organisations, we still know relatively little about the party's regional leaders. The Gauleiter, possibly more than any other of Hitler's lieutenants, was accorded a high degree of autonomy as a 'viceroy of the Reich' in return for his unquestioning personal loyalty to Hitler. These leaders were able to exploit their proximity to the Führer in order to pursue their own objectives as regional overlords. In this respect, Noakes' study of the Gauleiter provides a good example of how 'working towards the Führer' could also be used to pursue individual and regional ambition.

While it is to be expected that party members, and especially the Gauleiter with his personal relationship with Hitler, would have been at the forefront of 'working towards the Führer', the extent to which senior public servants were prepared to operate within the framework of Nazi objectives is perhaps more surprising. Anthony McElligott's work on the Weimar Republic has already explored some of the continuities between the profoundly anti-democratic attitudes and practices of conservatives and their 'routine compromises' with the Third Reich.[32] Building on an existing interest in the political role of the judiciary,[33] McElligott examines its uneasy role in the Nazi regime. Despite the leadership's intermittent hostility towards the courts, especially where individual judges were not felt to be working *hard* enough towards the Führer, the judiciary as an institution nevertheless accommodated itself to the overall aims of the regime, not least, McElligott argues, because it shared many, if not most, of the ideological precepts underpinning the Third Reich.

The practices that governed the formulation and implementation of policy within the Reich also characterised approaches to governance in occupied

Europe. In his study of the administration of the Netherlands under Nazi rule, Bob Moore examines the working relationship between, on the one hand, Dutch civil servants and, on the other, functionaries from the Reich who brought with them their experiences of working towards the Führer without instructions from above and applied them in the new context of the occupation. Moore, who has established himself as one of the principal authorities on the occupation of the Netherlands,[34] shows how the technocratic objectives of the Dutch bureaucracy converged with the ideological aims of the Nazi occupiers with chilling effect, not unlike the German judiciary. Using the example of a national registration system, the study illuminates the ways in which the strictly functional – and functionally amoral – approach of the bureaucracy was used by the Nazis to pursue their genocidal objective against the Jews.

The implementation of the Führer's will in occupied Europe was located within the broader attempt to create a new political culture constructed on a coincidence of Reich and local interests, and on small mundane acts of complicity and even of enthusiasm. This, it was hoped by many, would underpin and give meaning to a more enduring 'new order', as Tim Kirk shows in his case study of German cultural policy in the Balkans. This project was relatively unproblematical closer to home, as Kirk's earlier work on Austria has demonstrated,[35] but encountered greater scepticism in South-East Europe. Here, the local authoritarian elites were initially prepared to articulate their own aspirations within the framework of a '*Völkerfamilie*', whose common objectives were to be determined by the German '*Führungsvolk*'. As the tide of the war turned, however, it became clear from the regular reports to Vienna from this region that public opinion, even among former collaborators, was turning overwhelmingly against the Reich.

Germany's enemies carefully documented such shifts in public opinion. Pauline Elkes, Kershaw's doctoral student at the University of Sheffield,[36] in her contribution shows how the German Section of the British Political Warfare Executive (PWE) monitored the popular mood within the Reich with the intention of using such information to target volatile groups with propaganda and so undermine civilian morale. The weekly reports she utilises were not unlike the Nazi regime's own internal reports, and evidence a high level of accuracy. The PWE thus discerned the mood swings of Germany's wartime population on the home front. Increasingly, the reports showed a marked deterioration in the public mood. In spite of this evidence, however, the PWE concluded that while positive popular support was fading, there was nevertheless a passive acceptance of the regime. And Churchill's cabinet took this as justification for Roosevelt's 'total surrender' policy: there was thus no basis for working with a latent domestic resistance to Hitler in Germany itself. These findings – erroneous in Elkes's view – shaped both the way the Allies responded to the more resolute resisters of July 1944 and the way they would deal with Germany once hostilities had ended.

A rapprochement between the Allies and the 'bomb plot' conspirators would, however, as Hans Mommsen shows here, have been very problematical in *other* respects. The nature of the resisters' plan for a post-Hitler Germany revealed the extent to which they shared common nationalist objectives with the Führer, if not to the same degree: after all, it had perhaps been easier for the country's elites to work towards the Führer as long as he was already articulating their own ambitions for Germany. The resistance of 1944, as the Allies knew, was a 'resistance without the people' (indeed, in some respects a resistance *against* the people).[37] The resisters, above all Moltke, clung to their belief in a utopian European future, in which Germany would continue to play a leading role. The Casablanca Conference, and the Allies' insistence on unconditional surrender, had, of course rendered that goal impossible long before July 1944.

Hans Mommsen's discussion incorporates many of the themes of the collection, and appropriately so, in so far as they reflect the extent to which he and Ian Kershaw take a common approach to understanding the Third Reich and its place in the history of Germany and Europe in the twentieth century. Mommsen's influence on Kershaw, and Kershaw's own influence on a wider historiography of twentieth-century Europe, extend far beyond the contributions here, and have helped shape the perspectives that inform them.[38] But Kershaw's influence also extends beyond the mere academic. All the contributors to this volume, in particular his former students, have known him over the years as a loyal friend and wise adviser. And in many ways John Breuilly's personal appreciation of Ian that closes this volume speaks for them, too, and resonates with their gratitude.

Notes

1 International Council for Philosophy and Humanistic Studies, *The Third Reich*, Introduction by Jacques Rueff (London, 1955).

2 Karl Dietrich Bracher, *The Nazi Dictatorship: The Origins, Structure and Consequences of National Socialism*, trans. Jean Steinberg, Introduction by Peter Gay (London, 1971).

3 Hans Mommsen, *Beamtentum im Dritten Reich: Mit ausgewählten Quellen zur nationalsozialistischen Beamtenpolitik* (Stuttgart, 1966); Martin Broszat, *Der Staat Hitlers: Grundlegung und Entwicklung seiner inneren Verfassung* (Munich, 1969), trans. John Hiden as *The Hitler State: The Foundation and Development of the Internal structure of the Third Reich* (Harlow, 1981); see also Hans Mommsen, 'National Socialism: Continuity and Change', in Walter Laqueur (ed.), *Fascism: A Reader's Guide. Analyses, Interpretations, Bibliography* (Harmondsworth, 1976), pp. 151–92.

4   Ian Kershaw, *Der Hitler-Mythos: Volksmeinung und Propaganda im Dritten Reich*, Schriftenreihe der Vierteljahrshefte für Zeitgeschichte, 41 (Stuttgart, 1980); English trans. *The Hitler Myth: Image and Reality in the Third Reich* (Oxford, 1987).

5   The SD reports were compiled by the *Sicherheitsdienst* (Security Service) of the SS and have appeared in digested form as *Meldungen aus dem Reich 1938–1945: Die geheimen Lageberichte des Sicherheitsdienstes der SS*, ed. Heinz Boberach (17 vols; Herrsching, 1984). The exiled reports have likewise been collected in a digest and published as *Deutschland-Berichte der Sozialdemokratischen Partei Deutschlands (Sopade), 1934–1940* (7 vols; Salzhausen, 1980).

6   Ian Kershaw, *Popular Opinion and Political Dissent in the Third Reich: Bavaria 1933–1945* (Oxford, 1983).

7   Martin Broszat, Elke Fröhlich and Falk Wiesemann edited vol. 1 and, with Anton Grossmann, also vols 2–4 of *Bayern in der NS-Zeit*, Veröffentlichung im Rahmen des Projekts 'Widerstand und Verfolgung in Bayern 1933–1945' im Auftrag des Bayerischen Staatsministeriums für Unterricht und Kultus bearbeitet vom Institut für Zeitgeschichte in Verbindung mit den Staatlichen Archiven Bayerns (6 vols; Munich and Vienna, 1977–83). A selection of the contents of the six-volume work is published in Martin Broszat and Elke Fröhlich (eds), *Alltag und Widerstand, Bayern im Nationalsozialismsus* (Munich, 1987).

8   Martin Broszat, 'Resistenz und Widerstand: Eine Zwischenbilanz des Forschungs-projekts', in Broszat *et al.* (eds), *Bayern in der NS-Zeit 4* (Munich, 1981), pp. 691–709. An excerpt from this essay has now been published in English: Martin Broszat, '*Resistenz* and Resistance', in Neil Gregor (ed.), *Nazism* (Oxford, 2000), pp. 241–2.

9   Ian Kershaw, *Hitler 1889–1936: Hubris* (Harmondsworth, 1998), p. 507; on work-ing-class responses to the economic crisis of 1935, see Ian Kershaw, 'Social Unrest and the Response of the Nazi Regime', in Francis R. Nicosia and Lawrence D. Stokes (eds), *Germans Against Nazism: Nonconformity, Opposition and Resistance in the Third Reich. Essays in Honor of Peter Hoffmann* (New York and Oxford, 1990), pp. 157–74.

10 Ian Kershaw, 'Alltägliches und Außeralltägliches: Ihre Bedeutung für die Volksmeinung 1933–1939', in Detlev Peukert and Jürgen Reulecke (eds), *Die Reihen fast geschlossen: Beiträge zur Geschichte des Alltags unterm Nationalsozialis-mus* (Wuppertal, 1981), pp. 273–92.

11 *Ibid.*, p. 279.

12 Ian Kershaw, 'The Persecution of the Jews and German Popular Opinion in the Third Reich', *Yearbook of the Leo Baeck Institute*, 26 (1981), pp. 261–89.

13 Ian Kershaw, 'How Effective Was Nazi Propaganda?' in David Welch (ed.), *Nazi Propaganda: The Power and the Limitations* (Kent, 1983), pp. 180–205; and 'German Public Opinion during the Final Solution: Information, Comprehen-sion, Reaction', in Asher Cohen, Joav Gelber and Charlotte Wardi (eds), *Compre-hending the Holocaust: Historical and Literary Research* (Frankfurt, 1988), pp. 145–58.

14 Cf. Hermann Graml, *Antisemitism in the Third Reich* (Oxford, 1992); Christopher Browning, 'Zur Genesis der "Endlösung": Eine Antwort an Martin Broszat',

Vierteljahrshefte für Zeitgeschichte, 29:1 (1981), pp. 97–109; and : *Essays on Launching the Final Solution* (Cambridge, 1992).

15   Ian Kershaw, 'Improvised Genocide? The Emergence of the "Final Solution" in the Warthegau', *Transactions of the Royal Historical Society*, 6th series, 2 (1992), pp. 51–78; see also *idem*, 'Arthur Greiser – Ein Motor der "Endlösung" in Ronald Smelser, Enrico Syring and Rainer Zitelmann (eds), *Die braune Elite 2* (Darmstadt, 1993), pp. 116–27.

16   Tim Mason, 'Intention and Explanation: A Current Controversy about the Interpretation of National Socialism', in Lothar Kettenacker and Gerhard Hirschfeld (eds), *Der 'Führerstaat': Mythos und Realität. Studien zur Struktur und Politik des Dritten Reiches*, trans. as *The 'Führer State': Myth and Reality. Studies on the Structure and Politics of the Third Reich* (Stuttgart, 1981), pp. 23–41.

17   Ian Kershaw, *The Nazi Dictatorship: Problems and Perspectives of Interpretation* (London, 2000), pp. 69–92. The original references are to Norman Rich, *Hitler's War Aims: Ideology, the Nazi State and the Course of Expansion* (2 vols; London, 1992 [1973–74]), p. 11; Hans Mommsen, *Beamtentum im Dritten Reich* (Stuttgart, 1966), p. 98; and 'Nationalsozialismus', in C. D. Hermig (ed.), *Sowjetsystem und demokratische Gesellschaft: Eine vergleichende Enzyklopädie* (7 vols; Freiburg, 1966–72) vol. 4 (1971), column 702.

18   Ian Kershaw (ed.), *Weimar: Why Did German Democracy Fail?* (London, 1990); Ian Kershaw and Moshe Lewin (eds), *Stalinism and Nazism: Dictatorships in Comparison* (Cambridge, 1997).

19   See the articles collected in *Russian Review*, 45:4 (1986), including Geoff Eley, 'History with the Politics Left Out – Again?', pp. 385–94, which discusses the relationship between developments in the historiography of Germany and similar trends in the historiography of the USSR, and *Russian Review*, 46:4 (1987).

20   Ian Kershaw, '"Working towards the Führer": Reflections on the Nature of the Hitler Dictatorship', *Contemporary European History*, 2:2 (1993), pp. 103–18, here 104.

21   *Ibid.*, p. 113; *idem*, '"Cumulative Radicalisation" and the Uniqueness of National Socialism', in Christian Jansen, Lutz Niethammer and Bern Weisbrod (eds), *Von der Aufgabe der Freiheit: Politische Verantwortung und bürgerliche Gesellschaft im 19. und 20. Jahrhundert. Festschrift für Hans Mommsen zum 5. November 1995* (Berlin, 1995), pp. 323–36; the notion originated with Hans Mommsen.

22   Kershaw, 'Working towards the Führer', p. 116. The speaker was Werner Willikens, state secretary in the Food Ministry, first cited in Jeremy Noakes and Geoffrey Pridham (eds), *Nazism 1919–1945: A Documentary Reader*, vol. 2: *State, Economy and Society 1933–1939*, p. 207.

23   Detlev J. K. Peukrt, 'The Genesis of the "Final Solution" from the Spirit of Science', in Thomas Childers and Jane Caplan (eds), *Re-Evaluating the Third Reich* (New York, 1993), pp. 234–52.

24   Kershaw, 'Working towards the Führer', pp. 115–17.

25   Ian Kershaw, *Hitler*, Longman series 'Profiles in Power' (Harlow, 1991), p. 104; *Hitler 1889–1936: Hubris* (Harmondsworth, 1998); and *Hitler 1936–1945: Nemesis* (New York and London, 2000).

26   Martin Broszat, 'Zur Einführung: Probleme der Hitler-Forschung', in Kershaw, *Der Hitler-Mythos*, p. 7.

27   Richard Bessel, *Political Violence and the Rise of Nazism: The Storm Troopers in Eastern Germany 1925–1934* (Yale, 1984); and *Germany After the First World War* (Oxford, 1993).

28   *Die Tagebücher von Joseph Goebbels. Sämtliche Fragmente*, ed. Elke Fröhlich, commissioned by the Institut für Zeitgeschichte and in conjunction with the Bundesarchiv, part 1, *Aufzeichnungen 1924–1941* (4 vols and provisional index; Munich, 1987); *Die Tagebücher von Joseph Goebbels*, ed. Elke Fröhlich, commissioned by the Institut für Zeitgeschichte and with the support of the Russian State Archive Service, part 1: *Aufzeichnungen 1923–1941* (7 of 14 vols, vol. 3, vol. 2–vol. 9 published to date), part 2: *Diktate 1941–1945* (15 vols; Munich, 1993–).

29   David A. Welch, *Nazi Propaganda, the Power and the Limitations* (London, 1983); *Propaganda and the German Cinema 1933–1945* (Oxford, 1985); and *The Third Reich: Politics and Propaganda* (London, 1993).

30   Helen L. Boak, 'The Status of Women in the Weimar Republic', PhD thesis, University of Manchester, 1983; '"Our Last Hope": Women's Votes for Hitler – A Reappraisal', *German Studies Review*, 12 (1989), pp. 289–310; 'Women in Weimar Politics', *European History Quarterly*, 20 (1990), pp. 369–99; and 'National Socialism and Working-Class Women Before 1933', in Conan Fischer (ed), *The Rise of National Socialism and the Working Classes in Weimar Germany* (Oxford, 1996), pp. 163–88.

31   Jeremy Noakes, *The Nazi Party in Lower Saxony 1921–1933* (Oxford, 1971).

32   Anthony McElligott, *Contested City: Municipal Politics and the Rise of Nazism in Altona, 1917–1937* (Ann Arbor, MI, 1998).

33   Anthony McElligott, 'Authority, Control and Class Justice: The Role of the *Sondergerichte* in the Transition from Weimar to the Third Reich', *Criminal Justice History*, 15 (1995), pp. 209–33; and 'Dangerous Communities and Conservative Authority: The Judiciary, Nazis and Rough People, 1932–1933', in Tim Kirk and Anthony McElligott (eds), *Opposing Fascism. Community, Authority and Resistance in Europe* (Cambridge, 1999), pp. 33–47.

34   Bob Moore, *Victims and Survivors: The Nazi Persecution of the Jews in the Netherlands, 1940–1945* (London, 1997).

35   Timothy Kirk, *Nazism and the Working Class in Austria* (Cambridge, 1996).

36   Pauline Elkes, 'The Political Warfare Executive: A Re-Evaluation Based on the Intelligence Work of the German Section', Ph.D thesis, University of Sheffield, 1996.

37   Ian Kershaw, 'Widerstand ohne Volk'.

38   Evan Burr Bukey, *Hitler's Austria: Popular Sentiment in the Nazi Era, 1938–1945* (Chapel Hill, NC, 2000); R. J. B. Bosworth, *The Italian Dictatorship: Problems and Perspectives in the Interpretation of Mussolini and Fascism* (London, 1998).

1

Catastrophe and democracy: the legacy of the world wars in Germany

Richard Bessel

Introduction

In a lecture delivered in Stuttgart in October 1991, shortly after German uni-fication, Fritz Stern referred to a conversation he had had with the French Jewish sociologist Raymond Aron in Berlin in April 1979. Aron, who had stud-ied in Cologne and then Berlin between 1930 and 1933, commented – 'in a somewhat melancholy manner' according to Stern – 'It could have been Ger-many's century' ('Es hätte Deutschlands Jahrhundert sein können'). In 1979 Aron's melancholy seemed justified: Germany still was divided; in the centre of Berlin one still could see ruins left from the Second World War; memories of the National Socialist dictatorship and the war were still too close to be dis-cussed with complete openness. Musing on this comment twelve years later, Stern agreed: 'Aron was right: it could have been Germany's century; at the beginning of the century Germany was the country of dynamic advancement.'[1] However, that great future was not to be; instead, the 'dynamic advancement' of the first half of Germany's twentieth century led to two world wars and two defeats, to Nazi dictatorship, to mass murder and moral depravity on an unparalleled scale, to untold human misery and to the liquidation of German sovereignty. The dynamism at the beginning of the twentieth century pro-pelled Germany down a path not to glory but to catastrophe.

Nevertheless by the end of the twentieth century Germany had emerged as a peaceful, prosperous, and united democracy. The catastrophic history of Germany during the first half of the century not only marked the low point in Europe's tortured path to and through modernity: it formed the prehistory to the remarkable and ultimately successful second half of Germany's twentieth century. The story of Germany's, and Europe's, twentieth century was not just about war, violence, mass murder and destruction: it was about getting out from under the greatest outburst of violence and bloodletting in the history of humanity. Over the past few decades a main preoccupation of historians of modern Germany – with Ian Kershaw most prominent among them – has been to explain the path *into* Nazism and war: How did Hitler capture power?

How did a political system develop which could imprison and murder hundreds of thousands and, finally, millions of the people within its grasp? How did Germany push Europe into a war even more bloody and destructive than the First World War? How was humanity pushed down the road to Treblinka? Rather less thought was given to the questions which, for us and for the world we inhabit, may be even more important: how were the survivors able to emerge from those horrors, and how did this shape the post-war world? We have devoted great attention to how people got into war and Nazism, but only in recent times has similar attention been given to how people got back out.

The remarkable contrast between the two halves of 'Germany's century' stems in large measure from the contrasting legacies of the two world wars, how Germans emerged from violence and war in 1918 and in 1945. The melancholic assessment which may have seemed appropriate during the Cold War also revolved around the legacy of two lost world wars: a first war which had destroyed the stability of the old regime and bourgeois society, and had paved the way for a doomed democracy and vicious dictatorship; and a second war which provided the stage for a descent into barbarism and which led to the destruction of Germany as a sovereign state and a power at the centre of Europe. However, our perspective now is a different one: the post-war era has ended, and Germany is no longer divided as a consequence of the settlement in 1945. Looking at Germany's twentieth century from the perspective of the beginning of the twenty-first, it appears that the First World War brought Germany into catastrophe and that the Second World War allowed Germany to emerge from it, although at the most terrible cost imaginable. How the two world wars could have had such profoundly contrasting outcomes is one of the great underlying themes of 'Germany's century' – a century which ended not with the Red Army at the gates of Auschwitz and on the roof of the Reichstag, but with a democratic, stable and unified Germany within secure borders and at peace with her neighbours.

The legacy of the First World War

The First World War has long been regarded as the great 'civilisation break', which tore apart nineteenth-century Europe and thrust Europeans into the 'colder world of modernity',[2] the catastrophe which sent the Continent spiralling down into its 'age of extremes'. With hindsight, the pre-1914 world appeared to many as peaceful and stable. Looking back during the late 1980s at his childhood before the First World War, Werner Wachsmuth (born in 1900, and from 1946 to 1969 director of the University Hospital in Würzburg) observed:

> The word that best characterises life in the [German] Empire until the assassination in Sarajevo in 1914 is, I dare say, the word 'tranquillity'. It was neither the

calm before the storm nor the calm of idleness, rather it was the feeling of security. Fear like we know today and have known for years, and like that which has gripped the majority of humanity was unknown to us back then. All the more so the news from Sarajevo hit us unexpectedly, like a bolt of lightning from the sky, and at a stroke altered our carefree world.[3]

The history of the newly unified German empire, which had been characterised by relative peace, growing prosperity and apparent political stability, ended in an orgy of destruction which left over 2 million Germans dead, the old imperial system of Prussia–Germany swept away, and a political culture and public sphere poisoned by bitterness, grief, instability, fear, division, militarism and violence.[4]

Germany certainly was a far more violent, less civil, place after 1918 than it had been prior to 1914, and there are considerable grounds for speaking, as George Mosse has done, of a 'brutalisation of German politics' in the wake of the First World War.[5] Politics and public life in Weimar Germany were characterised by the widespread acceptance and glorification of violence, by militaristic behaviour, by an unwillingness to accept the constraints imposed on Germany as a consequence of participation and defeat in the war, and by constant reference to a myth of war experience which reinforced the claims of aggressive nationalism. Yet the crumbling of civility in German civil society was not a product simply of an alleged brutalisation of the more than 10 million men who had fought the war in German uniform, survived and returned to their unhappy *Heimat*; the fact that the overwhelming majority of those men were able to reintegrate relatively smoothly with civil society suggests that other processes helped to poison the atmosphere of post-war Germany.[6] The profoundly damaging legacy of the First World War for Germany consisted of a complicated combination of ingredients.

To understand this legacy, it is worth considering just how peculiar the German experience of the First World War had been. The first point to emphasise is that the First World War was fought almost entirely outside Germany. With the exception of the fighting in south-eastern East Prussia during the first weeks of war, a campaign which left considerable destruction in this relatively thinly settled region in the far north-eastern corner of the Reich, the battles of the First World War did not take place on German soil. At the end of the war there were no German counterparts to the moonscapes of northern France, which, in the words of the geographer Albert Demangeon, had been 'transformed into a desert, a wild steppe', and where in November 1918 the ten northern *départements* contained a civilian population only a little over half that recorded in the census of March 1911.[7] Germany, by contrast, had been left physically intact. Except for the inhabitants of some villages and towns in south-eastern East Prussia and the more than 700,000 people who had fled to Germany after the war from territories ceded to France, Denmark and Poland,

Germans generally had not lost their homes as a result of the conflict. The damage which the war did to the German economy was not immediately visible; the country still looked physically much as it had done prior to 1914.

Second – and this is something which Germany had in common with the other major Western combatant powers of the First World War – almost all the war casualties were military. The numbers of German military casualties were enormous: roughly 2 million killed (1.9 million from the army, almost 35,000 from the navy, and a further 100,000 missing and presumed dead) and over 4.8 million wounded.[8] At the same time, relatively few German (or, for that matter, British or French) civilians died directly as a result of the war. Certainly some civilians died earlier than they might otherwise have done as a consequence of wartime hardships, in particular the lack of sufficient food and heating; women's deaths attributed to tuberculosis and pneumonia rose noticeably (in the case of tuberculosis from 40,043 in 1914 to 66,608 in 1918, in the case of pneumonia from 35,700 in 1914 to 74,468 in 1918); and the influenza epidemic of 1918 claimed the lives of 72,464 men and 102,130 women within Germany in October and November.[9] However, it seems fairly clear that, while their lives were made miserable by shortages of food and fuel, German civilians did not actually starve to death,[10] and the number of additional civilian deaths during the war years, over and above those which would have been expected in peacetime, pales into insignificance when set alongside the enormous military casualties. The fact that the front and the home front were almost completely separate gave Germany's First World War its peculiar character.

With hindsight, it seems that, rather than setting the pattern for a new era of industrial warfare, the startlingly low proportion of civilian deaths during the 1914–1918 conflict was something which neither replicated what had happened in the wars of the past nor would be repeated in the wars yet to come. This peculiar character of the First World War had a number of important consequences. For one thing, it meant that almost all the casualties were young-adult and middle-aged males. The war did not take its deadly toll on all sections of society, but almost exclusively on this particular section of it. For another, it meant that the home front, the *Heimat*, remained largely intact, both physically and socially. Of course, families and communities suffered terribly as a consequence of the deaths of roughly 15 per cent of the 13.5 million men mobilised at some stage for military service;[11] few households were left untouched by the loss of a son, a husband, a father, a brother. In addition to the millions of dead, the war left behind a trail of suffering and dependence, as hundreds of thousands of Germans looked to the State for support as a result of the war: in 1926 there were 792,143 war invalids; 361,024 war widows; 849,087 children who had lost a father in the war; and 62,070 orphans, who were in receipt of state benefit.[12] The war left a country full of widows, orphans, and cripples, and with a demographic imbalance that would remain for decades. Nevertheless the basic physical, social, economic and cultural structures of German communities were left largely intact. Most Germans still lived in their old homes, still worked at their old jobs, and still resided in their old towns and villages, even after the upheavals caused by the 1914–18 conflict.

The fact that so much of Germany's physical and social fabric remained was extremely important for the legacy of the First World War. In particular, it meant that remembering the war, mourning the war-dead and suffering the effects of loss and disability took place in families and communities which for the most part had been left largely in one piece. In this context it could seem possible to return to the happier world of Germany before August 1914, since that world had been shaken but not demolished. German civil society was deeply damaged and deformed, not least by war-related inflation;[13] but in its main outlines it survived – to fight another day. The same can be said of the country as a whole. As Hagen Schulze noted some time ago, in the Introduction to his general history of Weimar Germany, a most remarkable and yet ignored aspect of the Versailles settlement was that 'the German Reich, apart from some adjustments to the borders, survived the World War as a whole at all'.[14] Instead, Germans concentrated their gaze on what they had lost – on the loss of Alsace-Lorraine and, particularly, of territories in eastern Prussia – on the 'bleeding frontier' with Poland and on the alleged injustice of the post-war settlement.[15] Germans could choose to focus on the injustices, hardships and disruptions they perceived, but within a country which essentially had remained in one piece.

The anger and anguish which these hardships and disruptions triggered were immense, all the more so because one still hoped, indeed expected, that things could and should return to 'normal'. Lives and communities had been disrupted, not smashed, leaving Germans desperately concerned to put their world back in order and desperately upset and incensed at the disorder around them.[16] There certainly appeared to be ample justification for anxiety almost everywhere one looked. Particular concern arose over crime. In the wake of the First World War Germany experienced a massive rise in crime, due in part to the deterioration in the power of government to exercise effective control over civil society, in part to the extreme political unrest of the period, in part to the continuing material shortages (especially of food), and in part to the rampant inflation (as Germans did not necessarily conduct their 'flight into real goods' – *Flucht in die Sachwerte* – within the law).[17] The number of criminal convictions, which had fallen sharply during the war, rose rapidly after the soldiers returned, exceeding pre-war figures in 1920 and reaching a peak of nearly half as many again, compared with the 1913 figure, in the hyperinflation year of 1923.[18] Of particular concern were the numbers of women and adolescents convicted – in 1923 these were, respectively, 53 per cent and 59 per cent in excess of the 1913 figures. Of course, this change in the composition of the convicted population reflected to some extent the fact that 2 million young men had not returned from the battlefield to prey on German society after the war, but that is not how people saw it; instead, it provided apparent evidence of a moral universe falling apart.

The high levels of juvenile crime in particular (among youth whose 'sense of authority has been widely undermined'[19]) seemed to prove that, after years when millions of fathers were absent, discipline and with it orderly family life had disintegrated. The 'far-reaching demoralisation and brutalisation' of the young resulted allegedly from the fact that 'respect for parents, teachers, authorities, etc., has declined among young people to a quite terrifying degree', as 'insolent, brutal, and presumptuous behaviour, accompanied by an unbridled pursuit of pleasure, has spread among wide circles of our youth'.[20] Ordered relations between the sexes seemed under threat. Divorce rates during the early 1920s were more than double those of the pre-war years.[21] Despite lack of hard evidence, medical authorities and social services became convinced that they faced an epidemic of venereal disease, as a result (in the words of the socialist eugenicist and secretary of the German Society for the Combating of Venereal Diseases Georg Loewenstein) of the 'devastating effect' of the war 'with its enormous shocks to all bourgeois standards'.[22] Many reacted to the post-war world as did the future chancellor Heinrich Brüning, who, when he returned from the war to Berlin in March 1919 (with its filthy streets as a result of a strike by dustmen), felt that he witnessed a 'picture of complete moral chaos'.[23] Germany seemed to be a country which had gone to the dogs, where (according to a Bavarian report of popular opinion from early 1920) public life was becoming 'almost like an orgy of frivolity . . . under the slogan: after us the deluge'.[24]

The suggestion here is that such expressions of shock and moral outrage were a reflection, paradoxically, as much of the degree to which things remained in place as of the degree to which things had fallen apart. The point is, and this helped to give the moral panic of post-1918 Germany its sharp edge, that Germans still had a great deal to lose. After the First World War the failure to achieve a post-war transition from disorder to order was accompanied by a widespread conviction that this transition could and should have been accomplished, that it should have been possible to resume life in the old grooves. After the Second World War, by contrast, such illusions were impossible to maintain; it was clear that 'the deluge' really had occurred.

A particularly fateful aspect of Germany's flawed post-war transition and of the legacy of the First World War was the continued glorification of things military, of militarism, in a country where the military establishment had been defeated and the armed forces severely restricted. The culture of war lived on, but outlets for channelling that culture were limited. It is this problem, and not just an inability of some veterans of the trenches to readjust to civilian life after the experience and camaraderie of the trenches, which was revealed by the growth of the Freikorps. It is well known that many men who subsequently made a name for themselves in the 'Third Reich' – Reinhard Heydrich, Erich Koch, Manfred von Killinger and Martin Bormann, to name but a few – had made their political debut in Freikorps units. For some veterans of the trenches, being a 'political soldier' in Weimar Germany proved more attractive than settling peacefully into civil society – as, for example, was the case with the Silesian SA leader Edmund Heines, who, from the time he volunteered for war service as a 17-year-old in 1915 until he was murdered along with Ernst Röhm in the 1934 'night of the long knives', lived a life in uniform in a succession of military or paramilitary organisations (at least when he was not in prison).[25] Yet it would be misleading to assume that such biographies were typical. For one thing, the vast majority of the soldiers of the First World War did not dedicate themselves to paramilitary politics after November 1918: most of the 6 million German soldiers demobilised in late 1918 and early 1919 just wanted to go 'home at any price'.[26] For another, there are indications that many of the roughly 250,000 men who joined the Freikorps had not seen military service during the war, but instead were school-leavers looking for their war after the Armistice.[27]

This second point is particularly telling: that young men who had not been compelled to go to war sought to do so in the wake of the 1914–18 conflict. Although the violence of the Freikorps during the early days of the Weimar Republic was definitely a minority pastime, it did presage the widespread interest in paramilitary politics in inter-war Germany – where hundreds of thousands of young men joined paramilitary formations and where, as Wolfram Wette has observed, during the 1920s pacifists became the 'best hated people' in the country.[28] Doubts about the wisdom of military adventures and about a commitment to warlike policies, while perhaps fairly widespread, remained largely a private affair, not the stuff of public posturing.[29] This contrasts sharply with what occurred in Germany after 1945, when pacifism held great attraction and where joining paramilitary organisations was impossible. After 1918, militarism remained alive and well in the wake of military defeat and in the absence of a large military establishment and of conscription; after 1945, the catastrophe of Nazism, total defeat and Allied occupation created a context in which, finally, German militarism was dealt a mortal blow.

The fact that, far from being undermined, militarism emerged after the First World War in an even more virulent strain, had much to do with the divisions which characterised German politics and society during the Weimar Republic. To be sure, those divisions were a product of the collapse of the old regime and the German Revolution of 1918–19, but it was the war which had provided the necessary catalyst for that collapse and revolution. A large proportion of the

German population remained bitterly antagonistic towards the new – republican – Government. The First World War was followed by a veritable civil war within Germany, which left hundreds dead in violent confrontations, domestic military campaigns involving paramilitary formations and revolutionary militias as well as a militarised police force which on occasion acted almost as an army (e.g. in central Germany during the bloodshed of March 1921),[30] coup attempts and their suppression, and frightful campaigns of political assassination which claimed the lives of (among others) a finance minister (Matthias Erzberger), a member (Hugo Haase) of the revolutionary Council of People's Commissars which had assumed governmental responsibility in November 1918, and a foreign minister (Walther Rathenau).[31] German post-war politics became, to a terrifying degree, a politics of hatred, and remained so throughout the Weimar period.

At the same time, the German memory of the First War remained a largely coherent one. That Germany bore no particular guilt for the outbreak of the war, that German armies had stood their ground against a world of enemies and had been undefeated in battle, that Germany had been 'stabbed in the back', that the Versailles Peace Treaty was an unfair, vindictive and crippling settlement imposed on the Reich – these assertions were broadly accepted in Weimar Germany, despite their rather tenuous relationship to historical fact. It was not so much the memory of the war itself that was a matter of dispute, but who owned it. Politicians sought to identify themselves with the soldiers of the First World War, and their service at the front was a matter of pride. Ultimately the most successful in this regard was that former corporal on the Western Front Adolf Hitler, but the degree to which even the Centre Party politician Heinrich Brüning identified with his war service provides a striking contrast with the former *Wehrmacht* officer and, subsequently, Social Democratic Chancellor Helmut Schmidt a generation later. All political parties rejected the Versailles settlement and sought to present themselves as defenders of German interests, and appeals based on the generally accepted myth of the war experience bridged the political spectrum. Almost everyone could agree about the nature of the war which Germany had fought and lost, and on that basis the memory of the war could become a weapon in the vicious disputes which characterised political life in Weimar Germany.

A telling example of how the imagined war could be situated in this political landscape is the shrill complaint of one Walter Kosinsky, a disabled veteran who suffered for years as a result of having lost his teeth in a grenade attack and who directed his 'flaming protest' to the Prussian minister for welfare in October 1931:

> Is that the thanks of the Fatherland, when a 'Welfare Office for War Invalids' today wants to know nothing more about disabilities stemming from war service and

would like to get rid of the victims of the war with remarks of the most insulting nature? We war victims really do not recognise the burden which our welfare signifies for the German economy; we feel ourselves free of guilt, for ultimately no one can reproach us about our willingness to make sacrifices. Also, an enrichment at the expense of the people is far from all our thoughts[. . .]

With glowing devotion I volunteered to help defend my Fatherland. With smashed limbs and a broken body I stand, thirteen years after the end of the War, with the question still on my lips: Will anyone help me, give back my health? Where are the homesteads we were promised? Where is employment, bread, fraternity? Emergency decrees and cuts have increased the misery of numerous families of war victims to a point where they are unbearable. Hands off the rights of the war victims! They have every right to an improvement of their situation![. . .]

Most honoured Herr Minister! I have worked my way through all agencies, from the War Invalids Office to the Main Pensions Office, regarding the fulfilment of my requests. I cannot bear yet another negative reply to my present request. The consequence of that would be a reorientation of my person in a political direction. I would ask Dr. Goebbels and [Wilhelm] Kube [Nazi Party *Gauleiter* in Brandenburg] most cordially to present my pension file to the Reichstag and to help me to my rights.[32]

The remarkable thing about this protest is not so much that its author already was in receipt of a monthly disability pension of RM 57.50 (which was roughly what an employed labourer could hope to earn, at a time when not many labourers were employed), but its political references. Without seeming to draw breath, Kosinsky moved from phrases taken word-for-word from an appeal to the 'conscience of the public' made by the social democratic Reich Association of War Invalids, War Veterans and War Dependants (*Reichsbund der Kriegsbeschädigten, Kriegsteilnehmer und Kriegshinterbliebenen*) at a rally in Stettin during the previous April ('Hands off the rights of the war victims! They have every right to an improvement of their situation!', etc.[33]) to a threat to take his case to two leading Nazi members of the Reichstag. Politicians of almost all persuasions could subscribe to the popularly accepted notion of the war and its consequences; the question was which of them would be able to instrumentalise it most effectively in the bitterly divided political culture of Weimar Germany.

The general point that the Weimar Republic remained hostage to myths about the war has been made forcefully by George Mosse.[34] According to this interpretation, the 'myth of the war experience' was used to legitimate the war (and war in general), and to take the place of the reality of the war experience. Warlike and militaristic politics resonated widely when based on a mythical imagination of the First World War which provided a foundation for irresponsible and unrealistic demands; it was easier to risk a second such war if one remained unwilling to face the harsh and depressing realities of the first. This, in Mosse's view, helped enable the acceptance, indeed glorification, of war despite the horrors which so many Germans (and others) had experienced from 1914 to 1918. It allowed Germans to avoid facing the harsh economic and political realties of a lost war, and to cling to a belief that if only the Versailles *diktat* could be overturned their post-war problems would disappear. The legacy of the First World War for Germans therefore was, first and foremost, one of illusions, illusions which formed the one point of consensus in Weimar politics. This allowed the maintenance of unrealistic expectations that were deeply destructive of democracy, which requires a degree of realism, as well as civility, to function. It was a fatal weakness of Weimar democracy that the one point of political integration was so profoundly corrosive and provided the basis for a widespread acceptance of a politics of hatred – hatred against Versailles, against foreigners, against Jews, against people of different social and economic classes. It was a politics the best and most successful practitioners of which were the Nazis, who in this sick post-war society were able to mobilise hatred to form the greatest and most broadly integrative political movement that Germany and Europe had ever seen.

What was it that allowed this to happen after the First World War but not after the Second? Of course there are many factors which can be cited, but a key point about the aftermath of the First World War in Germany seems to be that, while it created enormous upheaval, much nevertheless was left intact – so that in effect much of the old society was in a position to respond coherently, and destructively, to the advent of the new. The fate of Germany after 1945 was very different.

The legacy of the Second World War

After the Second World War, Germans faced a set of problems which put even those after 1918 in the shade. After the amazing successes of Germany during the second half of the twentieth century, it is possible to lose sight of how daunting those problems were. The huge, overarching challenge was how to build a democratic political system and civil society after the contaminating experience of Nazi dictatorship, in a destitute country with a smashed political and economic infrastructure and a profoundly damaged society, with at least 8 million former members of the Nazi Party,[35] with roughly 12 million Germans who were refugees and another 14 million who also were homeless. The scars left by the Second World War were unimaginably deep. More than twice as many Germans were killed in the Second World War as in the First, including some 600,000 as a consequence of Allied bombing. In 1947, out of 100 German men born in 1924, 23 had been killed in combat, had died or were missing, 2 were still in Soviet captivity, 31 had been seriously wounded and 5 less seriously wounded, and 2 had been rendered incapable of work by illness or accident; only 37 enjoyed full health.[36] The German urban landscape was largely one of rubble. The Nazi regime had managed to achieve total defeat, and the consequences were unavoidable wherever one cared to look.

In striking contrast to what had happened during the First World War, during the 1939–45 conflict millions of Germans encountered deadly and destructive violence *within* Germany. As noted above, during the 1914–18 conflict, the violence of war was experienced for the most part (i.e. with a few exceptions such as the military campaign in East Prussia in 1914) far away, at the front, in foreign countries and in environments different from those at home. During and immediately after the Second World War violence was visited on Germans within Germany in a variety of ways: through the massive Allied bombing, which increased in the last stages of the war (and reached its peak during the early months of 1945); through the terror which the Nazi regime turned on its own population, particularly as the German war effort faltered; through the terrible final battles which took place on German soil during the last months of the war; through the rape, largely but not exclusively by Soviet troops, of hundreds of thousands of German women as the war ended; through other assorted acts of violence (from the stealing of bicycles, watches and farm animals to violent assault and murder) committed by the victorious soldiers who streamed into Germany in 1945; through mass homelessness; through the often brutal expulsion of millions of Germans from their homes because they had had the misfortune of living on the wrong side of the new Oder–Neisse frontier. Scarcely less than for those who had been at the front, for those whose war had been on the home front the violence was not just a matter of abstract imagination: it was real.

First and foremost, this meant that Germans within Germany, as well as soldiers at the front, had witnessed violent death. During the First World War, violent death had been limited largely to the front, far removed from the daily lives of the majority of the German population. During the Second World War it was not just German *soldiers* who were confronted with violent death: so too were the elderly, women and children – children who would come of age in the post-war German states. A few years ago, the historian Konrad Jarausch wrote of his memories of the end of the Second World War as a young child, in a passage which begins with corpses:

> My own memories begin with a derailed train, lying with broken windows in the Landshut station, from which my mother wanted to distract my attention so as to keep me from seeing the dead. Since my father had already died in Russia in 1942, we had been evacuated from our Magdeburg apartment at the cloisters of Our Dear Lady and moved to a farm in Lower Bavaria in order to escape the bombing that would destroy our possessions. I can hardly recall the actual end of the war and only remember that suddenly the Polish labourers were gone, and an emaciated man in a torn uniform appeared, claiming to be my uncle.[37]

Another story, of a young boy who had not had the good fortune to leave
Magdeburg before the war ended, is the account by Manfred Uschner of the
most important formative experience of his childhood. Uschner was born in
1937, 'the first of three children of a poor working-class family in Magdeburg',
and later became personal secretary (*persönlicher Referent*) to SED Politburo
member Hermann Axen. He remained in that position for fourteen years until
his dismissal in February 1989. His wartime experience was, quite literally,
burned into his consciousness:

> As a seven-year-old, together with my sister Hannelore who was three years
> younger, I experienced the heavy Anglo-American bombing attack on Magde-
> burg on the 16th of January [1945]. As we were awakened at 20:45 in great haste
> by grandmother and grandfather and hurriedly dressed, the roofs of the rooms
> and the external walls of the building already were falling in. We found ourselves
> in the middle of a flaming inferno. Running out into the narrow interior court-
> yard (*Hinterhof*), our grandmother was hit by a phosphorous bomb. Only 10 to
> 15 meters away from us she burned before our eyes and ears, screaming, around
> which her loyal Alsatian [German shepherd] was jumping to the last second.
> Grandfather could do nothing, pulled us children through the building's hallway
> into the street and hurried back. In the chaos as the walls of the building collapsed
> I lost my sister, and only found her again in a bomb crater along the iced-over
> Elbe near the Magdeburg Finance Office, in which the glowing red skies were
> reflected. The next day we found our way through burning Magdeburg over
> mountains of burnt corpses. Magdeburg lost around 15,000 citizens that night.
> Only when we had reached the flat of our grandparents on our mother's side on
> the other side of the city was our shock released. Held by the adults, we screamed
> and raged for hours.
>
> This terrible experience burned itself into us for ever. I have never shaken loose
> from it. And it was the reason why I became political, why I asked political ques-
> tions, why I acted in a political way.[38]

This seems not only a (self-)justification for a political career in the German
Democratic Republic and an illustration of how the post-war East German
'anti-fascist–democratic' order attracted support despite its painfully obvious
shortcomings. It also is an example of how the politics and culture of the post-
war era reflected the legacy of the war, and of many people's intense desire (in
both East and West Germany), born of the experience of the violence of the
Second World War, not to see a repeat of a descent into war.

Another important consequence of the terrible visitation of violence on the
German population was that it left many, if not most, with a profound sense of
their own victimhood.[39] To be sure, after the First World War many Germans
had convinced themselves that they had been victims, but this was on a rather
abstract – and politically focused – level; they may have felt hard done by, but
relatively few German civilians themselves had been bombed, made homeless,

raped or expelled from their towns and villages. To be sure, in 1945 Germans were experiencing the sort of thing that their regime had inflicted deliberately on much of the rest of Europe's peoples. However, the fact that Germans shared the misery of other Europeans in 1945 did not mitigate their shock and sense of injustice at what was happening to them; indeed, the catastrophes they faced after the Second World War led many Germans to focus on their own terrible tribulations and to lose sight of what had happened to others, to those who had been on the receiving end of Nazi occupation policies.

The point here is that the nature of Germany's Second World War, particularly in its final stages – and one should not overlook the fact that the last months of the war were by far the most costly in terms of German casualties[40] – led to a widespread sense of victimhood and a turning inwards. The firsthand experience of violence, on the part of civilians as well as soldiers, provided a social and psychological base for the development of post-war East and West German societies for the overwhelming desire for 'security' and for the strength of pacifist and antimilitarist sentiment after the Second World War – among a people, as Michael Geyer has noted, 'not known for harboring antimilitary sentiments'.[41] So much had been destroyed, physically, socially, psychologically; a people desperately seeking stability had to face the most profound instability in both personal and public life. Germans saw themselves as the objects, not the subjects, of their own history: they had been bombed, shot at, raped, thrown out of their homes, occupied by foreign powers. That these experiences were a consequence of the aggression and crimes of a Nazi Government which had enjoyed widespread support may have seemed valid on an abstract plane, but in concrete terms Germans saw themselves as objects, as victims. This was reinforced by the fact that so large a proportion of the people on the receiving end of the violence had been women. The majority of the refugees who moved westwards, ahead of the invading Soviet Army, in the organised *Treks* in 1945 had been women and children,[42] as had the majority of the roughly 10 million Germans evacuated from the cities in order to escape the bombing from 1943 onwards. Precisely those people who, in 'normal' times, are regarded as responsible for creating and maintaining a stable home formed a disproportionate number of the uprooted.

The fate of German women was central to the perceptions and understandings which framed the post-war transition – not least because women formed so large a proportion of the population after the death and capture of millions of soldiers. The German population was overwhelmingly female precisely during those years (1945–48) which Germans regarded as having been the worst of the entire century (worse, indeed, than the war years!).[43] The preponderance of women over men was most extreme in the Soviet zone, where 7,379,546 men and 9,934,188 were counted in October 1946 (i.e. 73,330 fewer men but 2,229,941 more women than on the same territory in May 1939).[44]

Among young adults, not surprisingly, the imbalance was far greater.[45] In the western zones, where (according to 1946 census statistics charting unmarried men and women) those described as marriageable males were outnumbered by the available women by more than two to one,[46] the preponderance of women over men also was striking. The disruption of German women's lives after the Second World War was profound – and of a quite different order than what their mothers had experienced a quarter of a century previously, when many had been widowed though their homes and daily routines had remained largely intact. For millions of women, the prospect of return to a 'normal' life after 1945 seemed remote. Hundreds of thousands had been raped;[47] millions were widowed or had husbands languishing in PoW camps; and millions more were homeless. Altogether, the Second World War left over 1 million widows in Germany.[48] In 1950, of the 15.4 million households in the Federal Republic 3.8 million were headed by women, either on their own (1.7 million) or with dependants (2.1 million).[49] The patterns of private lives had been disrupted by war as never before in modern history.

Alongside the loss of loved ones and the profound disruption of 'normal' family life, probably the most important and enduring consequence for Germans of the Second World War was homelessness. The scale of this homelessness was truly unprecedented and provides a striking contrast with what had happened during the post-1918 period: altogether roughly 26 million Germans – a figure approaching one-third of the entire German population – had lost their homes at the end of the Second World War. The lack of housing cast a shadow over people's lives for years, as millions of Germans were compelled to share poorly heated overcrowded dwellings, in which privacy was conspicuous by its absence. In 1950, there were 900,000 refugees plus more than 1.3 million people in the Federal Republic living in what were described as 'emergency quarters' and in 'accommodation outside of flats'.[50] In that same year, more than two-fifths (41 per cent) of all 'normal dwellings' in the Federal Republic were inhabited by more than one household. No less important than the physical hardship this meant for millions of people was the sense of being uprooted which the loss of one's home, of one's *Heimat*, signified for the individuals involved. A revealing description of what such a loss could mean was offered in June 1995 by Fritz Stern, who had left his native Breslau as a 12-year-old in 1938: 'What does it mean to lose one's *Heimat*? In the first instance it leads to the loss of possessions, of one's livelihood. Yet much deeper lies the human–spiritual loss. *Heimat* signifies safety/security, it also shapes the largely "unconscious self-consciousness" or – to use the modern expression – it shapes identity.'[51] Millions of individuals who had lost their homes and communities needed somehow to reconstruct their sense of themselves after 1945.

The loss and disorientation this signified were felt most acutely by the Germans who had been expelled from their homes and communities to the east of the new Oder–Neisse border as well as from German communities in Czecho-slovakia and South-Eastern Europe. Millions were uprooted and transplanted; in 1950, one-sixth of the entire population of the Federal Republic (roughly 7.9 million people) were refugees, and in the German Democratic Republic the proportion was even higher – roughly one-quarter (4.06 million people).[52] Rainer Schulze has summed up well the social and psychological difficulties they faced:

> In the vast majority of cases, the refugees were not able to settle in established groups with their social networks still intact. Many of the old village communi-ties or neighbourhoods had been torn apart during the flight itself, whilst those that had managed to remain intact were broken up by deliberate Allied policies of redistribution, which were designed to prevent the development of revisionist movements. In consequence, individual refugees lost the social and emotional support of the communities in which they had grown up. Their sense of isolation was intensified by a dispersal and intermingling of the religious denominations: Protestant refugees were frequently settled in predominantly Catholic districts, and Catholics in areas which had previously been exclusively Protestant. Tradi-tional ties and ways of life, as well as a sense of identity, were thus destroyed in a manner which was little short of traumatic for many refugees.[53]

They had lost their old *Heimat* forever and with it the social networks which had sustained them in their daily lives; new social networks, new everyday rhythms, a new sense of themselves, would have to be built in a new and often strange environment.

In particular, the flood of refugees brought social upheaval to the country-side, which during the war largely had not seen the sort of destruction which the Allied bombing brought to German cities.[54] The destruction of the urban housing stock, as well as the largely rural origin of many refugees, made it nec-essary for most of them to be settled in the countryside both in the western occupation zones and in the Soviet zone. The *Länder* which received the great-est proportion of refugees were overwhelmingly rural: Schleswig–Holstein in the west (33.2 per cent of whose population consisted of refugees in 1950) and Mecklenburg in the east (43.3 per cent of whose population consisted of refugees in 1949).[55] The population of some rural areas doubled almost overnight, as for example was the case in the rural district of Demmin (near Greifswald, in the north-east of the Soviet occupation zone), where the popu-lation soared from roughly 53,000 to over 100,000 after the war, despite the fact that the town of Demmin itself had been largely destroyed.[56] Even before the upheaval of expropriation and land redistribution (in the east), this spelled massive social disturbance, particularly in those parts of the country which hitherto appeared largely to have been spared such disruption.

While it is difficult to pin down precisely the effects of flight, homelessness, life in temporary camps (sometimes previously used for prisoners-of-war or wartime forced labourers), and of adapting to a new environment after having lost property, possessions and social networks as well as loved ones, the disorientation clearly was extreme. One refugee from Siebenbürgen (Transylvania) in Romania, who arrived as a 21-year-old in Hamburg in 1945, observed: 'When I came to Hamburg after the war in 1945 I had nothing. No permit to move into the city, no residence permit . . . And in the war back then I was no one, knew no one.'[57] Many refugees thought initially that their stay in the west would be temporary, that they would be able to return home. Gradually, the truth of their predicament became apparent, and they had to undergo a long, slow process of coming to terms with their new environment. The shock of expulsion and the harsh life in spartan reception camps frequently led to a 'refugee neurosis', characterised by exhaustion, apathy, fearfulness and irritability.[58] More generally, what had happened at the war's end created an overwhelming concern to deal with the pressing personal need to build a new home and a new life in a new *Heimat*.

The social upheaval which flowed from millions of Germans moving westwards did not end in the late 1940s. The division of Germany ensured that it continued: between 1950 and August 1961, 3.6 million Germans left the German Democratic Republic for the west (while some 487,000 moved in the other direction).[59] Instability, upheaval, disorientation, migration thus continued to shape the lives and perspectives of a large proportion of the German population. Take, for example, the case of one post-war resident of the city of Celle, in Lower Saxony: he had come from the Baltic, was resettled during the war in the *Wartheland* in occupied Poland, had fled to Thuringia ahead of the advancing Soviet Army and then on to southern Germany (after making various intermediate stops) before he settled in Celle.[60] Such biographies were far from uncommon in post-war Germany; they also served to change the nature of local society. To take an example from Celle once again: a recent article about students at the city's Hermann-Billung-Gymnasium includes a photograph of the graduating class of 1955: eight members of the class had come from either Celle or the surrounding *Landkreis*; another eight came from the GDR or Berlin, and a further six came from east of the Oder–Neisse. Only a minority of the graduating class of the local gymnasium, which may be regarded as representative of the established (and future) bourgeoisie of postwar Celle, had deep roots in the city. The teacher, too, was an outsider: he had come from Thuringia.[61]

While the extent of destruction and disorientation after 1945 was enormous – and far greater than that after 1918 – it was difficult for Germans to find a public focus for responding to the legacy of the Second World War. This can be seen in a number of spheres. One such concerns the sort of militaristic veterans' politics which had plagued Germany after the First World War and which was prohibited after the Second; there would be no reprise of organisations such as the Stahlhelm, whose spokesmen might, as had one regional Stahlhelm leader in 1928, publicly proclaim their hatred for the democratic State.[62] In both East and West Germany, Allied-imposed political systems had determined that German militarism would be prevented from rising again. In the former, the 'anti-fascist–democratic' and then socialist order left no space for nostalgic or irredentist veterans' politics; for those so inclined, there was the prospect of internment in the 'Special Camps' of the Soviet occupation authorities.[63] In the latter, the occupying powers prohibited the payment of military pensions during the 1945–49 period and banned veterans' organisations, leaving no institutional framework around which veterans' politics might coalesce;[64] and when, in 1950, a War Victims' Benefits Law was passed in the Federal Republic, indirectly affecting one-fifth of the West German population, the debates which surrounded its enactment did not call the political system into question.

Another sign of the lack of a public focus for attention to the legacy of the war is the general absence of monuments to the German military dead of 1939–45. The contrast with the aftermath of the First World War is striking.[65] There were a number of obvious and understandable reasons for this, including the Allied directive of May 1946 banning monuments or memorials designed to maintain the German military tradition or to glorify war, the political commitments of the post-war German regimes (particularly of the GDR, which was littered with memorials to Soviet military dead of the Second World War but not to German, and where public commemoration of the Wehrmacht dead was prohibited), and the criminal nature of the regime for which German soldiers had fought between 1939 and 1945. In addition, there were the consequences of the redrawing of Germany's eastern borders: much of the country as it had existed before the war, and many of the places where German soldiers had fallen, lay out of reach to the east of the new border. Altogether, this meant that after the Second World War there were not the public spaces available for presenting and affirming a 'myth of the war experience', to use George Mosse's formulation, as there had been after the First.

The redrawing of Germany's borders, the physical uprooting of a large proportion of the German population, and the division of the country into two hostile states with, from May 1952, a fortified closed border between them, meant that Germans could not easily visit possible sites of mourning. Where can the homeless mourn their losses, and how can they frame their memories, without access to sites of memory and sites of mourning which, at other times, have been accessible to those left behind after war? This problem was compounded by the fact that so large a proportion of the German war-dead were missing – which meant that for a long time those left behind could not be sure that their absent loved ones were still alive. In the mid-1950s roughly one-quarter of West Germans claimed a relative missing in action in the east or still held in a prisoner-of-war camp.[66] This gave rise to peculiar answers to the problem of how one mourns the missing: to cemeteries containing headstones for the missing, to ceremonies in which candles were lit in memory of those of whom there were no remains, to vigils, processions and the burning of beacons in memory of the missing.[67] Well into the 1950s uncertainty remained as to how to mourn the absent dead.

However, the legacy of war after 1945 involved more than dealing with what had happened to others – to the difficulty of finding a focus for the memory of and the mourning of the dead: it also involved the difficulty of dealing with the memory of one's own experience. After the First World War, Germans could locate and represent their own, perhaps ambiguous, actions within a public framework which was unambiguous – of participation in a just war, allegedly forced on Germany, that Germany had fought against a world of enemies; after the Second World War, and the exposure of the monstrous crimes of the Nazi regime, that option was not available. The memory of the Second World War included that of involvement in a monstrous criminal regime, even if many Germans did their best to forget it.[68] This was not a matter just of participation in the major war crimes, of participation in campaigns of deportation and mass murder, but also of day-to-day involvement in the racism, immorality and criminality of the Nazi regime. Millions of Germans had profited from the crimes of the regime. They had enjoyed relatively high wartime standards of living made possible through the brutal exploitation of conquered peoples. They had benefited from racism at the workplace, where the use of millions of foreign labourers in the German war economy created a 'racial' hierarchy of work, and where, as Ulrich Herbert has observed, 'the practice of racism became a daily habit, part of everyday life'.[69] And they profited from the robbery of Jews who had either left Germany stripped of their assets or, from 1941, were sent off to be murdered. In Hamburg, as Frank Bajohr has shown, at least 100,000 German citizens took advantage of public auctions of stolen Jewish property during the years 1941–45 to snap up bargains.[70] The Nazi regime contaminated almost everyone it touched. That contamination too was part of the legacy of Germany's Second World War, and there was no easy and publicly acceptable way to deal with it. Not surprisingly, after 1945 Germans preferred not to dwell on this part of their past. The overwhelming problems which Germans faced in their personal lives – homelessness, the loss of millions of their own loved ones, expulsion from their own homes, economic destitution, the gigantic task of rebuilding the physical environment – made it relatively easy to push the ghosts of their immediate past out of public sight.

In West Germany, it was not until the late 1960s that those who had lived through, and profited from, the 'Third Reich' were really challenged publicly about what they had done between 1933 and 1945. The challenge came from a new generation then coming of age – the generation of those born after the

Second World War, who did not know war and the dirty compromises which their parents had made, and who were raised in a society which, at least from the late 1950s, was largely rebuilt, prosperous and apparently 'normal'. Furthermore, it came at a time when key aspects of the war's legacy were fading from the scene – when the generation of those who had suffered most in both world wars, the people born in the 1880s and 1890s, was passing away, and when the refugees were ceasing to play a significant role as *refugees* in West German public life.[71] To the east of the German–German border, the GDR's official anti-fascist propaganda line, which viewed Nazism as an imposition by capitalist interests rather than as a racist populism with disturbingly broad support, left no public space in which to confront these unwelcome aspects of one's own immediate past.[72] Thus the anti-fascist propaganda line of the East German regime served as a handy cover for avoiding uncomfortable facts about the Nazi past and the legacy of the Second World War, until the post-war era finally ended with the dismantling of the Berlin Wall in 1989.

The quandary confronting Germans after 1945 was one of how to confront the difficult legacy of the Second World War, a legacy which there was no easy way to represent in public and which could not easily be incorporated into some myth of the (Second World) war experience. The response of many Germans to this quandary after 1945 was to concentrate on their private sphere. A popular politics of hatred, built on a public memory of the war, such as had developed during the Weimar Republic, was impossible to develop in the post-war world. The colossal failure and the total defeat of Nazi Germany had delegitimised the old German nationalism; Allied occupation and tutelage, denazification, limited sovereignty and the Cold War circumscribed the political options; within Germany the terrible physical consequences of the war, and the huge task of rebuilding, could not but preoccupy the survivors. Yet while the possibilities for dealing publicly with the legacy of the war were largely circumscribed, an alternative was left open, at least to West Germans – to focus on their overwhelming private concerns. After the worst of the immediate post-war tribulations were behind them, West Germans were able to build something of a 'normality' in the private sphere; tremendous energies were channelled into rebuilding 'normal' family life – a sphere where government policy and popular desires were on the same wavelength;[73] and economic recovery during the 1950s made this possible. In the East, however, the new regime committed itself to a new, Soviet-inspired, political project and drove the population from one upheaval to another. Soviet occupation policies had undermined economic recovery, and Communist politics interfered with a focus on the private concerns which were so important after the horrors of the Second World War, effectively making it difficult if not impossible for Germans in the GDR to seek and to find their little piece of 'normality'. West Germans were able to deal with the legacy of the war privately and largely successfully, while East Germans were not, and millions left their socialist Fatherland to find 'normality' in the west.

Conclusion

The contrast between the ways in which Germans dealt with the legacy, respectively, of the First and the Second World War is profound, and is one of the key themes in the history of twentieth-century Europe. It may seem paradoxical, but the legacy of the Second World War, which was far more destructive than that of the First, ultimately was dealt with rather successfully, while Germany's path after the lesser damage left by the First World War had been one of terrible and ruinous failure. After 1918, when Germans had greater freedom about how to deal publicly with the legacy of the war, Germany never fully emerged from the post-war era. Weimar Germany did not have the time to emerge from the damaging legacy of the First World War, before that legacy contributed to the capture of power by a gang of racist criminals who plunged the world into war once again. After the Second World War, Germans were able to overcome the legacy of war, and to achieve a stable democratic society. This was thanks in large measure to the more profound and far-reaching effects of the upheaval, which forced (West) Germans' back to their private lives and concerns, to the limitations on political expression and room for manoeuvre created by the defeat of the Nazi regime and by foreign military occupation and political division for more than four decades, and to an economic boom which allowed people to rebuild their private sphere and enjoy good times once again.

Germany's twentieth century was framed by catastrophe and democracy. The failure of German democracy and civil society after 1918 and their success after 1945 were due in large measure to the nature of the catastrophes which preceded them, to the contrasting legacies of the two wars and to the ways in which those legacies were dealt with. Now, after more than half a century has passed since Germany was a threat to the civilised world, we can see how catastrophe paved the way for democracy. This is a remarkable success story, but one which came at a terrible cost: the bountiful harvest of the second half of the Germany's twentieth century was fertilised with the bones of the first. It *was*, in the end, 'Germany's century'.

Notes

1   Fritz Stern, *Verspielte Größe: Essays zur deutschen Geschichte des 20. Jahrhunderts* (Munich, 1996), p. 11: 'Die zweite Chance? Deutschland am Anfang und am Ende des Jahrhunderts'. The title of the essay collection, which begins with this lecture, underscores the point: *Verspielte Größe* – 'squandered greatness'.

2 Cora Stephan, 'Der Große Krieg und das kurze Jahrhundert', in Rainer Rother (ed.), *Die letzten Tage der Menschheit: Bilder des Ersten Weltkrieges* (Berlin, 1994), p. 29.

3 Werner Wachsmuth, 'Wir vertrauten einem intakten Staat', in Rudolf Pörtner (ed.), *Kindheit im Kaiserreich: Erinnerungen an vergangene Zeiten* (Munich, 1989), p. 113.

4 On the role of violence in Weimar politics, see Bernd Weisbrod, 'Gewalt in der Politik: Zur politischen Kultur in Deutschland zwischen den beiden Weltkriegen', *Geschichte in Wissenschaft und Unterricht*, 43 (1992), pp. 391–404; Dirk Schumann, *Politische Gewalt in der Weimarer Republik 1918–1933: Kampf um die Straße und Furcht vor dem Bürgerkrieg* (Essen, 2001).

5 George L. Mosse, *Fallen Soldiers: Reshaping the Memory of the World Wars* (New York and Oxford, 1990), pp. 159–81.

6 Richard Bessel, *Germany After the First World War* (Oxford, 1993).

7 Albert Demangeon, *Le Déclin de l'Europe* (Paris, 1920), pp. 33–4, quoted in Hugh Clout, *After the Ruins: Restoring the Countryside of Northern France after the Great War* (Exeter, 1996), p. 3; for the population figures, M. Huber, *La Population de la France pendant la Guerre* (Paris 1931), p. 490, cited in Clout, *After the Ruins*, p. 53.

8 Reichswehrministerium, *Sanitätsbericht über das deutsche Heer (Deutsches Feld- und Besatzungsheer) im Weltkriege, 1914–1918* (Berlin, 1934), vol. 3: *Die Krankenbewegung bei dem Deutschen Feld- und Besatzungsheer*, pp. 12, 31.

9 *Statistisches Jahrbuch für das Deutsche Reich 1924/25* (Berlin, 1925), pp. 44–9; *Statistisches Jahrbuch für das Deutsche Reich 1927* (Berlin, 1927), pp. 38–41.

10 Avner Offer, *The First World War: An Agrarian Interpretation* (Oxford, 1989), pp. 45–53; Bessel, *Germany After the First World War*, pp. 38–40.

11 See Robert Weldon Whalen, *Bitter Wounds: German Victims of the Great War, 1914–1939* (Ithaca, NY, and London, 1984), p. 39; Rudolf Meerwarth, 'Die Entwicklung der Bevölkerung in Deutschland während der Kriegs- und Nachkriegszeit', in Rudolf Meerwarth, Adolf Günther and Waldemar Zimmermann, *Die Einwirkung des Krieges auf die Bevölkerungsentwicklung, Einkommen und Lebenshaltung in Deutschland* (Stuttgart, 1932), pp. 57–64.

12 Whalen, *Bitter Wounds*, pp. 156–7.

13 See Gerald D. Feldman, *The Great Disorder: Politics, Economics and Society in the German Inflation, 1914–1924* (New York, 1993), esp. pp. 513–75; Martin Geyer, *Verkehrte Welt. Revolution, Inflation und Moderne: München 1914–1924* (Göttingen, 1998).

14 Hagen Schulze, *Weimar: Deutschland 1917–1933* (Berlin, 1982), p. 15.

15 See Richard Bessel, 'Eastern Germany as a Structural Problem in the Weimar Republic', *Social History*, 3:2 (1978), pp. 199–218.

16 See the perceptive concluding remarks in Geyer, *Verkehrte Welt*, pp. 397–9.

17 On 'everyday stealing', see *ibid.*, pp. 261–3.

18 *Statistisches Jahrbuch für das Deutsche Reich 1930* (Berlin, 1930), p. 556.

19 Niedersächsisches Hauptstaatsarchiv, Hann. 122a/XI, no. 1031, ff. 22–6: Regierungspräsident to Oberpräsident, Stade, 10 Sept. 1919.

20 *Ibid.*, ff. 33–6: Regierungspräsident to Minister des Innern, Aurich, 18 Sept. 1919; see also Geyer, *Verkehrte Welt*, pp. 70–5, 265–73.

21 *Statistisches Jahrbuch für das Deutsche Reich 1921/22* (Berlin, 1922), p. 48; *Statistisches Jahrbuch für das Deutsche Reich 1924/25* (Berlin, 1925), p. 51. The number of divorces in Germany, which had averaged 15,633 per annum between 1909 and 1913, peaked at 39,216 in 1921.

22 Dr Georg Loewenstein, 'Kritische Bemerkungen und Beiträge zur Statistik der Geschlechtskrankheiten (1910–1921)', offprint of the *Zeitschrift für Bekämpfung der Geschlechtskrankheiten*, 20, pp. 8–12; see also Bessel, *Germany After the First World War*, pp. 233–8.

23 Heinrich Brüning, *Memoiren 1918–1934* (Stuttgart, 1970), p. 44.

24 Archiwum Panstwowe w Poznanie, Rejencja w Pile, no. 92, f. 1: 'N-Bericht vom 8. Januar 1920'.

25 On Heines's career as a soldier and 'political soldier', see Richard Bessel, 'Politische Gewalt und die Krise der Weimarer Republik', in Lutz Niethammer *et al.* (eds), *Bürgerliche Gesellschaft in Deutschland. Historische Einblicke, Fragen, Perspektiven* (Frankfurt am Main, 1990), pp. 391–2.

26 This according to a volume published in 1936 describing the return of the armies from the east; see Forschungsanstalt für Kriegs- und Heeresgeschichte (ed.), *Die Rückführung des Ostheeres (dargestellt aus den Nachkriegskämpfen deutscher Truppen und Freikorps)* (Berlin, 1936), p. 22.

27 For example, from Tilsit it was reported in March 1919 that 'numerous pupils of higher schools' had signed up while former soldiers often tried to disrupt recruitment campaign by the *Ostpreussische Freiwilligenkorps*: see Geheimes Staatsarchiv Berlin-Dahlem, Rep. 12/11a/2, ff. 189–90: The Magistrat to the Oberpräsident in Königsberg, Tilsit, 11 March 1919. In his study of the Freikorps, Hagen Schulze observed that students and school pupils formed an 'essential factor in the ranks of the volunteer units': Hagen Schulze, *Freikorps und Republik 1918–1920* (Boppard am Rhein, 1969), pp. 50–1.

28 Wolfram Wette, 'Ideologien, Propaganda und Innenpolitik als Voraussetzungen der Kriegspolitik des Dritten Reiches', in Militärgeschichtliches Forschungsamt (ed.), *Das Deutsche Reich und der Zweite Weltkrieg*, vol. 1: *Ursachen und Voraussetzungen der deutschen Kriegspolitik* (Stuttgart, 1979), pp. 85–8.

29 This appears true of popular opinion in the early years of the Third Reich as well. That there were widespread misgivings about the implications of the Nazi military build-up is suggested by the worries noted in the reports of the Social Democratic Party in exile following the re-introduction of conscription in March 1935. Reactions were 'very mixed', ranging from enthusiasm among young people and some of their elders who believed that this way 'the youth would finally learn discipline and order again' to fears about a new war and distaste for a new militarisation of daily life; particularly among veterans of the Great War, it was reported, there were veiled comments that 'they are not keen to experience the years 1914–1918 again'. See *Deutschland-Berichte der Sozialdemokratischen Partei Deutschlands (Sopade) 1934–1940, Zweiter Jahrgang 1935* (Frankfurt am Main, 1980), pp. 276–82, 412.

30 See Peter Lessmann, *Die preußische Schutzpolizei in der Weimarer Republik. Streifendienst und Straßenkampf* (Düsseldorf, 1989), pp. 103–19; Schumann, *Politische Gewalt in der Weimarer Republik*, pp. 109–39.

31   See Emil Julius Gumbel, *Vier Jahre politischer Mord* (Berlin–Friedenau, 1922).
32   Archiwum panstwowe w Szczecinie, Oberpräsidium von Pommern, no. 3938: 'Bitte des Kriegsbeschädigten Walter Kosinsky um Zahnersatz und Nachzahlung von Militär-Versorgungsgebührnissen', to Preuss. Minister für Volkswohlfahrt, Stettin, 18 Oct. 1931; discussed in Bessel, *Germany After the First World War*, pp. 279–80.
33   Archiwum panstwowe w Szczecinie, Oberpräsidium von Pommern, no. 3938: Reichsbund der Kriegsbeschädigten, Kriegsteilnehmer und Kriegshinterbliebenen, Gau Pommern, to the Oberpräsident, Stettin, 27 Apr. 1931.
34   See Mosse, *Fallen Soldiers*.
35   Michael H. Kater, *The Nazi Party: A Social Profile of Members and Leaders, 1919–1945* (Oxford, 1983), figure 1, p. 263.
36   'Kirchliche Rundschau', *Nürnberger Evangelisches Gemeindeblatt*, 22 Jan. 1950; cited in Neil Gregor, '"Is He Still Alive, or Long Since Dead?": Loss, Absence and Remembrance in Nuremberg, 1945–1956', *German History*, 21:2 (2003).
37   Konrad H. Jarausch, '1945 and the Continuities of German History: Reflections on Memory, Historiography, and Politics', in Geoffrey J. Giles (ed.), *Stunde Null: The End and the Beginning Fifty Years Ago* (Washington, 1997), p. 11.
38   Manfred Uschner, *Die zweite Etage: Funktionsweise eines Machtapparates* (Berlin, 1993), pp. 28–9.
39   See, for example, Michael L. Hughes, '"Through No Fault of Our Own": West Germans Remember Their War Losses', *German History*, 18:2 (2000), pp. 193–213; Robert G. Moeller, 'War Stories: The Search for a Usable Past in the Federal Republic of Germany', *American Historical Review*, 101 (1996); Robert G. Moeller, *War Stories: The Search for a Usable Past in the Federal Republic of Germany* (Berkeley, Los Angeles and London, 2001); Klaus Naumann (ed.), *Nachkrieg in Deutschland* (Hamburg, 2001).
40   Rüdiger Overmans, *Deutsche militärische Verluste im Zweiten Weltkrieg* (Munich, 1999), pp. 265–6. The majority of German military casualties during the Second World War came in 1944 and 1945, and the number of military casualties in the first five months of 1945 were greater than in 1942 and 1943 put together.
41   Michael Geyer, 'Cold War Angst: The Case of West-German Opposition to Rearmament and Nuclear Weapons', in Hanna Schissler (ed.), *The Miracle Years: A Cultural History of West Germany, 1949–1968* (Princeton, NJ, 2001), p. 376.
42   See Dorothee Wierling, 'Is There an East German Identity? Aspects of a Social History of the Soviet Zone/German Democratic Republic', *Tel Aviver Jahrbuch für deutsche Geschichte*, 19 (1990), p. 195; Dietrich Storbeck, *Soziale Strukturen in Mitteldeutschland* (Berlin, 1964), pp. 219ff.
43   Geyer, 'Cold War Angst', p. 383.
44   That is to say, 57.7 per cent of the population was female (or, put another way, for every 1,000 males there were 1,346 females): see Günther Braun, 'Daten zur demographischen und sozialen Struktur der Bevölkerung', in Martin Broszat and Hermann Weber (eds), *SBZ Handbuch. Staatliche Verwaltungen, Parteien, gesellschaftliche Organisationen und ihre Führungskräfte in der Sowjetischen Besatzungzone Deutschlands 1945–1949* (Munich, 1990), pp. 1070–1.
45   For example, in Saxony at the end of August 1947 31.1 per cent of the total population were adult men, 46.7 per cent were adult women and 22.2 per cent were

children under 14 years of age: see Bundesarchiv Berlin, DO-1-7, no. 268, ff. 24–30: Abteilung Schutzpolizei, 'Auszug aus dem Monatsbericht des Landes Sachsen August 1947', Berlin, 15 Oct. 1947.

46   See Robert G. Moeller, *Protecting Motherhood: Women and the Family in the Politics of Postwar West Germany* (Berkeley and Los Angeles, 1993), p. 27.

47   On rape in 1945, see Erika M. Hoerning, 'Frauen als Kriegsbeute. Der Zwei-Fronten-Krieg. Beispiele aus Berlin', in Lutz Niethammer and Alexander von Platow (eds), *'Wir kriegen jetzt andere Zeiten'. Auf der Suche nach der Erfahrungen des Volkes in nachfaschistischen Ländern* (Berlin and Bonn, 1985), pp. 327–46; Helke Sander and Barbara John (eds), *BeFreier und Befreite. Krieg, Vergewaltigungen, Kinder* (Berlin, 1992); Atina Grossmann, 'A Question of Silence: The Rape of German Women by Occupation Soldiers', in Robert G. Moeller (ed.), *West Germany under Construction. Politics, Society, and Culture in the Adenauer Era* (Ann Arbor, MI, 1997), pp. 33–52; Norman M. Naimark, *The Russians in Germany. A History of the Soviet Zone of Occupation, 1945–1949* (Cambridge, MA, 1995), pp. 69–140.

48   Elizabeth D. Heineman, *What Difference Does a Husband Make? Women and Marital Status in Nazi and Postwar Germany* (Berkeley, Los Angeles and London, 1999), p. 51. In addition, it should not be forgotten that there were nearly eight times as many German parents who had lost a child during the war as there were women who had lost a husband. This points to the peculiar and tragic position of the generation of Germans born during the 1890s: the generation which suffered the greatest casualties of the First World War and, in so far as they survived the 1914–18 conflict, were the parents of the dead and the missing of the Second World War. That was the generation which suffered intense loss in both world wars, which experienced upheaval, disorientation and trauma as perhaps did no other. See Gregor, '"Is He Alive, or Long Since Dead?"'.

49   Statistisches Bundesamt, *Die Frau im wirtschaftlichen und sozialen Leben der Bundesrepublik* (Wiesbaden, 1956), pp. 4, 6–7, cited in Moeller, *Protecting Motherhood*, p. 32.

50   Wolfgang Benz (ed.), *Deutschland unter alliierter Besatzung 1945–1949/55* (Berlin, 1999), p. 126.

51   Stern, *Verspielte Größe*, p. 285 ('Verlorene Heimat', lecture delivered on 1 June 1995 in Berlin).

52   Benz (ed.), *Deutschland unter alliierter Besatzung*, p. 124. Only about 370,000 of the refugees went to Austria, which is one of the most important, but often overlooked, differences between Austria and the other two successor states of the 'Third Reich'.

53   Rainer Schulze, 'Growing Discontent: Relations between Native and Refugee Populations in a Rural District in Western Germany After the Second World War', *German History*, 7:3 (1989), pp. 334–5.

54   There were exceptions to this: in particular, many rural communities and small towns in Brandenburg suffered enormous physical destruction in the final battles of the war.

55   Benz (ed.), *Deutschland unter alliierter Besatzung*, p. 125; Schulze, 'Growing Discontent', pp. 332–4.

56   There the *Landrat* estimated that 'roughly 70 per cent of the town ... lay in rubble

and ashes' at the war's end; the Soviet commandant banned the refugees from settling in the town, and they consequently were 'distributed among the villages': see
Mecklenburgisches Landeshauptarchiv, Schwerin, Kreistag/Rat des Kreises
Demmin, no. 46, fascs 62–4: (Der Landrat des Kreises Demmin) to the Präsident
des Landes Mecklenburg-Vorpommern (Demmin), 21 Nov. 1945.

57　Quoted in Albrecht Lehmann, *Im Fremden ungewollt zuhaus: Flüchtlinge und Vertriebene in Westdeutschland 1945–1990* (Munich, 1991), p. 42.

58　Benz (ed.), *Deutschland unter alliierter Besatzung*, p. 126.

59　*Ibid.*, p. 128. In addition – and this often is forgotten – roughly 800,000 West Germans emigrated between 1950 and 1960, three-quarters of them to the USA: see
Axel Schildt, *Moderne Zeiten: Freizeit, Massenmedien und 'Zeitgeist' in der Bundesrepublik der 50er Jahre* (Hamburg, 1995), p. 49.

60　Wolfram Lietz, 'Im Schmeltztiegel der höheren Schule. Wie Abiturienten aus dem
Osten über ihren Heimatverlust und ihre Integration in Celle dachten. Eine
Untersuchung an Bildungsgängen der 1950er Jahre aus dem Hermann-Billung-
Gymnasium Celle', in Rainer Schulze (ed.), *Zwischen Heimat und Zuhause:
Deutsche Flüchtlinge und Vertriebene in (West-)Deutschland 1945–2000* (Osna-
brück, 2002), p. 77.

61　Lietz, 'Im Schmeltztiegel der höheren Schule'.

62　See Volker R. Berghahn, *Der Stahlhelm, Bund der Frontsoldaten 1918–1935* (Düsseldorf, 1966), p. 113.

63　On the 'Special Camps', see Alexander von Platow (ed.), *Sowjetische Speziallager in
Deutschland 1945 bis 1990* (Berlin, 1998), vol. 1: *Studien und Berichte*.

64　See James M. Diehl, *The Thanks of the Fatherland: German Veterans after the
Second World War* (Chapel Hill, NC, and London, 1993); James M. Diehl, 'Change
and Continuity in the Treatment of the German *Kriegsopfer*', in Moeller (ed.), *West
Germany under Construction*, pp. 98–108.

65　See Sabine Behrenbeck, *Der Kult um die toten Helden: Nationalsozialistische
Mythen, Riten und Symbole 1923–1945* (Vierow bei Greifswald, 1996); Sabine
Behrenbeck, 'Between Pain and Silence. Remembering the Victims of Violence in
East and West Germany after 1949', in Richard Bessel and Dirk Schumann (eds),
*Life after Death: Approaches to a Cultural and Social History of Europe during the
1940s and 1950s* (Cambridge, 2003), pp. 37–64.

66　This (27 per cent) was the finding of an opinion poll conducted in 1955: see
Robert Moeller, '"The Last Soldiers of the Great War" and Tales of Family Reunion
in the Federal Republic of Germany', *Signs: Journal of Women in Culture and Society*, 24:1 (1998), pp. 129–45, here 130.

67　Gregor, '"Is He Alive, or Long Since Dead?"'; see also Alf Lüdtke, 'Histories of
Mourning: Flowers and Stones for the War Dead, Confusion for the Living –
Vignettes from East and West Germany', in Gerald Sider and Gavin Smith (eds),
Between History and Histories: The Making of Silences and Commemorations
(Toronto, Buffalo and London, 1997), pp. 149–79.

68　On the political history of the far-reaching campaign during the early years of the
Federal Republic to draw the line on the prosecution of crimes committed under
the Nazi regime, see Norbert Frei, *Vergangenheitspolitik: Die Anfänge der Bundesrepublik und die NS-Vergangenheit* (Munich, 1996).

69   Ulrich Herbert, *Hitler's Foreign Workers: Enforced Foreign Labor in Germany Under the Third Reich* (Cambridge, 1997), p. 396; see also Ulrich Herbert, 'Apartheid nebenan': Erinnerungen an die Fremdarbeiter im Ruhrgebiet', in Lutz Niethammer (ed.), *'Die Jahre weiß man nicht, wo man die heute hinsetzen soll': Faschismus-Erfahrungen im Ruhrgebiet* (Berlin and Bonn, 1983), pp. 233–66.

70   Frank Bajohr, *'Arisierung' in Hamburg: Die Verdrängung der jüdischen Unternehmer 1933–45* (Hamburg, 1997), pp. 331–8.

71   It is worth noting in this context that the Federal Ministry for Expellees, Refugees and War Invalids was dissolved in 1969.

72   See Olaf Groehler, 'Antifaschismus – vom Umgang mit einem Begriff', in Ulrich Herbert and Olaf Groehler, *Zweierlei Bewältigung: Vier Beiträge über den Umgang mit der NS-Vergangenheit in den beiden deutschen Staaten* (Hamburg, 1992), pp. 29–40.

73   On this, see especially Moeller, *Protecting Motherhood*.

2

Hitler–Goebbels–Straßer: a war of deputies, as seen through the Goebbels diaries, 1926–27*

Elke Fröhlich

In the Preface to his masterly study *Hitler*,[1] which has been widely read both within and outside of the international scholarly community, and in his many interviews Ian Kershaw has stressed that a key documentary source for the biography of Adolf Hitler, in addition to Hitler's own speeches and writings,[2] is the diary of Joseph Goebbels.[3] Unlike his many predecessors as biographers of Hitler,[4] who were able to avail themselves of only a small number of fragments,[5] Ian Kershaw has had access to large sections of Goebbels' diary,[6] which – given that Hitler's own archival records are, for various reasons, rather limited – he rates as an absolutely indispensable source.[7] Certainly, no other personal records from the inner circle of the National Socialist ruling clique rival the Goebbels diaries in scope or significance.

The diaries furnish Kershaw with, among other things, a diversity of data for his 'working towards the Führer' thesis which has aroused considerable interest in reviews[8] and in other books.[9] To take one example from many, he cites the diary in support of his argument that a variety of forms of working toward the Führer were in play during the phase of anti-Semitic radicalisation that began in April 1938 and culminated in the *pogrom* of November 1938.[10]

While writing the two volumes of his Hitler biography Kershaw had at his disposal, in addition to the four volumes of fragments from the years 1924–41, published in 1987, the fifteen typed volumes of Goebbels' diary dating from July 1941 to April 1945 and four handwritten volumes of the diary (from August 1938 to July 1941). He did not, however, have access to ten handwritten volumes and part-volumes (seven currently still in preparation and three meanwhile published) of the diary from the period between 1923 and 1938, which have since become available in complete form and which, in part, contain previously quite unknown notes on whole years or half-year periods.

Like the twenty-two volumes from March 1936 to April 1945 that have so far been published, with their 11,200 printed pages of pure diary text, the seven volumes that have not yet appeared are likely to provide further revealing details, shed new light on events that have already been widely described and analysed, such as the so-called Röhm *putsch*, or seizure of power, and give startling insights into the personality of the diarist himself, especially during the period before he came into contact with National Socialism. In what follows I single out a small portion of these unpublished diaries dealing with the early period of National Socialist efforts at usurpation in the Berlin *Gauleitung* (regional leadership), examining it from a mono-causal point of view to see whether it furnishes evidence for Kershaw's thesis, referred to above.

It should be borne in mind that this huge source rapidly became fragmented and that different parts of it found their way to a number of different countries. Discovering and publishing it has therefore been the work of decades (and sections of it still remain incomplete). For example, despite the extensive search for the remaining parts of the diary that has been conducted over the past twenty years, a fragment turned up in Paris in 2002, roughly fifty-five years after the first discovery of a diary fragment by a waste-paper dealer in Berlin (it ended up in the USA). It will be useful, therefore, to begin by devoting a few words to the extraordinary story of the provenance of the source and its evaluation.

The provenance[11] and publication history of the diary of Goebbels

It is known that Joseph Goebbels kept a diary between 23 October 1923 and 9 April 1945, consisting of 6,783 pages written in his own hand in 23 black oilcloth notebooks (German Standards Institute A5) and of approximately 36,000 dictated type-written folios (German Standards Institute A4, each containing only 14 lines in large type); of the latter, 34,906 folios are known to have survived and have been published. At the end of the war the diary existed in three different forms: the original handwritten entries in the twenty-three notebooks; the original first typescript drafts of the dictated entries, and the second drafts, scarcely distinguishable from them; and microfiches of the entire diary on film-coated glass plates, commissioned by Goebbels. Apart from a relatively small original batch of 500 folios from the years 1942–43, which remained in the German Federal Republic and were acquired by the Institute for Contemporary History (Institut für Zeitgeschichte) in Munich in 1961, all the other original materials fell into the hands of the occupying powers, the USA, the USSR and France. They therefore remained closed to scholars for decades and came into the public domain only in piecemeal fashion, as they were discovered.

A portion of the diary has been published in almost every decade of the past seventy years. In 1934 Goebbels himself published his own edited version of his daily notes on the takeover of government between January 1932 and March 1933.[12] This edition went through forty-two printings (totalling 700,000 copies) during the ten years that followed. The next publications of the diary all occurred after Goebbels's suicide, again in a piecemeal manner (each covering only a few months) and on the basis of paper originals. In 1948 Louis P. Lochner published a selection from the original papers for the years 1942–43, held at the Hoover Institution on War, Revolution and Peace at Stanford University.[13] The Hoover Institution also holds the handwritten original diary for the months between August 1925 and October 1926, which was published in 1960.[14]

Whereas the parts of the diary that were held in America were made available to researchers comparatively quickly, the authorities in the Soviet Union chose to keep back the material in their possession. Nevertheless, like their opposite numbers in the German Democratic Republic, they were prepared to exploit the worldwide interest in the diary both on financial grounds, because they hoped to reap substantial foreign-currency earnings, and for a political reason, because they believed that the diary might help stoke up a neo-Nazi movement within the Federal Republic. They microfilmed a portion of the glass plates held in Moscow, deposited the parent film in the State Archival Administration in East Berlin and arranged for a copy of the microfilm and a few duplicate glass plates to be transferred via an intermediary to the West, where the extensive fragments – which, despite conspicuous omissions, touched on every important event in National Socialist history – caused a sensation. The publishers Hoffmann & Campe bought the entire microfilm copy in 1972, but in 1977 published little more than the entries for the month of March 1945.[15] In 1980 the publishers gave the film to the Federal Archive, then in Koblenz, and the Institute for Contemporary History in Munich, under whose auspices all the diary fragments were published in 1987.[16] The fact that this edition was based, essentially, on microfilm materials, which had originated in the Communist east, persuaded many observers to doubt the source's authenticity. Nevertheless, a considerable body of circumstantial evidence, as well as script comparisons and content analyses, strongly suggested that it was genuine.

The situation eased only when nine military officers' trunks containing Goebbels' diary for the years 1941–45 were located in the documentation archive in East Berlin and subjected to analysis and assessment.[17] At last, paper originals had been discovered which were, in part, identical to those that had been recorded on the Moscow microfilm and which conformed in style to, and helped complement, those held in the Hoover Institution. Proof of authenticity had eventually been achieved. All the same, despite this wealth of newfound material, only a very limited reconstitution of the diary was still possible, since this partial source was in an altogether dismal condition: split up into pieces, and damaged by both fire and water. This was unpromising enough from the editorial point of view, but the situation was made more irksome because there was now a veritable scramble for Goebbbels's diary among competing academics, publishers and journalists. Matters were resolved only in 1992, when the glass plates dramatically turned up in the so-called Central State Special Archive in Moscow. This set of glass plates, equivalent to original documents, finally paved the way for the complete edition of the diary of Joseph Goebbels , twenty-two volumes of which are now available.

Although the new-found glass plates definitively complemented the hand-written volumes, with regard to the typewritten portions the editor was unable to locate roughly 120 glass plates, for the whereabouts of which neither the relevant archivists in the General Directorate of the Russian State Archive Service nor contacts in the Secret Service and the Foreign Ministry of the Russian Federation were able to account. Nor, for that matter, were any of those officials able to explain why the large collection of glass plates had now suddenly become available. On the other hand, what was firmly established as a result of locating the source was confirmation of the finding of the original notebooks by Yelena Rzhevskaya (German transliteration: Jelena Rshewskaja).[18] She had discovered some of the black noteooks in Hitler's bunker in 1945, identified them as Goebbels's diary and written a report on them. For decades it had been thought that they were lost. In 1992, after protracted negotiations with the Russian Foreign Ministry, I was able to inspect all of the thirteen diaries held in Moscow. Yelena Rzhevskaya had found no glass plates in 1945, nor did she know of the existence of any.

Richard Otte, a senior civil servant in the Reich Ministry of Public Information and Propaganda and Goebbels's personal secretary, said in 1981 that he was ordered by Goebbels to microcopy his diary onto glass plate negatives and that when this job (which took more than three months) was completed, in mid-April 1945, he packed the plates into boxes and placed them in a military officer's trunk which was then secured with steel bands and buried, in his presence, in a small wood between Caputh and Michendorf, south of Potsdam. Otte professed ignorance of whether or not this trunk had later been excavated.[19] Confronted with the microfiches that were among the rolls of film transferred from the Communist east, he insisted in successive interviews that they could not have been made from glass plates. Already by 1987 the obvious inconsistency in his position – on the one hand, his testimony that the glass plates had been buried and, on the other, his claim that it was quite impossible that the Soviets had found them – aroused the suspicion that he himself had played a part in their excavation, but that the matter had passed out of his control, with the result that he no longer wished to be associated with it. To the man whose discretion had earned him the nickname Reich Bearer of Secrets, nothing could have been more painful than the charge that he had revealed the whereabouts of the diary's volumes to the Communists, the arch-enemies of the boss to whom he had solemnly promised, on 22 April 1945, that he would take care of the diary volumes posthumously in his capacity as trustee.[20]

In fact, as early as 1954 the British had established[21] that a former official of the Reich Propaganda Ministry had offered to act as an informant to the French information service at the beginning of 1946. The French by no means regarded the notion of the notorious propaganda minister's buried diary volumes as a flight of fantasy, but in order to initiate the excavation they in turn had to inform the Soviets, since the alleged burial site lay within the Soviet zone of occupation. The Russians, no less fascinated by the prospect of finding the diary of Hitler's close confidant, immediately granted permission for a search to take place but with the proviso that the search party be made up of both French and Russians and under Soviet command. On 25 March 1946, at the spot near the small town of Michendorf described by Richard Otte, this search party recovered a padlocked metal chest in which they found seventy-seven boxes each containing roughly a dozen glass plates: that is, a total of 900–1,000 glass plates.[22] The latest extended research efforts by the Russian General Directorate and the archival administration of the French Foreign Ministry, whose help I have recently requested, confirm that this account of the burial of the glass plates is broadly correct.

During 1948 the French read and photocopied approximately half of the glass plates – 120 glass plates, or the contents of ten boxes were, according to British findings, transported from Berlin to Paris, where they were said to be stored in the archives in the Quai d'Orsay under the custody of a M. Outry.[23] According to recent French investigations, however, in 1948 the head of the French delegation to the Allied Committee handed over to the head of the Archival Mission of the French Foreign Ministry in Berlin only four boxes.[24] A visit to the archive of the French Foreign Ministry revealed that one of the four boxes (the only ones extant, with the shelf-marks 1, 2, 3 and 9) in fact contains nineteen well-preserved glass plates onto which Goebbels's diary for the summer of 1941 had been photocopied. This discovery of glass plates in Paris, fifty-five years after they had been excavated and ten years after the discovery of glass plates in Moscow, deserves to be called sensational.[25] There are no indications in the archive of the Quai d'Orsay concerning the whereabouts of the missing five boxes with the shelf-marks 4–8. If the glass plates that had been contained in these boxes were also photocopies of Goebbels's diary, which is very probable, their discovery would supply the final piece in the jigsaw of provenance.

It should be emphasised that if Goebbels's diary is eventually to be fully reconstituted, this will be done on the basis of surviving glass plates equivalent to the originals, not on that of the original papers. Even among the 23 handwritten volumes, 9 of the originals have yet to be located, although the texts are secure thanks to the survival of the glass plates.

In what follows, a small part of these materials is referred to in support of the thesis that Goebbels – first unknowingly and later consciously – was carrying out Hitler's private wishes when, acting out of rivalry and rancour, he challenged the power and influence of the Straßer brothers because they seemed to pose a threat to the leader; later, having consistently sought to restrain them, he would go on to help destroy them.[26]

Gauleiter Goebbels in accord with the Straßers

On 16 September 1926 Hitler appointed Gregor Straßer Reich director of propaganda; on 28 October 1926 he appointed Joseph Goebbels as Gauleiter (*Gauführer*, as the post was at first called) of Berlin. For each man the appointment was an important career move within the early Nationalsozialistische Deutsche Arbeiter Partei (NSDAP), though the promotions were not of equal significance. Gregor Straßer possessed incomparably more power and prestige in the Reich as a whole, both as a member of the old guard (the *alte Kämpfer*) who had taken part in the Hitler *putsch* and, specifically, through his position in the capital, where, together with his brother Otto, he dominated the National Socialist press with the publications of his Kampfverlag (Combat Press). A figure like Joseph Goebbels, a recent recruit to the party, who served Straßer as the humble editor of the latter's *Nationalsozialistische Briefe*[27] (National Socialist Letters) and who had been weakened, in the eyes of many party comrades, by his ambivalent behaviour at the Bamberg conference, was scarcely likely to appear to pose a danger. Indeed, apart from some occasional minor disagreements, the two at first worked together in complete harmony and mutual confidence.

In the summer of 1926 they were fully in accord when, at party headquarters, on Gregor Straßer's suggestion the idea was aired that Goebbels might be put in charge, initially for a provisional four months, of reorganising the NSDAP in Berlin, which had become hopelessly split.[28] In the course of a power struggle within the Berlin NSDAP, two main competing groups had emerged: the SA squads under the leadership of Kurt Daluege, who were mainly engaged in activity on the streets, preferably in the form of brawls with the Communists; and the groups around the Straßer brothers, which sought to win supporters through argument. Even after the *Gauleiter* Dr Ernst Schlange, a senior civil servant unable to impose his will, was granted leave on 20 June 1926 and replaced by his deputy Erich Schmiedicke, the feud between the SA and the Political Organisation continued, since both men were seen as Straßer supporters. The dispute escalated at the leadership meeting on 25 August 1926, when Daluege tried to secure the appointment of Heinz Oskar Hauenstein, the former leader of the Schlageter Frontbann group, as the next Gauleiter. Otto Straßer flew into a rage and slapped the hero in the face. The two factions within the Berlin NSDAP, which was weak enough in any case, became completely paralysed, and their self-lacerating behaviour threatened to deprive them of any remaining appeal.[29]

Goebbels hesitated for some time,[30] but finally decided to accept the Berlin post after Otto Straßer used the first Mark (Brandenburg) Freedom Day in Potsdam to court him. On 9 October 1926 Goebbels was met at the railway station in Berlin by Dr Straßer himself and was driven via the Avus circuit to Potsdam, where he was given an effusive reception. The next day there was a fairly large rally and march-past at the Brandenburg Gate, in the presence of the Straßer brothers, culminating in a speech by Goebbels to party comrades at the Berlin airship port. What probably persuaded him to plump for Berlin was his realisation, on 12 October, that an end had to be put to the plottings of the Straßers' adversary, Hauenstein: 'I am now determined to take over Berlin and run it. That's that!' (*GT*, 16 October 1926).[31] Goebbels intention was to create order in the Berlin *Gau* as the Straßers' man: quite plainly, he had succumbed to Dr Straßer's blandishments. The two men – each the possessor of a university doctorate – spent the evening together. They went on to make a whole night of it, in the company of Hans Steiger, a contributor to the *Berliner Abendzeitung* (of which Otto Straßer was the editor), and Erich Schmiedicke,[32] the acting-Gauleiter of Berlin – both Nazis close to Straßer. For the time remaining until the departure of Goebbels's train, Straßer again kept him company, on that occasion alone. In his enthusiasm, Goebbels declared that during those two hours they had become friends. The Straßer brothers fondly concluded that in Goebbels they had an ally who would loyally fight on their side and not compete with them in the metropolis. On 17 October Goebbels confirmed that he had decided to go to Berlin. In the final analysis, he, too, believed that Berlin was the centre that had to be conquered, however hopeless the task might appear.

Before leaving for the 'stone desert', as he termed Berlin (his aversion was very much in keeping with the *Zeitgeist*), Goebbels first travelled to Munich to discuss with Hitler the modalities of his new role, particularly in light of a new full-scale row that had meanwhile broken out in the Berlin NSDAP over, *inter alia*, a pistol challenge by Dr Straßer and the salary that Goebbels would receive as Gauführer. His comment on the situtation was both laconic and characteristic: 'I am to play the Saviour there' (*GT*, 1 November 1926). As so often, Goebbels took a colloquial expression, in this case 'den wilden Mann spielen', translatable roughly as 'play the villain', and gave it a twist. Here his words suggest that he was going to Berlin on behalf of his God, Hitler, in order to play the role of the saviour Christ, the son of God, and sacrifice himself to redeem the sins of the world – the world in this instance being represented by the 'cesspool of sin', as Goebbels habitually described Berlin. This image, the fruit of his strict Roman Catholic upbringing, was complemented a week later by a metaphor from Greek mythology, when he depicted himself as Hercules, summoned to cleanse the Augean stables of the Berlin NSDAP. Secularised Christianity and classical humanism were the twin intellectual foundations of his overblown belief that he was destined to serve at his leader's right hand.[33]

After Goebbels had been in Munich a few days, Hitler gave his approval to everything in respect of Berlin (*GT*, 6 November 1926). In concrete terms, Goebbels had obtained special permission to reorganise the party and purge it politically, without needing to call in the Munich Committee of Inquiry and Conciliation of the NSDAP, as laid down by party regulations. On the morning of 9 November 1926, one of the most symbol-laden days in National Socialist history, and indeed in German history altogether, Goebbels arrived in Berlin[34] to assume his post as Gauleiter, a position he was to retain until the demise of the National Socialist regime. On the same day he gave his first speech in his new capacity, at the memorial ceremony of the *Deutscher Frauenorden* (German Order of Women). He met Helene Bechstein, the wife of the famous piano manufacturer and one of Hitler's earliest female patrons, who was very nice to him, inviting him to lunch the next day.[35] When he arrived at the house, he found that Hitler, his 'boss' as he then still called him, was already present. After the meal Hitler told him[36] about the march to the Feldherrenhalle that had taken place exactly three years earlier. It seems that the story did not fail to make the desired impression. The very next day, still spellbound, Goebbels wrote respectfully: 'He is a creative man, with a claim to historical stature' (*GT*, 11 Novemner 1926). In this frame of mind he spent the evening working on a speech that he hoped would play an important part in the reorganisation of the Berlin *Gau* by bringing an end to the quarrelling and the decline in membership that had marked the party's recent history.

The next day Goebbels had lunch with the second most important man in the movement, Gregor Straßer. His impressions were very favourable, and he expressed his firm conviction that the two of them would become closer still in Berlin. If Gregor Straßer had been trying to influence Goebbels for his own ends, he was too late: the speech, for the crucial general members meeting in Spandau the same evening, was already completed. As Goebbels noted, he began it in fighting spirit and was victorious right across the board (*GT*, 12 November 1926), in other words, over Hauenstein and his supporters.[37] Anyone who continued the running battles between the Straßer–Schmiedicke and Daluege–Hauenstein camps was threatened with summary expulsion from the party. The Straßers would have had cause to be satisfied with this first contribution of Goebbels. In the meanwhile, however, Goebbels had dictated his first circulars and *Gau* orders, in which he not only confirmed Daluege in his position as SA leader but appointed him as his deputy. Immediately after this he again had lunch with Gregor Straßer, who either was unaware that Goebbels had installed an anti-Straßer figure as his deputy or did not especially regard the appointment as a threat. Straßer would seem to have signalled his assent because, had he not, it is unlikely that Goebbels would have ended his summing-up of the meeting with an expression of sympathy for the burly Lower Bavarian: 'Good, honest Gregor. I am fond of him' (*GT*, 12 November 1926).

On the afternoon of 14 November 1926, after a march through Neukölln which ended with Goebbels's people being badly beaten up by the Communists (he counted 4 men seriously hurt and 14 with light injuries), Goebbels was visited by Hitler. The Führer was accompanied by Emil Maurice, one of the first stormtroopers and, since the time of their imprisonment together in Landsberg, a member of Hitler's closest entourage. Also present were a friend of Goebbels, the caricaturist Hans Herbert Schweitzer (Mjölnir), his newly appointed deputy Kurt Daluege and the latter's sworn enemy Otto Straßer. The men sat together until late in the evening, thrown into raptures by Adolf Hitler. Hitler seems to have been touchingly kind to Goebbels in particular, the diary recording the childlike confession: 'I like him from the bottom of my heart' (*GT*, 15 November 1926). Although Goebbels was busy with a number of activities, he found time the following day to get Otto Straßer to report to him a lot of news from Elberfeld, where he had recently served as one of the three Gauführers of the Ruhr *Großgau* (*GT*, 15 and 18 November 1926). This again implies that, from Goebbels's point of view, his relationship with the Straßer brothers was still untroubled.

Goebbels's attack on Gregor and Otto Straßer: an instinctive working towards the Führer

According to the diary, the ceaseless daily round of speeches, memorial ceremonies, brawls at meetings, visits to the injured, and so forth, for all that they brought him to beseech God's help (*GT*, 18 November 1926), gave Goebbels profound satisfaction.[38] These self-styled successes (*GT*, 18 and 21 November 1926), largely brutish and bloody street battles with the Communists, strengthened him in his revolutionary resolve and made him less tolerant of people who, in his view, were lacking in radicalism. Gregor Straßer noticed this when Goebbels, after returning from a one-week speaking tour (he had also encountered Hitler in Essen, where the two had discussed organisational and policy matters), attacked him from a more leftward position. On 30 November 1926, clearly still in the grip of the fascination that Hitler was to exert over him for the rest of his life, and invested with the authority of a man to whom the 'boss' had granted as many as six audiences in four weeks, he gave 'fat old Gregor' a dressing-down that flew in the face of their actual relative status. Straßer, after all, was not only Reich director of propaganda and, as such, the superior of all Gauleiters in the area of propaganda, but the publisher of the *Nationalsozialistische Briefe* for which Goebbels wrote articles. The diary contains a disparaging judgement on Gregor Straßer couched in revolutionary language: 'Again, I really gave him what for. Deep down, Gregor Straßer[39] is a Bavarian petty bourgeois (*ein bajuvarischer Spießer*), not a revolutionary, not an ascetic, not a new man (*kein neuer Mensch*). Enough said!' (*GT*, 1 December 1926). Goebbels had previously used such contemptuous tones only about those he was preparing to drive from office.[40] His verdict that Gregor Straßer was 'not a new man'[41] was particularly damning, since in Goebbels's scheme of things it was only through new men that redemption and salvation were to be achieved.

Shortly after the speaking tour to Dessau and Weimar the first adverse comment is found on Dr Otto Straßer, with whom Goebbels had discussed the tactics they should adopt towards Hauenstein: 'I don't like Dr Straßer very much. There is a lot about him that is decayed and rotten. He has no feeling for asceticism. In this respect, incidentally, he is like his brother Gregor. I oughtn't to waste so much time worrying about him' (*GT*, 8 December 1926). Conscious of his newly gained proximity to power, he believed he would be able to mount an attack on Otto Straßer. In truth, the sun of Hitler's favour was shining on him. On the evening of 8 December he was travelling again, this time to Munich, where the next day he made a brilliant speech to a packed Hackerkeller. Following the speech Hitler, with Rudolf Heß and Emil Maurice, joined him and thereafter Hitler and Goebbels spent half the night chatting alone in the best of humour, fortified only by water. The following day Heß took Goebbels to Elsa Bruckmann's salon; in view of the prominent place in society occupied by the publisher's wife, Goebbels rightly took the invitation to be a mark of distinction. Afterwards at a small restaurant he had lunch with Hitler and the Bechsteins, and Hitler presented him with the first copy of the second volume of *Mein Kampf*,[42] an even greater mark of distinction, which inspired Goebbels to write in his diary: 'I sometimes want to shout for joy' (*GT*, 12 December 1926).

Thanks to a series of victories and successes (*GT*, 26 January 1927), his permanent irritation with the Straßers (*GT*, 17, 18 and 30 December 1926; 22 January 1927) briefly receded into the background. But by mid-February 1927 he could scarcely contain any longer his bloodthirsty rage against Otto Straßer.[43] He demanded a meeting with Hitler to clarify the situation, vowing that his future career within the National Socialist movement would be dependent on the outcome of the discussion.

Goebbels travelled to Munich on 23 February 1927, and Hitler collected him from his hotel the next day. Together they went to Hitler's apartment, where Hitler first reprimanded him for the anti-parliamentary article he had published at the beginning of the month, which had been harshly critical of Wilhelm Frick.[44] Goebbels, as he himself put it, readily 'swallowed' the rebuke, having already suspected that the article would land him in trouble.[45] 'Then suddenly Hitler stood up, reached out both hands and, as the tears ... came to his eyes, said, in so many words: "You're quite right! I took a fancy to you the first time I heard you laugh!"' (*GT*, 25 February 1927). And now they were friends, Goebbels concluded euphorically, receptive to the homoerotic overtones. Afterwards they were joined by others, including Ernst Count zu Reventlow, a leading figure in the Freedom Party[46] who had also been fiercely attacked by Goebbels in the same article, Erich Koch, district leader in the Ruhr *Gau*, and Franz Stöhr, a National Socialist deputy in the Reichstag, all of whom maintained the best of relations with the Straßers. Goebbels was not daunted by the make-up of the group. Confident of his Führer's affections, and oblivious of tactical niceties, he voiced his misgivings about the Straßers, whereupon, he wrote, 'Hitler amid tears, confessed his worries on the subject and there and then, set [me] above all the others' (*GT*, 25 February 1927). The effect of this on the Straßerites may have escaped the blissful protégé. Further proofs of Hitler's favour followed, into the late evening hours; then lunch together, a trip to the *Caféhaus* in the afternoon, dinner at a restaurant with Hitler and others, an Italian puppet theatre at the Volkstheater, and a final hour at the Fürstenhof before it was time to part. Not satisfied with having given him so many hours of his company, Hitler paid Goebbels a special honour by instructing Max Amann, already a successful and powerful publisher, to fulfill his literary ambitions. Soon after getting back to Berlin Goebbels entered into detailed discussions with Amann, who agreed to publish Goebbels's new book, *Wege ins Dritte Reich* ('Paths to the Third Reich')[47] – a decision that was calculated to give Goebbels particular satisfaction, as he regarded himself as first and foremost a writer. As well as arranging a new car (a seven-seater Opel), Amann declared himself willing to provide Goebbels with suitable financial support. Finally, Goebbels was offered the post of editor of the *Nationalsozialistische Monatshefte*, a journal that was to begin publication on 1 April (*GT*, 26 February 1927). This last was a 'Greek gift'. Admittedly, nothing in the diary indicates that Goebbels knew the project was originally the brainchild of Gregor Straßer, who had wanted to launch it with Oswald Spengler; although the plan had foundered in 1925, Gregor Straßer had never abandoned the idea.[48] Nevertheless, if he assumed the editorship, Goebbels would be bound to come into conflict with Straßer. He could certainly regard Hitler's many attentions as a reward for the work he had done in consolidating the Berlin NSDAP, but this offer would be a real test both of his willingness to take risks and of his loyalty to Hitler. It would show how ready he was to do battle with the Straßers on their own ground.

The fact that Goebbels, still wholly under Hitler's spell, had not yet addressed these questions is clearly shown by his reaction, two weeks later, when – to his surprise, as he stressed (*GT*, 8 March 1927), he was officially offered the post of editor of the *Nationsozialistische Monatshefte* by the party leadership. Only then did he assess the situation more realistically. Simultaneously overjoyed and filled with consternation, he wondered what Gregor Straßer, the editor of the *Nationalsozialistische Briefe*, and Paul Schmitz, its treasurer, would be likely to say.[49] The following day Goebbels – quite uncharacteristically – referred to the offer again, adding that from 1 July onwards the *Monatshefte* would be published in Munich by Adolf Hitler himself. Although this bait – the opportunity of working for the 'boss' in person – was of course even more tempting, he reacted cautiously and his emotions wavered between joy and fear. His dread of plots and his anxiety that he might become completely isolated within the National Socialist movement were entirely warranted.[50] Goebbels had nothing to gain from an overt literary antagonism with Straßer. Hitler, on the other hand, had everything to gain, if his two leading lights in the north were caught in a debilitating stand-off. The combatants would become yet more dependent on him, as the only person who could arbitrate between them.

A week later Goebbels had a crucial discussion with – what he described as – a very depressed Gregor Straßer, in the course of which Goebbels decided that it would be a mistake to embark on a fight with him (*GT*, 15 March 1927). He was fighting battles on many other fronts as it was, and the brawls at meetings and on the streets, the house searches, the raids, the shootings and the interrogations were all putting a strain on his nerves.[51] On the other hand, his trust that God would grant him success seemed to remain intact.[52]

Meanwhile, the quarrel between Goebbels and Dr Straßer was becoming ever more pronounced. Goebbels wrote of Straßer as having been a destroyer from the start (*GT*, 12 April 1927). Straßer reportedly wrote him an impertinent letter, but then, according to the diary (*GT*, 13 and 14 April 1927), performed a climb-down. Nevertheless, Goebbels seems to have been quite worried, as he now evidently began to look for an ally. He found one in the SA chief Kurt Daluege, who was indebted to him for his post as Goebbels's deputy and was beholden to him in other ways. It is not surprising, therefore, that on 15 April the two men reached complete agreement[53] (confirmed on 27 April) that Dr Straßer had to be removed. They did so on the firm assumption that they would have Hitler on their side. Goebbels's use of the verb *bekakeln*, a north German word denoting unconstrained discussion among intimates, alone indicates as much. The Bechsteins, with whom Goebbels was then on close social terms, also backed him in his antipathy to Straßer.[54] His self-confidence bolstered again, on 21 April Goebbels travelled by car to Hanover, where he gave a speech in the evening, and the next day travelled on to Essen, where the Ruhr *Gau* party rally was to take place in the presence of Hitler on Saturday and Sunday 23–24 April. When Goebbels arrived in Essen on the Saturday afternoon he must already have heard about the article on the consequences of the mixing of races that had been published earlier that day in Gregor Straßer's *Berliner Abendzeitung*. The ostensible subject of this article (which also appeared in other journals published by the Kampfverlag) was the malice and lies of Voltaire and the opportunism of the club-footed Talleyrand: in reality, its unmistakable target was Goebbels. Erich Koch, the Straßer supporter mentioned above, signed the contribution. Goebbels's response in his diary shows, however, that he suspected the Straßers of being the real authors. Enraged, he noted: 'The swine have published two vile essays [against] me in their rag. The bastards are in for it all right' (*GT*, 27 April 1927). That evening Goebbels spoke at a workers' meeting, while Straßer officially opened the *Gau* party rally. On the Sunday morning the speakers in the Essen Stadtbausaal were the Reichstag deputy von Reventlow, followed by Goebbels, while Straßer was the final speaker in the afternoon: a further confirmation of their relative status.

Shortly afterwards Hitler summoned Goebbels to his hotel room, where he gave him the opportunity to vent his fury with Straßer. Goebbels bluntly voiced his suspicion that the Straßers were behind the campaign against him, as Erich Koch, having the intellect of a minor railway official, would have been incapable of writing an article of this kind.[55] He gained the firm sense that Hitler shared his antipathy towards Dr Otto Straßer and would resolve the rivalry between them in Berlin in Goebbels's favour.[56] The meeting, interrupted only by the speech that Hitler had to deliver before more than 10,000 party comrades in the exhibition halls,[57] continued into the evening, and the diary claims that Hitler confessed frankly that Goebbels was one of the very few who was dear to his heart (*GT*, 27 April 1927). Previous professions of amity – part-and-parcel of the rituals of affection in these circles – had perhaps had a more cordial ring, but the next day, Monday 25 April, Goebbels also spent, along others, in full harmony with Hitler, so that he could look forward with apparently justified hope to Sunday 1 May, when Hitler would speak, at Goebbels's invitation, at the Clou nightclub in Berlin.

Hitler's arrival was planned for Friday 29 April 1927 (*GT*, 27 April1927). Goebbels looked forward ardently to the moment,[58] but he had to wait until Sunday 1 May before seeing him, and even then no private words were exchanged. There was no contact the following day either. Hitler went to see Reventlow, while Goebbels demonstratively went out into the country: he had no desire to join the crowd of toadies around the leader. Finally, on 3 May, he spent the whole day with Hitler always, of course, in the presence of other people whom he omits to identify, and was also with him over lunchtime on 4 May. But again no discussion about Straßer materialised (*GT*, 4 May 1927). Hitler's calculated withdrawal of favour clearly indicated, among other things, that he was disappointed by the meagre success of his appearance in Berlin.[59] Instead, as previously on 24 and 25 February, Goebbels had a long conversation with Amann, although this time nothing was said about publishing matters. Rather than discuss the editing of the *Monatshefte*, Amann chose to tell him about mischievous plottings (*GT*, 4 May 1927) surrounding the journal.

Nor were any financial promises made on this occasion: Goebbels was left to hope that the long talk which Amann, not Goebbels himself, was due to have with the 'boss' that evening would go a good way towards clarifying the situation.

At a large gathering at the *Kriegervereinshaus* (War Veterans' Hall) that same evening, Goebbels, disappointed by Hitler's behaviour, gave vent to his feelings about the press, complaining that the newspapers had shown almost no interest in Hitler's visit and that the few regional papers which did report it had been disdainful. A priest, Friedrich Stucke, was thrown out of the hall after some heckling, Goebbels's supporters administering the usual brutal beating. According to the diary, everyone had a whale of a time, but the outcome, twenty-four hours later on 5 May, was that the party was banned and the Gauleiter prohibited from speaking in public. In the view of many at the time, this seemed to set the seal on the failure of Goebbels's mission in the capital.[60] Hitler, though, did not share this view. Staying on in Berlin, the two had a long talk on 5 May and Hitler, knowing only too well from his own experience the harmful effects of a ban on party and speaking activities, reassured Goebbels that he would prevail. A battle-weary and depressed Gauleiter in the capital of the Reich was no use to the leader.

On 6 May Goebbels left Berlin for Stuttgart and, like Hitler himself, spoke there the next day at the *Gau* rally of the NSDAP.[61] In the evening he sought out Hitler in Dingelacker's Hall, where the meeting had just closed amid a howling din. According to the diary, the boss listened to his long report on the position in Berlin and fully supported him (*GT*, 11 May 1927). The following day, 8 May, each had a gruelling programme. In the morning they both spoke at the same meeting: first Goebbels, who, judging from the furious noise in the press, had overnight become a famous man for the Nazis (*GT*, 11 May 1927), and then Hitler. After the march by the SA, Hitler and the Gauleiters, Goebbels and Eugen Munder, spoke in front of the Altes Schloß. The day ended with a meal together and a trip to the theatre. Although the National Socialists had suffered a catastrophic political setback, Goebbels experienced some sense of satisfaction: he had received strong backing from Hitler and was certain that he was on the right path.[62]

This encouraged him not only to persevere with his brutal methods of agitation but to forge new plans. Among the latter was an ambitious project to launch his own newspaper in Berlin. This would enable him to pursue several goals at once. First, as a weapon of agitation a newspaper would be the best way for him to get around the ban on speaking and party activity. Second, as an incidental benefit, he would be able to inflict cold-blooded retaliation on Gregor Straßer, who had now dispensed with his services on the *National-sozialistische Briefe*.[63] Third, and most important, by establishing his own newspaper he would be attacking the Straßers at their most sensitive spot: at this time the Straßers' Kampfverlag constituted a comparatively large publishing force in the National Socialist world, particularly in northern Germany, producing several newspapers with a combined circulation of 7,826 copies.[64] That said, the Kampfverlag was also in competition with the Eher Verlag, which was under Hitler's influence and published the *Völkischer Beobachter*, the main organ of the NSDAP. The *Völkischer Beobachter* had begun appearing in a nationwide edition in February 1927 and, following complications, would be published in Berlin from 1930 onwards. Plainly, Goebbels did not stop to wonder whether the establishment of a weekly newspaper, with an initial print run of 2,000 copies, would interfere with Hitler's long-term plans, perhaps even damage them. He apparently foresaw no problems at all, convinced that all his financial and journalistic worries would be resolved by Hitler in Munich (*GT*, 10, 24 and 26 May 1927).

On the last weekend in May Goebbels arrived in Munich, evidently in possession of a firm appointment to see Hitler on the Friday.[65] He was, indeed, received by Hitler, and joyfully so, the diary says, but nothing was discussed. The Saturday morning then found Goebbels at Max Amanns's, where he learned that none of his many schemes had been set in motion. When Hitler called in, Goebbels contrived to accompany him briefly, outlining his newspaper project to him on the wing. Although Hitler seems to have cut him short, he gave his assent to the plan. 'Hurrah!' Goebbels commented (*GT*, 1 June 1927). It is clear, though, that on this occasion, in contrast with the visit to Munich on 24 February, Hitler largely withheld his favour. He freed little time for Goebbels, and his agreement to the newspaper project did not signify much, since he gave it in the knowledge that Amann had switched off the cash flow: by no means the only instance in which Hitler blessed an undertaking while simultaneously scotching it. Goebbels – who now sought, and found, another financial backer – either failed to notice these obvious changes in Hitler's attitude or refrained from acknowledging them when writing up his diary. At least three daily newspapers had a better sense of what had happened, referring to hostile brothers and reporting that Hitler had given Goebbels a good ticking-off.[66]

A little later, on 6 June, after a rainy Whitsun break, Goebbels met a Dr Steintel, who confirmed that the offensive article in the *Berliner Abendzeitung* of 23 April had been deliberately timed to coincide with the party rally. The Straßers, he said, viewed Goebbels as a disgrace to the movement, and a bogus author had been enlisted to bump him off incognito.[67] This glimpse into what had been going on behind the scenes at the Kampfverlag made Goebbels 'shudder'. 'That does it', he continued. 'A letter[68] will be going to Hitler immediately with an offer of resignation. Dr Straßer has to go. It's either him or me! I can't see any other solution' (*GT*, 7 June 1927). At the end of that day's entry he repeated his apodictic demand in telegraphic style, this time including Gregor Straßer in it: 'Then settling of accounts with Straßer family. Either they stay or I. Up to Hitler now!' Again he left the final verdict to Hitler. Straßer, in fact, saw matters in very much the same way, with the result that each new request for a decision served to strengthen the authoritarian tendency by which Hitler was becoming the final court of appeal within the party on key decisions concerning personnel.

And yet it was not in Goebbels's nature to wait passively for decisions to be taken. The alacrity with which he now made the case public, wringing a loyalty pledge from his supporters as he had sought to wring one from Hitler, created something of a *fait accompli*. He invited sixteen of his closest allies, including Steiger, Schweitzer and Daluege, to a meeting on 10 June[69] and spoke about the article and the background to it. There was general indignation. Goebbels asked for a vote of confidence, making clear that if he did not receive one he would not stay in office a day longer. His request either received a unanimous vote in favour[70] or was adjudged to have been unanimously approved without a vote.[71]

While this was happening, Gregor Straßer, in a long session with Hitler in the Osteria Bavaria restaurant in Munich, was arguing against the establishment of another NSDAP newspaper in Berlin. Hitler soothed him, and appears, moreover, to have agreed with him, as he usually did when Goebbels lodged a complaint against one or other of the Straßers.

On the question of Goebbels's offer of resignation, too, Hitler either temporised or made plain that he would not accept it. No written answer by Hitler is extant, and the diary makes no reference to one. Goebbels would undoubtedly have referred to such a letter had one arrived; he certainly noted the absence of one.[72]

After six months of conflict with the Straßers, as the campaign of vilification against him reached its first high point, Goebbels recognised what really lay behind it. He wrote: 'The conflict is not Straßer/Goebbels, it is Hitler/Straßer. I am simply the miserable wretch who has to do the donkey work' (*GT*, 15 June 1927). He had grasped that he was waging a war on Hitler's behalf by proxy: enabling his leader to get a better sense of the strength of his competitors and, if required, helping him to contain it.

The conflict continued: a conscious working towards the Führer

Goebbels had responded with instinctive anger and pugnacity to Hitler's desire that the successful and popular Reich director of organisation be kept in check; he had not taken conscious stock of his own actions. Nevertheless, even after he had become aware of the situation, Goebbels continued to volunteer as Hitler's 'patsy', despite sometimes seeing his anger as quite corrosive,[73] and he was utterly fed up with all the plotting.[74] He shouldered the burden because he believed that Hitler was loyally on his side. It can be safely assumed that Gregor Straßer likewise believed that he, too, had Hitler's full support.

It was only logical, therefore, that Goebbels once again went to Munich, counting on Hitler to take decisions that would resolve the situation[75] – as it was, also, that Hitler gave him assurances tailored to Goebbels's own psychological needs. Hitler played the part of a leader at his wits' end, one who wanted to get a proper grip on Goebbels's party (*GT*, 22 June 1927) but who would first have to come to Berlin to lay down the law. Goebbels was obliged to leave empty-handed. Back in Berlin, the exhausted protégé could not avoid the realisation that he was the object of undisguised hatred and contempt, notably on the part of the Reichstag deputies Wilhelm Frick and Erich Koch, both of whom he had roundly attacked, though also on the part of allies such as Hans Steiger, who had backed him at the 10 June meeting, described above.[76]

For the first time, he seems to have been assailed by a sense of real anxiety.[77] Not that it was sufficient in any way to dampen his hyperactive ambition. On 4 July the first issue of the weekly newspaper *Der Angriff* ('The Attack') was published,[78] and he also rushed from public function to public function, attending to his speaking obligations both in and outside of Berlin. He did not notice, however, or perhaps he refused to notice, that Hitler was failing to honour his promise to resolve the Straßer–Goebbels dispute. When Goebbels, on route to Vienna, found himself in Munich instead (having been refused permission to enter Austria by the Austrian Federal Chancellor's Office), he was dismayed to be told at party headquarters that Hitler was staying in Berlin.[79] He returned as quickly as he could and, five long days later, managed to speak to Hitler on 18 July, almost four weeks since their last meeting. To his relief he learned that Hitler had not yet had talks with the other side and would settle the matter once and for all at the members' general meeting. Once again, Hitler had contrived to give Goebbels the impression that he was absolutely behind him. Reassured, Goebbels noted that the Fürher was the Hitler 'of old' (*GT*, 18 July 1927).

The poorly attended general members'meeting, chaired by Gregor Straßer, took place at the end of July. As well as listening to dull reports on the financial and organisational state of the NSDAP, Hitler treated the audience to a 'brilliant' speech,[80] but there was no word of any decision with regard to the Straßer–Goebbels controversy. Goebbels spent the evening of 30 July alone with Streicher, and then stayed up till 5 a.m with Eugen Munder, one of the few people from whom, in his judgement, he could count on unconditional support (*GT*, 1 August 1927). The next day he and his fellow-visitors were shown round the rooms of the new party headquarters by Hitler who then travelled out with them to Schliersee, where Goebbels was holidaying, the latter hoping to spend a day or two with Hitler.[81] After their arrival, they went for a walk, on which they settled 'urgent questions', as Goebbels later noted. It was agreed that

Goebbels would 'speak at the party rally on "Forms of Propaganda"'. And then, amid the idyllic rural surroundings, Hitler spoke 'about his youth, his strict father and his good, hard-working little mother. About his beautiful sister, his mischievous pranks and so forth. And through it all you can see the Titan to come. He really is a great man!' The loyal Goebbels confided to his diary: 'And I stand erect behind him' (*GT*, 1 July 1927). That evening Hitler left, without having so much as touched on the feud with Straßer. No new date for resolving the conflict had been considered, though that was beside the point, as Goebbels had been so impressed by Hitler's trivial stories about his childhood that all thought of his own interests had given way to worshipful admiration.

Goebbels spent the rest of his holiday without seeing Hitler. Nor did he meet him at the Bayreuth Festival, though he had hoped to do so. At the beginning of September he seems to have felt he could no longer endure the pressure from the Straßers, and he offered Hitler his resignation in writing,[82] though he already knew from experience that such gestures cut no ice with Hitler. That same evening, he had an unexpected opportunity to meet Hitler. He commented: 'Strange: for the first time I am not looking forward to it', adding 'I shall tender the boss my resignation' (*GT*, 7 September 1927). His plan was thwarted, however, as Hitler arrived, not alone, but accompanied by his sister, his niece and a third woman. 'So of course we could not get on to our dispute', he wrote disappointedly. Instead '[w]e drove out to the Lunapark and enjoyed ourselves, as far as it went' (*GT*, 8 September 1927). The following day Goebbels wrote again to Hitler, reiterating his wish to stand down.[83] On 9 September, Rudolf Heß turned up at a somewhat early hour to collect him from party headquarters. Goebbels had not yet arrived, but after hearing what had happened, he sped off in order to join Hitler – only to find himself, with Hitler and the three ladies whose presence at the Lunapark had made all political discussion impossible, watching the film of the Nuremberg party congress. Goebbels noted in his diary: 'The boss was solemn and silent. What *are* we going to say about this awful situation? The ladies were merry and cheerful' (*GT*, 10 September 1927). Afterwards the company went to the Café Vaterland, then to the Schauspielhaus and finally to the 'Rheingold', where they 'laughed a lot'. They parted without having exchanged a word about the conflict. 'The situation is now the same as before', Goebbels concluded, quite correctly (*GT*, 10 September 1927). He had, however, regained sufficient energy to resume his struggle against the Straßers and, by the same token, his work in furtherance of Hitler's unspoken interests.

The pattern I have tried to describe and document with reference to a specific year was to recur repeatedly. The tide began to turn back in Goebbels's favour about a month later, when he happily reported that Straßer would now be 'wiped out' (*GT*, 14 September 1927).[84] As we know, this was not what came to pass: not then, at any rate. Nearly three years were to elapse before, in July 1930, Otto Straßer and his supporters were forced to leave the party, and two more years until, on 8 December 1932, Gregor Straßer relinquished all his posts.[85] Eighteen months after that, on 30 June 1934,[86] Hitler had Gregor Straßer murdered in connection with the so-called Röhm *putsch*. To Alfred Rosenberg, Goebbels's subsequent adversary among Hitler's ministers, the reason was clear: Gregor Straßer, Hitler's most important political adviser, had been unable to withstand the 'antagonism of Dr Goebbels'.[87]

Notes

Translated by Richard Deveson. Editors' note: in order to keep footnotes to a minimun, references to Goebbels's diary are shown in paranthesis in the text (*GT*, followed by date of entry).

1 Ian Kershaw, *Hitler, 1889–1936: Hubris*, German trans. (Stuttgart, 1998); *Hitler, 1936–1945: Nemesis* German trans. (Stuttgart, 2000); all citations are of the German edition.

2 For the National Socialist period up to 1933, see *Hitler. Reden, Schriften, Anordnungen: Februar 1925 bis Januar 1933*, ed. Institut für Zeitgeschichte, 6 vols in 12 part-volumes, with the supplementary volume *Der Hitler-Prozess 1924* (4 part-volumes and index volumes; Munich 1992–99).

3 Elke Fröhlich (ed.), *Die Tagebücher von Joseph Goebbels*, commissioned by the Institut für Zeitgeschichte and with the support of the Russian State Archive Service, part 1: *Aufzeichnungen 1923–1941* (14 vols; 7 vols publishd to date, vols 3, II–9), part 2: *Diktate 1941–1945* (15 vols; Munich, 1993–).

4 The most important biographies, in the author's view, are: Alan Bullock, *Hitler: A Study in Tyranny* (London, 1952, German trans., *Hitler: Eine Studie über Tyrannei*, Düsseldorf, 1953); Joachim Fest, *Hitler: Eine Biographie* (Frankfurt am Main, 1973); Marlis Steinert, *Hitler* (Paris, 1991; German trans. Munich, 1994).

5 Elke Fröhlich (ed.), *Die Tagebücher von Joseph Goebbels: Sämtliche Fragmente*, commissioned by the Institut für Zeitgeschichte and in conjunction with the Bundesarchiv, part 1: *Aufzeichnungen 1924–1941* (4 vols and provisional index; Munich, 1987–).

6 The 15-volume edition of the dictated entries and volumes 6–9 of the handwritten entries: see note 3 above.

7 Kershaw, *Hitler*, vol. 1, p. 10.

8 See, for example, the reviews by Volker Ullrich, 'Die entfesselten Barbaren', *Die Zeit*, 43 (2000); and Rudolf Augstein, 'Der unersetzliche Führer', *Der Spiegel*, 42 (1998).

9 See, e.g., Christian Count von Krockow, *Hitler und seine Deutschen* (Munich, 2001), pp. 189f.

10 Kershaw, *Hitler*, vol. 2 pp. 190ff.

11 On the provenance of Goebbels's diary, see the Introduction to Frölich (ed.), *Sämtliche Fragmente*; Elke Fröhlich, 'Joseph Goebbels und sein Tagebuch', *Vierteljahrshefte für Zeitgeschichte*, 35 (1987), pp. 489–522; Elke Fröhlich, 'A propos du

journal de Goebbels par l'Institut für Zeitgeschichte de Munich', *Francia*, 25:3 (1998), pp. 137–42; Hans Günter Hockerts, 'Die Edition der Goebbels-Tagebücher', in Horst Möller and Udo Wengst (eds), *50 Jahre Institut für Zeitgeschichte: Eine Bilanz* (Munich, 1999), pp. 249–64; Horst Möller, 'Die Tagebücher von Joseph Goebbels. Quelle, Überlieferung, Edition', in Klaus Oldenhage, Hermann Schreyer and Wolfram Werner (eds), *Archiv und Geschichte: Festschrift für Friedrich P. Kahlenberg* (Düsseldorf, 2000), pp. 673–83.

12 Joseph Goebbels, *Vom Kaiserhof zur Reichskanzlei: Eine historische Darstellung in Tagebuchblättern (Vom 1. Januar 1932 bis zum 1. März 1933)* (Munich, 1934).

13 Louis P. Lochner (ed.), *Goebbels Tagebücher aus den Jahren 1942–1943: Mit anderen Dokumenten* (Zurich, 1948).

14 *Das Tagebuch des Joseph Goebbels 1925/26: Mit weiteren Dokumenten*, ed. Helmut Heiber, Vierteljahrshefte für Zeitgeschichte series, 1 (Stuttgart, 1960).

15 Joseph Goebbels, *Tagebücher 1945: Die letzten Aufzeichnungen*, Introduction by Rolf Hochhuth (Hamburg, 1977); this collection contains the entries from 28 February to 10 April 1945.

16 Fröhlich (ed.), *Die Tagebücher von Joseph Goebbels*.

17 Agreement reached on 6 August 1987 between the Institut für Zeitgeschichte and the documentation centre of the State Archival Administration of the German Democratic Republic regarding the incorporation of the diary volumes for 1941–45, in particular 1944–45, within the ongoing IfZ edition, and final copying for that edition, at the beginning of 1990.

18 Jelena Rshewskaja, *Hitlers Ende ohne Mythos* (East Berlin, 1967).

19 Richard Otte in interview with the author, 4 May 1981; see Goebbels, *Tagebücher 1945*, where reference is made (p. 567) to an extensive unsuccessful search for this officer's trunk carried out in the early 1960s.

20 Otte in interview with the author.

21 Public Record Office, FO 370/2377, report dated 8 March 1954.

22 *Ibid.*

23 *Ibid.*

24 Letter from the French Foreign Ministry, Direction des Archives, Département des Archives courantes et intermédiares, 14 February 2002.

25 It should be noted, however, that these diary texts have already been published in the edition on the basis of a difference provenance strand, so that their contents are familiar. The discovery fills a gap of provenance, not of knowledge.

26 On the Straßers, see particularly: Douglas Reed, *Nemesis? The Story of Otto Strasser* (London, 1953); and *The Prisoner of Ottawa: Otto Strasser* (London, 1953); Reinhard Kühnl, *Die nationalsozialistische Linke 1925–1930*, Marburger Abhandlungen zur Politischen Wissenschaft 6 (Meisenheim am Glan, 1966); Ulrich Wörtz, 'Programmatik und Führerprinzip: Das Problem des Strasser-Kreises in der NSDAP', Doctoral thesis, Erlangen-Nuremberg, 1966; Otto Straßer, *Mein Kampf: Eine politische Autobiographie*, 3rd rev. edn (Frankfurt am Main, 1969); Udo Kissenkoetter, *Gregor Straßer und die NSDAP*, Vierteljahrshefte für Zeitgeschichte series, 37 (Stuttgart, 1978); Peter D. Stachura, '"Der Fall Strasser": Gregor Strasser, Hitler and National Socialism, 1930–1932', in Peter D. Stachura (ed.), *The Shaping of the Nazi State* (London and New York, 1978), pp. 88–1130; David Bankier, 'Otto

Strasser und die Judenfrage', *Bulletin of the Leo Baeck Institute*, 20:60 (1981), pp. 3–20; Peter D. Stachura, *Gregor Strasser and the Rise of Nazism* (London, 1983); Günter Barsch, *Zwischen den Stühlen. Otto Strasse: Eine Biographie* (Koblenz, 1990); Kurt Gossweiler, *Die Strasser-Legende:. Auseinandersetzung mit einem Kapitel des deutschen Faschismus* (Berlin, 1994); Udo Kissenkoetter, 'Gregor Strasser NS-Parteiorganisator oder Weimarer Politker?' in Ronald M. Smelser and Rainer Zitelmann (eds), *Die braune Elite: 22 biographische Skizzen*, 4th edn (Darmstadt, 1999), pp. 273–85; Patrick Moreau, 'Otto Strasser Nationaler Sozialismus versus Nationalsozialismus', in *ibid*, pp. 286–98.

27 Klaus F. Schmid, 'Die "Nationalsozialistische Briefe" 1925–1930: Programm, Anschauungen, Tendenzen. Anmerkungen zu innerparteilichen Diskussionen und Richtungskämpfen der NSDAP', in *Paul Kluke zum 60. Geburtstag, dargebracht von Frankfurter Schülern und Mitarbeitern* (Frankfurt am Main, 1968), pp. 111–26.

28 On the desperate state of the party, see reports by Muchow: Martin Broszat, 'Die Anfänge der Berliner NSDAP 1926/27', *Vierteljahrshefte für Zeitgeschichte*, 8:1 (1960), pp. 85–118, specifically p. 101. On the early history of the NSDAP in general, see e.g.: Albert Krebs, *Tendenzen und Gestalten der NSDAP: Erinnerungen an die Frühzeit der Partei* (Stuttgart, 1959); Dietrich Orlow, 'The Organizational History and Structure of the NSDAP, 1919–1923', *Journal of Modern History*, 37 (1965), pp. 208–26; 'The Conversion of Myth into Power: The Case of the Nazi Party, 1925–26', *American Historical Review*, 72 (1967), pp. 906–24; *The History of the Nazi Party*, vol. 1: *1919–1933* (Pittsburgh, PA, 1969); Albrecht Tyrell, *Führer befiehl – Selbstzeugnisse aus der Kampfzeit der NSDAP: Dokumentation und Analyse* (Düsseldorf, 1969); Peter Hüttenberger, *Die Gauleiter: Studie zum Wandel des Machtgefüges in der NSDAP*, Vierteljahrshefte für Zeitgeschichte series, 19 (Stuttgart, 1969); Werner Maser, *Der Sturm auf die Republik: Frühgeschichte der NSDAP*, 2nd edn (Stuttgart, 1973); Anthony J. Nicholls, *Weimar and the Rise of Hitler*, 2nd edn (London, 1979); Wolfgang Horn, *Der Marsch zur Machtergreifung: Die NSDAP bis 1933* (Königstein, Ts., and Düsseldorf, 1980); Albrecht Tyrell, 'Das Scheitern der Weimarer Republik und der Aufstieg der NSDAP', in Martin Broszat and Norbert Frei (eds), *Ploetz: Das Dritte Reich. Ursprünge, Ereignisse, Wirkungen* (Freiburg i. Br. and Würzburg, 1983), pp. 18–27; George L. Mosse, *Ein Volk, ein Reich, ein Führer: Die völkischen Ursprünge des Nationalsozialismus*, 2nd edn (Königstein, Ts., 1990); Hans-Günter Richardi, *Hitler und seine Hintermänner: Neue Fakten zur Frühgeschichte der NSDAP* (Munich, 1991); Wolfgang Schieder (ed.), 'Die NSDAP als faschistische Partei', *Geschichte und Gesellschaft*, special issue, 19:2 (1993); Wolfgang Schieder, 'Die NSDAP vor 1933: Profil einer faschistischen Partei', *ibid.*, pp. 141–54; Hans Mommsen, 'Die Illusion einer Regierung ohne Parteien und der Aufstieg der NSDAP', in Eberhard Kolb and Walter Mühlhausen (eds), *Demokratie in der Krise: Parteien im Verfassungssystem der Weimarer Republik* (Munich, 1997), pp. 113–39. There are many regional and local studies that are highly illuminating, covering the whole of the former area of the Reich: for Lower Saxony, see Jeremy Noakes, *The NSDAP in Lower Saxony, 1921–1933: A Study of National Socialist Organisation* (Oxford, 1971); for Swabia, Zdenek Zofka, *Die Ausbreitung des Nationalsozialismus auf dem Land: Eine*

regionale Fallstudie zur politischen Einstellung der Landbevölkerung [im Kreis Günzburg (Schwaben)] in der Zeit des Aufstiegs und der Machtergreifung der NSDAP 1928–1936 (Munich, 1979). The most recent regional study of which I am aware is Mathias Rösch, *Die Münchner NSDAP 1925–1933: Eine Untersuchung zur inneren Struktur der NSDAP in der Weimarer Republik,* Studien zur Zeitgeschichte, 63 (Munich, 2002).

29   Even Goebbels took a very dim view of the fractious Berlin NSDAP, which numbered only a few hundred party comrades in a city of 4 million people: 'We were a ludicrously small organisation. People had never even heard of us. They regarded us as intellectually rather limited sectarians': Joseph Goebbels, *Kampf um Berlin. Der Anfang,* 8th edn (Munich, 1935), p. 49.

30   In his diary he had been debating since the beginning of June whether he ought to go to Berlin (*GT,* 6 July 1926); for further diary evidence of his hesitation, see Ralf Georg Reuth, *Goebbels* (Munich, 1990), pp. 104ff. Reuth's biography is the most comprehensive yet published and in its wealth of material surpasses all its predecessors, including: Heinrich Fraenkel and Roger Manvell, *Goebbels: Eine Biographie* (Cologne, 1960); Helmut Heiber, *Joseph Goebbels* (Berlin, 1962; Munich, 1965); and Viktor Reimann, *Dr. Joseph Goebbels* (Vienna, 1971). There is still a need for a convincing and insightful account of Goebbels's transformation from a young idealist, with a secure social background and a classical education, into one of the men who bore prime responsibility for the crimes of the Third Reich.

31   The existence of this diary entry has long been known, but because of the poor quality of the source this particular passage has not been decipherable until now. It should be emphasised that all subsequent quotations from the diary, none of which has previously been published, should be treated with the critical caution appropriate to all sources, to say nothing of the extra care befitting the writings of professional propagandists. The reservations that Martin Broszat expressed, over forty years ago, with regard to the situation reports of the talented Berlin propagandist Reinhold Muchow remain, in my view, entirely applicable today and with equal force to Goebbels's diary: 'The picture of the development, goals and significance of the Berlin NSDAP and SA that is painted in the reports involves … a considerable amount of retouching. The way in which the writer, consciously or unconsciously, portrays himself in a favourable light, and is at the same time caught in the grip of ideological terms and intellectual categories that give a reflection of reality distorted by propaganda and Weltanschauung, impairs the evidential value of the information he provides, and indeed would lead us into error if we were to take the reports as literal statements of fact. Muchow [Authors note: in the present case, read Goebbels] passes over many matters in silence, merely hints at others, and constantly exaggerates. His assignment of an heroic role to the NSDAP, and the cynical, polemical and aggressive attitude he adopts towards political rivals and opponents, are in many ways typical of the National Socialist journalism of the time and, to a certain extent, an anticipation of the literary glorification of the struggle for Berlin that took place after 1933, when every possible effort was made to depict even the most provocative and crude acts of violence perpetrated against their political opponents by the SA, SS and Hitler

Youth as part of an heroic epic of revolutionary struggle': Broszat, 'Die Anfänge', pp. 85f.

32 Schmiedicke conveyed to Goebbels the wish of all the Berlin party comrades, including party comrade Gregor Straßer, that he should come to Berlin as Gauleiter: letter from Schmiedicke to Goebbels, 16 October 1926, reprinted in *Das Tagebuch des Joseph Goebbels 1925/26*, pp. 112f.

33 The early – unpublished – diary gives interesting insights into Joseph Goebbels's sense of mission: to give a single example: 'If Heaven gives me the life to do so, then I shall be a redeemer – I must mature for my mission' (*GT*, 27 December 1923). On his psychology, see especially Claus-Ekkehard Bärsch, 'Das Katastrophenbewußtsein eines werdenden Nationalsozialisten: Der Antisemitismus im Tagebuch des Joseph Goebbels vor dem Eintritt in die NSDAP', *Menora. Jahrbuch für deutsch–jüdische Geschichte*, 1 (1990), pp. 125–51; Claus-Ekkehard Bärsch, *Der junge Goebbels: Erlösung und Vernichtung* (Munich, 1995).

34 Reuth covers the period under discussion here in the chapter entitled '"Berlin": Ein Sündenpfuhl! Und dahinein soll ich mich stürzen? (1926–1928)' ('"Berlin". A cesspool of sin! And that's what I'm meant to plunge into? (1926–1928)': *Goebbels*, pp. 108–37. When writing this chapter, Reuth did not have access to the entries from the diary between 1 November 1926 and 13 April 1928, and he places too much reliance on the self-serving memoirs of Otto Straßer – on which see especially Ulrich Höver, *Joseph Goebbels ein nationaler Sozialist* (Bonn, 1992), pp. 14ff. Inevitably, therefore, he makes some mistakes: for example, the date of Goebbels's arrival in Berlin is given incorrectly. Moreover, Goebbels was not met at the station by Otto Straßer, who paid due regard to Goebbels's new authority. (Reuth is perhaps confusing this occasion with Goebbels's visit on 9 October, when he was indeed met at the station by Straßer.) According to Reuth, Goebbels gave his maiden speech on 9 November at the Kriegervereinhaus, where, significantly, he says, Goebbels was introduced by Otto Straßer. The diary makes no mention of this, nor of any witch's cauldron, or the like; indeed, the whole of Reuth's argument on p. 111 is based on unprovable assertions by Otto Straßer. In the rest of the chapter Reuth mentions the Straßers on only two more occasions.

35 It was Helene Bechstein, and not – as Reuth says (*ibid.*, p. 111) – Otto Straßer, who introduced Goebbels into Berlin society. Invitations to her parties in Berlin, and at the Bayerischer Hof hotel in Munich, were much coveted; she competed socially with Elsa Bruckmann for Hitler's favour. See also David Clay Large, *Hitler's München: Aufstieg und Fall der Hauptstadt der Bewegung* (Munich, 1998), pp. 196ff.

36 'After the meal we had a couple of hours to ourselves' (*GT*, 11 November 1926).

37 'Yesterday evening Hauenstein, the snooping antipole, wanted to use terror tactics and break up the meeting. His people had to leave the hall, and about fifty of them went. I am rid of the perpetual trouble-makers and carpers' (*GT*, 12 November 1926).

38 The moods that Goebbels documents are the diametrical opposite of those Reuth (*Goebbels*, pp. 115ff.) ascribes to him during this period. According to Reuth, Goebbels was constantly filled with anger and annoyance.

39 Although the surname was spelt Straßer, Goebbels sometimes spelt it with a double 'ss'. For ease of reading the spelling has been standardised here.

40   For example, about Axel Ripke, the Gauführer for Rhineland North, and Helmuth
     Elbrechter, a prominent figure in the same *Gau*; the diary contains plentiful com-
     ments on both men.

41   Goebbels's characterisation of the new man occurs in the diary's entries for the
     end of 1923 and the beginning of 1924.

42   When Goebbels had been given the first volume of *Mein Kampf*, bound in leather
     and with a dedication, for Christmas in 1925, his joy had been comparatively
     restrained (*GT*, 29 December 1925). The first volume of *Mein Kampf* was pub-
     lished on 18 July 1925, the second on 10 December 1926. After May 1930 the two
     volumes were published in a single-volume popular edition.

43   'Until I destroy the bastard'; 'He's what's hellish about the movement' (*GT*, 19 and
     22 February 1927).

44   'Parliamentisierung?', *Nationalsozialistische Briefe*, 1 February 1927.

45   'There'll be a terrific fuss about it again. But I'll struggle through. I can't allow our
     movement to be condemned to die on the hotbed of Parliament' (*GT*, 4 January
     1927).

46   Shortly afterwards Reventlow, along with a fairly substantial portion of the north
     German German-National [*Völkisch*] Freedom Party, went over to the NSDAP,
     where he initially supported the Straßer tendency.

47   Joseph Goebbels, *Wege ins Dritte Reich: Briefe und Aufsätze für Zeitgenossen*
     (Munich, 1927).

48   See Kissenkoetter, *Gregor Straßer und die NSDAP*, p. 32; Oswald Spengler, *Briefe
     1913–36* (Munich, 1963), pp. 291f., 397f.

49   'I still have to work this out. I am doing a good job of making new enemies for
     myself' (*GT*, 8 March 1927).

50   'Happy about it as I am, I am also appalled by the string of intrigues that have
     already ensued. The Straßer family is seething. Their wretched Marxist influence
     is gradually being broken. Schmitz from Elberfeld has written me a letter teemig
     with suspicions. I am alone again … All that sustains me is the certainty that Hitler
     is on my side' (*GT*, 9 March 1927).

51   'You certainly need strong nerves'; 'It's like living in the midst of a war' (*GT*, 23 and
     24 March 1927).

52   After a meeting at which his brave Brownshirts and the Reds conducted the oblig-
     atory brawl with chair-legs, Goebbels confessed: 'The good Lord is on our side. I
     believe this faithfully, almost like a child' (*GT*, 31 March 1927).

53   'Dr Straßer is intolerable. Away with him, then! The sooner, the better. If Hitler
     comes, we shall have a cosy chat about it' (*GT*, 16 April 1927).

54   'They all hate this gross usurper' (*GT*, 20 April 1927).

55   Letter from Koch to Goebbels, 26 April 1927, reprinted in *Das Tagebuch des Joseph
     Goebbels 1925/26*, pp. 120f.

56   'I lodge complaints about Straßer. He is entirely of my opinion. He hates Dr Straßer.
     There will now be a decision about the Berlin business' (*GT*, 27 April 1927).

57   On Hitler's speech to the *Gau* party rally in Essen on 14 April 1927, see *Hitler.
     Reden, Schriften, Anordnungen*, vol. 2: *Vom Weimarer Parteitag bis zur Reich-
     stagswahl: Juli 1926–Mai 1928*, ed. with a commentary by Bärbel Dusik, part 1:
     'July 1926–July 1927', document 110, pp. 283f.

58 'And by this time tomorrow, Hitler will be here. I am looking forward to it like a child'; 'And tomorrow Hitler comes!'; 'I am now sitting and waiting expectantly. The boss is coming. I am looking forward to it very much. It is going to be a milestone in our development tomorrow … The good Lord likes me'; 'Hitler is here … He is the Leader!' (*GT*, 28, 29, 30 April and 2 May 1927).

59 On Hitler's speech in Berlin on 1 May 1927, see *Hitler. Reden, Schriften, Anordnungen*, vol. 2, part 1, document 113, pp. 287–90. See also 'Hitlers erste Rede in Berlin', *Völkischer Beobachter*, 3 May 1927; 'Herr, laß uns nicht feige sein', *ibid.*, 5 May 1927.

60 Reuth, *Goebbels*, p. 121.

61 On Hitler's speeches in Stuttgart on 7 and 8 May 1927, see *Hitler. Reden, Schriften, Anordnungen*, vol. 2, part 1, documents 116 and 117, pp. 291–5.

62 'He is completely on my side … The boss is good to me … How I revere and love this man!' (*GT*, 11 May 1927).

63 'Today the N.S. Briefe come out without me. Revenge is a dish best eaten cold. Patience! Wait till our newspaper arrives!' (*GT*, 18 May 1927).

64 Statement by Gregor Straßer, June 1927, Minutes, n.d., 'Bestätigung der Richtigkeit vom 16.6.1927 mit der schriftlichen Erwiderung von Gregor Straßer', n.d., reprinted in *Das Tagebuch des Joseph Goebbels 1925/26*, p. 133.

65 'On Friday in Munich many things will be cleared up, I am sure' (*GT*, 24 May 1927).

66 'Feindliche 'Brüder'', *Berliner Tageblatt*, 4 June 1927, and *Berliner Volkszeitung*, 4 June 1927; 'Bruderzwist im Hause Hitler', *Welt am Abend*, 4 June 1927. Hitler's denial was published under the headline 'Der Wunsch ist der Vater des Gedankens' in the *Völkischer Beobachter*, 25 June 1927.

67 Note by Dr Steintel, 17 June 1927, formerly held in Berlin Document Centre (BDC), today in Bundesarchiv (BA) and Mönchengladbach City Archive, collection 15/44/86, Joseph Goebbels.

68 Letter from Goebbels to Hitler, 5 June 1927, printed in *Das Tagebuch des Joseph Goebbels 1925/26*, pp. 121–3.

69 Minutes, n.d., 'Bestätigung der Richtigkeit vom 16.6.1927 mit der schriftlichen Erwiderung von Gregor Straßer', n.d., reprinted in *Das Tagebuch des Joseph Goebbels 1925/26*, pp. 127–34.

70 *Ibid.*

71 Goebbels's note in the diary says: 'Utter indignation. Now we shall get rid of the bastard. I hadn't thought he could be so stupid. Everyone on my side, unanimously' (*GT*, 11 June 1927).

72 'I am still expectantly waiting for Hitler's answer' (*GT*, 13 June 1927).

73 'Struggle with the Straßer combine right across the board. People are stirring and plotting against me in the most outrageous manner. Dietrich M.d.R. refuses to be editor on *Der Angriff*. Straßer sees this as an unfriendly act … I am no longer sleeping. The anger is devouring me' (*GT*, 17 June 1927).

74 'The row keeps on going … I am slowly getting fed up to the back teeth with it. What I should really like to do is to drop everything and sink into oblivion … You certainly have to hand it to the Straßers: they're clever workers and foxy bastards.' (*GT*, 17 June 1927).

75   'On Sunday evening I am going to Munich. And on Monday everything will be
     sorted out'; 'And on Monday in Munich everything should be resolved. Adolf
     Hitler will speak' (*GT*, 15 and 18 June 1927).

76   'A string of plots and calumnies. I'm at my wits end with all this dirt. The deputies
     are taking action: against me. Their "action committee". Dr Frick: *Der Angriff* is
     unnecessary. Marvellous! Koch shoots his big mouth off. The social traitor!' (*GT*,
     22 June 1927); 'The Honourable Deputies are causing problems upon problems
     … This parliament should be wiped out, root and branch. The road to life for the
     German people is over the dead body of this institution … Even our own deputies
     have already been badly corroded. That's why they hate it so profoundly when I
     protest against it. Just had a vehement set-to with Steiger. That has to go and
     happen too' (*GT*, 23 June 1927).

77   'My thoughts are running about all over the place, like hens when a fox has got into
     the henhouse. May God in His mercy make it all end well!' (*GT*, 23 June 1927).

78   Hans-Georg Rahm, *Der Angriff 1927–1930: Der nationalsozialistische Typ der
     Kampfzeitung* (Berlin, 1939); Ernest K. Bramstedt, 'Goebbels and His Newspaper
     Der Angriff', in Max Beloff (ed.), *On the Track of Tyranny: Essays Presented by the
     Wiener Library to Leonhard G. Montefiore, O.B.E., on the Occasion of His Seventi-
     eth Birthday* (London, 1960), pp. 45–60; Carin Kessemeier, *Der Leitartikler
     Goebbels in den NS-Organen Der Angriff und Das Reich* (Münster, 1967); Russel
     Lemmons, *Goebbels and Der Angriff* (Lexington, KY, 1994).

79   'A tricky business' (*GT*, 17 July 1927).

80   The speech of 30 July 1927 to the general members meeting of the NSDAP in
     Munich is printed in *Hitler. Reden, Schriften, Anordnungen*, vol. 2, , part 1, docu-
     ment 159, pp. 413–37; see also *Völkischer Beobachter*, 1–2 August 1927, pp. 1
     and 2.

81   'Hitler is also coming for a few days' (*GT*, 22 July 1927).

82   'Today a vast deal of anger, worry and trouble. Straßer's functioning at high pres-
     sure. I have written Hitler a long letter offering my resignation. I really want him
     to accept it. I can't bear things to carry on like this' (*GT*, 6 September 1927).

83   'At midday today I wrote to the boss again. Requesting to be relieved of my post.
     Now waiting for an answer tomorrow: either way!' (*GT*, 8 September 1927).

84   Six weeks later, the tide turned yet again: 'The election: time to get going. I shall be
     a leading candidate. In the evening with the boss, the Straßer peace treaty con-
     cluded. How long will it last?' (*GT*, 27 November 1927).

85   'Rumours that Straßer wants to carry out a palace revolution. This perpetual to-
     ing and fro-ing is such a strain. Boss has had letter from Straßer: resigns all his
     party posts. Phoney reasons, leading the party into government and so forth.
     None of it valid, naturally. Wants to be a minister … Everyone very depressed, but
     nobody is with Straßer. Str[aßer's] move doesn't surprise me. A back-stabber'
     (*GT*, 9 December 1932). In the next diary entry he calls Straßer a 'dead man' and
     voices his gratification that six years of struggle have now borne fruit. For the pos-
     sible connection between Straßer's resignation and his murder, see, among other
     documents, Hinrich Lohse (former Gauleiter of Schleswig–Holstein), IfZ Archive,
     ZS 265, p. 51. In that record, made on 23 January 1953, Lohse also gives an account
     of Straßer's reasons for his departure from the party and his resignation of his

posts, as traßer stated them on 8 December 1932 to the regional inspectors who had been summoned to the Reichstag. According to Lohse, Straßer characteristically gave the following personal reasons: 'I view the personnel, and personal, aspect of the problem as the ever-widening[!] spread of plotting within the Führer's close entourage, and as personal slights and injuries which, in my position, I simply cannot stand for any longer. Naturally, I have also had occasional need to see and speak to the Führer, on purely personal as well as professional grounds. When I go to the Kaiserhof, or into the Brown House in Munich, I always come across the same people. On these visits I am usually then told little, or at any rate nothing precise[!], about impending issues of the day or about political discussions and the current state of consultations between individuals or groups or parties. I have no wish, however, to rank below Göring, Goebbels, Röhm *et al.*: if they receive invitations, then I am entitled to be done the honour of being invited too. This, though, has never yet happened as far as the Führer is concerned. I feel this to be a slight, a personal humiliation, which I have not deserved and which I am no longer willing to put up with. My energies and my nerves, I might add, are exhausted. I have effected my departure from the party and am now going to the mountains to recuperate': *ibid.*, p. 27.

86 In his diary Goebbels – who had accompanied Hitler throughout the action – recorded the death of his great foe with remarkably little emotion (*GT*, 1 July 1934). His ambivalent role during the so-called Röhm *putsch* has not yet been properly studied.

87 Hans-Günter Seraphim (ed.), *Das politische Tagebuch Alfred Rosenbergs 1934/35 und 1939/40* (Munich, 1964), p. 48.

3

Mobilising women for Hitler: the female Nazi voter

Helen Boak

I

'We gained more women than all the other parties together', boasted Hitler.[1] While this is patently untrue as, in those areas where men and women voted separately, the NSDAP rarely managed to win over 50 per cent of the female vote, it is clear that in Protestant areas in 1932 the NSDAP was receiving more votes from women than from men.[2] My aim in this chapter is to explore how such a self-confessedly male party as the NSDAP mobilised the female vote, the reasons for its success with female voters and the type of woman who might have voted for the NSDAP. To what extent did the Nazis' methods of mobilising women voters differ from those of the other major political parties in the Weimar Republic? Is it possible to discern a distinctive appeal to women in Nazi propaganda?

It is now twenty years since Thomas Childers provided a comprehensive analysis of the political parties' election campaign appeals within a broader study of the formation of the Nazi constituency and two studies in German have since analysed the propaganda appeals of the NSDAP and the *Sozialdemokratische Partei Deutschlands* (SPD).[3] None of these studies concentrates on the parties' attempts to win women's votes, an omission recently rectified by Julia Sneeringer who has examined the parties' printed appeals to women in Berlin to investigate how they attempted to win women's votes and how their propaganda constructed women as political actors.[4] In exploring the new mobilisation strategies and the new areas of propaganda which the parties of the Weimar Republic believed they had to produce in order to win women's votes, one can not only provide an insight into the electoral politics of the Weimar Republic but also throw light on the role electoral propaganda played in mobilising women voters, and, thereby, contribute to the debate on the effectiveness of propaganda in winning votes for specific parties.

For many years historians have assumed that the success of the NSDAP's propaganda contributed significantly to its rise to power, though this view was questioned by Richard Bessel who argued that both the function and the effectiveness of Nazi propaganda had not been analysed in any depth. Bessel emphasised the role played by social and political culture and the failure of the Weimar system in the rise of the Nazis.[5] His view finds support in the work of Oded Heilbronner who, in his study of the NSDAP in the Black Forest, has shown that the Nazis' success at the polls is not to be seen as evidence of the effectiveness of the party's propaganda and organisation.[6] And yet Ian Kershaw has demonstrated the distinctiveness in the components, style and presentation of the Nazis' propaganda and the important role it played in creating an image for the party and in its success.[7] Taking its cue from both of these approaches, this chapter attempts to assess the shape, style and effectiveness of each party's propaganda in mobilising the female vote during the Weimar Republic in order to guage the distinctiveness of Nazi propaganda and its relative success in mobilising women voters.

II

German women aged 20 and over were given the vote by the Council of People's Delegates on 12 November 1918, barely ten years after German women had been granted complete freedom of association, that is the right to attend political meetings and join political parties, and it became imperative for women's groups and the political parties to educate and mobilise women voters for the forthcoming elections to the National Assembly.[8]

Throughout the Weimar Republic the main vehicles for the political parties to spread their message to the female electorate, which the parties perceived from the outset as a discrete constituency, were written propaganda and meetings. Women party members were instrumental in the provision and organisation of both, as winning women's votes quickly became the remit of the parties' women's sections or committees, although the KPD (*Kommunistische Partei Deutschlands* – German Communist Party) did try unsuccessfully to convince men that winning women's votes was the work of the whole party.[9] Radio was in its infancy during the Weimar Republic and was barred from use as a political medium, except on rare occasions. The principle of keeping politics off the radio may have had grave consequences for women's political education, as Kate Lacey argues, because of its capacity to reach women within their own homes.[10] The majority of the female electorate consisted probably of housewives: in 1925 women aged 20 or over numbered 21,025,998; 12,710,070 were married, though 37,539 of them were under 20.[11] Women, whose use of public space outside the home was, as Karen Hagemann has noted, 'extraordinarily circumscribed', could be educated about politics in the home, at work, in churches, within the organisations they joined or by attending the segregated meetings, indoor and out, held by the political parties.[12]

The parties' general public meetings tended to consist of a lecture and discussion on political issues of the day and were frequently held in public houses, places in which many women, particularly those of the older generation, felt uncomfortable. Women's meetings, held in the evenings or, frequently, in the afternoons, were addressed primarily by women speakers talking about women's issues. In 1924 the SPD's women's organisation realised that women preferred to have a mixture of culture, entertainment and political enlightenment at these meetings, and in the late 1920s the KPD, too, began to include entertainment within its meetings or to hold 'coffee and cake afternoons'.[13] In the late 1920s the SPD, the KPD and the NSDAP began to show slides and propaganda films at their meetings, and though these did not reach a wide audience they were popular.[14] By the later years of the Weimar Republic gender-specific demonstrations and rallies became the favoured means of the SPD and KPD to win women voters, and these were often focused on an issue of concern to working-class women, such as abortion or the struggle against fascism. These demonstrations were thought to be more attractive to younger women, as older women were considered to prefer the smaller meetings for women that were held indoors. In February 1931 over 3,000 women attended the Hamburg SPD's first women's anti-Nazi mass meeting to which men were not admitted.[15]

But as Karen Hagemann has shown, women's exclusion from numerous political events brought about in the early years of the Republic by the location and content of the parties' meetings and demonstrations, became greater with the militarisation and the increasing use of violence in political life, which, in turn, only increased the need for the segregation of public political activities in which women could participate.[16] Both Richard Bessel and Thomas Childers have demonstrated that the use of violence was a fundamental part of the Nazis' mobilisation strategy, and in the early 1930s Germany's streets became a battle-ground as the parties' paramilitary wings, clad in their uniforms, and with flags and insignia, fought for supremacy.[17] German women were for the most part excluded from this militarisation of German political life, though in 1932 the KPD made much of the violent attack by SA men on a young Communist woman.[18] Members of the KPD's Red Women and Girls' League wore uniforms and marched in military formation, and the members of the Nazi Women's Association similarly had uniforms and insignia. Nazi women also attempted to disrupt the women's meetings held by other parties.

German women were showered with printed matter prior to the elections to the National Assembly, as the parties which had previously refused to support the call for female suffrage were now quick to welcome women into political life. The female turnout for the elections to the National Assembly appear to indicate that the propaganda campaign to get women to vote was successful, though whether women went to their polls in response to the propaganda campaign launched by both women's groups and the political parties, because of the novelty-value of the vote, because they were aware of the serious situation in which the country found itself or because they were keen to do their duty cannot be ascertained. The percentage of women eligible to vote who made use of their right exceeded that of men in some areas where provision was made for men and women to vote separately; but on the whole it is estimated that the female turnout at 82.3 per cent was just lower than the male turnout at 82.4 per cent, the smallest difference in the male and female turnout recorded in the Weimar Republic.[19] Figures reveal that there was a low turnout among men under 25 as many of them were perhaps imprisoned abroad or still in uniform and making their way home. The figures also reveal that younger women were more likely to have made use of their vote than were older women, and that women in the towns and cities also made greater use of their right to vote than did those in the country.[20] Older women living in the country could, therefore, be seen to be harder to mobilise than younger urban women.

Childers has noted that each political party speedily adopted its own political language and imagery to distinguish itself from its rivals in the most significant medium of the Weimar Republic – print – and that they targeted their appeals at clearly defined occupational groups.[21] How did the parties formulate their appeals to women voters, the majority of whom were housewives and whose status in society came from their husbands or male heads of households? Printed matter included leaflets, pamphlets and posters during election campaigns; but it is from the brochures detailing the parties' views on women's issues, or those describing the activities of their female politicians and the reprints of the parties' petitions to the Reichstag relating to women's concerns throughout the Weimar Republic that the parties' attitudes to women's role in society can best be gleaned.

The brochures reveal that the three socialist parties, the SPD, USPD (*Unabhängige Sozialdemokratische Partei Deutschlands* – German Independent Socialist Party) and the KPD, demanded the recognition of women's equal right to work, equal pay for equal work, equal educational opportunities, equal unemployment benefits and better worker protection for women. However, the SPD was party to the demobilisation decrees at the war's end, and it voted in favour of the dismissal of married female civil servants in 1932. The KPD was the only party to vote against this law, but it also voted against the 1927 law governing the employment of women before and after childbirth because it did not consider its provisions extensive enough. Both the SPD and USPD called for equal legal status between men and women. All the socialist parties wished for contraceptive devices to be readily available, and whereas the SPD campaigned for a reduction in the penalties defined in the paragraphs in the penal code relating to abortion, both the USPD and the KPD favoured their abrogation. The SPD supported the introduction of divorce on the grounds of irreconcilable differences, whereas the KPD believed marriage should be seen as a private contract.[22]

The right-liberal DVP (*Deutsche Volkspartei* – German People's Party), in its guiding principles of 1919, advocated the political, economic and legal equality of the sexes. It gave its full support to and recognition of the work of woman as mothers and rearers of the next generation.[23] It did not support married women's right to work, the DVP fraction in the Berlin City Council calling in 1930 for the dismissal of all the city's married women civil servants and white-collar workers whose husbands earned a normal wage.[24] The DDP (*Deutsche Demokratische Partei* – German Democratic Party) allowed its Reichstag delegate Dr Marie-Elisabeth Lüders to champion the rights of professional women, especially civil servants, and the DStP (*Deutsche Staatspartei* – German State Party), the DDP's successor party, abstained from voting on the proposed law to dismiss married women civil servants in 1932. Both the DDP and the DVP said little on the issues of abortion or contraception but it was Marie-Elisabeth Lüders who led the campaign for divorce reform, supported by her party and the DVP.

The Centre Party's guiding principles of 1918 called for women's participation in all areas deemed to be in accordance with their feminine nature.[25] It did not believe implicitly in a woman's right to work and it instigated the law to dismiss married female civil servants in 1932. The Catholic Church regarded abortion as murder and was steadfastly and vociferously opposed to any form of contraception or reform of the divorce laws.[26] The *Deutschnationale Volkspartei* (DNVP) guidelines on women's issues called for equal pay for work of equal value and equal employment and promotion opportunities, though it did nothing to help turn those pronouncements into fact. The DNVP believed that 'the German woman is indispensable as the guardian of the moral and religious foundations of family life and of the nation'. It was fundamentally opposed to any relaxation in the abortion or divorce laws, and called on the Reichstag to introduce measures to combat the fall in the birth-rate.[27]

In contrast to the other parties, the NSDAP had no agreed guidelines on its position on women's role in society, and the only reference to women in the Nazi Party programme of 24 February 1920 was in connection with the protection of mothers and children (point 21) as part of its plan to improve the nation's health.[28] The party published no brochures detailing its views on the role of women. What was written came from female adherents of Nazism or as brief parts of larger works by Hitler, Rosenberg and Darre.[29] The lack of clear policy guidelines allowed some flexibility in Nazi views on women's role in employment. While Gregor Strasser promised working women equality in a National Socialist state, Hermann Esser said that the Nazis would remove all women and girls from every public office and job. The view was also propounded that women's employment should be restricted to those areas specially suited to women's nature and their role as mothers. The Nazis were prominent in the campaign against married working women in the early 1930s, calling for the dismissal of all married working women and their replacement by men who could do their work.[30] Nazi views on the primacy of women's role as mothers and preservers of the purity of the German race never wavered, however. The NSDAP did not support any relaxation in the abortion laws and even called for anyone who tried artificially to impede the natural fertility of the German race, by abortion or contraception, to be imprisoned for treason.[31]

Alone of the political parties the NSDAP refused to allow women to hold positions of leadership or to represent it at any level. The Nazis believed strongly in separate spheres for men and women: politics, the military and the judiciary were not thought suitable occupations for women. Women's sphere was primarily within the home and family, and one Nazi woman expressed the view that the role of housewife should be recognised as a profession.[32]

In their electoral propaganda the political parties tended to appeal to women in their roles as wife and mother, addressing social and cultural issues, though the working woman was not totally ignored, particularly by the KPD, the SPD and the DDP. The number of leaflets aimed at women soon fell after 1918, perhaps because of financial constraints, or the targeting of new groups, especially young people in the late 1920s and early 1930s, or because the parties believed that such propaganda was not necessary to mobilise the female vote. Electoral campaign leaflets tended to contain closely typed text on A4 paper, often coloured. Key words and phrases would appear in large bold print. A minority of the leaflets contained illustrations, frequently with caricature representations of other parties. In the first two elections of the Weimar Republic the leaflets concluded with an application form for party membership. The National Socialist Freedom Party in the December 1924 election also used this practice, with applicants having to sign that they were of German blood.[33]

Women usually wrote those electoral leaflets and pamphlets aimed at women, whereas the parties tended to employ graphic designers for their election posters, some of which were reproduced as postcards. The socialist parties had some notable artists to call upon, for example Käthe Kollwitz or John Heartfield, while the NSDAP bemoaned its lack of notable poster designers.[34] Gerhard Paul has noted that in urban areas election campaigns were fought primarily through the medium of posters and at meetings. He refers to 'the poster war' during every Weimar election campaign. In addition to hoardings on walls, kiosks and advertising columns, posters were displayed on election lorries and by men with sandwich boards. Whereas people could easily discard leaflets, posters were permanently visible, although Goebbels believed that they lost their effectiveness after eight days.[35]

Most posters were aimed at the electorate in general, with a minority being targeted at women. While these posters can give insight into the parties' views on how the women's vote could be won, it is impossible to determine their impact on women (or on men). We not know whether posters or any form of propaganda aimed at women played any role in persuading them to vote for a given party, nor whether women were more susceptible to the general political posters and propaganda of the parties than to the gender-specific ones. While it is relatively easy to detect some of the veiled messages in the parties' election posters – for example, the use of different scripts or colours (the SPD and the DDP tended to use the black, red and gold of the Republic, whereas the DNVP and, increasingly the DVP, used the imperial colours of black, red and white) – it is more difficult to pick up some of the allusions to Germany's cultural heritage.

In 1918–19 the SPD's poster stressed its belief in 'equal rights and equal duties', and throughout the Weimar Republic the SPD's posters appealed to women in a variety of guises – young working woman, wife, mother and responsible citizen.[36] In its leaflets the SPD emphasised its commitment to women's rights and promised better education and better worker protection. With the loss of 5 million votes between the elections to the National Assembly and the 1920 Reichstag election, and the fall in the numbers of women party members and of women in the trades union movement, the SPD reviewed the organisation of women's meetings and in 1924 the SPD newspaper *Vorwärts* began to publish a weekly supplement entitled *Die Wählerin* ('The Female Voter') during election campaigns. In 1927 the women's organisation decided to target women factory workers, believing that the party's current structures for factory agitation among women were insufficient as its representatives in factories were overwhelmingly male and they spent very little time trying to win women for the party. Throughout the Weimar Republic young working women were particularly hard to win, as they now had available to them a range of cultural and leisure activities, such as the cinema or dances, and were not as dependent on the SPD as their parents and grandparents had been for providing cultural and group activities.[37]

In 1930 it is likely that the SPD slogan 'Work for the father! Bread for the children!' found favour among women .[38] The theme of work and bread was subsequently adopted in 1932 by the Centre Party, the DVP and the NSDAP. Although the Nazis had begun to disrupt SPD meetings in late 1929, the SPD women's leader Marie Juchacz never once referred to them in an election speech in Hanover. However, with the success of the NSDAP at the polls in September 1930, when it polled 18.3 per cent of the vote and won 107 seats to become the second-largest party, the SPD's women's organisation turned its attention to raising awareness of Nazi attitudes to women. In December 1930 it published a poster, entitled 'Women, this is what will happen to you in the Third Reich', depicting a woman on her knees tying the bootlaces of a Nazi holding a whip (figure 3.1). It called on women to fight the Nazis by joining the Social Democrats. Similar posters followed, but were not part of any election

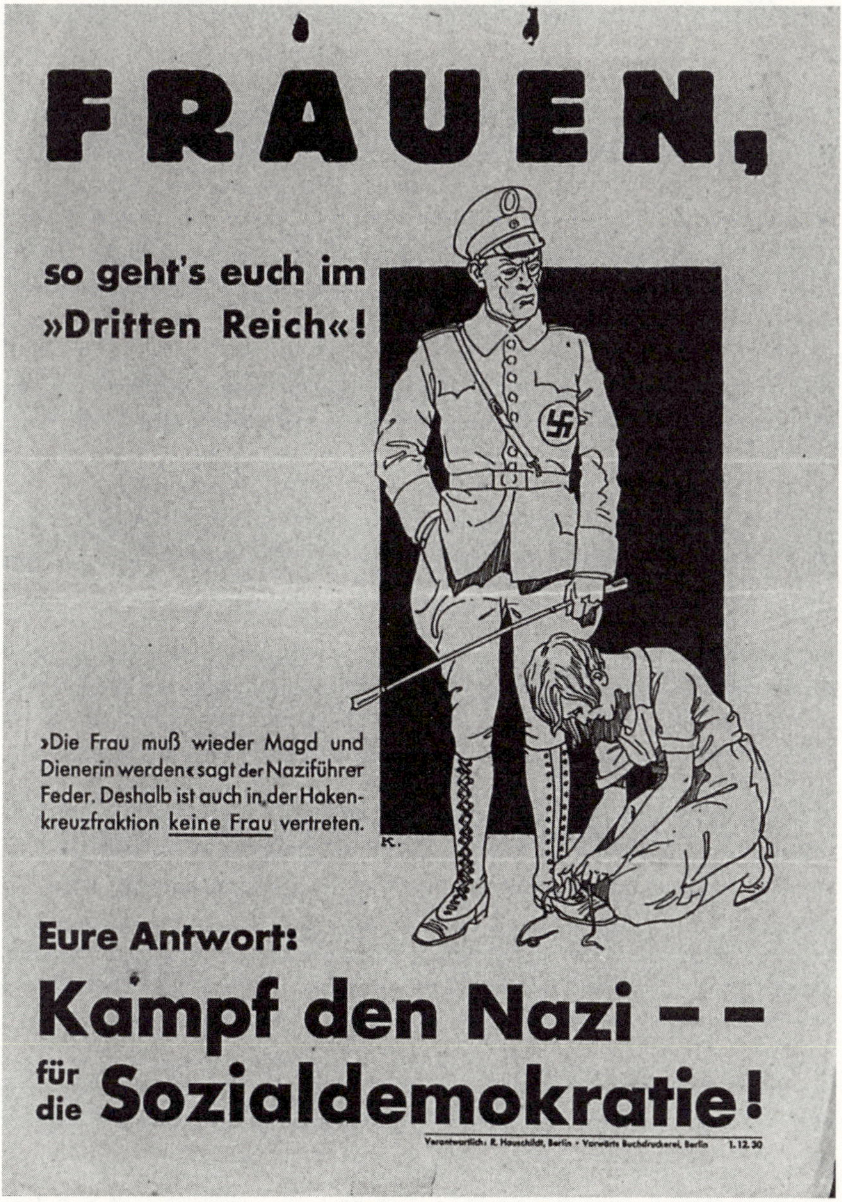

3.1 Anti-Nazi poster issued by the SPD, December 1930

campaign. The SPD women's section produced a slide lecture on Nazism, and in 1931 the largest number of women's meetings were held by the SPD since 1919, with 12 per cent of its local organisations having film or slide evenings.[39] In February 1932 the SPD produced a 227-page book entitled *National Socialism and Women's Issues. Material for Information and Use in the Struggle.*[40] In a 1932 electoral leaflet in which the SPD claimed that 'the German woman fights for a democratic Germany in the ranks of the SPD', the SPD criticised both the NSDAP and the KPD. In a leaflet for the Prussian *Landtag* election in April 1932, the SPD depicted a before and after scenario, with the Nazis courting women's votes and then throwing women out of politics. Women were reminded that they were in the majority and that the Nazis believed that blue- and white-collar women workers had no right to work. Mothers were told that the Nazis needed the masses for mass murder in a future war, whereas a victory for the SPD would mean an extension of women's rights, consolidation of peace and the education of young people to aid reconciliation between nations.[41] In the Reichstag elections of 1932 women were exhorted to vote SPD for freedom, welfare and peace or for freedom, work and peace.[42]

Throughout the Weimar Republic the SPD, with few exceptions, gained a higher share of the male than of the female vote, though the difference between the two narrowed. One reason offered for this decrease is that working-class men transferred their vote to the KPD.[43] The difference between the shares of the male and female votes going to the KPD was the largest of all the major political parties in the Weimar Republic. The party with the most radical platform on women's issues benefited least from women's suffrage.

The KPD's election leaflets and the pamphlets it produced between elections called unceasingly for equal pay for equal work, better worker protection for working mothers and a revocation of the laws concerning abortion. It praised the Soviet Union for its policies on women. There were few women-specific posters during the Weimar Republic, though depictions of women were frequently to be found in *Die Kommunistin* and the illustrated *Arbeiter-Illustrierte-Zeitung*. Eric Weitz writes of the party 'lurching from one image to another in the search for the way to appeal to women'.[44] A December 1924 poster of a haggard mother holding her baby and an emaciated child clutching her with a message that only the KPD was fighting for an end to the abortion laws is indicative of the many portrayals, several by Käthe Kollwitz, of downtrodden mothers that permeated the KPD's publications. A 1930 poster provides another image – that of the healthy young woman, left arm held aloft in a call to arms.[45] The language used in KPD propaganda tended to be militaristic and the front page of its general women's magazine, *Der Weg der Frau*, continued this military theme in October 1932 with a depiction of a mother wearing a gas mask putting a nappy on her baby, also wearing a gas mask, with the heading 'In the Third Reich every woman will have a man'.[46]

In its written propaganda the KPD did not portray women's work outside the home as an unremitting joy but stressed the low wages, long working hours and lack of protection. While this kind of propaganda can be understood as an attempt to win working women by advocating equal pay for equal work, such depictions can hardly have encouraged women to go out to work, which, according to Marxist theory, was a prerequisite for women's emancipation. The KPD had probably the most centrally directed organisation of all the parties for attempting to win women as members and voters. However, throughout the Weimar Republic there were complaints that not enough was being done, especially by men, to win women for the party.[47]

The Communists tried a variety of methods to attract women. In 1924 a three-pronged campaign was suggested for the elections: housewives could be approached while shopping for food; women workers could be canvassed in the factories; and mothers could be won over by the campaign against the abortion laws. In 1925 the party set up the Red Women and Girls' League and, according to Arendt, it became the main instrument for agitation among working-class women in the middle years of the Weimar Republic.[48] The KPD also set up the women's delegates' movement, one women being elected to represent fifty women at each meeting, to be held in factories and dole queues.[49] However, this targeting of women in factories and dole queues meant that the majority of women were ignored. Therefore, some areas decided to hold women's evenings, mixing entertainment and a lecture, or 'coffee and cake afternoons'.[50] The KPD, particularly its Working Group of Social Welfare Organisations, was instrumental in setting up the mass movement against the abortion laws which took to the streets in 1931; but the party, concerned about a large organisation of women it could not control, proved itself organisationally and ideologically unable to rise to the challenge of converting them to the party.[51]

Separate voting statistics reveal that the DDP received a marginally higher share of the male than of the female vote, in spite of the party's proud proclamation in 1918–19 that it was 'the party of women'. Its posters stressed its belief in women's rights and it produced a plethora of leaflets aimed at urban women – housewives, domestic servants, white- and blue-collar workers, women teachers and civil servants – promising them better working conditions and improvements in their promotion prospects.[52] In its posters after 1919 the DDP abandoned the call for women's rights and appealed to German women as mothers, though in its leaflets it continued to address issues of women's rights, especially those of working women. By 1930 the DDP's successor party, the DStP, was urging women to vote for calm and order. The DStP stood for recovery, not destruction, peace not civil war, unity not fragmentation, the people's community not the class struggle.[53] In 1932 it directly criticised the NSDAP's policy on women. A double-sided leaflet had caricatures of Hitler,

Feder, Goebbels and Strasser, quoting them and exhorting German women and girls to defend their womanhood, their families, their children, their dignity and their rights as human beings and citizens.[54] By 1932, however, the DStP had become almost insignificant in electoral terms, as had the other liberal party, the DVP.

In its leaflets to women the DVP stressed its commitment to preserving Christian and patriotic ideals and to protecting German Christian family life. It claimed to be 'the party of the German family' and also called for respect for women's rights and their work within the family and as employees.[55] In 1932 it produced an anti-Nazi booklet which drew attention to Nazi policies on women in public life. It called on women to vote DVP to ensure that women continued to have influence in public life and employment. The DVP also promised work and bread for the German people and the maintenance of order and high standards in public life in the German State.[56] Statistics from the districts where men and women voted separately reveal that the DVP received a marginally higher share of the female vote than it did of the male.[57] The one constant in DVP propaganda aimed at women is its emphasis on the German Christian family, an emphasis shared by the DNVP whose propaganda also contained a more nationalist ethos.

Throughout the Weimar Republic the DNVP consistently polled a higher share of the female than of the male vote in Protestant areas.[58] The DNVP based its propaganda for women on the twin pillars of religion and nationalism, as two posters clearly illustrate: one of 1928 depicts a grandmother and her granddaughter praying together; the other, of 1932, shows an older and a younger woman standing either side of the imperial flag under the heading 'German Women, German Loyalty', a phrase from the national anthem that appeared in DNVP propaganda throughout the Republic.[59] In its poster for the National Assembly elections the DNVP called on women to 'wake up and do your duty. The election will determine Germany's and your children's future. Help to save them. Vote German National' (figure 3.2). In 1918–19 and in the 1920s the DNVP aimed its written propaganda at a range of women – country women, housewives, white-collar workers, civil servants – and praised German women as the guardians of the German home, the German Christian family and Christian marriage. It stressed its support for religion, the home, freedom, law and order. [60] There is a noticeable absence of DNVP electoral material aimed specifically at women after 1928, though in 1932 it produced an anti-Nazi leaflet.[61]

The Centre Party was the party that benefited most from female suffrage throughout the Weimar Republic. In its posters targeting women it depicted an idealised vision of mother and child, against the background of a cross. The Centre Party's sister party in Bavaria, the BVP (*Bayerische Volkspartei* – Bavarian People's Party), shared this tendency, though here the blue and white

3.2 DNVP poster to the National Assembly

colours of Bavaria were prominent.[62] In its written propaganda the Centre Party called upon Christian women to preserve the Christian family and protect Christian schools and charitable organisations. It preached the sanctity of marriage and respect for women as wives and mothers, portraying itself as the bulwark against radicalism. The only reference it made to women's employment was a promise for improved worker protection.[63] In 1932, in a leaflet for the Bavarian *Landtag* election, Thusnelda Lang-Brumann, a BVP delegate to the Reichstag, asked 'What does a sensible woman want with Hitler?' and drew attention to Nazi pronouncements on women's role in public life and employment, and on religion.[64] The most noticeable thing about Centre Party propaganda aimed at women is, however, its paucity. Sneeringer has commented that the Centre Party took women for granted:[65] the party was well-aware that Catholic women's organisations and the Roman Catholic Church would mobilise its female voters.

The NSDAP was slow to target female voters, and it is generally assumed that it was not until the early 1930s that the Nazis believed that the women's vote would have to be actively won.[66] Although it produced no leaflets aimed at women in 1928, the party did produce a poster depicting three women, a mother holding her child, and a nurse and a young woman sitting at a desk, with the words 'Mothers, working women, we vote National Socialist'.[67] No leaflets or posters directly targeting the female vote were produced by the party in the 1930 election, but for the Reich presidential elections in 1932 it produced at least two, in one of which a woman is depicted, seated at a table holding a baby, her child and husband standing behind, with the inscription 'Millions of men without work, millions of children without a future'. Women were exhorted, in Germanic script, to 'save the German family'. In another poster, with a woman holding her hand to her mouth in a gesture of despair, her two children clinging to her, women are asked to think of their children. Hitler as the saviour of the family and Germany was a theme in other Reich presidential election posters in which figures of women appear: 'Our Last Hope' (figure 3.3) and 'Against Hunger and Despair'. In the posters for the presidential elections women are seen to be in despair, but in the NSDAP's July 1932 Reichstag election poster we see a drawing of the faces of two self-assured, happy women, with the simple inscription 'We Women Vote List 2 National Socialist'.[68] The newly created Nazi Women's League also produced a poster in 1932 with a woman and her two children looking towards the swastika sun rising, a church in the background. German women are exhorted to join together while German girls are told that they belong to the Nazis.[69] Here national rebirth through the NSDAP is combined with an acceptance of the significance of religion in women's voting patterns.

In its leaflets in 1932 the Nazis took issue with the other parties' propaganda concerning their views on women's role in society. One leaflet, for the Reich

3.3 Reich presidential election poster 1932

presidential elections, stated that the claims that Adolf Hitler wanted to drive women from their jobs and that the Nazis wanted to destroy the family were slanderous lies propounded by the newspapers of the 'system parties'. It went on to ask a range of women what the parties had done for them over the past thirteen years. Hitler's speech at the Sport Palace, in which he claimed that the Nazis regarded women as men's life companions, but that it was men's responsibility to ensure that women do not have to work to earn the daily bread and children should be seen as a joy, not a burden, was quoted at length. Women were asked to vote for Hitler and thereby rescue their jobs, family and children for the future. In a leaflet entitled 'What does Hitler want?' people were told that Hitler desires peace, order, thrift and high standards in public life, but not civil war, corruption, inflation or double-earners, the latter a reference to married working women.[70]

The NSDAP was increasing its appeal to women voters from 1930 onwards, so that by 1932 it was polling almost as high a share of the female as of the male vote in Protestant areas, and in Catholic areas the difference between the shares of male and female votes going to the Nazis was narrowing.[71]

This brief overview of party propaganda reveals that the parties of the Weimar Republic which benefited most from female suffrage were those that emphasised women's role within the family and Christian values. The parties' written propaganda reveals finely nuanced differences in the parties' attitudes to women's issues, and in the style and language in which they were expressed. Yet the lack of gender-specific propaganda furnished by the Centre Party, the DNVP after 1928 and the NSDAP before 1932 would suggest that women were not influenced greatly in their voting choice by gender-specific electoral propaganda. Women may have been attracted by a party's electoral propaganda on wider political, economic or foreign policy issues, where its stance may have been more distinctive.

III

As has been noted, propaganda alone did not mobilise the female vote. Winning women's votes was one of the tasks of the parties' women's committees, although some depended heavily on the help of existing women's organisations, with which many of the Reich Women's Committee members had links. The dependence of the Centre Party on Catholic women's organisations and the Catholic Church itself has already been noted. The liberal DDP was able to turn to local middle-class women's associations. The DNVP and, to a lesser extent, the DVP depended on local Protestant women's associations to mobilise women. In early 1919 the chair of the DNVP Reich Women's Committee Margarete Behm wrote to the wives of vicars to ask for their support in getting women to vote DNVP.[72] The DNVP could also depend on the rural housewives' associations and nationalist leagues to mobilise women in its support, at least until 1930. Thereafter some women in those organisations turned to the NSDAP, as did young Protestant women in the youth movement.[73] In some areas women from other organisations, such as the *Königin Luise Bund*, took part in Nazi rallies.[74] The NSDAP, believing that politics was a dirty business from which women should be kept unsullied, did not have a women's committee and therefore had no discrete organisation to entrust with winning women's votes for the party. While in other parties women worked closely with the male leadership on various issues, including its stance on women's representation, this was not the case within the NSDAP.[75]

The party's female adherents were joined together in various organisations, the best known being Elsbeth Zander's German Women's Order Red Swastika (DFO), founded in Berlin in 1923 and recognised by Hitler in 1926. The Order's aim was to remove women from the turmoil of party politics and to direct them towards social and welfare work; its tasks included running soup kitchens for the party and nursing SA men wounded in skirmishes with political opponents. It came under the direct jurisdiction of the party in 1928, and by December 1930 it was reported to have some 160 branches with around 4,000 members.[76] Other local Nazi women's groups were set up, at the instigation of women, in the mid-1920s in Plauen, Nuremberg, Kassel, Frankfurt and Hamburg, and the failure of the male leadership to coordinate women's activities allowed them some degree of independence and autonomy.[77]

It was partly in an attempt to control and coordinate women's activities within the party that the Nazi Women's Association (*Nationalsozialistische Frauenschaft*, NSF) was set up with effect from 1 October 1931. At all levels the NSF was under control of the male party leadership. Its remit included providing economic help such as soup kitchens, lessons in hygiene, indoctrination of party ideas and in educating German women to buy only German goods. Another of its tasks was to win women's votes for the party. By the spring of 1933 it had founded branches in all Germany's towns and larger villages.[78]

Ian Kershaw has noted that 'the quantity of Nazi propaganda amounted to a qualitative distinction from other bourgeois parties'.[79] The same might be said of its meetings, as in 1930 the Nazis held some 34,000 meetings and in the next two years held considerably more meetings than the SPD and KPD. Party activity was noted in the partisan press, though Paul notes that the NSDAP achieved more success at the polls when it received favourable comments in the bourgeois press.[80]

Childers claims that in 1932 the Nazi propaganda leadership inundated women with political literature emphasising religious and cultural themes, and that this propaganda was successful in mobilising women for the party, especially in Protestant areas.[81] However, as it is clear that gender-specific electoral propaganda did not play a decisive role in determining women's votes, other elements must have played a part in a woman's decision to vote for the NSDAP. Some historians have referred to Hitler's charismatic appeal for women, citing Rauschning's description of 'front seat women' with 'their expression of rapturous self-surrender, their moist and glistening eyes'.[82] The police had noted the presence of women at Hitler's rallies in the 1920s: when Hitler spoke in Heidelberg for the first time, on 6 August 1927, there were 1,000 women in his audience of 2,500.[83]

Had women only voted in the Reich presidential elections in 1932, however, Hindenburg would have won in the first round.[84] The NSDAP's attraction for women cannot have centred on Hitler alone, though contemporary observers noted Hitler's ability to 'address each member of his audience separately' and to 'deal with many of the grievances familiar to workaday people' in readily understandable language.[85] A Hitler rally in the early 1930s was an event judged well worth the cost of admission, with its singing, marching, flags, military music – and Hitler, portrayed as the one man who could save Germany and lead Germans to the promised land of the Third Reich.[86] But very few women who voted NSDAP will have heard Hitler speak. It has been noted that men followed the example set by local notables in joining the party, and this might also hold some explanatory power for women's political choices. The leaders of Nazi women's groups in Baden, for example, were wives of respected middle-class men, and the wives and daughters of local landowners and business magnates were seen at Hitler's rallies.[87] Meanwhile historians have offered a variety of reasons for explaining the Nazi female vote.

Renate Bridenthal believes that the Weimar Republic failed to bring women emancipation and tentatively suggests that a Nazi vote might be seen as one rejecting women's supposed economic emancipation.[88] This view resonates with the Nazis' claim to 'emancipate women from emancipation' and to emancipate women from employment, not from men.[89] Leila Rupp believes that the NSDAP was attractive to women because it shared their belief in the importance of their roles as wives and mothers; Childers, too, believes that women were drawn to Nazism by its anti-modernism and espousal of the three Ks – *Kinder, Kirche, Küche*.[90] Jill Stephenson believes that Hitler's promise of a husband for every women and a job for every husband was attractive to young women in monotonous factory or clerical work.[91] William Brustein has emphasised the part played in attracting voters by the NSDAP's coherent and innovative programmes for tackling the economic crisis; and Marit Berntson and Brian Ault have argued that these would have been attractive to single middle-class women, drawn by the promise to remove married women from paid employment, freeing up the employment market for them.[92]

These proposed reasons for women's support of Nazism highlight material self-interest. Richard Evans, however, thinks that some women voted NSDAP because they wanted to see the destruction of the Weimar Republic.[93] Michael Phayer sees an attraction for Protestant middle-class women in Nazi calls for national renewal, under Hitler's leadership, and in the NSDAP's pro-natalism and support for mothercare services.[94] Others have referred to the appeal of the Nazis' nationalism. As one upper-middle-class woman from Hamburg noted: 'every person who thinks and feels as a German, the bourgeois, the farmer, the aristocrat, the prince, the intelligentsia, stands by Hitler. It is the nationalist movement.'[95] Elizabeth Harvey has noted that the growth of nationalism among young Protestant women in the early 1930s, coupled with the Nazis' emphasis on the roles of women as wives and mothers, and their fight against decadent Weimar culture, led Protestant young women to support Nazism.[96]

Yet it is impossible to determine why German women voted for the NSDAP. As was noted above, it is possible that women were drawn in by the global image created by the NSDAP's electoral propaganda, meetings, marches, para-military units, flags and symbols, or by the party's stand on a particular aspect or aspects; they might have been following the example set by their husbands or male heads of households. The problem with many studies is that they treat the female electorate as an undifferentiated constituency. For the critical question is: *which* women were susceptible to Nazism?

Ian Kershaw has noted that the NSDAP was the only party to successfully corner the right-wing vote.[97] It benefited from the collapse of the liberal parties and won votes from the DNVP. It also, however, won voters from the SPD and first-time voters. Childers has referred to the NSDAP as a 'catch-all party', and it was a party to which all women, regardless of class, were susceptible unless they were staunch Catholics, especially in the countryside, committed ideologically to another party or affiliated to the labour movement.[98] Evans has noted the prominence of women in those groups – older voters such as pensioners – which are known to have supported the NSDAP; but it is clear that, by 1932, the NSDAP was attracting votes from Protestant women, young and old, of all classes in the towns and in the countryside.[99]

It is clear that prior to 1932 the NSDAP was attracting women's votes without targeting women as an electoral group. It did not actively seek to win the female vote until 1932, when it not only realised the significance of women's votes but was forced to repudiate the propaganda of other parties concerning its views on women's role in employment and public life. The concentration of all the other parties on attacking the NSDAP's purported policies on women meant, as Julia Sneeringer has noted, that women's rights became an election issue in 1932 for the first time since the beginning of the Republic.[100] But the way in which millions of women cast their vote in 1932 ensured that women's rights would be absent from the electoral agenda for some considerable time.

Notes

1 N. H. Baynes, *The Speeches of Adolf Hitler 1922–1939* (Oxford, 1942), p. 530.
2 As women were the majority of the electorate, however, this did not mean that the NSDAP received a higher share of the female than of the male vote. See Helen L. Boak, '"Our Last Hope": Women's Votes for Hitler – A Reappraisal', *German Studies Review*, 12 (1989), pp. 289–310. In two Bavarian strongholds, Ansbach and Dinkelsbühl, the NSDAP did poll 50 per cent or more of women's votes in November 1932 and March 1933: *Zeitschrift des bayerischen statistischen Landesamtes*, 63 (1931), pp. 93–4; 65 (1933), pp. 103–4.
3 Thomas Childers, *The Nazi Voter: The Social Foundations of Fascism in Germany, 1919–1933* (Chapel Hill, NC, and London, 1983); Daniela Janusch, *Die plakative Propaganda der Sozialdemokratischen Partei Deutschlands zu den Reichstagswahlen 1928 bis 1932* (Bochum, 1989); Gerhard Paul, *Aufstand der Bilder: Die NS-Propaganda vor 1933* (Bonn, 1990).
4 Julia Sneeringer, *Winning Women's Votes. Propaganda and Politics in Weimar Germany* (Chapel Hill, NC, and London, 2002).
5 Richard Bessel, 'The Rise of the NSDAP and the Myth of Nazi Propaganda', *Wiener Library Bulletin*, 33 (1980), pp. 20–9.
6 Oded Heilbronner, 'The Failure that Succeeded: Nazi Party Activity in a Catholic Region in Germany, 1929–32', *Journal of Contemporary History*, 27 (1992), pp. 531–49.
7 Ian Kershaw, 'Ideology, Propaganda, and the Rise of the Nazi Party', in Peter D. Stachura, *The Nazi Machtergreifung* (London, 1983), pp. 162–81.
8 *Reichsgesetzblatt 1918*, 153 (12 November 1918), p. 1304. Kurt Eisner had proclaimed female suffrage in Bavaria on 7 November 1918: *Die Frau im Staat*, 10:11 (November 1918), p. 1.
9 On the parties' women's groupings and their role see Helen Boak, 'Women in Weimar Politics', *European History Quarterly*, 20 (1990), pp. 369–99. On the KPD see BAK, R45IV/17, pp. 19ff. and 'Frauenarbeit ist nicht Arbeit der Frauen der Partei, sondern Arbeit der Partei unter den Frauen', in Forschungsgemeinschaft Geschichte des Kampfes der deutschen Arbeiterklasse um die Befreiung der Frau, *Dokumente der revolutionären deutschen Arbeiterbewegung zur Frauenfrage 1848–1974* (Leipzig, 1975), pp. 98–100.
10 Kate Lacey, 'From *Plauderei* to Propaganda: On Women's Radio in Germany, 1924–35', *Media, Culture and Society*, 16 (1994), pp. 589–607. Paul notes that the Brüning cabinet permitted party propaganda on the radio for the July 1932 election. Hitler was not, however, heard on the radio until after 30 January 1933: Paul, *Aufstand*, p. 196.
11 Additionally, some 2,987,011 women were widowed or divorced, of whom 623 were under 20. Of the married women, 790,598 were employed outside of the home in blue- or white-collar work; of the widowed and divorced, 380,859. Married women numbering 3,645,326 were classed as employed, 2,501,335 women were classed as family helpers, 309,160 as independent workers (primarily homeworkers) and 44,233 as domestic servants: calculated from figures in *Statistisches Jahrbuch für das deutsche Reich 1932*, pp. 12–13; *Statistik des deutschen Reiches,*

402, pp. 452–3. There were 18,769,662 men over 20.

12 Karen Hagemann, 'Men's Demonstrations and Women's Protest: Gender in Collective Action in the Urban Working-Class Milieu in the Weimar Republic', *Gender and History*, 5 (1993), pp. 101–19.

13 Karen Hagemann, *Frauenalltag und Männerpolitik: Alltagsleben und gesellschaftliches Handeln von Arbeiterfrauen in der Weimarer Republik* (Bonn, 1990), pp. 539–41, 563; Adelheid von Saldern, 'Modernization as Challenge. Perceptions and Reactions of German Social Democratic Women', in H. Gruber and P. Graves (eds), *Women and Socialism* (Oxford, 1998), pp. 95–134; Karen Hagemann, '"Equal But Not the Same": The Social Democratic Women's Movement in the Weimar Republic', in Roger Fletcher (ed.), *Bernstein to Brandt. A Short History of German Social Democracy* (London, 1987), pp. 133–43; Eric D. Weitz, *Creating German Communism, 1890–1990: From Popular Protests to Socialist State* (Princeton, NJ, 1996), pp. 221, 223–4; Atina Grossmann, 'German Communism and New Women: Dilemmas and Contradictions', in Huber and Graves (eds), *Socialism*, pp. 135–68.

14 James Wickham, 'Working-Class Movement and Working-Class Life: Frankfurt am Main during the Weimar Republic', *Social History*, 8 (1983), pp. 315–43; Paul, *Aufstand*, pp. 187–94; Janusch, *Propaganda*, pp. 35–6.

15 Hagemann, *Alltag*, pp. 546–7

16 Hagemann, 'Demonstrations', pp. 105, 107–9.

17 Richard Bessel, 'Violence as Propaganda: The Role of the Storm Troopers in the Rise of National Socialism', in Thomas Childers (ed.), *The Formation of the Nazi Constituency 1919–1933* (Totowa, 1986), pp. 131–46; Thomas Childers, 'Voters and Violence: Political Violence and the Limits of National Socialist Mass Mobilization', *German Studies Review*, 13 (1990), pp. 481–98.

18 Landesarchiv Berlin (LAB), Z. Sg. 2088, 'Arbeitende Frauen und Mädchen'; Sneeringer, *Winning*, pp. 256–7.

19 In Bremen 79.8 per cent of men and 87.7 per cent of women made use of their vote, in Baden 89.2 per cent of men and 83.7 per cent of women: R. Hartwig, 'Wie die Frauen im Deutschen Reich von ihrem politischen Wahlrecht Gebrauch machen', *Allgemeines Statistisches Archiv*, 17 (1928), pp. 497–512. Hofmann-Göttig's figures reveal that 14,572,345 women out of 17,710,872 eligible voters did so (82.3 per cent); for men the figures were 12,572,345 out of 15,051,114, highlighting the fact that women were the majority of the electorate and that a lower female turnout, or share of the vote, did not necessarily mean the actual number of women voting was smaller than the number of men: Joachim Hoffmann-Göttig, *Emanzipation mit dem Stimmzettel: 70 Jahre Frauenwahlrecht in Deutschland* (Bonn, 1986), pp. 27–8.

20 In Mannheim, for example, 69.2 per cent of eligible male voters aged 20 did so, as did 78.6 per cent of men aged 21–25 and 86.3 per cent of men over 25; for women these figures were 78.4, 78.2 and 81.5 per cent, respectively: Hartwig, 'Wie die Frauen', pp. 502–5.

21 Thomas Childers, 'The Social Language of Politics in Germany: The Sociology of Political Discourse in the Weimar Republic', *American Historical Review*, 95:2 (1990), pp. 331–58; and 'Languages of Liberalism: Liberal Political Discourse in

the Weimar Republic', in Konrad H. Jarausch and Larry Eugene Jones (eds), *In Search of Liberal Germany: Studies in the History of German Liberalism from 1789 to the Present* (Oxford, 1990), pp. 323–59.

22 *Protokoll über die Verhandlungen des Parteitages der SPD*: Weimar, 1919, p. 465; Görlitz, 1921, p. 15; Heidelberg, 1925, p. 8; Magdeburg, 1929, p. 235; *Die Gleichheit*, 29:14 (1919), p. 105; *Die Kommunistin*, 3:6 (1921), pp. 412; BAK, Z. Sg. 1.65/77, 'Frauen im Kampf um Brot und Freiheit'; BAK, Z. Sg. 1.91/7, Proceedings of the USPD's Women's Conference held in Leipzig, November 29–30, 1919, pp. 518–21; Zentrale der KPD, *Referentenmaterial: Mutter und Kind in Deutschland und Russland* (Berlin, 1926), pp. 14–15; Ernst Kahn, *Der internationale Geburtenstreik* (Berlin, 1930), p. 69. Various divorce petitions found in BAK, Nachlass Lüders 232. On the law to dismiss married female civil servants see Helen Boak, 'The State as an Employer of Women in the Weimar Republic', in W. R. Lee and E. Rosenhaft (eds), *The State and Social Change in Germany 1880–1980* (Oxford, 1990), pp. 61–98.

23 BAK, R45II/62, pp. 109–24, 'Grundsätze der DVP'.

24 BAK, Nachlass Lüders 135, press-cutting from the *Deutsche Allgemeine Zeitung* of 3 December 1930.

25 BAK, Z. Sg. 1.108/7, pamphlets entitled 'Zentum und neue Zeit' and 'Zentrum und politische Neuordnung'.

26 'Die christliche Ehe. Enzyklika des Papstes Pius XI vom 31. Dezember 1930', *Archiv für Bevölkerungsfragen*, 1 (1931), pp. 24–56.

27 BAK, Z. Sg. 1.44/8, 'Richtlinien der Deutschnationalen Volkspartei für Frauenfragen'. DNVP petition of 7 March 1928 found in BAK, Nachlass Lüders 233. Scheck says that the DNVP reviewed its guidelines in 1933: Raffael Scheck, 'Women on the Weimar Right: The Role of Female Politicians in the Deutschnationale Volkspartei (DNVP)', *Journal of Contemporary History*, 36 (2001), pp. 547–60.

28 Roderick Stackelberg and Sally A. Winkle, *The Nazi Germany Sourcebook* (London and New York, 2002), pp. 63–6.

29 Hans-Jürgen Arendt, Sabine Hering and Leonie Wagner (eds), *Nationalsozialistische Frauenpolitik vor 1933* (Frankfurt am Main, 1995), pp. 19–22.

30 Sofia Rabe, *Die Frau im nationalsozialistischen Staat* (Munich, 1932), pp. 9–12; petition no. 408 to the Prussian *Landtag* found in Archiv des ADLV, packet 16.

31 Wilhelm Frick, *Die Nationalsozialisten im Reichstag 1924–1931* (Munich, 1932), pp. 63ff.; Leila Rupp, 'Mother of the *Volk*: The Image of Women in Nazi Ideology', *Signs: Journal of Women in Culture and Society*, 3 (1977), pp. 362–79.

32 Arendt, Hering and Wagner (eds), *Frauenpolitik*, pp. 30–1; Rabe, *Frau*, p. 7.

33 LAB, Z. Sg. 240, leaflet entitled 'Deutsche Männer und Frauen Gross-Berlins!'

34 Paul, *Aufstand*, pp. 151–2.

35 Berlin had 3,000 hoardings and there were almost 31,000 in another 2,423 German towns: Paul, *Aufstand*, pp. 96, 151ff.

36 A range of SPD posters is to be found on the website of the Archiv der Sozialdemokratie, Friedrich-Ebert-Stiftung at www.fes.de/archiv.

37 Hagemann, *Frauenalltag*, pp. 539–41, 563; Adelheid von Saldern, 'Modernization', p. 120.

38 Janusch, *Propaganda*, pp. 122–4; Paul, *Aufstand*, p. 247. The same slogan was used

in the 1932 Prussian *Landtag* election: Thomas Friedrich, *Berlin: A Photographic Portrait of the Weimar Years 1918–1933* (London, 1991), p. 224.

39 Hagemann, *Alltag*, pp. 546–7; Donna Harsch, *German Social Democracy and the Rise of Nazism* (Chapel Hill, 1993), pp. 67, 83.

40 BAK, Z. Sg. 1.90/43.

41 LAB, Z. Sg. 2088, leaflets entitled 'Wir Wählerinnen sind die Mehrheit in der Nation', 'Mütter'; BAK, Z. Sg. 1.90/41, 'Die deutsche Frau kämpft für ein demokratisches Deutschland in den Reihen der SPD'. In another leaflet it reminded female workers in agriculture and the wives of male agricultural workers that women formed the majority of the electorate and their vote would be decisive.

42 Childers, *The Nazi Voter*, p. 289; Evangelisches Zentralarchiv, Berlin (EZA), 1565/94; leaflet entitled 'Frauen Mütter' found at http://library.fes.de.library/netzquelle/rechtsextremismus/plak11.html

43 Boak, '"Our Last Hope"', p. 293.

44 Weitz, *Creating German Communism*, p. 205.

45 Karen Hagemann and Jan Kolossa, *Gleiche Rechte – Gleiche Pflichten?* (Hamburg, 1990), p. 68; Karen Hagemann (ed.), *Eine Frauensache: Alltagsleben und Geburtenpolitik 1919–1933* (Pfaffenweiler, 1991), p. 115.

46 Silvia Kontos, *Die Partei kämpft wie ein Mann* (Frankfurt am Main and Basle, 1979), p. 62.

47 See note 9 and 'Die Arbeit unter den Frauen', in Institut für Marxistische Studien und Forschungen, *Arbeiterbewegung und Frauenemanziption 1889 bis 1933* (Frankfurt am Main, 1973), pp. 69–71.

48 Hans-Jürgen Arendt and Werner Freigang, 'Der Rote Frauen- und Mädchenbund – die revolutionäre deutsche Frauenorganisation in der Weimarer Republik', *Beiträge zur Geschichte der Arbeiterbewegung*, 21 (1979), pp. 249–58.

49 Forschungsgemeinschaft Geschichte des Kampfes der deutschen Arbeiterklasse um die Befreiung der Frau, *Die Frau und die Gesellschaft* (Leipzig, 1974), pp. 97–100; Hans-Jürgen Arendt, 'Das Reichskomittee werktätiger Frauen 1919–32', *Beiträge zur Geschichte der Arbeiterbewegung*, 23 (1981), pp. 743–8.

50 Atina Grossmann writes of Helene Overlach, the leader of the Reich Women's Bureau from 1927 and a KPD delegate in the Reichstag from 1928 to 1933, taking her own brochures round the yards of Berlin tenement buildings, her guitar strapped to her back: Atina Grossmann, 'German Communism and New Women', p. 152; Weitz, *Creating German Communism*, p. 224.

51 Grossmann, 'German Communism and New Women', pp. 152–4. On the whole 1931 campaign see Atina Grossmann, *Reforming Sex: The German Movement for Birth Control and Abortion Reform 1920–1950* (Oxford, 1995), pp. 76–106.

52 LAB, B/219, 'Das Wahlrecht', B/217, 'Wir demokratischen Frauen!', B/229, 'Deutsche Frauen', B/222, 'Hausangestellte', B/227, 'An die Hausfrauen!', B/196, 'An die Arbeiterinnen!', B/197, 'An die weiblichen Angestellten', B/197, 'An die Lehrerinnen!'. Larry Eugene Jones comments that the DDP distributed 20 million leaflets for the National Assembly elections, of which a quarter were aimed at women: Larry Eugene Jones, *German Liberalism and the Dissolution of the Weimar Party System, 1918–1933* (Chapel Hill, NC, and London, 1988), p. 22. Sneeringer

found 53 DDP leaflets from 1918–20 aimed at women: *Winning Women's Votes*,
p. 22.

53 LAB, 2088, 'An die deutschen Frauen!'; BAK, Z. Sg. 1.27/6, 'Frauen aller Stände –
wir rufen euch auf!', 'Deutsche! Halt! Rufen wir Frauen'. Childers has noted the
DDP was the only political party to attempt to construct a new language of democratic participation in the Weimar Republic: Childers, 'Social Language of Politics in Germany', p. 326.

54 LAB, Z. Sg. 240. The first page is depicted in Sneeringer, *Winning Women's Votes*,
p. 235.

55 BAK, Z. Sg. 1.42/7, 'Die Frau und die DVP', 'Deutsche Frauen, deutsche Mütter'.

56 Elisabeth Schwarzhaupt, *Was hat die Frau vom Nationalsozialismus zu erwarten?*
(Berlin, 1932); EZA 1565/94, 'Ein Wort an die Frauen!'

57 Gabriele Bremme, *Die politische Rolle der Frau in Deutschland* (Göttingen, 1956),
p. 72.

58 *Ibid.*, p. 70.

59 Janusch, *Propaganda*, pp. 173, 178; Hagemann and Kolossa, *Rechte*, p. 69. Phayer
claims that Protestant women were more nationalistic than Catholic women:
Michael Phayer, *Protestant and Catholic Women in Nazi Germany* (Detroit, 1990),
pp. 35–7.

60 LAB, Z. Sg. 241/1024, no. 60, 'Die deutsche Frau'; BAP, 62DAF3/695, 'Wir wissen,
was wir am 4. Mai zu tun haben, wir deutschen Frauen!', 'Beamtinnen und
weibliche Angestellte aller Berufe', 'Wir deutschen Frauen in Stadt und Land',
'Wir Landfrauen', 'Deutsche Frauen'; EZA, 1565/94, 'Deutsche Frauen, was wird
aus Euren Kindern?', 'Was sagen die Reichstagswahlen den Arbeiterinnen?',
'Junge Arbeiterin', 'Warum müssen Christen wählen?', 'Schwestern, Hebammen,
Wohlfahrtspflegerinnen!', 'Warum wählt die deutsche Frau?'

61 Sneeringer also notes the lack of material and claims there was just one leaflet,
aimed at housewives, in 1930: Sneeringer, *Winning Women's Votes*, pp. 177–9; 1932
leaflet found in BAP, 60Vo2DNVP 490.

62 Sneeringer, *Winning Women's Votes*, p. 151; Janusch, *Propaganda*, p. 189.

63 BAK, Z. Sg. 1.108/9, 'Für Ordnung, Ruhe und Sachlichkeit', 'Deutsche Frauen –
Wahrheit, Freiheit, Recht'; LAB, B/68, 'Einig und Treu!', 'Deutsche Frauen!'; BAK,
Z. Sg. 1.108/7 'Der Sozialismus und der Würde der Frau'.

64 BAK, Kleine Erwerbungen 65/4, pp. 69–73.

65 BAK, Z. Sg. 1.108/9, 'Für Ordnung, Ruhe und Sachlichkeit', 'Deutsche Frauen –
Wahrheit, Freiheit, Recht'; Sneeringer, *Winning Women's Votes*, p. 92.

66 Boak, '"Our Last Hope"', p. 301; Jill Stephenson, Claudia Koonz, Thomas Childers
and Gerhard Paul date the targeting of women voters to 1932: Childers, *The Nazi
Voter*, p. 198; Jill Stephenson, 'National Socialism and Women Before 1933', in
Stachura (ed.), *Machtergreifung*, pp. 33–48; Claudia Koonz, 'Nazi Women before
1933: Rebels Against Emancipation', *Social Science Quarterly*, 56 (1976), pp.
553–63; Paul, *Aufstand*, p. 217. Only 5 of the 168 Nazi posters seen by Paul were
directly targeted at women.

67 Sneeringer, *Winning Women's Votes*, p. 161.

68 Posters to be found in Paul, *Aufstand*.

69 Hagemann and Kolossa, *Rechte*, p. 172.

70 Leaflets found in LAB, Z. Sg. 2088.

71 Boak, '"Our Last Hope"', pp. 298–301.

73 On the Protestant Women's League's mobilisation of women for the National Assembly see Carol Gale Woodfin, 'Reluctant Democrats: Women of the Protestant *Frauenhilfe* and Weimar Politics 1918–1933', PhD thesis, University of Nashville, 1997, pp. 69–70; Nancy Reagin, *A German Women's Movement: Class and Gender in Hanover, 1880–1933* (Chapel Hill, NC, and London, 1995), pp. 204, 234; Renate Bridenthal, 'Organized Rural Women and the Conservative Mobilization of the German Countryside in the Weimar Republic', in Larry Eugene Jones and James Retallack (eds), *Between Reform, Reaction and Resistance* (Oxford, 1993), pp. 375–405; Elizabeth Harvey, 'Serving the *Volk*, Saving the Nation: Women in the Youth Movement and Public Sphere in Weimar Germany', in Larry Eugene Jones and James Retallack (eds), *Elections, Mass Politics and Social Change in Modern Germany: New Perspectives* (Cambridge, 1992), pp. 201–21.

74 This happened in Neulussheim and Karlsruhe in Baden from 1926: Staatsarchiv Freiburg, 317/1257d–e, police report of 1 December 1926; Johnpeter Grill, *The Nazi Party in Baden 1920–1945* (Chapel Hill, NC, and London, 1983), p. 223.

76 NSDAP Hauptarchiv, reel 89, folder 1865, frame 80, announcement sheet no. 23 of the Berlin police headquarters of 1 December 1930. On the German Women's Order see Jill Stephenson, *The Nazi Organisation of Women* (London, 1981), pp. 23–58.

77 Michael H. Kater, 'Frauen in der NS-Bewegung', *Vierteljahrshefte für Zeitgeschichte*, 31:2 (1983), pp. 202–41; Koonz, 'Nazi Women', p. 558; and 'The Competition for a Women's Lebenraum, 1928–1934', in Renate Bridenthal, Atina Grossmann and Marion Kaplan (eds), *When Biology Became Destiny: Women in Weimar and Nazi Germany* (New York, 1984), pp. 199–236.

78 The number of women in the DFO rose from 4,000 in August 1930 to 10,000 in September 1931. Figures for the Nazi Women's Association reveal 19,382 members in December 1931, rising to 109,320 a year later: Arendt, Hering and Wagner (eds), *Frauenpolitik*, pp. 325–6. For the foundation of the NS-Frauenschaft see Stephenson, *Nazi Organisation of Women*, pp. 44–58.

79 Kershaw, 'Ideology', p. 174.

80 Paul, *Aufstand*, pp. 125–6, 185–6.

81 Childers, *The Nazi Voter*, pp. 259–60.

82 Hermann Rauschning, *Hitler Speaks* (London, 1939), p. 259; Joachim C. Fest, *The Face of the Third Reich* (London, 1970), p. 265; Hans-Peter Bleuel, *Strength Through Joy: Sex and Society in Nazi Germany* (London and Edinburgh, 1972), p. 46; Claudia Koonz, *Mothers in the Fatherland: Women, the Family and Nazi Politics* (London, 1986), p. 60.

83 Staatsarchiv Freiburg, 317/1257 d–e, police report of 1 November 1927; Grill, *Nazi Party*, p. 223.

84 Hindenburg received 51.5 per cent of the female and 44.2 per cent of the male vote in the first round, Hitler 26.5 per cent and 28.3 per cent, respectively. In the second round Hindenburg received 56 per cent of the female and 48.7 per cent of the male vote, Hitler 33.6 per cent of the female and 35.9 per cent of the male: Arendt, Hering and Wagner (eds), *Frauenpolitik*, p. 332.

85 Katherine Thomas, *Women in Nazi Germany* (London, 1943), pp. 21, 23–5.

86 *Ibid.*, pp. 23–5; Koonz, *Mothers in the Fatherland*, p. 65.

87 Kershaw, 'Ideology', p. 172. Thomas, *Women in Nazi Germany*, p. 27. Dr Hildebrand's wife led the Karlsruhe branch of the DFO and Dr Endemann's wife was noted for her propaganda activity: Grill, *Nazi Party*, p. 590.

88 Renate Bridenthal, 'Beyond "*Kinder, Küche, Kirche*": Weimar Women at Work', *Central European History*, 6 (1973), pp. 148–66; Richard Evans, 'German Women and the Triumph of Hitler', *Journal of Modern History*, 48 (1976), on-demand supplement.

89 Rabe, *Frau*, pp. 6, 9.

90 Rupp, 'Mother of the *Volk*', p. 375; Childers, *The Nazi Voter*, p. 267.

91 Stephenson, 'National Socialism', pp. 44–5; Koonz also believes that Hitler's 'promise to provide a husband for every woman ... had great appeal': Claudia Koonz, 'Mothers in the Fatherland: Women in Nazi Germany', in Renate Bridenthal and Claudia Koonz (eds), *Becoming Visible: Women in European History*, 2nd edn (Boston, MA, and London, 1987), pp. 445–73.

92 William Brustein, 'Nazism Through Democracy: Why 14 million Germans Voted for the Nazi Party', *Research on Democracy and Society*, 3 (1996), pp. 327–52; Marit A. Berntson and Brian Ault, 'Gender and Nazism: Women Joiners of the Pre-1933 Nazi Party', *American Behavioral Scientist*, 41 (1998), pp. 1193–218.

93 Richard Evans, *Comrades and Sisters: Feminism, Socialism and Pacifism in Europe 1870–1945* (Brighton, 1987), p. 185.

94 Phayer, *Protestant and Catholic Women*, pp. 42–55. On reasons why Protestant working-class women may have been drawn to Nazism see Helen Boak, 'National Socialism and Working-Class Women before 1933', in Conan Fischer (ed.), *The Rise of National Socialism and the Working Classes in Weimar Germany* (Oxford, 1996), pp. 163–88.

95 Jeremy Noakes and Geoffrey Pridham, *Nazism 1919–1945*, vol. 1: *The Rise to Power 1919–1934* (Exeter, 1983), pp. 80–1; Berntson and Ault, 'Gender and Nazism', pp. 1201, 1211.

96 Elizabeth Harvey, 'Gender, Generation and Politics: Young Protestant Women in the Final Years of the Weimar Republic', in Mark Roseman (ed.), *Generations in Conflict* (Cambridge, 1995), pp. 184–209.

97 Kershaw, 'Ideology', p. 177.

98 Childers, *The Nazi Voter*, p. 265; and 'The Social Bases of the National Socialist Vote', *Journal of Contemporary History*, 11 (1976), pp. 17–42.

99 Evans, *Comrades and Sisters*, p. 184.

100 Sneeringer, *Winning Women's Votes*, p. 231.

4

'Working towards the Führer': charismatic leadership and the image of Adolf Hitler in Nazi propaganda

David Welch

In 1941, at the height of Germany's military success, Joseph Goebbels informed his officials in the Ministry for Popular Enlightenment and Propaganda that his two notable propaganda achievements were, first, 'the style and technique of the Party's public ceremonies; the ceremonial of the mass demonstrations, the ritual of the great Party occasion, and, second, that through his 'creation of the Führer-myth, Hitler had been given the halo of infallibility, with the result that many people who looked askance at the Party after 1933 had now complete confidence in Hitler'.[1]

Ian Kershaw, who has subjected the relationship between Hitler and the German people to a systematic analysis, has demonstrated that Hitler was indeed the most vital legitimising force within the regime.[2] More recently, Kershaw's position is set out in a phrase that has become synonymous with his work, namely: 'working towards the Führer'. According to Kershaw, the 'vision' embodied in Hitler's leadership claim served to funnel a variety of social motivations, at times contradictory and conflicting, into furthering – intentionally or unwittingly – Nazi aims closely associated with Hitler's own ideological obsessions.[3] The concept of 'charismatic authority' and the '*Führerprinzip*' (leadership principle) are central to Kershaw's interpretation of the workings of the Hitlerian state. Although Kershaw's work is closely associated with the manner in which different groups within Germany received the Hitler-myth, his body of work, including the massive two-volume biography of Hitler, has rarely dwelt on the dissemination of images of 'charismatic authority' in Nazi propaganda.[4] For a contemporary audience, the overriding image of Hitler drawn from old Nazi newsreels is one of a deranged demi-god 'milking' large rallies of the faithful. Surprisingly, few scholarly works have analysed in depth the different ways in which Hitler was portrayed in National Socialist propaganda. How was Hitler presented to the German people, and did the images of the Führer change during the course of the Third Reich? It is my intention in this chapter to explore the various ways in which Hitler was disseminated in Nazi propaganda and how those images shaped German public opinion.

The cult of the leader, which surpassed any normal level of trust in political leadership, is central to an understanding of the appeal of National Socialism, and it was undoubtedly the most important theme cementing together Nazi propaganda. The Nazis turned to *völkisch* thought (a product of nineteenth-century German Romanticism) and the notion of *Führerprinzip*, a mystical figure embodying and guiding the nation's destiny. In *practical* terms this meant that decisions came down from above instead of being worked out by discussion and choice from below. The roots and antecedents of such a concept are more complex and derive from many sources: the messianism of Christianity; the thaumaturgic kings of the Middle Ages; the Nietzschean 'superman' of *völkisch* mythology, and rightist circles in Germany prior to the First World War. However, the Nazi belief in the *Führerprinzip*, as it found expression in Germany after 1933, stemmed partly from the distaste which Germans felt towards the nineteenth century for the determining of policy by the counting of votes, and partly from the way in which Nazi philosophers such as Alfred Bäumler had reinterpreted Nietzsche's concept of the 'triumph of the will' in terms of individual genius. The *Führerprinzip* was to be based on a very special personality, one possessed of the will and power to actualise the *Volksstaat*. That will and power would be realised in the man of destiny – resolute, uncompromising, dynamic and radical – who would destroy the old privileged and class-ridden society and replace it with the ethnically pure and socially harmonious 'national community' (*Volksgemeinschaft*). By implication it would be the antithesis of democracy. The extreme fragmentation of Weimar politics, which was increasingly seen in terms of a failure to govern, served only to make such leadership qualities appear all the more attractive.

The period between the re-founding of the NSDAP in 1925 and the Reichstag elections of July 1932, when the Nazis emerged as the largest political party in Germany, marks a sea-change in their fortunes. Nevertheless it is important to remind ourselves just how insignificant Hitler and the NSDAP were to the centre stage of Weimar politics in the period leading up to their electoral breakthrough. The onset of the Depression, with its devastating effects on the German middle and working classes, helped win support. But, equally, much of the success must be attributed to the creation of the Führer-myth and the movement's quasi-religious identification with its leader Adolf Hitler. Nazi propaganda that depicted Hitler as an uncompromising opponent of the Weimar Republic had the effect of setting Hitler apart from other politicians tainted by their association with the Weimar system, which had now become synonymous with political humiliation and economic failure.

Symbolic of the intensification of the 'cult of leader' was the compulsory 'Heil Hitler' greeting for all party members. Heinrich Hoffmann, Hitler's official photographer, produced a series of stylised postcards showing Hitler in different resolute poses. In the last days of the 1932 election campaign, amidst a sea of coloured election posters, the Nazis confidently produced a strikingly effective black-and-white election poster consisting of Hitler's disembodied head against a black background. Below the face, in white capitals, was simply 'HITLER'. No electioneering slogan was thought necessary: the juxtaposition of face and name was considered sufficient. Hitler's familiarity in an age when the mass media was only just being recognised as a potent political force had been established largely by his astonishing election schedule. By taking to the skies in his *Deutschlandflug*, accompanied by the slogan 'The Führer over Germany', Hitler addressed major rallies in twenty different cities within a period of only six days. Writing in *Der Angriff* during the 1932 election campaign, Goebbels heralded Hitler as 'the Greater German, the Führer, the Prophet, the Fighter that last hope of the masses, the shining symbol of the German will to freedom'.[5] The umbilical bond within this 'charismatic community' became so closely identified with the absolute authority of its leader that when Germans voted in elections in the early 1930s, the ballot card referred not to the NSDAP but to the 'Hitler Movement' (*Hitlerbewegung*).

In opposition the NSDAP relied largely on Hitler's speeches and the party press to convey its message. Once in power the Nazis took control of the means of communication by establishing the Ministry for Popular Enlightenment and Propaganda (*Reichministerium für Volksaufklärung und Propaganda* – RMVP). How did the monopoly of power change the manner in which Hitler as Führer was presented in Nazi propaganda? Did this image change during the course of the Third Reich – and particularly after 1939 and the outbreak of war? Moreover, was there a distinction between the way in which he was presented to the party faithful and the manner in which he appeared in national propaganda?

Bearing in mind Goebbels's 1932 electioneering slogan, I wish to keep the themes of Hitler as Führer, prophet and fighter very much to the fore in the following analysis. I do not, however, intend to restrict myself to a chronological narrative.

'Führer-power' operated at a number of levels. For disparate activists within the NSDAP, Hitler as undisputed 'Führer' represented the unifying force of the movement. Embodied in the notion of the *Führerprinzip* was recognition on the part of all the different interests within the party of where power resided. As such the *Führerprinzip* governed the organisational structure of Nazism and provided it with its unique source of legitimacy. For the mass population who were not party members, on the other hand, Hitler filled a vacuum created by the sudden loss of the monarchy in 1918.[6] Nazi propaganda presented him as a contemporary *Volkskaiser* who transcended party politics, but a leader who demanded unconditional loyalty and obedience in order to bring about the *Volksgemeinschaft*. This mass recognition proved particularly important in persuading non-Nazi elites to accept Hitler's authority in the crucial transitional period immediately after the 'seizure of power'.

From 1933 the personality cult surrounding Hitler burgeoned. The first manifestation of this since the take-over of power was the extraordinary adulation that accompanied Hitler's forty-fourth birthday on 20 April 1933. Poems were written in his honour; towns and cities conferred honorary citizenships and the commercial exploitation of the Führer cult created an entire industry of *kitsch*. Bronze plaques, pewter plates, drinking goblets, even thimbles, were manufactured in industrial quantities to honour the Führer ('*unser Volkskanzler*'). Families sent in orchestrated photographic portraits with personal messages ('You have given me the will to live') and requests ('When will I see you next?') to Hitler. Towns and villages vied with one another to change their historic names to Hitlerhöhe, and proud parents requested permission to christen their daughters 'Hitlerine'. Anything from a tree to a bridge was considered worthy of a dedication to Hitler.[7] Such *kitsch* was, according to Michael Burleigh, 'the last refuge of the deranged, the desperate, the opportunistic and the pompous'.[8] For the party faithful, expressions of love and faith in their Führer continued largely unadulterated until the last days of the Reich.

Propaganda, although manufactured, was able to tap popular sentiments and a genuine hero-worship. The aim of Goebbels's propaganda was to transform Hitler from merely a popular party leader into a symbol of national unity. To that end, the Nazis embraced art in its widest context. *Kulturpolitik* was an important element in German life, but the Nazis were the first party systematically to organise the entire cultural life of a nation.[9] In contrast to the ephemera of the mass media, art was considered a more meaningful and lasting celebration of the achievements of the regime and the genius of its leader. Art was to provide a lead to the rest of the mass media on how Hitler was to be commemorated.

As the Nazi revolution was to bring about a new consciousness, one which would transcend the political structure, it followed that artists, too, had a revolutionary role to play.[10] Under the Nazis, art was seen as an expression of race and would underpin the political renaissance that was taking place. Whereas modernism was associated with 'decadent' Jewish-liberal culture, art under National Socialism would be rooted in the people as the true expression of the spirit of the 'People's Community' (*Volksgemeinschaft*). 'Art must not be isolated from Blood and Soil', wrote the art historian Kurt Karl Eberlein in 1933; and, writing in *Deutsche Kulture-Wacht* in 1933, Professor Max Kutschmann proclaimed:

> The deeply convinced National Socialist artist must logically lift his work – be it a simple flower picture or the last judgement – from the sticky miasma of an aesthetic baseness into the pure and cool air of devoted service for his people. In this way, with each of his works, he becomes – quite unwittingly – the proclaimer of that phi-

losophy. In his work the philosopher will appear purer than in the hard battlefield of daily politics . . . we must go forward. If we don't have a National Socialist art, National Socialism will be deprived of its strongest and most effective armour'.[11]

As a failed artist himself, Hitler held strong views about art. At the height of his power, Hitler gave a succinct summary of his concept of culture and the role of artists in a speech delivered on 18 July 1937 at the opening of the House of German Art in Munich, which was intended to house officially approved art:

> During the long years in which I planned the formation of a new Reich I gave much thought to the tasks which would await us in the cultural cleansing of the people's life; there was to be a cultural renaissance as well as a political and economic reform . . . As in politics, so in German art-life, we are determined to make a clean sweep of empty phrases . . . The artist does not create for the artist. He creates for the people, and we will see to it that the people in future be called to judge his art. No one must say that the people has no understanding for a really valuable enrichment of its cultural life . . . The people in passing through these galleries will recognise in me its spokesman and counsellor. It will draw a sigh of relief and gladly express its agreement with this purification of art . . . The artist cannot stand aloof from his people . . .'[12]

In this speech, Hitler compared his own views with those expressed by the modern artists whose works were being displayed simultaneously in another building under the title of 'Degenerate Art' and intended to demonstrate the extent to which the German nation had been corrupted by an international conspiracy of Jews and Bolsheviks. The 'alternative' exhibition of 'Degenerate Art' was an extraordinary statement, even for the Nazis, of art that was to be abominated. Why, one might ask, did Hitler go to such lengths to convey his disgust for modern art? In his speech opening the rival exhibition, Hitler talked of modern art as being an expression of a worldview that had become 'adulterated' through the mixing of races and ideas. This had resulted in 'misformed cripples and cretins, women who inspire only disgust, men who are more like wild beasts . . .'. Nazi racial theory underpins both Hitler's contempt for modernist art and the idealised Nordic alternative that would embody the 'new human type'. Hitler's aesthetics were based on genetics. In his view, only 'Aryans' were capable of creating what he referred to as 'true' art. At stake was not merely German culture, but Germany itself: 'As in politics, so in German art-life, we are determined to make a clean sweep of empty phrases'. For Hitler, modern art spelt racial corruption – what he referred to as 'cultural Bolshevism'. Opening the House of German Art, Hitler spoke of art's duty to embody the 'experiences of the German people' and to 'express the essential character of the abiding people' as an 'eternal monument'.[13]

Hitler was not averse to being viewed as an artist, particularly as the 'artist–statesman', and as such he was projected by German propaganda as the protector of the artistic heritage of Germany and (final) arbiter of artistic taste. Adolf Ziegler expressed this succinctly at the opening of the 'Degenerate Art' exhibition: 'As in all things, the people trust the judgement of one man, our Führer. He knows which way German art must go in order to fulfil its task as a projection of the German character.'[14] The art of the racially pure culture was to overcome class allegiance and forge a new 'national community'. Artists therefore were responsible for visualising National Socialist ideology. Robert Bötticher, the president of the Art Teachers' Association, left no doubt from where this inspiration stemmed:

> Now the whole nation walks again united and relentlessly into the light. Where did this light come from? It came from the depths of the German people, from the older generations, from the peasants, whose blood is still linked to the soil . . . But most of all, the light came from one man, a man who kept his soul pure, who has not been corrupted by wrong education and culture, as millions among us have; the light came from Adolf Hitler.[15]

Artists in the Third Reich thus had a political role in depicting the nature of the regime, its racial roots and antecedents, and its 'everyday life'. In effect artists were commissioned to 'visualise' or to give visual expression to National Socialist ideology. This is where Kershaw's notion of 'working towards the Führer' is a helpful and revealing metaphor for the manner in which policy was implemented in the Third Reich. In order that art should reflect the ideological precepts of National Socialism, it was imperative that artists, while not necessarily having to transmogrify into 'little Hitlers', should be sympathetic towards the aims and ideals of the regime. Accordingly a 'cleansing' process of *Entjudung* eliminated Jews and other political undesirables from working in German cultural life.[16] The striking feature of the 'nazification' of German cultural life was the alacrity with which intellectuals, writers, artists and academics collaborated in the process. In some cases this could be put down to idealism but more often than not 'self-coordination' (*Selbstgleichschaltung*) was an opportunistic means of career advancement.[17]

A distinction should be made (although not about quality) from the outset between art sponsored by the Nazi Party for the party and the art in more general use. The so-called party art, depicting Nazi leaders or events, was an important element of art production. Portraits of Hitler dominated, of course, but party-sponsored art encouraged artists to glorify the achievements of the movement and particularly the exploits of the SA and the SS. Not surprisingly, stereotypical images of lantern-jawed stormtroopers proliferated (with the artist Elk Eber particularly prominent). Typical of this genre are Hermann Otto Hoyer's *SA Man Rescuing Wounded Comrade* (1933) and Richard Spitz's *Nazi Vision of Greatness* (1933). Examples of Nazi-sponsored painting for a wider audience would include Adolf Wissel's politically correct 'blood and soil' characters such as the *Peasant Women* (1938) and *Farm Family from Kahlenberg* (1939).

In cultivating the Führer cult, the depiction of Hitler was both essential and sensitive. While photographs of Hitler appeared regularly in the German press and provided the day-to-day contact between leader and people, artists, film-makers, poets, and musicians were commissioned to depict Hitler in a more stylised fashion illustrating different aspects of the Führer's work, his moods and his 'genius'. Whatever the form chosen, it would have to accord with official Nazi art policy. The SS weekly *Das Schwarze Korps* summed up the significance of such representation:

> The Führer is the highest gift to the nation. He is the German fulfilment. An artist who wants to render the Führer must be more than an artist. The entire German people and German eternity will stand silently in front of this work, filled with emotions to gain strength from it today and for all times. Holy is the art and the call to serve the people. Only the best may dare to render the Führer.[18]

Not surprisingly a carefully constructed image of the Führer emerged. Hitler was often painted in full body and invariably alone which, according to Peter Adams, was in order to convey his divine role:[19] a seated portrait, on the other hand, would have looked too relaxed and familiar, though there are rare examples of Hitler in such a familiar pose (compare Jacob's 1933 portrait of Hitler in party uniform). Invariably the portraits are extremely formal and Hitler, rather than sitting, is 'enthroned' like some modern monarch (never looking entirely convincing – as this did not correspond to the Führer myth). I chose such a painting by an unknown artist for the cover of my own book on Hitler *Profile of a Dictator*. Largely due to the Führer myth, Hitler was never painted in his home surroundings, as to have done so would have diminished his mythical qualities and made him appear 'ordinary'. On the rare occasions Hitler is depicted in a group context he dominates the painting. A typical example is Emil Scheibe's *Hitler at the Front* (1942–43) in which the Führer is centre-stage, surrounded by awe-struck soldiers taking a welcome break from the fighting and eager to fraternise with their commander-in-chief (Hitler ispainted in full military uniform and trenchcoat). This is a rare glimpse of the 'relaxed' Führer, clearly enjoying the experience, his determination, nevertheless, expressed by means of the clenched right fist grasping his buckle. In *Mein Kampf* Hitler had written about his own experiences of the First World War and the aloofness of German generals. Scheibe's painting is, no doubt, intended to be a corrective and to show the humane side of the Führer. During (or more strictly after) a military campaign Hitler insisted on having his photograph taken with the troops in some informal and relaxed capacity such as sharing a meal with them at the front. In another group painting, *Portrait of the Führer* (1940) by Georg Poppe, Hitler is depicted as a messiah-like figure 'blessing' a mother and child and surrounded by representative 'disciples' from *Volksgemeinschaft* at the Frankfurt Physicians' Corporation.

More familiar are the portraits by specially commissioned 'court' artists such as Conrad Hommel, revealing Hitler as an authoritative and pensive *Feldherr* (Supreme Commander of the Armed Forces). Typical was Hommel's 1940 portrait *The Führer and Commander-in-Chief of the Army*: Hitler, in military uniform, is seen juxtaposed against a stormy sky, gazing into the distance with the map of the world at his feet. More prosaic were the familiar ceremonial 'Portraits of the Führer' – either in uniform (Franz Triebsch, 1939) or in civilian clothes (Walter Einbeck, 1938)

Similarly, Fritz Erler's stylised *Portrait of the Führer* (1937) imposes a stiff-looking Hitler on a rooftop in front of a monumental Nazi life-sculpture of a warrior figure brandishing a sword in one hand and the German eagle in the other. Hitler is surrounded by sculptural implements and architectural stone slabs, with the newly opened House of German Art just visible in the background. This is Hitler the artist and sculptor. Sculpture was even more susceptible to political interference than was painting, no doubt because scultures dominated public spaces in a way that paintings did not. The image of the idealised male nude is a quintessential expression of the 'new man' or warrior hero that figured so prominently in Fascist propaganda. The male body, displaying steely masculinity, dominated National Socialist sculpture. Equally prominent were sculptures celebrating the peasant, the heroic worker and German womanhood – generally in the form of the fertile female in a state of radiant happiness (that is; motherhood). Interestingly enough, unlike other authoritarian regimes in the twentieth century that eulogised their leaders in massive monuments and statues, Nazi monumental relief rarely included Hitler, who was confined to the more restrained busts or portraits

Artists were also commissioned to commemorate the more prestigious public works' schemes that had been inspired by Hitler. The building of the autobahns proved particularly popular and figured heavily in state-sponsored art. Carl Protzen, for example, painted the grandiose building schemes in *The Führer's Roads* (1940). It is a very poor and unimaginative painting, and representative of the poverty of imagination that characterised art in the Third Reich.

Artists and party functionaries often employed familiar Christian imagery when writing about Hitler or depicting him in their art. Indeed the Führer's closest companions were called his 'apostles', while he himself was often referred to as 'the saviour'.[20] The most extraordinary deification of Hitler was Taust's *Hitler and God* which positions Hitler speaking with his back to the audience, a halo framing the back of his head and a star-like swastika lighting the sky. Hermann Otto Hoyer called the myth-laden painting of Hitler speaking to his early followers *In the Beginning Was the Word* (*Am Anfang war das Wort*). This painting, included in the 1937 Exhibition of German Art, has overt religious connotations: a young Hitler stands on a dias in familiar pose addressing a group of early disciples (which includes a sprinkling of women) who are listening intently to his words. An SA man stands behind him holding the party flag and the light that hovers above Hitler appears to be illuminating the room.

Poster art also played an important role in Nazi propaganda. A number of artists worked on poster design. Posters and paintings often complemented each other. One of the most famous propaganda posters, for example, proclaimed: 'All Germany Listens to the Führer on the People's Receiver'. Interestingly Hitler does not appear on the poster; instead a huge crowd is gathered around a 'people's radio' (*Reichsvolksempfänger*) listening intently to the words of their leader – 'people's receivers' were designed with a limited range, which meant that Germans who purchased them were unable to receive foreign broadcasts. The poster was used to encourage all Germans to buy one of these (subsidised) uniform radio sets as an act of faith in the regime.[21] The poster captured in a crudely dramatic form the propaganda potential of the medium for the dissemination of National Socialist ideas and the importance attached to radio-listening in the Third Reich. Artists, on the other hand, were expected to capture the *spirit* of community listening. Paul Mathias Padua, for example, showed a typical 'Aryan' family listening solemnly to the radio in their living-room under the title *The Führer Speaks*. As well as the *Reichsvolksempfänger*, the painting featured a picture of Hitler on the wall (a painting within a painting). It was exhibited at the 'Great German Art Exhibition' in 1940. Similarly, Hubert Lanziger's painting *The Flag Bearer*, which depicted Hitler as a Teutonic warrior in the form of a medieval knight on horseback in the style of Dürer, became a popular print and poster in many German households. Hitler was also used in posters to recruit young people into the Hitler Youth. Perhaps the most famous recruitment poster of all is a painting of Hitler's arm saluting the ranks of marching uniformed Hitler Youth with the slogan: 'The Hand (Hitler's) that Guides the Reich; German Youth Follow it in the Ranks of the Hitler Youth'. In 1936 The League of German Girls (*Bund deutscher Mädel*), the female counterpart of the Hitler Youth, produced its own recruitment poster that showed a young 'Aryan' girl and the caption: 'You, too, Belong to the Führer'. Hitler's thoughts and speeches were also reprinted on posters. In 1941 the party's propaganda department produced a poster (and a postcard) containing the most inflammatory extract from Hitler's 'prophecy' speech to the Reichstag on 30 January 1939: 'Should the international Jewish financiers succeed once again in plunging the nations into a world war, the result will be not the victory Jews but the annihilation of the Jewish race in Europe – Adolf Hitler.' The poster was distributed to party branches throughout the Reich.

An often neglected medium of propaganda iconography is the postage stamp. The stamp proved an ideal vehicle for Nazi propaganda, and it was used to mark events in the Nazi calendar, from the Saar Plebiscite (1934), the War Hero's Day (1935), the Day of Youth Obligation, anniversaries of the 1923 Hitler '*putsch*' in Munich, to the production of the 'People's Car' (*Volkswagen*), the 1936 Olympic Games and the 'winter-help' programme. Stamps were also used to commemorate Hitler himself. Interestingly enough, however, Hitler's portrait did not appear on a official Reichpost stamp until 5 April 1937 when a miniature sheet was released with a block of four stamps of Hitler's portrait above the slogan 'Wer ein Volk retten will, kann nur heroisch denken' ('Whoever Wishes to Rescue a People Can Only Think Heroically'). Thereafter special stamps were issued nearly every year to celebrate Hitler's birthday. No other Nazi Party personage was represented on an official stamp issue. Stamp issues contributed to Hitler's elevation and to some extent reinforced the widely held view that Hitler was different from other party officials.[22]

The year 1937 marked a turning-point for National Socialist stamp design. Following the propaganda success of the 1936 Berlin Olympic Games, a wider range of Nazi motifs appeared on stamps. During 1938 a new portrait of Hitler was issued on a larger stamp that carried a surcharge many times the face-value of the stamp. It was issued to commemorate both Hitler's birthday and the Reich Party Congress.[23] The 1939 issue was a striking black-and-white design of Hitler in dramatic pose as the all-powerful orator, speaking from the podium. The 1939 issue also celebrated the newly instituted 'Workers' Day' on 1 May . In 1940, with Germany at war, a gentler image of Hitler was issued of the Führer affectionately greeting a small child carrying a bouquet of flowers. After 1940, further issues depicted Hitler in military uniform in the pose of Feldherr. This series was used also in occupied territories. By the beginning of 1942 Hitler's portrait had become an everyday image rather than one specifically associated with special party events.[24]

Prior to the outbreak of the Second World War the theme of 'Hitler the prophet' was intended, according to Goebbels, to help generate a new political faith amid the misery that had followed the First. In the transitional period from opposition to government, Hitler was to awaken a new sense of national identity after the humiliation of defeat in the Great War and the *Diktat* of the Treaty of Versailles. 'Germany Awake' ('*Deutschland erwache*') was a familiar propaganda slogan employed by the Nazis in the 1930s. The artist Karl Stauber produced 'Germany Lives', a widely disseminated poster showing a resolute Hitler in full party uniform, one hand holding the Nazi standard, the other clenched as a fist. In the background are hundreds of loyal followers waving swastikas, and from the heavens above, where the German eagle hovers protectively, a shaft of light descends and frames Hitler in a halo effect.

Film, too, was used by the Nazis to project the Hitler myth, though the projection of the Führer cult posed certain problems for Nazi film-makers. As Hitler embodied the 'true' will of the German people, there was no limit to his imagined protean capacity. Any dramatisation of such a God-like figure on the cinema screen would be considered blasphemous. Instead, they chose the great figures from German history to project the Hitler prototype. Thus, during the Third Reich, a number of historical extravaganzas were filmed, in which the appeal to Nazi nationalistic sentiment was made through the inclusion of great figures from Germany's past – poets (Friedrich Schiller), sculptors (Andreas Schlüter), scientists (Paracelsus), explorers (Carl Peters), indistrialists (Der Herrscher), statesmen (Bismarck), and kings ('Der grosse König'). All of them can be seen as part-projections of Hitler, who was exalted in Nazi propaganda as an amalgam of such geniuses. [25]

The documentary film of the 1934 Reichsparteitag, which was commissioned by Hitler, is an exception to the rule: Leni Riefenstahl's *Triumph des Willens* ('Triumph of the Will', 1935), in which the theme of Hitler as a long-awaited saviour or prophet was introduced, opens with a slow fade-up of the German eagle and the film's title, along with the caption:

Twenty years after the outbreak of the First World War,
Sixteen years after the beginning of Germany's time of trial,
Nineteen months after the beginning of the rebirth of Germany,
Adolf Hitler flew to Nuremberg to muster his faithful followers . . .

The opening sequence of the film celebrates the apotheosis of Hitler. It is worthy of particular attention as it is a statement of *Triumph des Willens*' key theme. Through a break in the clouds we see an aeroplane and suddenly appear in a clear sky. Medieval Nuremberg, its towers and spires wrapped in the mist, appears below. As the plane becomes more defined the overture to *Die Meistersinger* slowly merges into *Horst Wessel Lied*, just as the old Germany has given way to the new. By means of magnificent aerial photography, the streets of Nuremberg are seen lined by thousands of marching Germans, all in perfect formation, creating the first geometric pattern of humanity to be shown in the film. The aeroplane eventually makes contact with the earth and taxis to a halt. The German people await its leader. Hitler emerges, in uniform, to acknowledge the cheers of the crowd surging forward to greet him.

Throughout the film, Hitler is seen always in isolation, photographed from below so that he appears to tower above the proceedings around him. Furthermore, it is not without symbolic meaning that Hitler's features appear invariably against a backdrop of clouds and sky. The triumphant journey from the airport through Nuremberg is used to juxtapose the essential loneliness of the Führer with shots of the masses. The camera is placed behind Hitler, concentrating on his arm extended in the Nazi salute. There follows a montage sequence of Hitler's arm and individual faces picked out in the crowd, with close-ups of Nuremberg's great statues looking on approvingly. As if to reinforce the message that the saviour has descended from the heavens and is among his people, Hitler's car stops for a mother and her little girl to present flowers to the Führer. Whenever Hitler is shown in the film he is depicted as a singular figure, while any individuality of the people is submerged in the symmetry and order that characterises the mass scenes.[26]

Similarly, the notion of Hitler as some god-like being in whom Germany's youth was to place its faith found expression in the numerous 'invocations' that children were expected to recite 'religiously'. Typical is the following from an invocation that children in Cologne were instructed to recite at the NSV children's lunch programme:

Before meals:

Führer, my Führer, bequeathed to me by the Lord,
Protect and preserve me as long as I live!
Thou has rescued Germany from deepest distress,
I thank thee today for my daily bread.
Abideth thou long with me, forsaketh me not,
Führer, my Führer, my faith and my light!
          Heil, mein Führer!

After Meals:

Thank thee for this bountiful meal,
Protector of youth and friend of the aged!
I know thou hast cares, but worry not,
I am with thee by day and by night.
Lie thy head in my lap.
Be assured, my Führer, that thou art great
          Heil, mein Führer![27]

Children were an important component in the projection of the Führer cult and were omnipresent whenever Hitler was undertaking official ceremonial duties. No visit to a town or village, or even to a rally, was possible without the photo-opportunity of a child presenting flowers to the Führer. Surrounding Hitler with surrogate children compensated for his lack of family and allowed propagandists the opportunity to present the Führer as the benign and compassionate father-figure of the nation. In 1936 on Hitler's forty-seventh birthday he received a delegation of children representing the Reich Food Estate. The visit was, as usual, heavily choreographed consisting of speeches, incantations and songs. The celebration, which was filmed for the cinema newsreels, finished with children singing the following typically syrupy and sentimental song that had been especially written for the occasion:

Dear good Führer
We love you very much,
We wish to present you with flowers
With out tiny little hands

Then you will love us too.
Dear good Führer
We love you very much
You have the best spot
In our little heartlets
We love you very much.[28]

Praising Hitler in this manner may be viewed as a variation of Kershaw's 'working towards the Führer'. Quasi-religious liturgical responses took on many different guises. They were not confined to small children who knew no better. As we have seen, the construction of the autobahns was intended to represent the technological superiority of a National Socialist Germany under the inspirational leadership of Adolf Hitler. A special German newsreel (*Deutsche Wochenschau*) devoted to Nazi technological and architectural achievements inspired the following accompanying verse about the building of the motorways. Once again, 'faith' is stressed as the tie between the nation and the Führer:

A ribbon of stone doth span our land,
A people hath built with all its might,
Stands ready now for a new fight.
The Führer's mind did think it out,
A faithful people brought it about.
A triumph of power, the work is done.
The first battle has been won.
A people free of want and shame,
The future calls with higher aim.
The Führer gives us faith again.[29]

Another expression of 'faith' in the Führer was the oath of allegiance. Various groups saw this as a means of registering their support for Hitler and the regime. The National Socialist Sisterhood (*Nationalsozialistische Schwesternschaft*), set up in response to the dramatic fall in denominational nurses, made great propaganda capital by taking an oath of allegiance to the Führer at carefully staged ceremonies. (Nuns, working as nurses, had been forbidden by their bishops to assist in operations performed under the Law for the Prevention of Hereditary Ill Offspring. This allowed the National Socialist Sisterhood to claim that it was guaranteeing the future of efficient nursing in hospitals. The Catholic Church came to realise that it had handed the regime a propaganda coup by this prohibition, and in 1940 the nuns were released from it.[30])

An event of more lasting political significance occurred in August 1934 (just over a month after the culling of the SA), when Hitler changed the oath of allegiance sworn by the Reichswehr. Until July 1934, the oath of allegiance taken by the Reichswehr was as follows: 'I swear by God this holy oath that I will serve my people and fatherland at all times as a worthy soldier and will be ready at

any time to risk my life for this oath.' On 2 August 1934, the day of Hindenburg's death and the day on which Hitler assumed the office of president of the
Reich and supreme commander of the armed forces, the oath was changed to:

> I swear by God this holy oath that I will render unconditional obedience to the
> Führer of the German Reich and People, Adolf Hitler, the Supreme Commander
> of the Armed Forces, and as a worthy soldier I will be ready at all times to risk my
> life for this oath.

In changing the oath in this manner Hitler had established the binding obligation of the Reichswehr to himself. Once again these ceremonies were filmed
and shown throughout the Reich in the cinema newsreels and were also
(in)famously captured in Riefenstahl's *Triumph des Willens*.[31]

The ritual of the mass meeting was an important element in the projection
of the Führer cult. Uniforms, bands, flags and symbols were all part of
Goebbels's propaganda machine to increase the impact of Hitler's strong
words with strong deeds. This is the fundamental rationale behind the constant display of Nazi symbols in posters and in films like *Triumph des Willens*
and the weekly German newsreels. In projecting the image of the strong leader
to an audience that had come to associate the Weimar Republic and the Treaty
of Versailles with national ignominy, *Triumph des Willens* portrayed Hitler as a
statesman of genius who had single-handedly rebuilt the nation and staunchly
defended Germany's territorial rights over the hegemony imposed by foreigners. Similarly, a veritable industry of paintings and posters showed Hitler in
familiar 'renaissance pose' with the propaganda slogan: 'One People, One
Nation, One Leader' ('*Ein Volk, ein Reich, ein Führer*') – to be used to great
effect in 1938 with the *Anschluss* (union) with Austria. However, the determination to feel and be united was not enough: the Nazis had to give public testimony to this 'unity'. Nazi rallies (particularly the annual party congress at
Nuremberg) were theatrical pieces carefully staged to create such an effect. To
Hitler's possessive call 'Hail My Men!' the thousands roared back 'Hail My
Führer!' This also explains why the Nazis repeatedly staged 'national moments'
(*Stunden der Nation*) when Hitler's speeches would be broadcast simultaneously throughout the Reich. On such occasions life would come to a standstill,
demonstrating the sense of national community by which the individual par-
ticipant in the ritual, moved by Hitler's rhetoric and swayed by the crowd,
underwent a metamorphosis 'from a little worm into part of a large dragon', as
Goebbels later wrote.[32]

Although Goebbels was quick to exploit such hero-worship there was
nonetheless a genuine outpouring of adulation that took on the characteristics
of a religious movement. Propaganda alone could not have manufactured
what one writer has referred to as a 'politics of faith'. For a brief period in the
mid-1930s Hitler's standing as a *national* leader was unmatched by any previ-

ous German leader – including Bismarck. By 1936 Nazi propaganda had proclaimed him a leader of genius who had single-handedly restored Germany's international reputation, masterminded economic recovery and re-established law and order. These were not specifically *Nazi* achievements: they were achievements of which any German politician or statesman would have been proud. As such they transcended party politics, and even sections of the community opposed to Nazism were forced into grudging admiration. According to Kershaw, 1936 was the year in which Hitler began to believe his own myth: 'That you have found me, among so many millions is the miracle of our time! And that I have found you, that is Germany's fortune.' Had the German people realised the nature of Hitler's haphazard style of leadership, his cavalier attitude to the day-to-day affairs of state and the ensuing administrative chaos, then public perception might have shifted. On the other hand, when he was preparing for an important speech he would often engage in a frenzy of activity. Kershaw noted that the public image was vital: 'He remained, above all, the propagandist *par excellence*.'[33] Hitler now viewed himself, no doubt encouraged by his own propaganda, as irreplaceable.

Nonetheless, Goebbels's manipulatory skill alone could not have created the quasi-religious faith in Hitler demonstrated by large sections of the German population. Without concrete achievements Hitler could not have sustained his positive image as Führer. By the spring of 1939 Sopade had identified the reduction in unemployment and a series of foreign policy successes as the two major achievements consolidating Hitler's position. In domestic politics, Hitler was recognised for having won the 'battle for work', building the autobahns, and generally revamping the economy. Although industrial workers continued to view the 'economic miracle' in terms of longer hours and low wages, they nevertheless welcomed the restoration of full employment and the social welfare schemes for the poorer sections of the community. The middle class, which had benefited from the rearmament boom of the mid-1930s, remained devoted to Hitler, who they saw as the father-figure of the regime.[34]

By appearing to stand above the day-to-day realities of the regime, Hitler acted as a kind of medieval monarch, as a positive symbol, a focus of loyalty and of national unity. Hitler was presented as not just another party leader but as *the* leader for whom Germany had been waiting – a leader who would place the nation before any particularist cause. The nature of Hitler's position as charismatic leader, as the Führer of the German people, rested on his continuing ability to detach himself from day-to-day politics with the result that he was never personally associated with the worst extremes of the regime. Different social groupings, ranging from the industrial working class to church leaders continued to perceive Hitler as a 'moderate', opposed to the radical and extreme elements within the movement. One of most significant achievements of the propaganda construction of the 'Führer myth' was success in separating

Hitler from the growing unpopularity of the Nazi Party itself. 'Ordinary' Germans rationalised corruption and oppression by reassuring themselves that all would be well 'if only the Führer knew': in other words, the modern equivalent of the medieval separation of the 'good king' from his wicked advisers.

Much of Hitler's popularity after he came to power rested on his achievements in foreign policy. A recurring theme in Nazi propaganda prior to 1939 was that Hitler was a man of peace, but one who was determined to recover German territories 'lost' as a result of the Treaty of Versailles. To that end, cartoons were used as a form of short-hand. Compare, for example, a 1936 cartoon in the right-wing magazine *Kladderadatsch* entitled 'The Seed of Peace, Not Dragons' Teeth', which appeared after Germany's illegal occupation of the Rhineland, but presents Hitler as the 'sower of peace'. Hitler is shown sowing seeds; behind him, blowing a heavenly cornet, stands an angel of peace and hope.[35] Providing that foreign policy propaganda could show the achievements of revisionism without the shedding of German blood, then it was relatively easy to feast on the consensus that favoured reversing the humiliation of the post-war peace settlements. From the moment in 1936 when Hitler ordered German troops to re-occupy the demililtarised Rhineland until the Munich Settlement in 1938 which gave the Sudentenland to Germany, Hitler had successfully carried out a series of audacious foreign policy coups that won him support from all sections of the community. He was now widely acclaimed, enjoying unparalleled popularity and prestige.

There was a basic contradiction, however, between propaganda that presented the Führer as a 'man of peace' and an ideology that was inexorably linked to struggle and war. Obsessed by territorial expansion in the East, Hitler confirmed to his military commanders at the Hossbach Conference, in November 1937, that 'Germany's problems can only be solved by means of force'. A year later, after he had sent troops into Austria to secure the *Anschluss* and had acquired the Sudentenland at the Munich Settlement, Hitler summoned to Munich 400 of the regime's leading journalists and media experts, and instructed them in their role in the coming war: 'It is absolutely necessary gradually to prepare the German people psychologically for the coming war and to make it clear to them that there are some things which only force, not peaceful means, must decide.'[36] Goebbels now switched track and claimed that war was unavoidable and was being forced on Germany by aggressive and unresponsive foreign powers. Anticipating Germany's expansion as a major world power, propaganda set out to psychologically prepare for war and mobilise the nation as a 'fighting community'. An ominous slogan of the period proclaimed: 'Today Germany, Tomorrow, the World'.

When the war came, Hitler's astonishing run of *Blitzkrieg* victories, culminating in the fall of France, confirmed Goebbels's propaganda presenting him as not only a great statesman but a military strategist of genius who confounded even his own generals. Goebbels now embarked on the third element in the construction of the Hitler myth: namely Hitler as the fighter, the great commander-in-chief. Following the triumph of *Blitzkrieg* in Poland, the popular demand for pictures of Hitler at the front resulted in the publication of Heinrich Hoffmann's *With Hitler in Poland* (1939), a photographic glorification of Hitler's leadership qualities and his military genius. The photographs illustrated different aspects of the Hitler-myth: Hitler visiting German soldiers wounded in the Polish campaign; sharing field mess with his troops; at the front conducting operations; and, finally, his triumphal 'liberation' of Danzig. The book proved to be one of the most widely distributed party wartime publications.[37]

The first reactions in Germany to the victories in the West were ecstatic. Nazi propagandists struggled to find new superlatives to express the 'unshakeable loyalty' of his 'following'. A *Filmwochenschau* special edition was produced to mark Hitler's fiftieth birthday, the celebrations for which became a unique day of thanksgiving.[38] Following the entry of German troops into Paris on 14 June and the official French capitulation in Compiegne on 22 June, one party official from Swabia was moved to declare: 'All "well-meaning" citizens recognised wholly, joyfully, and thankfully the superhuman greatness of the Führer and his work.'[39] Hitler's standing among the population reached its highest point with the signing of the armistice with France on 22 June 1940. If ever there was widespread enthusiasm for the war in Germany, then this was probably the period when it existed. It overshadowed even the general discontent about the coal shortages and the workings of the rationing system. The secret police (SD) reports claimed that the military victories had integrated the population behind Hitler's war aims: 'as a consequence of the military victories, an unprecedented solidarity has developed between the front and the domestic population, as well as unprecedented solidarity amongst the whole population'.[40]

The victory over France marked the high point of Nazi propaganda, but was to prove the last great military success the Germans celebrated. Nevertheless, the special Deutsche Wochenschau of Hitler – *Triumphant Return to Berlin* – released to celebrate the fall of France, testifies to the remarkable popularity of the cult of the Führer. The train journey back to Germany from France and particularly his arrival in Berlin where he is greeted by *Bund deutscher Mädel* girls and adoring women is a powerful reminder of the emotional manner in which the Hitler myth was portrayed. The final scene culminates with Hitler, accompanied by Goering, on the balcony of the Reich Chancellery, receiving the adulation of an ecstatic crowd gathered on Wilhelmsplatz in Berlin. Such triumphalism was captured in the poetry of SA Sturmführer Heinrich Anacker. The campaign in France presented Anacker with the opportunity to celebrate Hitler as the 'greatest military commander of all times'. In poems such as *Der graue Rock* ('The Grey Coat') and *Der Führer bei seinen Soldaten* Hitler is presented as the first soldier of the Reich, sharing the dangers of the battle with his men. In *The Führer in Compiègne*, Germany's humiliation at the end of the Great War is reversed:

> Now as Commander of Greater Germany's Army he leads
> It to victory from the Argonne Forest to the sea.
> Motors thunder and roar
> Announcing the triumph of German arms
> In the forest of Compiègne.

According to Anacker, Hitler's very presence appeared to guarantee victory:

> Unseen the eagle of eternal glory circled . . .
> Everything that happened was conceived by Hitler
> Who, weighed down with care, leads us to the dawn![41]

Seduced by military conquest supported by propaganda, German public opinion appeared to have been convinced that Hitler was in command of the situation and the final victory assured. Once again, however, it is unwise to make sweeping generalisations. Although there was a feeling of euphoria within Germany, the SD reports reveal that there was still a strong desire for an end to the war.[42] Fuelled by a 'united Europe' theme that rationalised *Blitzkrieg* as 'liberating' Europe from the Jewish-Bolshevik threat, the populace was still able to be persuaded that all Hitler wanted from the war was a 'just and lasting peace and living space for Germans'. It was deemed, therefore, that the Führer's fifty-first birthday was to be celebrated not by loud fanfares and endless parades, but by a nation fighting and working. In his birthday address, broadcast to the nation, Goebbels reaffirmed the 'people's love, obedience, and trust in the Führer'.[43]

The war started to turn against Hitler in the winter of 1942–3, though it would take some time before military reverses had any noticeable effect on his popularity. While the standing of his party deteriorated considerably, Hitler's personal standing remained remarkably high. Following the catastrophe of Stalingrad, however, a defeat for which he was held responsible, Hitler's popularity began to decline. With final victory proving elusive, propaganda struck a new note of heroic resistance, and stoicism, or 'holding out' (*Durchhalten*), replaced the earlier enthusiastic superiority. Out of the distorted shadow of Nazi history a new film on Frederick the Great was released in the spring of 1942 entitled *Der grosse König* ('The Great King'). The Great King was clearly modelled on Hitler. The film illustrated the heroic attitude of Frederick II during the critical phases of the Seven Years' War and the enduring faith of the Prussian people in their leader. The film was particularly suited to a depressed nation that had encountered military reverses for the first time since the end of the First World War. Goebbels believed that such a message would greatly lift morale.[44] On 19 April 1942, Goebbels gave a radio address to mark Hitler's fifty-third birthday. He praised *Der grosse König*'s emotional qualities, and then posed the question: 'What is the lesson to be learnt from the film?' He argued that it was not economic resources or military potential, but superior leadership that decided wars. At a time when German forces were encountering the miseries of defeat and a Russian winter, and the German population at home was forced to reappraise the omnipotence of its Führer, *Der grosse König* formulated, with a view to Stalingrad, one of the first expressions of the need for endurance throughout the war: 'Prussia will never be lost as long as the King lives!' – a slogan that was repeated time and again. Despite Goebbels's denials, such slogans were clearly meant to apply to Hitler.[45]

When the Führer had been paraded as an 'utterly great' historical figure, photographs and newsreels showed a relatively young-looking and vigorous Hitler as the brilliant architect of German victories. From the end of 1942 (that is, before the defeat at Stalingrad), a more sober image of Hitler began to emerge. After the surrender of the German 6th Army at Stalingrad in January 1943, Hitler retreated into an increasingly illusory world and refused to speak to his people. On his fifty-fourth birthday, in April 1943, 'indelible furrows on his face', formed by long nights without sleep, were evident. 'Could one draw the face of our people,' Goebbels asserted, 'it would, during the course of this war, probably reveal the same deep changes which we observe with earnest pride in the face of the Führer.'[46] Hitler's health was clearly deteriorating, and photographs of him that appeared in the press were heavily censored. The more rarely Hitler appeared to the masses, the more Goebbels realised the necessity of pointing to his symbolic image. 'One felt everywhere the need to see him, even if only his photograph, in order to gain strength from glancing at him . . .'.[47]

One suggestion for improving morale was to give the Führer a higher profile in German propaganda. According to the SD, in April 1943, the German public wanted to see and hear the Führer more often 'in order to keep alive the contact between leader and nation'. There was a widespread belief that he had become too reclusive. There had also been much speculation about the (poor) condition of his health. In fact on 21 March 1943, Heroes' Memorial Day, Hitler had spoken to the nation in a radio broadcast for the first time since Stalingrad. He had confided to Goebbels that he felt like an 'old propagandist' and wanted to use the speech to make a fierce attack on Bolshevism.[48] The routine attack on Jewry and Bolshevism, which was delivered in a dreary monotone, made little impression on the people and prompted further rumours about Hitler's poor health. The excited anticipation and the resulting disappointment were profound.[49] The lacklustre reaction to the speech was further evidence that Hitler's popularity was in decline and that this decline had been markedly accelerated by Stalingrad. In April, the Reich Chancellery reported that *Gau* headquarters had noticed a sharp increase in the number of political jokes involving Hitler. Some jokes were treasonous, such as the one that had been doing the rounds since the autumn of 1940: *Question*: 'An airplane carrying Hitler, Goering and Goebbels crashes. All three are killed. Who is saved?' *Answer*: 'The German people.' Two more jokes in particular are worth citing for the manner in which they illustrate not only a prevailing resignation but a loss of confidence in Hitler: 'What's the difference between the sun and Hitler? The sun rises in the East, Hitler goes down in the East.' And 'Zarah Leander (a popular film actress) is summoned to the Führer's headquarters. Why? She has to sing "I know there'll be a miracle one day, every day".'[50]

The increasingly rare public appearances by Hitler meant that Goebbels worked harder than ever to maintain the Führer myth. Revealingly, his reluctance to address the nation was not compensated by an increase in Hitler iconography. In fact by the end of 1943, the Führer cult had ceased to develop in terms of new images or propaganda slogans. There are few examples of state-commissioned art at that time presenting Hitler in a new and revitalised light. This cannot be explained solely by the exigencies of war as the Propaganda Ministry was spending huge amounts of money on other projects and campaigns. In May 1943 the party's propaganda department suggested a new slogan for a poster campaign, 'The Führer Is Always Right', which was not taken up. Instead the artist R. Gerhard Zill painted a half portrait of Hitler with a look of heroic fortitude, standing in shadow next to a chair, with the slogan 'Adolf Hitler is Victory' ('Hitler ist der Sieg'). Released shortly after the disaster of Stalingrad, this painting became the most widely distributed poster of the Führer in the final period of the war.

In April 1944 the *Deutsche Wochenschau* celebrated Hitler's fifty-fifth birthday. It was to be one of the last appearances Hitler made in the German newsreels. At an NSDAP concert on the eve of his birthday (and with Beethoven's *Eroica* being played), Goebbels offered the party's congratulations to Hitler and reaffirmed the nation's faith in him: 'We want to assure him that he is able to rely on his people absolutely in this great struggle – that he is today as he always was – our Führer!' The scene in the concert hall is followed by shots of a bomb-damaged Berlin recovering from an Allied sortie. In the background, just visible, slogans can be seen daubed on the ruins and on banners hanging from windows. As the commentator says that this is the German people's gift to Hitler, the camera pans in to reveal a demonstration of the nation's unbending will: 'Our walls may break but our hearts do not – as long as the Führer lives!'

In the summer of 1944 the intelligence reports confirmed a short-lived revival of trust in the Führer following the failure of the 20 July plot against him. By portraying the 'Officers' Plot' as a cowardly unpatriotic act, Goebbels organised well-attended demonstrations of 'spontaneous expression of the views of our people about the foul attempt on the Führer's life'.[51] The propaganda minister exploited the attempted assassination to show that the hand of providence was guiding Hitler by resurrecting the slogan 'Hitler is Victory'. In the final year of the war Goebbels attempted to breathe new life into the Führer cult by once again depicting Hitler as a latter-day Frederick the Great, ultimately triumphant in the face of adversity. It was the same message as *Der grosse König*'s – if only Germans would fight as the Prussians had done during the Seven Years' War. He even quoted a letter from Frederick the Great to his sister Amalia written in 1757, in which the king commented that 'victory and death were the only alternatives'. Goebbels promised that 'if the German people kept faith with the Führer, Hitler would produce a 'similar victory'.[52]

However, the overwhelming majority of the population now accepted that the war was irretrievably lost. Hitler no longer addressed the nation, and he had virtually disappeared from the cinema screens and the rare photographs that had escaped the censor revealed his declining physical and mental state. The penultimate *Deutsche Wochenschau* was released in March 1945 and contained the last, fleeting, appearances of Hitler and Goebbels, acting out roles that had changed little over twelve years.[53] One of the last images of Adolf Hitler is a photograph taken on 20 March 1945 in the courtyard of the Reich Chancellery showing the Führer decorating members of the Hitler Youth for defending the capital of the Third Reich as Russian troops closed around Berlin. It is a poignant historical footnote revealing an old and disillusioned man – utterly defeated by the turn of events and the ensuing chaos. It is in stark contrast to the hundreds of images of Hitler that suggested superman status. Even as late 29 April 1945, the day before Hitler committed suicide in his bunker, a Berlin newspaper was insisting that Hitler would remain steadfast with his people and 'wherever the Führer is, there is victory'.[54] With Berlin about to fall, no amount of propaganda could sustain such an alarming flight from reality. The 'Hitler myth' and the Third Reich were on the verge of extinction.

The hagiography that had started with Hitler the prophet and saviour swiftly became Hitler the Führer-figure. The *Weltanschauung*, or secular worldview, that underpinned such a deification was accompanied by its own ritualistic political liturgy that allowed first the party and then the wider German community to enter into a mystical identification with its leader. The Führer was then transmogrified into a superman – a combination of supreme statesman and commander-in-chief – Hitler the warrior. The images of Hitler that appeared in Nazi propaganda reflected the different aspects of charismatic leadership. After his triumphant return to Berlin following the fall of France, Hitler did indeed seem like a god – the wielder of magic. Throughout, the *Nibelungentreue*, the Germanic faithfulness of the followers, was evoked as a kind of mystical – *völkisch* – identification between the Führer and the people.

By the end of 1943, the magic had begun to wane and Hitler no longer held the nation spellbound. In the final months of the Third Reich, the only army that Hitler could muster was a part-time militia made up of old men and young boys. They, too, would have to be surrendered to the *Deutschtum* myth of heroic sacrifice. The German people recognised, albeit belatedly, the hollowness of the images of the Führer that they had, in part, constructed. Hitler spoke of himself as a man called by providence to restore Germany to greatness, but he chose not to survive the defeat of his people. He took his own life cursing the German people for failing to match up to an image of himself that had been largely constructed by propaganda.

Notes

1 R. Semmler, *Goebbels, the Man Next to Hitler* (London, 1947), entry for 12 December 1941, pp. 56–7.

2 See Ian Kershaw, *Der Hitler-Mythos: Volksmeinung und Propaganda im Dritten Reich* (Stuttgart, 1980), translated into English as *The 'Hitler Myth': Image and Reality in the Third Reich* (Oxford, 1987); and more briefly 'The Führer Image and Political Integration: The Popular Conception of Hitler in Bavaria during the Third Reich', in G. Hirschfeld and L. Kettenacker (eds), *Der Führerstaat: Mythos und Realität* (Stuttgart, 1981), pp. 133–63.

3 See Ian Kershaw, '"Working towards the Führer": Reflections on the Nature of the Hitler Dictatorship', *Contemporary European History*, 2:2 (1993), pp. 103–18. Although Kershaw is most closely associated with the 'structuralist' historians, he rejects their most controversial claim that Hitler was a 'weak dictator'.

4 Ian Kershaw, *Hitler 1896–1936: Hubris* (London, 1998), and *Hitler 1936–1945: Nemesis* (London, 2000).

5 *Der Angriff*, 5 March 1932, quoted in E. Bramsted, *Goebbels and National Socialist Propaganda 1925–1945* (Michigan, 1965), p. 201.

6 For an analysis of the way in which the Kaiser had been portrayed in German propaganda during the First World War see, David Welch, *Germany, Propaganda and Total War, 1914–1918* (London, 2000).

7 The tastelessness of this commercial exploitation forced Goebbels in May 1933 to ban the use of Hitler's image on commercial products: see R. Steinberg, *Nazi Kitsch* (Darmstadt, 1975); Kershaw, *Hubris*, p. 484.

8 M. Burleigh, *The Third Reich: A New History* (London, 2000), p. 213. The largest swastika was made out of trees, in a wood north of Berlin, with a diameter of 100 metres, and could be seen from the sky.

9 The Reich Chamber of Culture (*Reichskulturkammer*) proved crucial in the systematic reorganisation of German cultural life; for an analysis see, David Welch, *The Third Reich: Politics and Propaganda*, 2nd edn (London, 2002), pp. 32–57; Alan E. Steinweis, *Art, Ideology, and Economics in Nazi Germany. The Reich Chambers of Music, Theater, and the Visual Arts* (Chapel Hill, NC, and London, 1993). F. Spotts, *Hitler and the Power of Aesthetics* (London, 2002).

10 Interestingly enough this was not to include Hitler's early work as a struggling

artist. In 1937 Hitler decreed that no one should write about his drawings and forbade any exhibitions of his work. A few years later he banned the sale of his work abroad. See, P. Adams, *The Arts of the Third Reich* (London, 1992), p. 44; also B. Hinz, *Art in the Third Reich* (Oxford, 1980).

11 *Deutsche Kultur-Wacht*, 1 (1933), p. 6, quoted in Adams, *Arts of the Third Reich*, p. 71.

12 The full speech can be found in Welch, *Third Reich*, pp. 203–8.

13 There is considerable irony in the fact that an estimated 20,000 people per day visited the exhibition of 'Degenerate Art' and that it eventually toured thirteen venues in Germany and Austria, being seen by 3 million people: *ibid.*, p. 203; see also Stepahnie Barron and Peter W. Guenther (eds), *Degenerate Art: The Fate of the Avante-Garde in Nazi Germany* (New York, 1991).

14 Adolf Ziegler, opening of the Degenerate Art exhibition, quoted in Adams, *Arts of the Third Reich*, p. 122. Hitler was a great patron of the arts and any work of art that could claim to be 'purchased by the Führer' was highly prized.

15 Adams, *Arts of the Third Reich*, p. 21.

16 For a detailed account of this process see A. E. Steinweis, 'Cultural Eugenics: Social Policy, Economic Reform, and the Purge of Jews from German Cultural Life', in G. R. Cuomo (ed.), *National Socialist Cultural Policy* (New York, 1995), pp. 23–38.

17 For a detailed analysis of the film see David Welch, *Propaganda and the German Cinema 1933–1945* (Oxford, 1983; new rev. edn, I. B. Tauris, 2002), pp. 5–18. Joachim Fest has claimed that for many intellectuals the arrival of Hitler on the political scene acted as a 'healing process' from their existential despair: Fest, *Hitler: Eine Biographie* (Frankfurt, 1976), p. 635.

18 *Das Schwarze Korps*, 19 June 1935, p. 12, quoted in Adams, *Arts of the Third Reich*, p. 171.

19 *Ibid.*, p. 171.

20 See David Welch, *Hitler: Profile of a Dictator* (London, 2001), pp. 22–3.

21 During 1933, 1.5 million sets were produced, and in 1934 the figure for radio sets passed the 6 million mark. By the beginning of the war over 70 per cent of all households owned a radio set – the highest percentage anywhere in the world: Welch, *The Third Reich*, pp. 38–43.

22 Norbert Frei has claimed that the explanation for his absence from stamp issues was Goebbels's desire to disassociate the Führer from the failings of the party to honour its election promises. Such failures, according to Frei, were officially blamed on party functionaries and regional officials: N. Frei, *National Socialist Rule in Germany. The Führer State 1933–45* (London, 1993).

23 The surcharge was reportedly collected for charitable donations in line with the propaganda slogan encapsulating the 'People's Community' – 'The Community Before the Individual'.

24 Much of this information on the postage stamp has been gleaned from J. Lamont, 'Propaganda and the Postage Stamp. An Examination of the Postage Issues of the Third Reich', unpublished MA dissertation, University of Kent at Canterbury, 1997.

25 For analyses of all these films see, Welch, *Propaganda and the German Cinema*, pp. 123–58.

26   For a more detailed analysis of the film, see *ibid.*, pp. 125–34.

27   J. Neuhäusler, *Kreuz und Hakenkreuz: Der Kampf des Nationalsozialismus gegen die katholische Kirche und der kirchliche Widerstand* (Munich, 1946), p. 251, quoted in G. Mosse, *Nazi Culture: Intellectual, Cultural and Social Life in the Third Reich* (London, 1966), p. 241.

28   B. Heiber and H. Heiber (eds), *Die Rückseite des Hakenkreuzes* (Munich, 1993), pp. 148–9, quoted in Burleigh, *The Third Reich*, p. 215. The theme of young children 'helping the Führer' appears in numerous school textbooks. Typical is the following taken from a 1935 school reader. A boy and a girl are seen presenting Hitler with flowers. The girl tells 'Mein Führer': 'I know you well and love you like Father and Mother, / I shall always obey you like Father and Mother, / And when I grow up I shall help you like Father and Mother, / And you will be proud of me like Father and Mother': see L. Pine, 'Nazism in the Classroom', *History Today*, 17:3 (April 1997), pp. 22–7. For a more detail exploration of children's literature as propaganda see, C. Kamenetsky, *Children's Literature in Nazi Germany* (Ohio, 1984),

29   Quoted in Adams, *Arts of the Third Reich*, p. 215.

30   See, G. Lewy, *The Catholic Church and Nazi Germany* (London, 1964), p. 263.

31   The initiative to change the oath came in fact from the Reichswehr, which played into Hitler's hands: see David Welch, *The Hitler Conspiracies* (London, 2001), pp. 146–7. The film *Triumph des Willens* also captured the swearing of allegiance to Hitler by 52,000 *Arbeitsdienst* (members) gathered on the Zeppelin Field. The extent to which the occasion was conducted like a religious ceremony is striking: see Welch, *Propaganda and the German Cinema*, pp. 132–3.

32   J. Goebbels, *Der Kampf um Berlin: Der Anfang* (Munich, 1932), p. 18. The original term, of course, came from the second volume of Hitler's *Mein Kampf*: see *Hitler's Mein Kampf*, introduced by D. C. Watt (London, 1969), p. 430.

33   Kershaw, *Hubris*, p. 535.

34   *Deutschland-Berichte der Soziademokratischen Partei Deutschlands (Sopade-Berichte)* (Frankfurt 1980): see vol. 5 (Febuary, 1938), p. 175; vol. 6 (July, 1939), pp. 757–8; for a further discussion see Welch, *The Third Reich*, pp. 60–73.

35   *Kladderadatsch*, 22 March 1936, cited in David Welch, *Modern European History, 1871–2000* (London, 2000), pp. 149–51.

36   Full speech reprinted in Z. A. B. Zeman, *Nazi Propaganda* (Oxford, 1973), pp. 212–25.

37   See R. E. Herzstein, *The War that Hitler Won: The Most Infamous Propaganda Campaign in History* (London, 1979), pp. 189–94.

38   For an account of the detailed preparations for the newsreel, see F. Terveen, 'Der Filmbericht über Hitlers 50. Geburtstag: Ein Beispiel nationalsozialistischer Selbstdarstellung und Propaganda', *Vierteljahrshefte für Zeitgeschichte*, 7:1 (1959), pp. 75–84.

39   See Kershaw, '*Hitler Myth*', pp. 153–5.

40   H. Boberach, *Meldungen aus dem Reich: Auswahl geheimen Lagerichten des Sicherheitsdienst der SS 1939–44* (Berlin and Neuwied, 1965), p. 77.

41   The poem is quoted in J. Baird, *To Die for Germany: Heroes in the Nazi Pantheon* (Bloomington and Indianapolis, 1990), p. 207.

42 See Boberach, *Meldungen*, pp. 102, 153.

43 J. Goebbels, *Die Zeit ohne Beispiel: Reden und Aufsätze aus den Jahren 1939–41* (Munich, 1941), pp. 284–5.

44 In his diary he noted: 'With this film we will make politics . . . It is an excellent expedient for the soul of our people and in the process of creating the necessary German resistance needed to see us successfully through the war'. IfZ, *Goebbels Tagebuch*, entry for 19 February 1942.

45 For a detailed analysis of the film see Welch, *Propaganda and the German Cinema*, pp. 147–53.

46 The full 'Führergeburtstag' speech of 1943 is reprinted in J. Goebbels, *Die Steile Aufstieg. Reden and Aufsätze aus den Jahren 1942/3* (Munich, 1944), pp. 252–62.

47 J. Goebbels, *Das eherne Herz: Reden und Aufsätze aus den Jahren 1941/2* (Munich, 1943), p. 291.

48 For the full conversation between Hitler and Goebbels see *Die Tagebücher von Joseph Goebbels*, ed. E. Fröhlich, vol. 2: *Diktate 1941–45* (Munich, 1993), pp. 593–5.

49 Kershaw, *Nemesis*, p. 556.

50 Cited in J. Noakes, *Nazism 1919–1945*, vol. 4: *The German Home Front in World War II* (Exeter, 1998), pp. 548–9.

51 M. G. Steinert, *Hitlers Krieg und die Deutschen* (Düsseldorf, 1970), pp. 475ff; Kershaw, *'Hitler Myth'*, p. 216; Welch, *Hitler Conspiracies*, pp. 169–75.

52 See Welch, *Propaganda and the German Cinema*, p. 152; Bramsted, *Goebbels and National Socialist Propaganda*, p. 448.

53 For a brief discussion of the newsreel see Welch, *Third Reich*, pp. 154–5.

54 *Der Panzerbär*, 29 April 1945; interestingly enough, this headline is on p. 2.

5

'Viceroys of the Reich'?
Gauleiters 1925–45

Jeremy Noakes

Gauleiters, the regional leaders of the political organisation (PO) of the NSDAP, were the key figures within the Nazi Party and, by 1943 at the latest, they had acquired the dominant role in German government in the provinces. Yet surprisingly little has been written about them. One reason for this may be that the PO of the Nazi Party in the field has been assumed to have been relatively unimportant by comparison with, for example, the Staff of the Führer's Deputy (later Party Chancellery) of Rudolf Hess and Martin Bormann, the SS, or Goebbels's Propaganda Ministry. This assumption has in turn been the result of the relative neglect of German domestic affairs during the Second World War. Only through the research of the past decade or so has it become clear how important the PO of the Nazi Party became on the German home front between 1939 and 1945 and it was the Gauleiters who reaped the main benefits of that increase in power.[1] Yet a growing awareness of the importance of the Gauleiters during the war years has not been matched by an increase in research into their role more generally. Indeed, not a great deal has been added to the picture provided by Peter Hüttenberger's excellent pioneering work published in 1969.[2] In particular, we lack detailed studies of the activities of individual Gauleiters,[3] a fact that is no doubt due in part to a dearth of sources in many cases and which has not been compensated for by the few self-justifying Gauleiter autobiographies that have appeared since 1945, although they do provide the occasional interesting insight.[4] In the absence of such studies the historian is forced to make do with evidence of the activities of Gauleiters provided by the diaries and memoirs of other political actors and by studies of various aspects of the regime and its activities in which the Gauleiters played a part. The aim of this chapter is to provide a brief survey of the current state of our knowledge about the role of the Gauleiters in the Third Reich.[5]

The early years 1925–33

The position of Gauleiter was first instituted following the re-founding of the NSDAP in February 1925 after Hitler's release from prison following his abortive Munich *putsch*.[6] During the first phase of the party's existence (1919–23), faced with competition from rival *völkisch* groups, Hitler had been very concerned to ensure the dominant role of Munich headquarters under his leadership, and so it had dealt directly with the various local branches outside of Munich without any intermediate body coming between them. Moreover, since the vast majority had been in the south of Germany, and particularly in Bavaria itself, there was no need for an elaborate regional organisation.

In 1925, the NSDAP was still strongest in Bavaria, above all in Franconia in the north, and also in the neighbouring state of Thuringia. However, the party was no longer largely confined to south Germany. Now, as a result partly of the notoriety which Hitler had acquired through the Munich *putsch* and subsequent trial, and partly because of the frustration created by the disintegration of the *völkisch* movement into warring factions during 1924, there were pockets of Hitler supporters scattered all over Germany. And, with the threat posed by a rival *völkisch* party, the Deutschvölkische Freiheitspartei (DVFP), it was vital for the NSDAP quickly to establish an effective organisation outside its traditional base in Bavaria, and this inevitably involved creating a regional structure, though it was not yet clear what form it would take. In the 1925 statutes branches were to be organised in 'provincial organisations' (*Landesverbände*) and then into *Gaus* 'according to need'.[7]

At this early stage, Hitler and his agent in north Germany, Gregor Strasser, had little choice as to whom to appoint as regional leaders since the main aim had to be to maximise declarations of support for Hitler among those who claimed leadership of the *völkisch* movement in their particular areas. Moreover, they had little information about the candidates involved. For example, Strasser was obliged to appoint Josef Klant, an elderly and cantankerous intriguer, as Gauleiter of Hamburg for want of a better alternative.[8] Individuals would contact headquarters declaring their loyalty to Hitler and request recognition as Gauleiters of the NSDAP. Sometimes Gauleiters were elected by the local branches in their area. Josef Bürckel of the Palatinate, for example, was elected Gauleiter on 3 March 1926, despite the fact that the rival incumbent had been appointed with the support of a representative of the Munich headquarters.[9] When he informed Munich of his election he was welcomed but was requested to fill in a membership form since he was not yet registered as a member!. His confirmation by Hitler did not come until February 1927. At this stage, the boundaries of the various *Gaus* tended to stretch as far as the individual Gauleiters' influence reached, and sometimes they were fixed by mutual agreement between neighbouring Gauleiters with minimal involvement from Munich. In March 1926, the leaders of *Gau* Rhineland North and

Gau Westphalia initiated a merger to form *Gau* Ruhr and initially they adopted a collegial form of leadership in which there were three Gauleiters – Karl Kaufmann, Erich Koch, and Franz von Pfeffer, a clear breach of Hitler's *Führerprinzip*.

For the time being, Hitler was content to tolerate this situation. Apart from the fact that he had little alternative, given the limited resources of his Munich headquarters, it coincided with his notion of 'organic development' and his belief in the importance of leadership. Indeed, it reflected his view of life as a struggle for the survival of the fittest. However, even at this early stage there were limits to the extent to which Hitler was prepared to tolerate the independent actions of the Gauleiters, and, in February 1926, he was forced to block a potentially dangerous development, namely the attempt by Gauleiters in the north and west of Germany to form a 'working group' in rivalry with the Munich headquarters.[10] This move was not aimed at Hitler himself; indeed the 'working group' hoped to win him over. It was prompted by personal, political and organisational disagreements with the Munich party officials. In fact, the working group, which included as members or associates most of the Gauleiters in the north and west of Germany, was far too disparate in terms of the views and personalities of its members to represent a significant threat to Munich. However, Hitler could not afford to permit such a challenge to continue; and so, at a meeting in Bamberg on 16 February 1926, he asserted his authority over the issuess of the organisation and the programme.

Following his success at Bamberg, Hitler for the first time formalised the position of the Gauleiters. A revision to clause 6 of the party statutes, issued on 22 May 1926, stated that local branches would be organised into *Gaus* as required, that the Reich headquarters would work only with local branches and *Gaus*, and that the Gauleiters were to be appointed by the Reich headquarters.[11] Then, on 1 July 1926, 'Guidelines for *Gaus* and local branches of the NSDAP' for the first time formally defined the role of the Gauleiter and tightened the control of the Munich headquarters over the party regions.[12] Gauleiters were 'responsible in the first instance for the regular conduct of business and the uniform implementation of the movement's goals as well as for their propagation through the founding of new branches'. They were further responsible for handling the correspondence between the local branches and the Reich headquarters, as well as for sending in the membership dues, applications for membership and resignations on the dates designated by headquarters. At the same time, Munich laid down that, while the Gauleiter could appoint his deputy, the appointment required Munich's approval. However, the most important point, as far as the future of the Gauleiters was concerned, was the statement that 'since the NSDAP represents a large working group, smaller working groups as combinations of individual *Gaus* have no justification'. This clause ensured that in future Gauleiters were prevented from working together independently of the party headquarters; there were to be no more frondes.

However, during the thin years 1925–28, the Reich headquarters lacked the resources to keep a tight control over the party in the regions, and much of its activity devolved on the Gauleiters. The *Gau* headquarters were often housed in their private houses and flats, and much depended on their personal initiative and on their organisational competence, which was often limited. In this situation Gauleiters continued to retain a considerable measure of autonomy from Munich. But this was in line with Hitler's thinking. For, provided the Gauleiters fulfilled their organisational and financial obligations to Munich and adhered ideologically to the basic party line, they were free to develop their own style of running their *Gaus* and of propaganda. The only criterion on which they were judged was success in winning new members and voters. Hitler was happy for Gauleiters to emphasise aspects of Nazi ideology appropriate to the political and social environment of their particular *Gaus*. Thus, in his speech to the party's general meeting in Munich on 22 May 1926 he referred to the success of the NSDAP among such varied populations as the 'lively Franconians' in Nuremberg and the 'significantly cooler north Germans in the Ruhr district' as indicating the correctness of Nazi ideology. He continued:

> Perhaps it will take on a local colouring everywhere; that doesn't matter. In principle everybody is marching towards the same goal. It may well be that in this or that district a particular aspect will receive special emphasis. But the aim everywhere is to convert people to the political creed of National Socialism, whether in Hamburg, Munich, Nuremberg or Elberfeld, whether in Baden or East Prussia.[13]

In practice *Gaus* did indeed tend to reflect the nature of their respective political cultures and the individual characters and preoccupations of their Gauleiters. Thus, for example, whereas the *völkisch* nationalist components of Nazi ideology predominated in Franconia in the rabid anti-semitism of Julius Streicher in Nuremberg and the quasi-religious rhetoric of Hans Schemm in Bayreuth, Nazism's 'socialist' dimension predominated in the industrial Ruhr through the anti-capitalist and anti-bourgeois rhetoric of young radical leaders such as Dr Joseph Goebbels, Karl Kaufmann and Erich Koch.

The other side of this extensive degree of autonomy granted to the Gauleiters was Munich's general unwillingness to get involved in the bitter personal rivalries which marked the years 1925–29 and which resulted in a substantial turnover of Gauleiters during this period. For, despite the fact that, under clause 9 of the party's statutes, the *Gau* organisation had the same dictatorial structure as the Reich headquarters, Gauleiters often found it difficult to assert their authority against rivals, particularly against the *Gau* SA leadership. Their success in doing so varied from *Gau* to *Gau* depending on the local circumstances and on the political skill and forcefulness of the Gauleiter concerned. However, even a Gauleiter as tough and dynamic as Josef Bürckel of the Palatinate had not managed firmly to establish his position until as late as 1929.[14]

To begin with, Hitler was wary of imposing his authority too forcefully.[15] As late as 1928, for example, in the case of Gauleiter Dinter of Thuringia who was trying to use the NSDAP as a vehicle for his cranky religious views, Hitler insisted that the more influential Gauleiters should be consulted before a decision was reached on his expulsion. Moreover, even when Hitler did intervene to appoint new Gauleiters his intervention was often prompted by local initiatives rather than by a coherent personnel policy. The extent to which the Gauleiters considered that they had secured their positions through their own efforts and the significance of their role in the development of the party in their areas encouraged them to adopt a proprietorial attitude to their *Gaus*, leading them to resent outside interference from Munich. A striking instance of this occurred in 1931 when Hitler decided to replace the *Gauleiter* of Halle-Merseburg, Paul Hinkler. On the arrival of Rudolf Jordan, who was to replace him, Hinkler drew a pistol declaring: 'This *Gau* is a combat *Gau* and not an administrative district, not a province. This *Gau*...that's me...I am the *Gau*! And that's an end to it.'[16]

The year 1928 marked something of a turning-point in the history of the Nazi *Gaus*, since in September the party leadership responded to its poor election result in the Reichstag election of the previous May (2.8 per cent) by rearranging the boundaries of most of the *Gaus* on the basis of those of the Reichstag electoral districts, so that each *Gau* corresponded to an electoral district. This reflected the priority the party now gave to the electoral path to power. Moreover, from now onwards, the party's fortunes began to turn. By 1930, Hitler felt strong enough to act swiftly to suspend the Gauleiter of Mecklenburg, Friedrich Hildebrandt, who had criticised his links to industry. Indeed, by 1930, the growing self-confidence of the Munich headquarters, fed by the rapid increase in the number of members and the increase in resources which they brought, coupled with concern about the damage caused by the breakaway of Otto Strasser and his followers to form the Black Front, encouraged the party leadership to tighten control over the Gauleiters.[17] For example, with the appointment of Dr Joseph Goebbels as head of the propaganda department, election campaigns were increasingly directed centrally from Munich, with the *Gaus* subjected to more and more detailed instructions.[18] Gregor Strasser, now head of PO, aimed to turn the Gauleiters into an effective leadership corps at regional level whose actions would be controlled and coordinated by Munich.[19] This culminated in the introduction, on 9 June 1932, of a new system involving the appointment initially of two Reich inspectors: Paul Schulz, covering the north; and Robert Ley, the south.[20] This was followed, on

17 August, by the further appointment of ten provincial inspectors (*Landesin-spekteure*), composed of leading Gauleiters, each of whom was made responsible for supervising a number of *Gaus*, although their responsibilities were in fact limited.[21] This resulted in the creation of, in effect, first- and second-class Gauleiters and subordinated the Gauleiters more effectively to Strasser's organisation department, which now came between them and Hitler.

These developments had, in turn, prompted the Gauleiters to strengthen their control over their own *Gaus*.[22] They acted in part to be able to respond to the increasing demands of the Reich headquarters and in part to secure their own position within their *Gaus* against potential rivals. Their response took the form, first, of an increase in the *Gau* bureaucracy in order to cope with the increase in membership and the growing complexity of the party, with its proliferation of organisations geared to particular functions and social and economic groups; their second response was to create a clique of loyal supporters, placed in key positions both within the *Gau* headqurters and in the field as district leaders.[23] This was especially important for the increasing number of Gauleiters, such as Erich Koch of East Prussia, who had been brought in from outside the area to take over a *Gau* that was failing and who, therefore, had to establish their authority in the face of local suspicion or even hostility. They often took their cliques with them if they were moved to other posts.

Hitler had accepted Strasser's organisational reforms of 1931–32, but was clearly unhappy about them. So he seized the opportunity provided by the latter's resignation in December 1932 to abolish the *Gau* inspectors, strengthen the Gauleiters' position, and restore the direct relationship between himself and the individual Gauleiters. Thus, in his important December memorandum on the party's reorganisation he insisted, first, that the Gauleiter was the movement's representative in his area and that the more emphasis that was given to the importance of his position the more effectively he would be able to fulfil this task. For, by being deeply rooted in his area he would be able 'to keep control of the movement even in critical times'.[24] Second, 'as representatives of the supreme leader of the movement', the Gauleiters were to be 'subordinated solely to him personally'.[25] As 'the most important representatives of the Führer . . . it is my wish and will that *their position in the movement should be as sovereign a one as possible*. But let them also feel themselves to be and act as sovereign representatives of the party.'[26]

After 1933 the *Gau* system remained largely intact, apart from changes created by territorial acquisitions. Between 1933 and 1937 there were 31 *Gaus*, and 42 from 1938 to 1945.[27] The fact that *Gaus* such as Franconia, Saxony and Mecklenburg continued to exist, although their boundaries did not correspond with the electoral districts, indicates that, despite the 1928 reform, other factors had exerted an influence on the party's regional organisation. Indeed, as Walter Ziegler suggests, the *Gau* system was shaped by 'a mixture of regional traditions, practical considerations, propaganda achievements, and interventions on grounds of personnel policy'.[28]

The Gauleiters

Who then were these Gauleiters? Peter Hüttenberger selected twenty-nine who were in office in 1932 and held it for a lengthy period after 1933, some until 1945, and who can therefore be seen as the core group. They were confessionally mixed, reflecting the confessional preponderance of the areas from which they came. Their average age in 1933 was 40. Nearly half (14) were from the so-called 'front generation' born between 1890 and 1900, 7 were born between 1880 and 1889, 3 in 1902, one in 1879 (Mutschmann) and one in 1876 (Telschow). Their social background was typically lower-middle class, but upwardly rather than downwardly mobile.[29] These were not social or occupational losers; on the contrary, most had respectable careers and several had been officers in the war. All but two (Kube of Kurmark and Meyer of Westphalia-North) had joined the party on its refounding in 1925, and all but one (Meyer) had been active in *völkisch* organisations prior to 1925, several as members of the NSDAP. In short, these were hard-line *völkisch* activists. Finally, of 45 Gauleiters who were in office after 1933, 18 of those appointed before 1933 were already closely connected with their *Gau* before they were appointed, 5 loosely connected and 6 with no connections. Of those appointed between 1933 and 1939 the ratio was 1:1:4 and 1939–1945 3:3;4.[30]

The characters and competence of the individual Gauleiters varied markedly. On the one hand, there were the tyrants like Josef Bürckel of the Palatinate, described as 'a doctrinaire schoolmaster type', with an inferiority complex and harbouring strong personal resentments, a choleric with a fondness for alcohol, but also 'a man of extraordinary dynamism, a huge desire for personal prestige and very sharp elbows'.[31] Martin Mutschmann ('King Mu'), who ruled Saxony like the old-fashioned mill owner he was, fits into this category, as do, among others, Erich Koch of East Prussia and Adolf Wagner of Munich-Upper Bavaria. But, at the other end of the spectrum there were nonentities like the former professional soldier and policeman Otto Telschow of Hanover-East, whose *Gau* was effectively run for most of the time by his deputy, Heinrich Peper; the mild-mannered former local government official, Karl Wahl of Swabia, a naïve *völkisch* true believer; and Karl Weinrich of Kurhessen, who, according to a report prepared for the Nazi Party headquarters by a visiting party inspector, dated 10.1.1932, lacked leadership qualities in every sphere because he lacked the requisite intelligence. Apparently, he resembled an old-fashioned NCO and, when holding major speeches in public, appeared ridiculous.[32]

Hitler was exceptionally loyal to his Gauleiters, showing remarkable tolerance of their excesses.[33] After 1933, only six Gauleiters were dismissed.[34]

Helmuth Brückner of Silesia was caught up in the SA purge, suspected of links with the homosexual clique round the Silesian SA leader Edmund Heines. Wilhelm Karpenstein of Pomerania was also dismissed in the wake of the Röhm purge, suspected of links with Strasser and having alienated Goering.[35] Wilhelm Kube of Kurmark was dismissed for writing an anonymous letter to the party judge, Walter Buch, accusing his wife of being Jewish, although he was rehabilitated in 1941 with his appointment as general commissioner in Byelorussia. Julius Streicher was suspended in 1939 for massive corruption associated with the 'Aryanisation' of Jewish property following the *Reichskristallnacht* and for a string of other excesses, not least doubting the paternity of Goering's son and hence Goering's virility. Hitler expressed extreme remorse for taking this step and his hope to rehabilitate Streicher in the future.[36] Following an intrigue by Bormann and Himmler, Josef Wagner, Gauleiter of Westphalia-South, was stripped of his office in 1941 for his family's close links with the Catholic Church and specifically for refusing permission for his daughter to marry an SS officer.[37] Finally, Karl Weinrich of Kurhessen was dismissed in 1943.[38] He had provided too few air-raid shelters for his *Gau* capital, Kassel, and spent the night of 23 October 1943, when Kassel suffered a major air raid, drinking with his party comrades and entered the city to rescue his furniture only after the all-clear had been given. Goebbels managed to persuade Hitler to replace him.

A number of Gauleiters died during this period (e.g. Carl Röver in 1942 and Adolf Wagner in 1944), and they, too, had to be replaced. Responsibility for replacements fell on Hess and Bormann, who tried to train-up suitable candidates in the Party Chancellery. But the pool was very limited.[39] On 23 June 1942 Goebbels noted: 'The Führer knows all the old *Gauleiters* extremely well, but he tells me that he doesn't have a proper overview of the young candidates. Nevertheless, he wants to bring forward the young ones.'[40] In fact, those appointed, such as Albert Hoffmann of Westphalia-South (1943), Hartmann Lauterbacher of Hanover-South-Brunswick (1940) and Paul Wegener of Weser-Ems (1942), appear to have acquitted themselves reasonably well.

The aim to establish Reich *Gaus*

Following Hitler's appointment as Reich chancellor on 30 January 1933, the Gauleiters came to play a key role in the Nazi take-over of power in the regions. It was they who, along with the SA leadership, initiated and coordinated the 'revolution from below' during the spring of 1933 – in other words, the campaign of intimidation by Nazi activists which forced the resignation of the non-Nazi state governments as well as numerous mayors in towns and cities all over Germany.[41] Most Gauleiters wished to acquire political dominance over their *Gaus*. They perceived the Nazi Party as a revolutionary movement which had the right to take over the State and use it to transform German society and its values in accordance with the ideology of National Socialism. As the party leaders in the provinces, they had 'conquered' their *Gaus* for the movement and so could claim the right to rule there as Hitler's representatives.

However, this raised the question of their future relationship with the state regional authorities who were officially responsible and who were subordinate to the state interior ministries, which were now also in the hands of Nazis.[42] As far as the Gauleiters were concerned, a very varied pattern emerged.[43] By the end of 1933, only 9 out of 30 Gauleiters were without a state office.[44] There was a Reich minister (Rust), ten *Reichsstatthalters*, 8 Prussian *Oberpräsidenten*, 2 state ministers (Wagner and Schemm), and 2 *Regierungspräsidenten* (Hellmuth and Wahl). However, the fact that a Gauleiter did not acquire a state position did not necessarily imply a lack of authority in his *Gau*. Josef Bürckel, for example, explicitly declined the position of prefect, or *Regierungspräsident*, in his *Gau*, the Palatinate.[45] He was conscious of his lack of the requisite legal and administrative training for the post; but, above all, he did not wish to be integrated in a subordinate role into the hierarchy of the Bavarian State. He wanted the dominant position in the *Gau* but not to become a civil servant in the process. Indeed, he summed up his attitude by asserting that 'the *Gauleiters* don't want a state position but they do want the responsible leadership, with the inclusion of the SA and SS'.[46] And in a speech to government officials in the Palatinate, on 3 May 1934, Bürckel made a distinction between government, as it had been traditionally conducted by the regional prefect (Regierungspräsident), and political leadership. He did not want National Socialism defined in legal clauses: 'I don't want to govern in the way it was done previously, I want to lead politically.'[47]

The key question for the future role of the Gauleiters was how this political leadership was to be achieved. During the Third Reich, Gauleiters came to aspire to a situation in which they would combine state and party authority in the *Gau* in their hands, delegating the technical aspects of government to professional civil servants but retaining the authority to make the important political decisions in their own hands. This notion of 'government without administration'[48] was, of course, an illusion. But it was after all the model of government already being implemented by Hitler, of whom they saw themselves as regional representatives. However, a major obstacle was the fact that the existing political and administrative boundaries within the Reich did not correspond with those of the *Gaus*. Thus, their goal, which emerged over the next few years, was a major reform of the internal structure of the Reich.[49] This would replace the historical division of the Reich into states (*Länder*) of very varied size and the overlapping boundaries of the various Reich government agencies (e.g. the Reich Finance Administration), which had come to be superimposed on those of the original German states after the unification of Germany in 1871. This incredibly complex and administratively irrational structure would be replaced by a system in which Germany would be divided into Reich *Gaus* in which all the state and party agencies would be subordinated to the Gauleiter.[50] The state agencies would still be legally subordinate to the Reich ministries, but the Gauleiters would be granted as much autonomy as possible within the overall guidelines set by the Reich Government in Berlin and they would remain directly responsible to Hitler. This goal did not represent a joint and coherent project on the part of the Gauleiters acting as a corps, but rather emerged through *ad hoc* initiatives from individual Gauleiters, often in response to particular problems they faced and to various political developments, notably the annexation of new territories to the German Reich, which gave a marked impetus to the notion of the Reich *Gau*.

These initiatives were supported at first by the Reich Interior Ministry, which wanted to use the Reich *Gau* as a strong *Mittelinstanz* to counteract the centrifugal tendencies of the Reich agencies, which were developing their own field organisations.[51] However, it assumed that the Reich *Gaus* would be integrated into the hierarchy of the Interior Ministry. But the Gauleiters had no intention of allowing themselves to become line managers of the Interior Ministry. In this they were supported by the Staff of the Führer's Deputy/Party Chancellery, who not only wished to increase the power of the party over the State but hoped eventually to subordinate the Reich *Gaus* to their office.

In practice, the Gauleiters pursued a dual policy. In the first place, they endeavoured to expand their power at the expense of the state authorities in their *Gau*. In the case of Prussia this involved them in a confrontation with the regional agencies of the Reich ministries, in particular those of the Reich/Prussian Interior Ministry; in the case of the *Gaus* in the other states they confronted their state governments and the Reich ministries. The problem here was that legislation passed during 1933–35 replaced the previous federal structure of the Reich, in which the individual states had considerable autonomy from the Reich, exercised through a range of independent responsibilities (e.g. for education), with a centralised system, in which the states were subordinated to the Reich ministries, in particular to the Reich/Prussian Interior Ministry.[52] Thus, even in those states (Saxony, Hessen and Lippe) where the Reichsstatthalter/Gauleiters had succeeded in taking over the state government, the state officials were still ultimately subordinate to their superiors in the Reich ministries in Berlin, while the Gauleiters continued to regard themselves as solely responsible to the Führer and were so regarded by Hitler.

The second string of the Gauleiters' policy was to try to expand the borders of their *Gaus* in order to make them as viable as possible as political, administrative and economic units in order to legitimise their demand for maximum political autonomy. In order to further their goal, several Gauleiters took up schemes for territorial and administrative reorganisation that had been developed in the 1920s (see below). However, here they found themselves confronted with the problem that Hitler had banned any discussion of reform of the Reich and, with only a few exceptions, consistently resisted requests for boundary changes, for fear of provoking major conflict and confusion between the various bodies concerned. In practice, where the boundaries of the *Gaus* and those of the states or Prussian provinces coincided, as for example in Saxony or East Prussia, tough and determined Gauleiters like Martin Mutschmann and Erich Koch could acquire a dominant influence over the state authorities, thereby in effect creating a Reich *Gau*, without the need for administrative reforms.

This emergence of Reich *Gaus* was perhaps most strikingly demonstrated in Hamburg where Gauleiter Karl Kaufmann managed to combine the positions of Gauleiter, Reichsstatthalter, and head of the state and municipal governments, as well as, through the 'Greater Hamburg Law' of 1937, extending the borders of the city state of Hamburg to include neighbouring parts of Prussia (Altona, Harburg-Wilhelmsburg and Wandsbek). This created what was in theory the first 'Reich *Gau*', although in practice the various Reich agencies were never integrated into the *Reichsstatthalterei*. However, Greater Hamburg provided a model for the future Reich *Gaus* in the occupied territories.[53] However, Hamburg also demonstrated the problems of such a concentration of power in one individual in terms of the difficulties of coordination and of his being swamped by material, leading to an inability to see the wood for the trees and with a consequent tendency for time and effort to be wasted on trivia.[54]

Another example of such a *Gau* was Thuringia, under its Gauleiter/ Reichsstatthalter, Fritz Sauckel. It was Sauckel's ambition to establish his dominance over the state of Thuringia and to expand the borders of his *Gau* until they corresponded with 'the Thuringian tribe'.[55] He had been appointed Reichsstatthalter in April 1933, but was thwarted in his attempt to take over the state government of Thuringia by Hitler's refusal in 1935 to confirm his appointment as prime minister. Nevertheless, the following year he did succeed in establishing effective control of the Thuringian government. For, after the death of Gauleiter Hans Schemm in an aeroplane accident, Sauckel was able to get rid of his rival, Fritz Wächtler, the minister of education, by securing the latter's nomination as Schemm's replacement. Then, as part of the consequent government reorganisation, he secured Hitler's agreement to the Interior Ministry being subordinated to him as Reichsstatthalter. The man appointed to conduct the actual business of the Interior Ministry was a confidant, namely the head of his office as Reichsstatthalter and simultaneously the chief of police in Weimar, Walter Ortlepp. Moreover, as part of this government reorganisation, Sauckel acquired responsibility for theatres, art institutions and the University of Jena from the Ministry of Education. Thus, as a result of this reorganisation of the Thuringian state government, Sauckel as Reichsstatthalter had concentrated power in his own hands and reduced Prime Minister Willy Marschler to a mere figurehead.

As far as the expansion of his Gau was concerned, in order to further his aim of making its borders correspond to 'those of the Thuringian tribe', Sauckel adopted plans for the reorganisation of central Germany developed in the mid-1920s, which required the inclusion of the Prussian district (*Regierungs-bezirk*) of Erfurt. However, this was blocked by Goering as prime minister of Prussia and so Sauckel had to adopt indirect methods. Thus, when in 1935 the Thuringian Minister of Justice Dr Otto Weber was appointed Regierung-spräsident of Erfurt, Sauckel appointed him a Thuringian state councillor, thereby retaining him nominally as a member of the Thuringian government. Moreover, in order to strengthen Weber's role as a link between Erfurt and Weimar, in 1936 Weber was appointed a member of the Thuringian State Planning Agency. However, Sauckel had to wait until 1 April 1944 when, as part of the reorganisation of the Prussian provinces of Hessen-Nassau and Saxony, the district of Erfurt was removed from the province of Saxony and established as a separate Prussian province under him as Oberpräsident.

Sauckel's attempt to evade Hitler's block on boundary changes in proceeding by stealth, using indirect methods, was typical. One method, for example, was for Gauleiters to try to create a regional economic sphere linked to their *Gaus* by merging economic institutions, such as chambers of commerce, with those of a neighbouring administrative district outside of their *Gaus*. The aim was to produce changes on the ground which would prejudice future border rearrangement in their favour. Jakob Sprenger of Hessen-Nassau, for example, was among the more ambitious and determined Gauleiters.[56] Having been appointed Reichsstatthalter of Hessen in 1933, he then succeeded in forcing out two successive prime ministers of Hesse and taking over the government himself in 1935. For, unlike the case of Sauckel in Thuringia, Hitler approved his appointment as prime minister. However, his ambitions went further and, adopting plans put forward by the Frankfurt am Main city authorities under Weimar to reorganise the Rhine–Main area, in 1933 he created a planning organisation as the first step towards the creation of a new province out of the Prussian district of Wiesbaden and the state of Hessen. The problem was, of course, that such actions invariably represented an encroachment on another *Gau* as well as being liable to provoke resistance from the central state authorities. Indeeed, continuing conflict between Gauleiters and between Gauleiters and the state authorities was structured into the situation. For a long time Sprenger found his ambitions blocked by the Oberpräsident of the Prussian province of Hessen, Prince Philip of Hesse, supported by Goering and Hitler. However, on 1 April 1944, following the dismissal of the prince of Hesse, he did indeed achieve part of his aim with his appointment as Oberpräsident of a new Prussian province of Nassau.

However, the main opportunity for Gauleiters to create Reich *Gaus*, in which both state and party authority at regional level were concentrated in their hands, was provided by the acquisition of new territory directly adjacent to the Reich. For such territories provided a kind of *tabula rasa* for constitutional and administrative experiments, since they were not already subject to the variety of party and state jurisdictions which hampered the consolidation of authority in the hands of the Gauleiters in the 'old Reich'.

The first Gauleiter to seize this new opportunity was Josef Bürckel of the Palatinate.[57] Indeed, Bürckel is another good example of how most Gauleiters wished both to secure maximum independence for their *Gaus* from the Reich authorities and to expand the range of their influence and if possible the borders of their *Gaus*. But in his case he was able to benefit from Germany's acquisition of new territory adjacent to his *Gau* (the Saar and Lorraine), which provided him with the opportunity, to some extent, to evade Hitler's block on administrative reform, since new arrangements had to be made to deal with these acquisitions. However, before these new territories had been acquired he had concentrated on trying to make himself independent of the Bavarian state authorities. For, despite being separated from it geographically by the state of Hessen, for historical reasons the Palatinate was part of Bavaria.

From 1933 onwards, Bürckel sought to achieve the Palatinate's complete separation from Bavaria and, at the same time, maximum autonomy from Berlin. Initially, he was thwarted by the Bavarian government, supported by the Reich Interior Ministry and by a ban, imposed by Hitler, on territorial changes. However, Bürckel was able to take advantage of his appointment as Reich commissioner for the Saar, following its reincorporation in the Reich in 1935, to acquire an increasing degree of independence from the state authorities in Munich, integrating the Saar with the Palatinate.[58] Finally, on 8 April 1940, he achieved a *de facto* complete separation of the Palatinate from Bavaria, in the shape of the new administrative district Saar–Palatinate. From that point onwards, Bürckel was effectively the ruler of both the Palatinate and the Saar.

Bürckel's success in reincorporating the Saar into the Reich prompted Hitler to appoint him on 13 March 1938 as 'Reich commissionner for the reunification of Austria with the Reich'. In Austria, unrestricted by existing *Gau* boundaries and able to ride roughshod over existing state jurisdictions, it was possible for the regime to introduce the Reich *Gau* model. Austria was divided into six Reich *Gaus* (Vienna, Lower Danube, Upper Danube, Salzburg, Steiermark, Tyrol), in which state and party authority were combined in what had now become a single institution, the office of Gauleiter/Reichsstatthalter. A year later, on 8 October 1939, Hitler used the opportunity presented by the incorporation within the Reich of territories in western Poland to create two new Reich *Gaus*, West Prussia and Posen/Wartheland.

Finally, after the occupation in June 1940 of Lorraine, which bordered on the Saar–Palatinate, Bürckel had succeeded in extending his power still further. For, following the Gauleiter's appointment as head of the German civil administration (CdZ) in the former French province, although Lorraine was not yet formally part of the Reich, Hitler gave instructions that the CdZ should be answerable directly to him and that he should act as if Lorraine was part of the Reich. This gave Bürckel the green light to begin integrating Lorraine with Saar Palatinate to form what was in effect, even though it was not officially titled as such, a new Reich *Gau*, which he named Westmark.

Bürckel owed his success in creating a *de facto* Reich *Gau* to his acquisition of new territory (the Saar and Lorraine), which had not formed part of the political–administrative structure of the old Reich. In these circumstances Hitler had been happy to move forward the Reich reform agenda.[59] Indeed, he regarded the Gauleiters as the most appropriate figures to govern and Germanise the newly incorporated territories since, unlike state officials, they would not feel restricted by rules and regulations. Thus, referring to Alsace and Lorraine – though the opinion applied to all the newly incorporated territories – he insisted that

> it was not a matter of creating regular conditions such as exist in the [old] Reich as quickly as possible, but the aim is rather to achieve the speediest possible germanisation of the districts. To achieve this goal a strong legal framewrok can only represent a limitation, while to achieve this goal any method is justified that leads to this goal quickly.[60]

However, as far as the 'old Reich' was concerned, Hitler adopted a cautious approach to administrative change. With his personalised view of politics he undoubtedly sympathised with the model of the Reich *Gau* under the control of the Gauleiter as the future shape of regional administration in Germany. Thus, according to a conversation with Goebbels, on 4 February 1941, he envisaged the break-up of Prussia into provinces and the creation of *Gaus* of varying size to introduce an element of competition among the Gauleiters and the possibility of promotion on merit.[61] He was also anxious to grant the Gauleiters as much autonomy as possible. Indeed, on one occasion he described them as 'viceroys of the Reich'.[62] In a conversation at dinner in his East Prussian headquarters, on 24 June 1942, in which he referred to the dangers of overcentralisation, he announced:

> The experience I gained while organising the Party during the *Kampfzeit* will stand me in good stead now that I have the organisation of the Reich in my hands. If at the time I made the Gauleiters into Kings of their Gau, who received from above only the broadest possible instructions, I now intend to give to our

Reichsstatthalters the same wide freedom, even if this should sometimes bring me into conflict with the Ministry of the Interior. It is only by giving the Gauleiters and the Reichsstatthalters a free hand that one finds out where real capability lies. Otherwise, there will eventually spring up a stolid stupid bureaucracy. And it is only by giving the regional leaders responsibility that one will obtain men eager to accept it, and thus form a nucleus from which to choose leaders of the highest posts in the State.[63]

While insisting that the Gauleiters should maintain the strictest possible discipline in obedience to orders from above, he insisted that 'of course the central government is not concerned with matters of detail which vary greatly in different parts of the country'.[64] However, despite his determination to strengthen the position of the Gauleiters, he had been concerned not to embark on the major territorial and administrative reorganisation of the Reich, which would be involved in the creation of a uniform system of Reich *Gaus* for fear of the political and administrative upheaval that it would create. Such a reform would have to await the end of the war.

Indeed most Gauleiters were operating in the 'old Reich' and, during peacetime, their political power was limited by rules and regulations. For the problem remained that, as a result of the abolition of the federal system through the legislation of 1933–35, the states had been largely reduced to field agencies of the Reich Government in Berlin so that, even where the Gauleiters were Reichsstatthalters and controlled the state (*Land*) government, their hands were to some extent tied. Thus, in a memorandum to Hitler, dated 27 January 1936, Sauckel compared the position of Reichsstatthalter to that of the 'English king in England. He can make quite a lot of his position through his energy and skill but largely outside the legal limits.'[65] However, in some cases the local party and state officials cooperated with one another to resist interference from Berlin – the 'Berlin swindle', as one Baden official later put it, reflecting long-standing anti-Prussian feelings.[66]

Prior to the war, the strongest weapon in the hands of the Gauleiters was, in general, their influence over personnel policy. To a large extent Gauleiters based their power on the exercise of patronage and endeavoured to ensure that key local state positions were filled by members of their *Gau* clique.[67] Their influence here derived in part from their right to issue certificates of political reliability to state officials who were being considered for appointment or promotion and to be heard on the appointment of mayors.[68] However, in practice, their influence in this sphere came from their ability to make life difficult in various ways for the incumbent of any state or local government post who proved objectionable in their eyes. In the case of state officials it was possible, up to a point, for the ministries in Berlin to sustain their officials in the provinces against a Gauleiter. However, because of the difficulties, it often seemed easier to replace the individual concerned with someone to whom the

Gauleiter did not object, either a candidate suggested by the Gauleiter himself or a compromise candidate.

The extent to which the party was able to, or indeed wished to, impose unqualified personnel on the state agencies varied from *Gau* to *Gau*. Thus, according to a report of the Reich Interior Ministry from 1943, whereas in the Prussian provinces of East Prussia, Hessen-Nassau and parts of the Rhineland more than half of the *Landräte* were unqualified party appointments, in Pomerania and in some parts of other provinces they were more or less in the minority, while in Bavaria, Baden and Württemberg all the Landräte appointed after 1933 were qualified and almost all were locals.[69] However, it is open to question whether this fact resulted in any significant obstacle being placed in the way of the Gauleiter achieving his goals, since, most *qualified* officials were prepared to cooperate and, as in the case of Hamburg, he could always bypass the established officials by creating 'special' commissioners and agencies to cover particular spheres of activity appointed from within his own *Gau* clique.[70]

In the case of local government officials the Gauleiters were in a far stronger position.[71] Some Gauleiters cooperated well with their mayors. Gauleiter Wahl of Swabia, for example, even interceded with Hitler and persuaded him to revoke his dismissal of the *Oberbürgermeister* of Augsburg.[72] However, according to the Oberbürgermeister of Stettin, Werner Faber,

in practice it is the case that the Oberbürgermeister and the political leaders cannot report anything to their superiors that does not have the Gauleiter's approval. The Oberbürgermeister has seriously blotted his copy book if he opposes a measure [of the Gauleiter's] or reports to his superiors about it; it doesn't even have to be a formal complaint.

In 1934, for example, there was a trial of strength between the Oberbürgermeister of Bremen, Richard Markert and the Gauleiter/Reichsstatthalter of Oldenburg–Bremen, Carl Röver, and the Gauleiter of Hanover-East, Otto Telschow. Despite the fact that Markert had the support of his senate, of leading figures in the commercial world of Bremen, and of his supervisory authority, the Reich Interior Ministry, and, despite his control of the city government and, since Bremen was a state, his status as head of a state government as well, Markert was forced out.[73] A similar trial of strength occurred in Düsseldorf in 1939.[74] The Reich Interior Minister Wilhelm Frick, the Prussian Prime Minister Hermann Goering, and the Gauleiter of neighbouring Essen Josef Terboven all favoured a particular candidate as mayor. But the Gauleiter of Düsseldorf Friedrich Florian objected to the appointment. On being requested for his opinion, Hitler was reported as having responded 'that agreement must exist between the Gauleiter and the senior officials in his *Gau*. If this agreement is undermined then the senior official must be recalled, even if he has given no cause for it, so that the work does not suffer in consequence.' As a result, mayors, even important ones, were rarely able to survive the hostility of their Gauleiter for long. The Oberbürgermeisters of Frankfurt am Main and Stuttgart, Fritz Krebs and Karl Strölin, managed to survive the hostility of their Gauleiters only because they had exceptionally strong party records and good connections at the highest level, and were very able. But, even so, they probably survived only because of the growing crisis during the last phase of the war.

Essentially, the Gauleiters' power was local. It was based on their position as Hitler's direct representatives in their *Gaus*. Their influence on national politics was minimal and after 1933–34 they felt themselves increasingly marginalised. In the words of Gauleiter Jordan, 'what was going on in the *Gaus* mattered less and less; we had suddenly become "provincial"'. There were continual complaints about their lack of knowledge of what was going on.[75] One reason for this lack of clout at national level was their inability to form a lobby. This was partly because of their individual rivalries but also because they were prevented from meeting together independently. Thus, an attempt by the Gauleiter of Westphalia-South to call a meeting of Gauleiters in December 1934 was blocked by Hess, who insisted that such meetings could be summoned only by Hitler or himself.[76] And in fact, in asserting its right to organise such meetings, the Staff of the Führer's Deputy was endeavouring to establish its leadership of the party.

Between 30 January 1933 and 1 September 1939, there were twenty-seven meetings of the Gauleiters of 1–3 days' duration, regularly chaired by Hess and occasionally attended by Hitler.[77] Important issues such as 'reform of the Reich' and 'Church and party' were on the agenda and, under Hess's chairmanship, there was evidently some discussion.[78] During the war, there were nineteen such meetings with a particular concentration during the years 1943–44 when Hitler clearly sought the comfort of the support of his loyal Gauleiters.[79] The Führer did not usually attend the meetings, which were organised by Bormann who appears to have set the agenda, although he invited them to a reception later at which he gave an address. Initially, the meetings were apparently designed to to keep the Gauleiters abreast, in general terms, of current developments, and there was little or no discussion. However, after Stalingrad, as the Gauleiters became increasingly involved in administration, the subject matter became more concrete and detailed, involving issues such as civil defence, evacuation and economic matters. The Gauleiters not only received instructions but were able to express their views and exchange experiences. These meetings, involving a subsequent pep talk from Hitler, may have helped to coordinate the implementation of policy and undoubtedly strengthened their corps spirit and boosted their morale.[80]

Populist strategies

As far as Hitler was concerned, the main role of the Gauleiters was to win their populations over to the regime and its key ideological tenets, and to maintain that support. With the take-over of power complete by the summer of 1933, the Gauleiters therefore felt the pressure to legitimise, in the eyes of the public at large, their claim to dominate their *Gaus*. They proceeded to do so through a variety of means designed to create the right image – that of a ruler who iden-tified himself with the people of his *Gau* and who would defend their interests. Particularly in the case of a Gauleiter, such as Bürckel, who was born or brought up in his *Gau*, there was also undoubtedly an element of genuine loy-alty to the locality involved. But even an 'imported' Gauleiter, such as Jordan in Halle-Merseburg, was anxious to make his mark. Thus Jordan noted after the war that he 'was perhaps so vain as to already see my name recorded in the his-tory of this landscape whose significance was as great in the present as it would be in the future'.[81]

The image that emerged was constructed by tapping into the tradition of the monarch as the 'father of the country' (*Landesvater*), the benevolent ruler of his people concerned for their welfare, but also the representative and patron of the culture and traditions of his land. It was a tradition that still resonated with large numbers of Germans. But this trope was modified by the image of the Gauleiter as a modern *Volksführer*, one of the people, but marked out for leadership by his quasi-military virtues of toughness, decisiveness, and deter-mination. He was a man of action and a leader who was looking forward rather than back, proud of the heritage of his *Gau* and yet engaged with the modern world. In general, the Nazi Party came to conceive of its main function in the Third Reich as 'the leadership of the people' (*Menschenführung*), and the Gauleiters were expected to take a prominent role in this.[82] Typical of their per-ception of this role is a statement by Hartmann Lauterbacher, the wartime Gauleiter of Hanover–South-Brunswick in his memoirs:

> I wasn't the type who sits behind a desk; I wanted to be on the front line, some-one who always engaged with people. And so I visited government offices just as sometimes I appeared as Harun al Raschid [i.e. incognito] ... And I talked to workers in the factories, to peasants, to students, but also to people in the street. This is what I felt and understood to be leadership.[83]

A key element in the self-perception of many Gauleiters was their quasi-pedagogic role.[84] Many had previously been teachers or had trained as teach-ers, and even those who had no such background often saw themselves in this role.[85] On 15 April 1937, for example, Gauleiter Dr Alfred Meyer of Westphalia-North, a trained economist and a mining official, explained to foreign diplo-mats in Berlin his view of 'the Gauleiter's most decisive task', namely '*Menschenführung*': 'This task cannot be done from an office desk. The

Gauleiter must really conquer the hearts, the trust, and the faith of the compatriots entrusted to him by the Führer on a daily basis.' As 'speakers and preachers of the National Socialist ideology' the main aim must be 'to explain the Führer's measures and those of the state man to man and thereby gradually convert the German compatriots to National Socialism'.[86]

In order to create and sustain this image of political leadership it was vital for the Gauleiters to maintain a dominant presence within the minds of their populations through maximising their public exposure. This was achieved partly through a constant round of public appearances. Every possible opportunity was taken for the Gauleiter to present himself to the population in some impressive or worthy setting: national celebrations, such as May Day or Mothers' Day; the visits of national leaders; *Gau* and district party rallies; ten-year anniversaries of the founding of local party branches; the ceremonial openings of cultural or charitable events; the start-up of major economic developments – any and every occasion was seized on to demonstrate a Gauleiter's leading role as the man who made things happen, the man to whom the populace owed gratitude for the improvement in its situation, or at least as the local representative of the regime which had achieved this. Moreover, the effect of these public appearances was reinforced by the use of the press. For most Gauleiters were able to use local newspapers to give additional prominence to their activities. For example, Meyer was the centre of attention in 604 articles, reports and official statements in 3,964 issues of the *National-Zeitung*, the main regional paper for Westphalia between 1 March 1933 and 31 March 1944, in other words approximately once a week.[87] During peacetime, when the paper was not obliged to devote space to reporting the war, he appeared even more frequently. Furthermore, his public presence was strengthened by the use of photographs. Between March 1933 and April 1944, a photo of Meyer appeared in the *National Zeitung* 211 times. Every third article about Meyer had a photo, and one-third of these photos was a portrait or a photo in which he was the dominant figure and a quarter showed him in the company of prominent national or international figures.

An important aspect of the Gauleiters' efforts to legitimise their position was their attempts to cultivate the local historical traditions and cultural heritage of their *Gaus*. There was in fact a tension in Nazi cultural policy.[88] On the one hand there was the centralising, homogenising thrust of Goebbels's propaganda ministry, which wished to subordinate cultural activities to the aim of uniting the nation in a national community and mobilising its spiritual resources for the goal of territorial expansion. On the other hand, there was the *völkisch* ideology which emphasised local and regional cultural features, with its notions of blood, soil and *Heimat*. Moreover, these ideas had a strong resonance for provincial cultural elites, the integration of which into the regime was considered important . This latter aspect of Nazi ideology and cultural policy provided an opportunity for the Gauleiters to exercise a measure of cultural autonomy. But there was always a degree of tension with Berlin over such matters as the appointment of theatre directors or the creation of *Gau* cultural organisations. Thus, for example, when eight Gauleiters appointed their own personal cultural staff officer the ministry tried with questionable success to persuade them to abolish those posts in the interests of 'a uniform Reich administration'.

Sometimes, this cultural engagement involved the creation of new traditions. For example, Gauleiter Meyer initiated an annual ritual on 21 June commemorating the 'martyrdom' of Ludwig Knickmann, a Nazi shot by Belgian soldiers during the Ruhr occupation in 1923.[89] Another common way of celebrating the *Gau*'s heritage was to commemorate famous local sons. For example, Meyer established festivals to commemorate Arminius, the Germanic tribal leader who defeated the Roman legions in the Teutoburg forest. He also established an annual book week to commemorate the local nineteenth-century Lippe playwright Christian Dietrich Grabbe, whose nationalist sympathies and plays about historical German figures, such as the emperors Frederick Barbarossa and Heinrich VI, made him a particularly appropriate figure for the Nazis to celebrate.[90]

However, undoubtedly the most striking example of a Gauleiter exploiting the local cultural heritage of his *Gau* was Sauckel's instrumentalising of the cultural prestige of his *Gau* capital, Weimar.[91] As the home of the two great classical writers, Goethe and Schiller, the philospher Herder and, at least temporarily, of J. S. Bach, and later, during its 'silver age' in the nineteenth century, associated with Liszt and Nietzsche, Weimar possessed enormous cultural prestige, and Sauckel determined to exploit this in order to raise the profile of his *Gau* and establish Weimar as a Nazi capital on a par with Munich, Nuremberg and Bayreuth. Moreover, in his aspiration to make Weimar the centre of a new National Socialist German classicism, he had the sympathy of a Weimar cultural establishment, which had strongly resented the town's association with the Republic and what it regarded as the latter's debasement of German culture through such manifestations as the Bauhaus, which for a time of course had been based in Weimar.[92] Indeed, this consensus in the rejection of modern cultural trends represented an important bridge between the new Nazi and old local *bürgerlich* elites. Sauckel and the head of the *Gau* cultural department, Hans Severus Ziegler, organised a whole series of events – *Gau* cultural weeks, annual book weeks, celebrations of German cultural icons associated with Weimar (e.g. Schiller in 1934, Bach and Luther in 1935), aided by numerous academics and cultural figures, who were ready and willing to put a National Socialist gloss on the Weimar heritage. Moreover, this harnessing of the *Gau*'s cultural past was not confined to Weimar, for Thuringia also contained the iconic castle the Wartburg, with its associations with Luther and the *Burschenschaften*, which were also heavily exploited.

Significantly, however, Sauckel distanced himself to some extent from the conservative cultural establishment of the town by making it clear that he wished his subjects not to wallow in the past but to see these great local figures as a spur to future cultural achievements. Thus, in his address on the occasion of the *Gau* cultural week in February–March 1934 he appealed to the citizens of Weimar

> not to rest on the laurels of a tremendous tradition, on the heritage which very great German men, who have given Weimar its reputation, fought to create, but now to create new things out of the spirit of National Socialism, the spirit of Adolf Hitler. Go to work, create new things and then the name of Weimar will remain unforgettable and you will create inestimable values for the future glory of Germany.[93]

The most striking manifestation of this attempt to adapt the heritage of Weimar to the new Nazi era was Sauckel's determination to leave his mark through new buildings. Thus, he was the first Gauleiter to build a '*Gau* forum' as the first stage of his plan to modernise Weimar 'in the spirit of National Socialism'. In a speech on 24 August 1939 he insisted that Weimar was not a 'sacred cultural cemetery': it needed to be wakened from its 'beauty sleep'. Its new buildings represented the 'essence and spirit' of the new age, the 'tempo and rhythm' of which were symbolised by Weimar's access to the new Autobahnen.

Sauckel was, however, by no means the only Gauleiter to attempt to leave his mark on his *Gau* through architecture. Indeed, Gauleiters embarked on a wide range of building projects – theatres, opera-houses, party buildings, housing estates, among others – designed to enhance their prestige and that of their *Gaus*. Gauleiter Meyer, for example, planned a massive project for his *Gau* capital Münster, involving new government and party quarters, with a large 'people's hall' and parade ground, and an enormous bell tower.[94] He also intended the renovation of the working-class district of the mining city of Gelsenkirchen. Finally, he envisaged constructing a huge cult centre on a hill below the ninteenth-century monument to Arminius. This complex of buildings, which was to commemorate the NSDAP's crucial victory in the Lippe-Detmold election of January 1933, was to be built in the neo-classical style and intended to become 'a new Acropolis'. All these plans had been agreed with Hitler and Speer; indeed, one of the incentives encouraging the Gauleiters to embark on such mammoth projects was to win the approval of Hitler. For the Führer could always be guaranteed to be interested in any architectural project; and, by demonstrating initiative and a 'grand vision' in this sphere, a Gauleiter could be sure to enhance his stature in Hitler's eyes. However, such megalomaniacal plans, which were paralleled by those of many other Gauleiters, of course reflected also their perceptions of themselves since they were considered appropriate expressions of their leadership roles.[95]

Much of the focus of the Gauleiters' engagement with high culture was on educating the ordinary 'compatriots', a particular feature of their quasi-pedagogic role. As Meyer put it in January 1938:

In the future, the party has the task of educating the German people in National Socialism and with all the means that are appropriate, not least with the help of art. Previously, the German worker has had little to do with art. Now he must free himself from the idea that art is not for him. Art has great tasks to fulfil, in particular for the working man. We must acquaint the people with the beauties of Germany and the works of the great German masters.[96]

Meyer, however, also exploited popular culture by patronising the famous Gelsenkirchen football club Schalke O4, which won several football league championiships during the 1930s. He attended matches and publicly honoured the victorious teams. Thus, he welcomed the team's victory in 1940 by announcing:

We in Gau Westphalia North are proud of our Schalke boys. They've managed to do it even in wartime under more difficult circumstances when part of the team is wearing military uniform and has fought bravely at the front . . . The presence of representatives of the state and the party and the Wehrmacht should prove to Schalke how closely bound to them we feel. They shall have the confidence of knowing, that even in the most difficult times, the whole of Westphalia is behind them.[97]

Another practice designed to convey their image as rulers who were in touch with their people was the introduction by several Gauleiters, rather in the tradition of benevolent rulers of the past, of regular times when 'compatriots' could see them to discuss their problems and grievances, offering the prospect of cutting through the red tape in order to correct possible injustices and alleviate hardships. Gauleiter Wahl of Swabia reserved two days of the week on which people could see him without witnesses, while Lauterbacher held surgeries in Hanover, Braunschweig, Hildesheim, and Göttingen which people could attend without prior arrangement, and he brought with him experts in various fields who could give advice.[98] Gauleiter Kaufmann of Hamburg introduced a weekly surgery in May 1933 and an 'Investigation and Advice Centre' to which Hamburg citizens could take their grievances against decisions by the city administration.[99] Between January 1935 and March 1937 over 15,000 complaints were made, some of which Kaufmann took up himself and satisfied against the prevailing rules. Such populist measures were clearly designed to distance the Gauleiters from the unpopular decisions of the state administration.

An important aspect of the attempt by the Gauleiters to legitimise themselves and the regime was to convey the impression that they were endeavouring to deal with the particular economic problems of their *Gaus*. Gauleiter Sauckel of Thuringia, for example, produced a 'Thuringian Film' premiered in

Berlin in March 1933 and designed to boost the state's tourist industry. He also established a 'Thuringia House' in Berlin in September 1933 as a showcase for the *Gau*'s industrial products, handicrafts and cultural achievements and intended to demonstrate that 'Thuringia is not only a state with a beautiful landscape, a state renowned for its intellect (*Geist*), but also an industrial centre'. Similarly, Gauleiter Karl Kaufmann of Hamburg endeavoured to meet the demands of both the business and the working-class communities of Hamburg. Hamburg's foreign commercial activities were seriously hampered by the increasingly autarkic policies being followed under the Four Year Plan of 1936 and its economy was increasingly dependent on state orders and subject to state controls. Describing himself as 'a travelling businessman (*Kaufmann*) for the firm of Hamburg', Kaufmann cultivated Hamburg's business leaders. He ensured that they gained from the Aryanisation of Jewish commercial operations in Vienna and lobbied for their appointment to senior positions in the German occupation administrations.[100] But he also tried to mollify the Hamburg working class by supporting the high wage structure in Hamburg, backing measures for improving the lot of dock workers in irregular employment and cracking down on increases in beer prices. These 'social populist' measures were clearly designed to convey the impression of the Gauleiter as a tough leader and 'a man of the people'. He replied to complaints about 'brown Bolshevism' by pointing out that 'total war in an industrial state is not only fought with arms and soldiers but above all with workers'.[101].

The biggest challenge facing the regime on coming to power had been mass unemployment. A striking example of a Gauleiter's involvement in solving this problem and the hardship it caused occurred in the Prussian province and *Gau* of East Prussia, where, on 26 July 1933, the Gauleiter and Oberpräsident Erich Koch proudly informed Hitler that unemployment had been banished.[102] Koch's remarkable (short term) success was based on a number of factors. But vital to it was the fact that he had succeeded in winning the support of the minister of the interior in Prussia, Hermann Goering, enabling East Prussia to receive preferential credits from Prussia and the Reich in order to finance a massive programme of work-creation projects for both rural and urban unemployed, which, temporarily at any rate, solved the problem.

Elsewhere, Gauleiters sought by varied means to relieve the crisis in their *Gaus*. In Hessen, for example, on 5 June 1933, Gauleiter Jakob Sprenger established a so-called Control Office for Work Creation to coordinate the activities of the Prussian and Hessen state authorities concerning work creation.[103] Factories in the Rhine–Main area were combed through for young workers who were forced into the Labour Service organisation to provide vacancies for older workers with families. And, on 23 September 1933, Sprenger invited Hitler to the start of construction on the first section of the Frankfurt–Darmstadt autobahn, plans for which had been prepared prior to the Nazis' accession to power.

The Gauleiter personally handed out spades to 700 unemployed workers and then headed their march to the building site accompanied by a band and, naturally, the local press.

Another striking example was Gauleiter Dr Otto Hellmuth of Lower Franconia, who, throughout the 1930s, endeavoured to transform the economic situation of the Rhön, a desperately poor and underdeveloped district in his *Gau*, through a comprehensive programme addressing the problems of transportation, agriculture and industry.[104] It envisaged the resettlement of a large proportion of the Rhön's population through the replacement of the large number of uneconomic smallholdings with larger, economically viable, productive hereditary farms (*Erbhöfe*) operated by racially sound proprietors instead of the physically and spiritually debilitated existing population. However, although the scheme appeared to reflect many of the key principles of Nazi ideology and despite official acknowledgement of the problems of the Rhön, in the end little of the 'Dr Hellmuth Plan' was realised. The high cost of this ambitious programme, the scepticism of the Reich authorities in Berlin, objections from the minister–president of neighbouring Thuringia, which contained part of the Rhön, and the local population's opposition to losing their land and being forcibly relocated combined to prevent its realisation. The story of the Dr Hellmuth Plan indicates both the role which a Gauleiter felt himself called on to fulfil and the limits of his influence without the backing of other agencies, particularly at Reich level.

But the most remarkable instance of a Gauleiter adopting a high profile in the alleviation of the effects of the economic crisis was that of Josef Bürckel, a Gauleiter on the radical 'socialist' wing of the party, acquiring the reputation of being a 'red Gauleiter'.[105] Declaring that 'the Palatinate has the wish to provide a model of true German Socialism for the Reich and to commit itself to the Socialism of Action', on 9 September 1933 he launched a so-called 'People's Socialist Aid Programme' to the accompaniment of mass meetings and the ringing of church bells throughout the province.[106] This programme required all wage- and salary-earners to contribute a percentage of their income – in the case of officials, twenty per cent. Those who objected had to reckon with a public 'shaming'. For the launching of this programme had been preceded, on 2 September, by a People's Socialist Law of Honour, which established 'a special moral claim', allegedly deriving from the people of the Palatinate, comprising a set of rules of behaviour with punishments for inappropriate conduct. Thus, according to Article 1:

> The compatriots (*Volksgenossen*), who are bound together by their Socialism will, as a totality, pronounce the punishment of anyone who offends against the essence and the content of the Socialist national community. Such a verdict will deny their right to call themselves compatriots and will remove from the totality the obligation of regarding them as compatriots.[107]

Protests against Bürckel's actions poured in from the ministries in Berlin and Munich, which strongly objected to their officials being forced to subscribe to this programme. However, it was not until the middle of 1934, following the creation of the monopoly for welfare collections of the National Socialist Welfare Organisation (NSV), that Bürckel was forced to merge his organisation with the NSV. Apart from raising his personal profile and channelling the revolutionary sentiments of the local SA, the aim of Bürckel's welfare organisation was 'to make the Palatinate stand on its own feet and make it no longer dependent on help from the Reich or the state' (Bavaria),[108] a further example of the desire of the Gauleiters to assert their independence. Moreover, Bürckel continued to push his own line against the Reich authorities. Thus, against the opposition of Goering, he took the initiative in introducing the payment of wages for public holidays, which was instituted throughout the Reich on 3 December 1937.[109]

These instances of Gauleiters taking on responsibility in 1933 for economic and social developments in their *Gaus* were just the start of an ongoing process of engagement. Thus, the office of *Gau* economic advisor played an increasingly important role in the local economy, notably in its control of the Aryanisation programme, in other words the more-or-less forcible acquisition of Jewish property.[110] For example, Gauleiter Sauckel of Thuringia used the Aryanisation programme to gain control of the Jewish armaments firm of Simson based in Suhl. Renamed the Wilhelm Gustloff Works and controlled by Sauckel through a holding company, the Wilhelm Gustloff Foundation, the firm provided Sauckel with an economic power base, enabling him to finance his projects and achieve at least partial independence from the financial control of the party treasurer.[111] The Gustloff Works acquired increasing importance in the German armaments' programme through its association with Buchenwald concentration camp, which provided labour for major projects, notably the construction of underground plants in Thuringia for the production of the V weapons and the M 262 jet-fighter.

Finally, as part of their public relations' efforts, Gauleiters endeavoured to record, underline and publicise their achievements for their *Gaus* with a series of publications. Significantly, these publications did not generally take the form of histories of the local party but rather of descriptions of the region, its geography, economy, history and cultural traditions, stressing the extent to which the Gauleiters and the local party organisations identified with their *Gaus* and took pride in the contribution which they had made to their well-being and future prosperity.[112]

The war years

With the outbreak of war civilian morale became an acute issue, especially given Hitler's paranoia about the revolution of 1918. It was not surprising, therefore, that he should have given responsibility for all matters pertaining to civilian defence to the Gauleiters in the shape of the new office of Reich defence commissioner (RVK) rather than, as in the First World War, to the district military commanders.[113] On 1 September 1939, thirteen Gauleiters were appointed to the new post, the boundaries of which coincided with those of the military districts. However, they were obliged to use the existing governmental machinery and, in practice, during the first successful phase of the war – until 1942 – the part played by the Gauleiters as RVKs was limited.

In November 1942, all forty-two Gauleiters were appointed RVKs and the growing crisis produced by the Allied bombing campaign and then by the threat of invasion provided the context for a rapid increase in their power, as almost all spheres of civilian life came to be subsumed under the term 'defence of the Reich'. Thus, by 1944, under various items of legislation, they had been given substantial if not total control over labour deployment, civil defence, evacuation, the treatment of foreign workers, exemptions from military service and the closing of inessential plants and businesses. The war years are also notable for the important part played by the Gauleiters in the radicalising of policies springing directly from Nazi ideology. This was most notorious in the case of Jewish persecution, where Gauleiter Bürckel and Gauleiter Robert Wagner of Baden took the initiative for the deportation of Jews under their jurisdiction to camps in Vichy France in 1940, while, in the following year, Goebbels of Berlin, Kaufmann of Hamburg and Baldur von Schirach of Vienna, all pressed, eventually successfully, for the deportation of Jews to Poland.[114]

After the assassination attempt on Hitler of 20 July 1944 and the appointment of Goebbels as 'Reich commissioner for Total War' on 25 July 1944 the Gauleiters' power increased still further, since, under a Hitler decree of 16 August, they were given the power of requesting information from and issuing instructions to all government agencies and businesses at regional and local levels.[115] By that time, as RVKs, the Gauleiters had become the effective rulers of their *Gaus*. In the final months of the war, true to their conception of their role of *Menschenführung*, they concentrated on mobilising their populations for the building of fortifications and the formation of the *Volkssturm*, or Home Guard, most notably in the cases of Koch in East Prussia and Karl Hanke in Breslau.

The increasing allocation of powers to the Gauleiters through legislation reflected Hitler's growing reliance on his most loyal supporters as the crisis deepened. 'The Gauleiters', Hitler told Goebbels on 20 August 1942, 'never cheat me. They are my most faithful and reliable colleagues. If I lost my faith in them. I would no longer know in whom to put my trust' and he repeated 'emphatically' that the Gauleiters were subordinated to him personally.[116] However, the increase in the Gauleiters' power was also a function of the developing situation in which they could seize the opportunity to expand their role. For, in the growing crisis, channels of communication from the centre to the periphery became less efficient and in what became a more or less permanent state of emergency rapid decisions had to be taken. Following the erosion of the authority and self-confidence of the state authorities, party officials alone had the political will and clout to take action, cutting through the red tape when necessary.

In that situation each Gauleiter saw his priority as being, overwhelmingly, the defence of the interests of his *Gau*. Thus, Goebbels complained that Gauleiters were using the air raids as a pretext by which to acquire 'enormous powers' in order to emancipate themselves from the central authorities in Berlin. As a result, the unauthorised actions of a number of Gauleiters were causing serious problems.[117] Gauleiter Florian of Düsseldorf was a particularly notorious example. 'For example, at a meeting in the Interior Ministry' he declared that, 'as far as he was concerned, "legal decrees" had no significance; he would do what his common sense told him to do'. Goebbels commented drily that 'if Florian had a healthy common sense then that wouldn't cause serious damage; but sometimes it is the complete opposite and so Florian will have to be rapped over the knuckles'.[118] Goebbels was constantly complaining that the Gauleiters were showing little 'community spirit', for example over evacuation measures and the hoarding of workers needed elsewhere, behaviour which affected him directly in his role as Gauleiter of Berlin. Thus, as early as June 1942, he was noting in his diary that 'the critical situation in the big cities, above all in Berlin, is the result of the Gauleiters' particularism. The more limited the supplies become the more the Gauleiters are inclined to hold back the stuff that is produced in their own Gau and on no account to export it'.[119]

It was, however, Albert Speer, the man in charge of the war economy, who complained most vigorously about the 'particularist' behaviour of the Gauleiters who, in protecting their own *Gau* economies by refusing to close inessential businesses and by hoarding food, labour and other materials, were damaging the overall war effort.[120]

As I have said, this 'particularist' behaviour reflected the Gauleiters' view of their role as it had developed since 1933, or even earlier, and also their sense of what the Führer expected of them, namely the maintenance of morale in their *Gaus*. Indeed, it has been argued that, in pursuing this policy, the Gauleiters were in fact acting as a stabilising factor for the regime as a whole, adjusting central measures to local needs and preventing potential unrest.[121] It has also been argued that it was only the energies unleashed by the polycratic rivalries and the ambitions of the party officials, notably the Gauleiters as RVKs, which enabled the regime to mobilise the resources that kept it going for so long.[122]

This question of the effectiveness of the Gauleiters during the later stages of the war is difficult to determine at the present stage of research. In his diaries

Goebbels oscillates between praise and criticism. It is, however, significant that, in February 1943, Hitler felt obliged to warn the Gauleiters about their lifestyles.[123] According to Goebbels, they showed no awareness of the seriousness of the situation, and were living 'as if we were enjoying complete peace. Above all, the consumption of alcohol has reached abnormally large proportions.'[124] Similarly, on 27 February 1943, Ernst Kaltenbrunner, the chief of the Security Police and SD, complained to Goebbels about the poor behaviour of a number of Gauleiters: 'They often spend days on end at their hunting lodges and pay no attention either to the leadership of their Gaus or to dealing with the urgent questions involved in total war.' Goebbels noted: 'something ought to be done about this', but then continued, significantly: 'but who has the authority to do it?'[125] The Gauleiters' effectiveness undoubtedly varied from individual to individual. Karl Weinrich of Kurhessen was an example of the less competent Gauleiters. At the other end of the spectrum there was Karl Kaufmann of Hamburg, who evidently dealt with the aftermath of the catastrophic raids on his city of July 1943 reasonably effectively. Also, while many of the older Gauleiters appear to have taken to drink or sunk into lethargy, the younger ones, such as Albert Hoffmann of Westphalia-South, Dr Hugo Jury of the Lower Danube, Hartmann Lauterbacher of Hanover-South–Brunswick, Paul Wegener of Weser-Ems, appear to have been more effective.[126] Only further research on the performance of individual Gauleiters will help to clarify this issue as indeed other aspects of the Gauleiters' activities. What is clear already, however, is that they played a major role in the history of Germany during the Third Reich and have hitherto been unwisely neglected by historians.

Notes

1 See above all Dieter Rebentisch, *Führerstaat und Verwaltung im Zweiten Weltkrieg: Verfassungsentwicklung und Verwaltungspolitik 1939–1945* (Stuttgart, 1989); also Jeremy Noakes (ed.), *Nazism 1919–1945*, vol. 4: *The German Home Front 1939–1945* (Exeter, 1998).

2 Peter Hüttenberger, *Die Gauleiter: Studie zum Wandel des Machtgefüges in der NSDAP* (Stuttgart, 1969). Dietrich Orlow's two-volume history of the NSDAP *The History of the Nazi Party*, vol.1: *1919–1933* and vol. 2: *1933–1945* (Newton Abbot, 1969 and 1973), contains useful material; see also Karl Höffkes, *Hitlers Politische Generäle: Die Gauleiter des Dritten Reiches* (Tübingen, 1986).

3 The only Gauleiter for whom there is a substantial number of studies is Josef Bürckel of the Palatinate. See: Hans Fenske, 'Josef Bürckel und die Verwaltung der Pfalz', in Dieter Rebentisch and Karl Teppe (eds), *Verwaltung contra Menschenführung im Staat Hitlers: Studien zum politisch–administrativen System* (Göttingen, 1986), pp. 153–72; E. D. H. Harrison, *Gauleiter Bürckel and the Bavarian Palatinate 1933–1940* (Leeds, 1986); Hans-Joachim Heinz, *NSDAP und Verwal-*

tung in der Pfalz: Allgemeine innere Verwaltung und kommunale Selbstverwaltung im Spannungsfeld nationalsozialistischer Herrschaftspraxis 1933–1939. Ein Beitrag zur zeitgeschichtlichen Landeskunde (Mainz 1994); Klaus-Michael Mallmann and Gerhard Paul, *Herrschaft und Alltag: Ein Industrierevier im Dritten Reich* (Bonn, 1991); Dieter Muskalla, *NS-Politik an der Saar unter Josef Bürckel: Gleichschaltung–Neuordnung–Verwaltung* (Saarbrücken, 1995); Dieter Wolfanger, 'Populist und Machtpolitiker. Josef Bürckel: Vom Gauleiter der Pfalz zum Chef der Zivilverwaltung in Lothringen', in Gerhard Nestler and Hannes Ziegler (eds), *Die Pfalz unterm Hakenkreuz Eine deutsche Provinz während der nationalsozialistischen Terrorherrschaft* (Landau, 1993), pp. 63–86. For other studies of individual Gauleiters, see: (on Sauckel) Ronald Smelser and Rainer Zitelmann (eds), *Die braune Elite: 22 biographische Skizzen* (Darmstadt 1989); (on Bürckel, Globocnik, Greiser, Robert Wagner) Ronald Smelser, Enrico Syring and Rainer Zitelmann (eds), *Die braune Elite*, vol. 2: *21 weitere biographische Skizzen* (Darmstadt, 1993); Frank Bajohr, 'Gauleiter in Hamburg. Zur Person und Tätigkeit Karl Kaufmanns', *Vierteljahrshefte für Zeitgeschichte*, 2 (1995), pp. 267–95; Kurt Gayer, 'Wilhelm Murr. Gauleiter und Reichsstatthalter von 1933–1945', in Kurt Gayer and Heinz Krämer (eds), *Die Villa Reitzenstein und ihre Herren: Die Geschichte des baden-württembergischen Regierungssitzes* (Stuttgart, 1988), pp. 119–30; Franz Kühnl, *Hans Schemm. Gauleiter und Kultusminister (1891–1935)* (Nuremberg, 1985); Heinz-Jürgen Priamus, 'Alfred Meyer – Selbstinszenierung eines Gauleiters', in Heinz-Jürgen Priamus and Stefan Gosch (eds), *Macht der Propaganda oder Propaganda der Mach: Inszenierung nationalsozialistischer Politik im 'Drittten Reich' am Beispiel der Stadt Gelsenkirchen* (Essen, 1992), pp. 48–67; and 'Regionale Aspekte in der Politik des nordwestfälischen Gauleiters Alfred Meyer', in H. Möller, A. Wirsching and W. Ziegler (eds), *Nationalsozialismus in der Region: Beiträge zur regionalen und lokalen Forschung und zum internationalen Vergleich* (Munich, 1996), pp. 175–98.

4 Alfred E Frauenfeld, *Und trage keine Reu: Vom Wiener Gauleiter zum Generalkommisar der Krim. Erinnerungen und Aufzeichnungen* (Leoni, 1978); Rudolf Jordan, *Erlebt und erlitten: Weg eines Gauleiters von München bis Moskau* (Leoni, 1971) and *Im Zeugenstand der Geschichte: Antworten zum Thema Hitler* (Leoni, 1983); Albert Krebs, *Tendenzen und Gestalten der NSDAP: Erinnerungen an die Frühzeit der Partei* (Stuttgart, 1959); Hartmann Lauterbacher, *Erlebt und mitgestaltet: Kronzeuge einer Epoche 1923–1924: Zu neuen Ufern nach Kriegsende* (Preussisch Oldendorf, 1987); Baldur von Schirach, *Ich glaubte an Hitler* (Hamburg, 1967); Karl Wahl, '...es ist das deutsche Herz': *Erlebnisse und Erkenntnisse eines ehemaligen Gauleiters* (Augsburg, 1954); and *Patrioten oder Verbrecher: Aus 50jähriger Praxis, davon 17 als Gauleiter*, 3rd edn (Heusenstamm, 1975). See also Goebbels's diaries.

5 For useful recent surveys see Walter Ziegler, 'Die nationalsozialistischen Gauleiter in Bayern. Ein Beitrag zur Geschichte Bayerns im Dritten Reich', *Zeitschrift für bayerische Landesgeschichte*, 58 (1995), pp. 427–60; and 'Gaue und Gauleiter im Dritten Reich', in Möller *et.al.*, *Nationalsozialismus in der Region*, pp. 139–60; and Kurt Düwell, 'Gauleiter und Kreisleiter im Dritten Reich', in *ibid.*, pp. 161–74.

6 For the early history of the party see Orlow, *The History of the Nazi Party*, vol. 1;

Wolfgang Horn, *Führerideologie und Parteiorganisation in der NSDAP (1919–1933)* (Düsseldorf, 1972), Albrecht Tyrell (ed.), *Führer befiehl . . . Selbstzeugnisse aus der 'Kampfzeit' der NSDAP: Dokumentation und Analyse* (Düsseldorf, 1969). On the role of the Gauleiters see Hüttenberger, *Die Gauleiter*, pp. 13–74.

7 See clause 6 of the Satzung der NSDAP/NSDAV, 11 August 1925, in *Hitler: Reden, Schriften, Anordnungen Februar 1925 bis Januar 1933* (hereafter, *Hitler: Reden*), vol. 1: *Die Wiedergründung der NSDAP 1925–Juni 1926*, ed. Clemens Vollnhals (Munich, 1992), p. 149. 'Gau' to designate a district organisation had already been used by youth groups in the nineteenth century, and was being used by other right-wing organisations in the immediate post-war period.

8 See Albert Krebs, *Tendenzen*, pp. 40ff.

9 See Wolfanger, 'Populist und Machtpolitiker', p. 65.

10 On the North and West German 'working group' (*Arbeitsgemeinschaft*) see, in addition to the works mentioned in note 6: Jeremy Noakes, *The Nazi Party in Lower Saxony 1921–1933* (Oxford, 1971),pp. 56–86; and Joseph Nyomarkay, *Charisma and Factionalism in the Nazi Party* (Minneapolis, MN, 1967), pp. 71–109.

11 *Hitler: Reden*, vol. 1, p. 463.

12 *Ibid.*, vol. 2: *Vom Weimarer Parteitag bis zur Reichstagswahl Juli 1926–Mai 1928*, part 1: 'Juli 1926–Juli 1927', ed. Bärbel Dusik (Munich, 1992), pp. 1–2.

13 *Ibid.*, vol. 1, p. 445.

14 Hans Fenske, 'Die Pfälzische NSDAP', *Mitteilungen des Historischen Vereins der Pfalz*, 85 (1987), p. 359.

15 For the following see Hüttenberger, *Die Gauleiter*, pp. 45ff.

16 Jordan, *Erlebt und erlitten*, pp. 28–9.

17 On Otto Strasser and the Black Front see Patrick Moreau, *Nationalsozialismus von links: Die 'Kampfgemeinschaft Revolution' arer Nationalsozialisten und die 'Schwarze Front' Otto Strassers 1930–1935* (Stuttgart, 1985).

18 See Detlef Mühlberger, 'Central Control versus Regional Autonomy: A Case Study of Nazi Propaganda in Westphalia, 1925–1932', in Thomas Childers (ed.), *The Formation of the Nazi Constituency 1919–1933* (London, 1986), pp. 64–103.

19 See Udo Kissenkötter, *Gregor Strasser und die NSDAP* (Stuttgart, 1978), pp. 145ff. and Peter D. Stachura, *Gregor Strasser and the Rse of Nazism* (London, 1983), pp. 86ff.

20 Adolf Hitler 'Verfügung', in *Hitler: Reden*, vol. 5: *Von der Reichspräsidentenwahl bis zur Machtergreifung April 1932–Januar 1933*, part 1: 'April 1932–September 1932', ed. Klaus. A. Lankheit (Munich, 1996), p. 158.

21 Adolf Hitler 'Verfügung', in *ibid.*, pp. 310–12.

22 For the following see Hüttenberger, *Die Gauleiter*, pp. 56ff.

23 Josef Bürckel, Gauleiter of the Palatinate, for example, operated through a clique which he later used to staff his offices in the Saar, Austria and Lorraine. It was comprised of locals and Nazi activists of long standing. In Baden the clique of the Gauleiter Robert Wagner, composed largely of native Badenese and long-term völkisch activists, 'represented the only segment of the party that remained relatively stable': see Johnpeter Horst Grill, *The Nazi Movement in Baden 1920–1945* (Chapel Hill, NC, 1983), p. 422.

24 Adolf Hitler: 'Denkschrift über die inneren Gründe für die Verfügungen zur Her-stellung einer erhöhten Schlagkraft der Bewegung', 15 Dec. 1932, in *Hitler: Reden*, vol. 5, part 2, 'Oktober 1932–Januar 1933', ed. Christian Hartmann and Klaus Lankheit (Munich 1998), p. 277.

25 Adolf Hitler, 'Denkschrift über die inneren Gründe für die Verfügungen zur Herstellung einer erhöhten Schlagkraft der Bewegung', 20 Dec. 1932, in *ibid.*, p. 295.

26 *Ibid.*; italics in the original.

27 For the following see Hüttenberger, *Die Gauleiter*, pp. 79ff.

28 Ziegler, 'Gaue und Gauleiter', p. 143.

29 See Ronald Rogowski, 'The Gauleiter and the Social Origins of Fascism, *Comparative Studies in Society and History*, 19 (1977), pp. 399–430.

30 Ziegler, 'Gaue und Gauleiter', p. 149.

31 Wolfanger, ' Populist und Machtpolitiker', p. 67; the final words quoted are from Hans Kehrl, a key figure in Speer's ministry.

32 Rebentisch, 'NS Revolution', p. 234.

33 See Hüttenberger, *Die Gauleiter*, pp. 200ff.

34 Although Fritz Wächtler of Bayerische Ostmark/Bayreuth was murdered by the SS in the final stages of the war and Josef Bürckel of the Palatinate was marginalised in 1944 and died in mysterious circumstances shortly afterwards.

35 Robert Threvoz, Hans Branig *and Cecile Lowenthal-Hensel* (eds), *Pommern 1934/ 35 im Spiegel von Gestapo-Lageberichten und Sachakten. Darstellung* (Cologne and Berlin, 1974), pp. 44–5.

36 See the entry for 28–9 Dec. 1941 in *Hitler's Table Talk. Hitler's Conversations Recorded by Martin Bormann* (Oxford, 1988), pp. 153ff.

37 See Martin Moll, 'Der Sturz alter Kämpfer. Ein neuer Zugang zur Herrschafts-analyse des NS-Regimes', *Historische Mitteilungen der Ranke-Gesellschaft*, 5 (1992), pp. 30–6; and Jordan, *Im Zeugenstand*, pp. 186ff.

38 See Rebentisch, 'Die nationalsozialistische Revolution', p. 245 and *Die Tagebücher von Joseph Goebbels* (hereafter, *TB Goebbels*), part 2: *Diktate 1941–1945*, vol. 10: *Oktober–Dezember 1943*, ed. Volker Dahm (Munich, 1994), pp. 168, 189, 238.

39 See Orlow, *The Nazi Party*, vol. 2, pp. 268ff. and 356ff.

40 See *TB Goebbels*, part 2, vol. 4: *April–June 1942*, ed. Elke Fröhlich (Munich 1995), p. 583.

41 For three examples see: Grill, *The Nazi Movement*, pp. 243ff.; Lothar Meinzer, 'Die Pfalz wird Braun', in Nester and Ziegler (eds), *Die Pfalz*, pp. 37–62; and Dieter Rebentisch, 'Nationalsozialistische Revolution, Parteiherrschaft und totaler Krieg in Hessen (1933–1945)', in Uwe Schultz (ed.), *Die Geschichte Hessens* (Stuttgart, 1983), pp. 237ff.

42 On this issue see Peter Diehl-Thiele, *Partei und Staat im Dritten Reich: Unter-suchungen zum Verhältnis von NSDAP und allgemeiner innerer Staatsverwaltung* (Munich, 1969), pp. 37–74, 92–134.

43 See Hüttenberger, *Die Gauleiter*, pp. 79–80.

44 Josef Wagner was at that time Gauleiter of two *Gaus* – Silesia and Westphalia-South.

45 Diehl-Thiele, *Partei und Staat*, p. 100.

46 Wolfanger, ' Populist und Machtpolitiker', p. 67.

47 Fenske, 'Josef Bürckel', p. 158.

48 See Jane Caplan, *Government Without Administration: State and Civil Service in Weimar and Nazi Germany* (Oxford, 1988).

49 See Jeremy Noakes, 'Federalism in the Nazi State', in Maiken Umbach (ed.), *German Federalism: Past, Present, Future* (Basingstoke, 2002), pp. 113ff.

50 On the history of the Reich Gaus see in particular Dieter Rebentisch, *Führerstaat*, pp. 163–293.

51 See Günter Neliba, *Der Legalist des Unrechtsstaates, Wilhelm Frick: Eine politische Biographie* (Paderborn, 1992), pp. 115ff.

52 Notably the Law for the Reconstruction of the Reich of 30 January 1934: see Noakes, 'Federalism', p. 123.

53 See Bajohr, 'Gauleiter in Hamburg', pp. 270, 283.

54 *Ibid.*, p. 281.

55 For the following see Bernhard Post, 'Thüringen 1920 bis 1995: Von der Gründung des Landes bis zum Freistaat', in Bernhard Post and Volker Wahl (eds), *Thüringen Handbuch 1920–1995: Territorium, Verfassung, Parlament, Regierung und Verwaltung in Thüringen 1920–1995* (Weimar, 1999), pp. 38ff.

56 See Rebentisch, 'NS Revolution', p. 233; and *Verwaltung*, pp. 217–23.

57 For the following see Heinz, *NSDAP und Verwaltung*, pp. 141–241; and Jochen Klenner, *Verhältnis von Partei und Staat 1933–1945: Dargestellt am Beispiel Bayerns* (Munich, 1974), pp. 170–216.

58 See Muskalla, *NS-Politik*, pp. 295–336.

59 Although the fact that Hitler was not prepared to accede to Gustav Simon's request to form a Reichsgau by incorporating Luxemburg, of which he was CdZ, into his Gau Koblenz-Trier, suggests that Hitler was prepared to act only on a case-by-case basis: see Duvell, 'Gauleiter und Kreisleiter', pp. 169–70; and Horst Romeyk, 'Der Gau Moselland in der nationalsozialistischen Reichsreform', *Zeitschrift für westdeutsche Landesgeschichte*, 11 (1985), pp. 267–95.

60 Hüttenberger, *Die Gauleiter*, p. 150.

61 *TB Goebbels*, part 1: *Aufzeichnungen 1923–1941*, vol. 9: *Dezember 1940–Juli 1941*, ed. Elke Fröhlich (Munich, 1998), p. 127.

62 At the Reichsstatthalter conference on 22 March 1934, quoted in Martin Broszat, *Der Staat Hitlers* (Stuttgart 1969), p. 150.

63 *Hitler's Table Talk*, p. 533.

64 *Ibid.*

65 J. Noakes and G. Pridham (eds), *Nazism 1919–1945*, vol. 2: *State, Economy and Society 1933–1939* (Exeter 1984), p. 254.

66 See Michael Ruck, 'Zentralismus und Regionalgewalten im Herrschaftsgefüge des NS Staates', in Möller *et.al.* (eds), *Nationalsozialismus in der Region*, pp. 113–14.

67 On patronage as a political weapon of the Gauleiters see in particular Bajohr, 'Gauleiter in Hamburg', pp. 277ff.

68 See Peter Hüttenberger, 'Die "politische Beurteilung" als Herrschaftsinstrument der NSDAP', in Detlef Peukert and Jürgen Reulecke (eds), *Die Reihen fast geschlossen: Beiträge zur Geschichte des Alltags unterm Nationalsozialismus* (Wuppertal, 1981), pp. 107–28.

69 Ruck, 'Zentralismus', p. 115.

70 Bajohr, 'Gauleiter in Hamburg', p. 283.

71 See Horst Matzerath, *Nationalsozialismus und kommunale Selbstverwaltung* (Stuttgart, 1970); and 'Oberbürgermeister im Dritten Reich', in Gerhard Hirschfeld and Lothar Kettenacker (eds), *Der 'Führerstaat': Mythos und Realität. Studies on the Structure and Politics of the Third Reich* (Stuttgart 1981), pp. 228–54; and Jeremy Noakes, 'Oberbürgermeister and Gauleiter. City Government between Party and State', in *ibid.*, pp. 194–227.

72 Wahl, '. . . es ist das deustche Herz', pp. 233ff.

73 Noakes, 'Oberbürgermeister', pp. 208ff.

74 *Ibid.*, pp. 215ff.

75 See, for example, the entries in Goebbels's diaries for 26 Feb. 1940 and 30 Jan. 1943.

76 See Peter Longerich, *Hitlers Stellvertreter: Führung der Partei und Kontrolle des Staatsapparates durch den Stab Hess und die Parteikanzlwei Bormanns* (Munich, 1992), p. 12. According to Baldur von Schirach, Hitler regarded a meeting of more than three Gauleiters as a conspiracy: Baldur von Schirach, *Ich glaubte an Hitler* (Hamburg, 1967), p. 298.

77 For the following see Martin Moll, 'Steuerungsinstrument im "Ämterchaos"? Die Tagungen der Reichs- und Gauleiter der NSDAP', *Vierteljahrshefte für Zeitgeschichte*, 49 (2001), pp. 215–73.

78 See Lauterbacher, *Erlebt und mitgestaltet*, p. 227; he suggests (p. 238) that when Bormann took over this was no longer the case.

79 There are detailed accounts of the wartime Gauleiter meetings in Goebbels's diaries.

80 Based on the entry in Goebbels's diary, Christian Gerlach has argued that Hitler announced his decision to exterminate the European Jews at the Gauleiter meeting on 12 Dec. 1941. See Christian Gerlach, 'Die Wannsee-Konferenz, das Schicksal der deutschen Juden und Hitlers politische Grundsatzentscheidung, alle Juden Europas zu ermorden', in Christian Gerlach *Krieg, Ernahrung, Völkermord: Forschungen zur deutscen Vernichtungspolitik im Zweiten Weltkrieg* (Hamburg 1998), pp. 85–166, specifically pp. 117ff. For Moll's discussion of this thesis see 'Steuerungsinstrument', pp. 239ff.

81 Jordan, *Im Zeugenstand*, p. 156.

82 On the concept of '*Menschenführung*' see Rebentisch and Teppe (eds), 'Einleitung', in *Verwaltung*, pp. 7–32; and Eberhard Laux, 'Führung und Verwaltung in der Rechtslehre des Nationalsozialismus', in *ibid.*, pp. 33–64.

83 Lauterbacher, *Erlebt und mitgestaltet*, pp. 216–17; for similar sentiments see also Wahl, '. . . es ist das deutsche Herz', p. 110.

84 See, e.g., Jordan, *Erlebt und erlitten*, p. 72.

85 More than a quarter of Hüttenberger's core group of Gauleiters had trained as teachers.

86 Priamus, 'Regionale Aspekte', p. 180.

87 Priamus, 'Alfred Meyer', pp. 52ff.

88 For the following see Volker Daum, 'Kulturpolitischer Zentralismus und landschaftlich-lokale Kulturpflege im Dritten Reich', in Möller *et al.* (eds), *National-*

sozialismus in der Region, pp. 127–9.

89 For the following see Priamus, 'Regionale Aspekte', pp. 190–1.

90 *Ibid.*, pp. 182ff.

91 For the following see Lothar Ehrlich *et al.*, *Das Dritte Weimar: Klassik und Kultur im Nationalsozialismus* (Cologne, Weimar and Vienna, 1999).

92 See Justus H. Ulbricht, 'Von der "Heimat" zum "Trutzgau": Kulturgeschichtliche Aspekte der "Zeitenwende" 1933', in *ibid.*, pp. 163–218.

93 *Ibid.*, p. 210.

94 See Priamus, 'Regionale Aspekte', pp. 192ff.; and 'Alfred Meyer', p. 62.

95 For other examples of *Gau* building projects see Gauleiter Wahl of Swabia's plans for Augsburg described in his memoirs, '. . .*es ist das deutsche Herz*'; see also Albert Speer, *Spandau: The Secret Diaries* (London, 1976), pp. 104ff.; Gauleiter Jordan's plans in *Erlebt und erlitten*, p. 176; Kaufmann's plans for Hamburg in Michael Bose *et.al.*, '. . . *ein neues Hamburg entsteht . . .'. Planen und Bauen von 1933–1945* (Hamburg 1986), and Winfried Nerdinger (ed.), *Bauen im Nationalsozialismus: Bayern 1933–1945: Ausstellungskatalog* (Munich, 1993).

96 Priamus, 'Alfred Meyer', p. 63.

97 Priamus, 'Regionale Aspekte', p. 190.

98 Wahl, '. . . *es ist das deusche Herz*', p. 121; Lauterbacher, *Erlebt und mitgestaltet*, p. 181.

99 Bajohr, 'Gauleiter in Hamburg', p. 284.

100 *Ibid.*, pp. 287ff.

101 *Ibid.*, pp. 285ff.

102 See Dan P. Silverman, *Hitler's Economy: Nazi Work Creation Programs, 1933–1936* (Cambridge, MA, 1998), pp. 70ff.

103 For the following see Rebentisch, 'Nationalsozialistische Revolution', p. 239.

104 Silverman, *Hitler's Economy*, pp. 97ff.

105 Mallmann and Paul, *Herrschaft und Alltag*, pp. 82ff.; and Wolfanger, 'Populist und Machtpolitiker', p. 68.

106 For the following see Heinz, *NSDAP und Verwaltung*, 246ff., quoted statement on p. 247, Mallmann and Paul, *Herrschaft und Alltag*, pp. 119ff.; Wolfanger, 'Populist und Machtpolitiker', pp. 68–9.

107 Heinz, *NSDAP und Verwaltung*, pp. 260–2.

108 *Ibid.*, p. 249.

109 Timothy W. Mason (ed.), *Arbeiterklasse und Volksgemeinschaft: Dokumente und Materialien zur deutschen Arbeiterpolitik 1936–1939* (Opladen, 1975), pp. 438, 453; and Mallmann and Paul, *Herrschaft und Alltag*, pp. 134ff.

110 See Gerhard Kratsch, *Der Gauwirtschaftsapparat der NSDAP: Menschenführung, 'Arisierung', Wehrwirtschaft im Gau Westfalen-Süd* (Münster, 1989); and 'Der Gauwirtschaftsberater im Gau Westfalen-Süd', in Rebentisch and Teppe (eds), *Verwaltung*, pp. 173–207; and see Bajohr, 'Arisierung', pp. 173ff.

111 Jürgen John, 'Rüstungsindustrie und NSDAP-Organisation in Thüringen 1933 bis 1939', *Zeitschrift für Geschichtswissenschaft*, 1 (1974), pp. 412–22; and Michael T. Allen, *The Business of Genocide: The SS, Slave Labour and the Concentration Camps* (Chapel Hill, NC, 2002), pp. 190ff. and 238.

112 See, among others, Otto Dietrich, *Das Buch der deutschen Gaue: Fünf Jahre nation-*

alsozialistische Aufbauleistung (Bayreuth, 1938); the series of Gau studies in Paul Meier-Benneckenstein (ed.), *Die deutschen Gaue in Einzeldarstellungen: e.g. Hans Hertel, Thüringen* (Berlin, 1941); Hans Scherzer (ed.), *Gau Bayerische Ostmark: Land, Volk und Geschichte* (Munich, 1940); Rudolf Jordan, *Zwischen Harz und Lausitz* (Breslau, 1935).

113 On the Gauleiters role as RVKs see above all Rebentisch, *Führerstaat*, pp. 132ff. and *passim*; see also Hüttenberger, *Die Gauleiter*, pp. 152–94; and Karl Teppe, 'Der Reichsverteidigunskommissar: Organistion und Praxis in Westfalen', in Rebentisch and Teppe (eds), *Verwaltung*, pp. 278–302.

114 On the deportations to France see Paul Sauer, *Dokumente über die Verfolgung der jüdischen Bürger in Baden-Württemberg durch das nationalsozialistische Regime* (Stuttgart, 1966), vol. 2, pp. 236ff. On the role of the Gauleiters in the deportation of the German Jews to Poland in 1941 see Peter Longerich, *Politik der Vernichtung: Eine Gesamtdarstellung der nationalsozialistischen Judenverfolgung* (Munich, 1998), pp. 427ff.; and Götz Aly, *'Final Solution': Nazi Population Policy and the Murder of the European Jews* (London, 1999), p. 116.

115 Rebentisch, *Führerstaat*, p. 519.

116 *TB Goebbels*, part 2, vol. 5: *Juli–September 1942*, ed. Angela Stuber (Munich, 1995), p. 537.

117 *Ibid.*, vol. 9: *Juli–September 1943*, ed. Manfred Kittel (Munich, 1993), p. 144.

118 *Ibid.*

119 *Ibid.*, vol. 4: *April–Juni 1942*, ed. Elke Fröhlich (Munich, 1995), p. 635.

120 See Speer, *Inside the Third Reich*, pp. 218–19, 312–15, 396–7; and Goebbels's entry of 7 Oct. 1943 in *TB Goebbels*, part 2, vol. 10: *Oktober–Dezember 1943*, p. 71

121 Teppe, 'Der Reichsverteidigungskommissar', pp. 300–1; and Ruck, 'Zentralismus', pp. 118ff.

122 *Ibid.*

123 Entry for 8 Feb. 1943 in *TB Goebbels*, part 2, vol. 7: *Januar–März 1943*, ed. Elke Fröhlich (Munich 1993), p. 297.

124 *Ibid.*

125 Entry for 27 Feb. 1943, in *ibid.*, p. 428.

126 This is a very tentative statement gleaned from Goebbels's comments in his diaries: more research is needed to confirm or refute it.

6

'Sentencing towards the Führer'?
The judiciary in the Third Reich

Anthony McElligott

Between the outbreak of war in 1939 and its end in the spring of 1945, German courts worked overtime passing judgment on those the Nazi State decried as 'enemies of the people' (*Volksfeinde*). Thousands of Germans who, in peacetime, would probably have never seen the inside of a courtroom found themselves in those years caught up in an unremitting judicial terror that took away (limited) freedom, removed (circumscribed) civil status and callously destroyed life. We best know this judicial terror through the rabid declamations of Roland Freisler and the savage People's Court over which he presided from 1942 until his death during an Allied air raid in February 1945. On the one hand, to focus only on Freisler and this particular court, vicious as both were, distracts our attention from the role of the courts during the entire period and, in particular, from the wider legal community.[1] For there can be little disagreement among historians that the legal system in Germany between 1933 and 1945 became a key instrument of oppression in the Nazi State.[2] From the outset the judiciary facilitated a legal framework for political terror. At a ministerial meeting in the afternoon of 7 March 1933, the state secretary in the Justice Ministry, Franz Schlegelberger, eagerly agreed with Hitler on how 'the law had to adapt to [fit] conditions'.[3] What this was to mean in practice was that the political and racial aims of the regime were dressed in a cloak of legality; and that the judiciary actively constructed and maintained the legal architecture of the Third Reich, and thus facilitated its crimes from the outset.[4] That the judiciary was deeply implicated in the machinations of the Third Reich is today a given, but this premiss, on the other hand, equally can lead to an oversimplification in interpreting its role in the Third Reich. Thus to explain courtroom terror merely in terms of 'Nazi' or 'fascist' judges can also deny meaningful discussion.[5]

Indeed, a close examination of the judiciary during the Third Reich would reveal a less reassuringly straightforward picture. We would find a profession deeply divided and unsettled by the politics of the Third Reich; we would note the myriad personal and professional contradictions; we would discern a vast difference in outlook and action between its principal actors, the judges and public prosecutors – between those who actively collaborated or passively conformed, and those who were openly defiant or stubbornly dragged their feet; we would discover the everyday petty conflicts and rivalries between individuals and departments that characterised life in the Third Reich; and we would soon learn that both the adherence to professional discipline for some, and the allure of a rapid and successful career for others, in the end determined the degree to which one ingratiated oneself within the Hitler State.

Such a history of the judiciary during the Third Reich cannot be written here. My aim in this chapter is more modest: namely, to situate a discussion of the judiciary in terms that acknowledge both structure and individual agency along the lines first developed by critical historians of the Third Reich, Ian Kershaw among them.[6] By adopting this approach, I treat Hitler's judges and prosecutors as historical actors morally responsible for their actions by arguing that 'working towards the Führer' was as much a pragmatic self-interested course of action determined by a specific historical context as it was a consequence of pressure from the regime and a sign of a general willingness to serve Hitler's ideological aims. For, as Klaus Marxen has argued, the judiciary also saw the regime as a useful facilitator for realizing *its own* long cherished aim of restoring authoritarian law.[7]

I

The jurists who 'worked towards the Führer' were not necessarily ardent Nazis. As we know, their natural home tended to be in the nationalist and conservative camps of the German Nationalist People's Party (DNVP), or to a lesser extent in the German People's Party (DVP), and rarely in a Centre–Left party.[8] Apart from a handful of high-profile Nazi jurists, such as Hanns Kerrl, Roland Freisler, and Otto Thierack, all early joiners, the number of judges and prosecutors in the NSDAP was relatively small, with few of them openly declaring any sympathy for Nazism before 1933. Estimates of party membership prior to 1933 vary greatly, from Hermann Weinkauff's low figure of 30 out of 7,000 judges in Prussia – barely half a per cent – to Richard Schmid's rather imprecise 'massive numbers'. Local studies of individual courts after 1933 show that the balance between Nazi and non-Nazi personnel varies widely from place to place. Thus Weinkauff found of the 613 judges who worked at the Hamm High Court (*Oberlandesgericht*), only 1.6 per cent admitted to Allied interrogators after the war to having been members of the party. This is in stark contrast to Ralph Angermund's examination of the political orientation of sixty judges at the High Court in Cologne in the mid-1930s. He found that 6.6 per cent had been active Nazis prior to 1933, a figure that was very slightly higher than that of the High Courts in Hamburg and in Celle, and therefore may well be indicative of the national average.[9]

Even after March, unlike lawyers who seem to have flocked to the party, some judges and prosecutors appear to have been reluctant to commit themselves politically, while the party leadership also did not appear too concerned about membership.[10] Nevertheless, with the opening up of party membership in 1937, there was a discernible drift to the party, not only among younger judges but among senior jurists. By the beginning of 1941, 31 of the 34 presidents of the High Courts were members of the NSDAP (the three senior judges presiding at Düsseldorf, Berlin and Vienna, however, were not members). Of these, 10 had joined the party before 1933, 11 in 1933 (the so-called '*Märzgefallene*'), and 10 after that date. All of the 35 state chief prosecutors were members of the party, with 8 having joined during the republican period, 14 in 1933, and the remainder probably in 1937. By that date, membership of the party was clearly an advantage for gaining promotion to a higher grade, but the evidence also suggests that while non-membership could be a hindrance, it need not automatically block a career.[11]

The Reich justice minister himself is a prime example of this (as indeed is his state secretary, Franz Schlegelberger). Franz Gürtner is the quintessential conservative traditionalist who rose from modest origins to high office under the Republic (he served as Reich minister of justice in von Papen's cabinet), and who continued in office after 1933, serving Hitler until his unexpected death at 60 years of age in late January 1941. During the 1920s Gürtner had been a member of the right-wing German National Bavarian Middle Party (*Deutschnationale bayerische Mittelpartei*) who, together with other non-Nazis in Hitler's cabinet, finally became a party member in 1937, with the dubious honour of receiving the party's 'Golden Badge'.[12] The timing of his membership and whether it was voluntary (or 'involuntary', as Schlegelberger claimed was the case with him when, in 1938, Hitler 'decreed' his membership) are unclear. Earlier in his career, Gürtner had expressed a broad sympathy with Hitler's movement, at least in terms of its ideals, if not its methods (although as Bavarian justice minister in 1923 he was instrumental in procuring lenient sentences and then amnesties for Hitler and the co-conspirators of the 'Beer Hall Putsch'[13]). His membership in 1937, and that of Schlegelberger in 1938, can be seen as signalling the 'unity' of the cabinet (which, anyway by this time, was in decline as an instrument of government, and it wouldn't be until 1942 before the judicial system was finally led by the fanatical triumvirate of Thierack, Rothenberger and Freisler[14]).

The fact that Gürtner, as well as a number of senior judges, remained outside the party for so long exposes the limitations of the Nazi coordination (*Gleichschaltung*) of the judiciary.[15] The main targets of the Law for the Restoration of a Professional Civil Service and the Law for the Admission to Practice of Law (both passed on 7 April) were Jews and those considered politically unreliable. Yet, Schlegelberger sought – with some success – to intervene on behalf of jurists who had seen action during the First World War, or who had a father or son(s) killed in action.[16] In all, about a quarter of Prussia's (mostly younger) 3,515 Jewish lawyers were affected by the measures.[17] And, as Lothar Gruchmann shows, the implementation of those laws also varied widely between the different *Länder*.[18]

More likely than direct party membership was membership of the Association of National Socialist German Jurists (*Bund nationalsozialistischer deutschen Juristen*, or BNSDJ), founded in 1928 by a young and ambitious lawyer from Karlsruhe, Hans Frank. The BNSDJ grew steadily to around 1500 members by 1933, attracting many younger jurists in the ministerial bureaucracy, such as Wilhelm Crohne who joined in the autumn of 1932, and later rose to become the deputy-chairman of the People's Court.[19] Over the course of the Third Reich membership of this association became *de rigueur* for entry into the profession and for progress through the ranks. The members of the German Association of Judges (*Deutsche Richterverein*) became *de facto* members of the National Socialist League of Judges (*Nationalsozialistische Richterbund*), when the latter replaced the former in 1933 as the professional association for judges.

The Third Reich offered the prospect of greater professional mobility for those middle- and lower-level jurists prepared to participate in the aims of the regime. Table 6.1 is based on 780 active jurists from the former German Federal Republic who were serving as public prosecutors and judges in both civilian and military courts at the end of the war.[20] While some had begun their careers before 1933, professional development for the majority came to depend on – and mirror – the evolution of the Hitler State.

Table 6.1 Judges and prosecutors by age cohort

Age cohort	N	%
1890–1900	55	7.0
1901–5	371	47.0
1906–10	273	35.0
1911–15	87	11.0

Source: Compiled from Dr Norbert Podewin (ed.), *Braunbuch, Kriegs- und Naziverbrecher in der Bundesrepublik und in Berlin (West)*, reprint (Berlin, 1968,), pp. 147–87.

The eldest cohort of this group (those born in the final decade of the nineteenth century), aged 33–43 when Hitler came to power, would have been already established within the professional hierarchy in 1933. By the outbreak of war in 1939, they would have achieved positions of seniority or else would soon go on to do so (as in the case of Hans Hoyer, discussed below); and by 1944, they would be at the apex of their careers. Many of those from this group who joined the NSDAP in 1933 or in 1937 were most likely to have done so because they previously belonged to a political party, such as the German People's Party in Hamburg that switched allegiance *en bloc* in 1933, or for reasons of career opportunity, or perhaps as a result of peer pressure in 1937.[21] The next cohort, born in the years 1901–10 (broken down into two smaller cohorts in the table), would have finished their academic studies and be in the process of completing their training in 1933. By 1939, the older members of this cohort would be poised to take leading positions on the bench; a career cycle that would be almost, if not already, completed by 1944. If not convinced Nazis in 1933, they would almost certainly have aligned themselves with the Führer by 1937. The youngest cohort, those born roughly in the half-decade 1911–15, would have been students still in 1933, but assistant judges and prosecutors (*Assessoren*) in 1939 and full judges or prosecutors by 1944.

To ensure the crystallising of a corps of jurists who would serve Hitler's Third Reich, a special training camp was set up in 1933 in Jüterborg, south of Potsdam, where law students had to undergo rigorous physical and political education for a period of six weeks between preliminary and final exams in their final year at university.[22] With the opening of the Hanns Kerrl Training Camp in the summer of 1933,[23] the initial intake of forty-three trainees was kept under the strict supervision and constant surveillance of officials from the Justice Ministry and party; these experienced men weeded out those students considered 'unsuitable to serve the Third Reich as jurists'. Thus 'the first clever step was taken in the education of the young jurists to realize the ideas of the Führer'. Originally built for a total of 100 trainees, the camp's capacity was soon extended fivefold, and within three months 683 students had gone through its gates. Its success led to similar camps being established in other parts of the Reich. It was the youngest of the three cohorts, those born in 1911–15, that was exposed from the outset to the tenets of National Socialism, and was viewed at the time as the 'new generation of jurists' who would work towards the aims of the Führer State.[24]

Even though the above sample is a small one, barely 5 per cent of the total number of judges and public prosecutors serving the Third Reich, it provides some useful insights. As I have noted, the majority of jurists in the sample were men who were at an early or middle stage in their careers in 1933. These men, at least, were more likely to owe allegiance to a system that facilitated rapid professional mobility in contrast to the bleak state of affairs of the pre-1933 era when advancement appeared poor.[25] Thus 'working towards the Führer' opened up career opportunities for the ambitious and eager jurist. A particularly striking example of this is Schlegelberger's own son, Hartwig, who was born in 1913. Still a student in 1933, by June 1944, at the age of 30, he had advanced to the position of senior naval judge, involved in passing and carrying out death sentences against young sailors found guilty of desertion.[26] It may well be that Schlegelberger junior had benefited from his father's position in Hitler's Government. But it is a greater likelihood that he exemplifies the experience of many younger jurists for whom the Third Reich (and the war it unleashed) facilitated rapid advance.[27]

For those whose careers were less spectacular, but which nonetheless benefited from the opportunities offered by the Third Reich, Erwin Schüle's case can serve as an illustration.[28] Schüle was born in 1913 in Bad Cannstatt, near Stuttgart, where his father was a wine grower. After leaving secondary school in 1933 he promptly joined the SA and two years later the party. Schüle spent the next four years studying law and political sciences (*Staatswissenschaften*) in Tübingen and Königsberg, passing the first part of his legal training in the autumn of 1937 at the Oberlandesgericht in Stuttgart. In January 1938 he took up a junior post at the Lower Court in Weiltingen (Upper Bavaria), then continued his legal training at the Landgericht in Stuttgart, before finally qualifying in January 1941 at the age of 28 to serve as an assessor (assistant judge). Called up as a lieutenant, Schüle served on the Eastern Front as an adjutant with the 215th Infantry Division, and then, aged 30, transferred to the 253rd Infantry Division as a commander of a so-called special convict company (*Sonderstrafkompagnie*). Even though Schüle did not spend his wartime years as an active judge (as far as we can tell from the sources), his experience and socialisation cannot have been too far off that of his peers who did become wartime judges. Born in the glory years of the empire, these men's early experiences would have been marked by the turbulent and hungry years of war, revolution and inflation. Living in households of the middle classes, their teenage years would have been marked by the social and economic uncertainties of the Weimar Republic. Receptive to the appeals for national renewal under authoritarian leadership, some of these young men would have been, like Schüle, caught up in the violent political mobilisation of the nationalist right, before eventually succumbing to Nazism.[29]

Werner Johe's seminal study of the Hamburg judiciary showed how the party leadership relied on this younger generation of judges to carry out the Führer's will, a view apparently supported by the examples discussed above.[30] But it was not solely a younger fanatical cohort which manned the radicalised courts of the Third Reich. In Oldenburg, Dr Berthold Witte (a chairman of the bench –*Landgerichtsdirektor* – at the Regional Court) had joined the party on 1 May 1933; two years later, aged 47, he was appointed chief prosecutor at the Special Court (*Sondergericht*). His colleague Dr Hans Hoyer also joined the NSDAP in May 1933, and in his late-forties became the chairman of the Special Court from 1 January 1941. His career, like Witte's, had commenced in the 1920s; in 1930 he became a judge at the Provincial Court (*Landgerichtsrat*), and a year later took a senior administrative post with the Justice Ministry in Hamburg. In April 1935 he returned to the court in Oldenburg, and three years later was appointed presiding judge at the Criminal Court. Under his steward-ship, the Special Court gained a reputation for uncompromising ruthlessness. Through their senior court positions, Hoyer and Witte 'mentored' the more junior judges who came and went during their joint-tenure at the Special Court at Oldenburg, 'teaching by example' how to work towards the Führer. As beneficiaries of the Hitler State, they repaid it through a fervent desire to serve its aims.[31] Much the same could be said about those of their colleagues who, sharing broadly similar characteristics, complied with the dictates of the regime not because they were necessarily convinced Nazis but because it was opportune to do so. These men would later come to be known as the *Mitläufer*, or 'fellow travellers', who probably made up the largest group of jurists 'work-ing towards the will of the Führer'.[32]

II

As I noted above, the Reich Justice Ministry pledged its full support to Hitler during the cabinet meeting of 7 March 1933. This declaration, made by Schlegelberger who was deputising for the bed-ridden Gürtner, should be treated with some caution and not seen simply as a sycophantic desire to serve the will of the Führer.[33] Instead, we can view it as a contract between the bureaucracy and Hitler's cabinet whereby serving the new Government was made contingent on the latter's ability to restore the full authority of the State.

A key factor in this Faustian bargain was the view among conservatives that the State and its institutions had been undermined by the corrosive influence of a divided and weak Republic. The authority of the law in particular had suf-fered at the hands of republican reformers, leaving the judiciary demoralised and disoriented, so that by the end of the 1920s even senior judges at the *Reichsgericht* were speaking of a 'crisis of confidence' between judiciary and the Republic.[34] On a more popular level, a publication of 1931 carried the title *Gefesselte Justiz* ('Justice in Chains'), supporting the view that political inter-ference in the law had created a 'magna carta' for the 'dangerous, professional criminal' classes who held hostage law-abiding Germans.[35] By 1933 the calls for tougher law as a means of overcoming the 'crisis', had reached their loudest. Two young academics teaching in the law faculties of the universities of Tübingen and Göttingen, Georg Dahm and Friedrich Schaffstein, went further, arguing in a controversial pamphlet that for Germany to climb out of the 'cultural crisis' it had to abandon the liberal conception of law and opt for 'authoritarian law'.[36] The allegation that the Republic as a 'compromise state' had weakened the law can be challenged,[37] but in 1933 this notion chimed with a general mentality that had already attracted millions to Nazism.

It was against this background that, at the cabinet meeting on 21 March, Schlegelberger insisted: 'the judiciary would support with its utmost energy any government, but especially the present one of national renewal, whose efforts were directed at the protection of the state against acts of high treason and treason, as well as other similar important tasks'.[38] This meeting approved a raft of measures – not least the notorious Enabling Act and the introduction of the *Sondergerichte* – designed to strengthen the executive. It was Schlegelberger, Otto Meissner and other senior state secretaries who advised and formulated workable policies during these early critical cabinet meetings and which laid the foundations for Hitler's eventual dictatorship.[39] In return, the regime offered the Ministry the room for manoeuvre needed to implement a toughening of the law.[40] At this point, Schlegelberger, together with his like-minded colleagues in the higher bureaucracy, was working towards a conservative idea of an authoritarian nationalist state based on the 'people's will' rather than Hitler's personal rule. This was to change from 1934 (after the law of 13 July retrospectively justified the murders of 30 June, and thus also established the primacy of politics – and of Hitler – over the law, and from August of that year when judges and public prosecutors as civil servants were bound to Hitler by an oath of loyalty). After the war, Schlegelberger was to claim that it became clear to him only in 1937 that Hitler's Government was in fact a dictatorship; his participation in formulating laws and policy prior to this date was driven by the belief that he was contributing to the strengthening the conservative–authoritarian State. Indeed, even Nazi leaders such as Göring emphasised the primacy of the State.[41]

Judges expected Hitler as chancellor to succeed where von Papen had failed and to finally haul Germany from the morass.[42] The president of the German League of Judges (*Deutsche Richterbund*) welcomed the 'new will' of Hitler's Government to combat the crisis. His counterpart at the Prussian Association of Judges (*Preussische Richterverein*) also lauded Hitler, probably articulating what many believed and felt at the time:

> Prussia's judges and public prosecutors take the opportunity of Germany's national renewal to declare that it is their sincere aim to take part in the rebuilding of the German Reich and the German people's community in the area of the practice of law. Underpinning and supporting the honour and dignity of the new state created by the national revolution is valid for them too.[43]

This declaration was made on 20 March 1933, just one day before the passing of the Enabling Act and at a time when Hitler's personal position as dictator – or indeed that of the Nazis per se – was far from decided. But if these judges and their bosses in Berlin (i.e. Gürtner and Schlegelberger) believed they could instrumentalise the Führer to pursue a conservative jurisprudence, then Hitler equally believed that the law should serve the aims of his regime. Reflecting on this almost ten years after coming to power, Hitler told Thierack and Curt Rothenberger (respectively, newly appointed justice minister and state secretary): 'Justice is not an end in itself. It serves the maintenance of the human social order, an organism for which we thank culture and progress. Right is every means that serves this aim. Wrong is everything that does not. It is not the task of justice to be mild or hard. It is simply its task to satisfy this aim.'[44] Hitler had made clear the principle of judging according to 'healthy popular instinct' (*gesunde Volksempfindung*) rather than 'paragraphs' in his opening speech to the new Reichstag after the March elections in 1933, emphasising that the law had to protect the interests of the *Volk* (nation) above those of the individual, and that this alone justified the existence of the judiciary.[45] A flavour of this concept of law can be gauged from the discussion at the cabinet meeting of 7 March on how to deal with the alleged Reichstag arsonist van der Lubbe, when Hitler, along with Göring, insisted that van der Lubbe (and all other 'enemies' of the nation) should be strung up in the streets, regardless of legal niceties, because: 'The German public expects it above all else. He [Hitler] cannot accept the doctrine: "law is law" if it means that the entire life of the state collapses as a result.'[46]

Nevertheless, in spite of such statements, also parroted by those around him, Hitler went out of his way in 1933 to assure the judiciary that its autonomy was safe in his hands. Judges would still be accorded a wide discretion; for, as one his acolytes put it: 'The highest leadership of the state can only indicate the general direction, it cannot arbitrate in the many everyday conflicts; to this end, the judiciary, which stands above material interests, is called upon as the defender of the pure idea.'[47] In practice, this meant that the implementation of the law would still be left to the discretion of the individual courts, for the time being at least. Nevertheless, by the end of the year Gürtner, in line with the Nazi state justice ministers of Prussia (Hanns Kerrl), Bavaria (Hans Frank), and Saxony (Otto Thierack), as well as senior judges such as Dr Oegg from the Reichsgericht, were publicly airing their approval of a criminal law and courtroom practice that took into consideration 'healthy popular instinct' instead of legal text. Of course, Hitler would be the final arbiter of the public's mood,[48] but such exhortations did not necessarily contradict or 'direct' a judge's decision. For judges themselves in all probability shared the 'healthy popular instinct' that was being addressed at this time. Indeed, another judge at the Reichsgericht, Dr Schwarz, went so far as to state emphatically that the era of judicial 'false objectivity' was over and 'it was now in the interests of the nation to be partisan'. He coined a new maxim: "Reich law superseded state law, people's law superceded Reich law.'[49]

The institutional legitimising of the 'public mood' as a basis on which to sentence, and the focus on retribution rather than on the criminal and the crime, were among the chief elements of Nazism's contribution to German jurisprudence.[50] But it is worth noting that the concept is a fluid one, the constituency of which could be equally mutable. During the crisis years of the Weimar Republic and the early years of the Third Reich, it reflected concerns among the middle classes with rising socially and politically motivated crimes (their boundaries were often blurred). Throughout the Third Reich the 'public mood' also manifested itself in thousands of denunciations, as neighbours, family members and strangers avidly reported against one another.[51] But while it is true that the authorities were sensitive to public opinion at a more collective level, the frequent resort by individual judges to such a nebulous concept as the 'public mood' in justifying murderous sentences during the later years of the Third Reich can be questioned. More often than not, judges and prosecutors used the concept as a convenience for articulating their own prejudices and for doing what they believed the Führer required of them.[52]

III

As already suggested, 'healthy popular instinct' by the early 1930s demanded at the very least a containment of such crimes and their swift retribution through the application of a toughened law. The re-introduction of twenty-six *Sondergerichte* in March promised to deliver such a practice, and was welcomed for that reason by state prosecutors and judges.[53] The Special Courts were not exclusive to the Third Reich. They had existed in various guises since the First World War and had the overt aim of dispensing the desired tough summary justice against those seen as challenging either the political or the social order.[54] With the Nazis in government, they focused on 'completely exterminating all opponents of the Third Reich, particularly Communists and Social Democrats', and any other potential opposition, a task in which they appear to have largely succeeded by the mid-1930s.[55] Whereas summary courts, or a speeding up of the judicial process in the ordinary courts (permitted under paragraph 212 of StPO – the code governing court procedure), had previously been both temporary and limited in scope, under the Third Reich the *Sondergerichte* increased in number (there were fifty-five by the beginning of the war), and they also became permanent tribunals displacing regular courts. Together with the People's Court, introduced the following year and which stood at the apex of the court system, the Special Courts epitomised the judicial process of the Third Reich.[56]

While indictments for treason remained the prerogative of the People's Court, and to a lesser extent that of the Reichsgericht, the Special Courts made steady inroads on the competence of the regular courts. The Law Against Malicious Attacks on the State and Party and for the Protection of the Party Uniforms (*Heimtückegesetz*), passed in December 1934 and thereby replacing the earlier decree of 21 March 1933, allowed the jurisdiction of the Special Courts to spread beyond their original remit of dealing with 'politically motivated crime' (defined by the notorious Decree for the Protection of People and State, of 28 February). A previous change in the law, in May 1933, allowed for tougher sentencing in a number of cases.[57] By the late 1930s, these punitive courts were dealing almost exclusively with *bagatelle* and social crime, as recent research has shown, which could comprise as much as 80 per cent, if not more, of their caseload.[58] A decree of 20 November 1938 passed all indictments to the Sondergericht where the crime was considered grave or where public opinion 'demanded' it, so that the 'competence of the special court now covered practically all important criminal cases'.[59] They thus came to represent the 'non dramatic side of repression' in the Third Reich.[60]

The onset of war a year later saw the passing of a raft of emergency decrees that gave the Special Courts almost unlimited jurisdiction (the People's Court continued to deal exclusively with cases of treason), from the Special Wartime Penal Code in August 1939 to the law of 21 February 1940. In between these two measures were a number of decrees that transformed mundane petty misdemeanors (and, indeed, hitherto entirely innocent activity) into acts against the State and the war effort. Of the many pieces of wartime legislation, those most widely applied against the civilian population were the Decree Against Persons Harmful to the National Community and the Supplementary Decree to the Penal Provisions for the Protection of the Military Strength of the Nation (5 September and 25 November 1939).[61] These wartime decrees were particularly vague in their wording, leaving a wide margin for interpretation. The result was a radicaling of sentencing, especially in courts with particularly zealous personnel. Whereas previously a defendant might have expected a light custodial sentence for a minor crime, judges could now invoke penal servitude, or, as they did increasingly during the later war years, even the death penalty for the same crime.[62] The 'crimes' that came before the courts ranged from what would be considered criminal in any society to those that were a product of the regime's manipulation of the law. In mid-October 1939 Gürtner issued a secret circular setting up a special department that was to look into means by which to extend and intensify the sentences of the Special Courts, especially against so-called 'harmful persons' (*Volksschädlinge*). This department was also charged with formulating a new clause to add to the criminal law that would make the death sentence mandatory for grievous bodily harm.[63] Crimes deemed capital offences had already been increased at the inception of the Third Reich, and they were extended to other activities now deemed 'criminal', until by 1943 they covered some forty-six 'crimes'. Thus many indiscreet acts that previously might have received mild censure now warranted a death verdict, so that such activities as listening to the foreign broadcasts of the BBC, or engaging in loose talk (rumours), carrying out or abetting an abortion, or scavenging among the rubble of bombed-out houses, could result in swift and lethal retribution by the courts.[64]

While it should be acknowledged that these war-specific crimes only ever constituted a small though radically increasing proportion of the total number of crimes that came before the courts between 1940 and 1943, the period for which data are available, the distribution of crimes before the courts suggests a particular concern of the regime with public morale based on access to food and goods, on the one hand, and its priorities for boosting war-time production, on the other hand.

Table 6.2 Distribution of war-specific crime (%)

Offences	1939	1940	1941	1942	1943
v. consumer regulations		25.2	40.5	44.2	44.7
v. war economy decrees	4.0	8.5	15.9	19.3	22.5
v. harmful persons decree	77.2	33.8	16.4	12.0	12.8
v. foreign broadcasts decree	16.3	9.5	3.7	2.4	1.7
Illegal association with PoWs	1.3	21.9	22.5	21.6	17.8
v. violent criminals decree	0.9	0.9	0.9	0.5	0.3
Total war-specific crimes	220	8,700	19,273	42,153	29,649
Total crimes	298,851	266,223	20,766	345,150	77,332

Source: adapted from Jeremy Noakes (ed.), *Nazism 1919–1945*, vol. 4: *The German Home Front in the Second World War. A Documentary Reader* (Exeter, 1998), p. 136.

At the same time, the data reveal the regime's particular concern with certain types of behaviour. Thus sexual relations between German women and foreign workers, and especially prisoners of war (PoW), were frowned on for both racial and security reasons, and were pursued with increasing zeal by the authorities, so that prosecutions rose from just below 2,000 in 1940 to over 9,000 in 1942.[65] Such relationships – never more than around one-fifth of all war-specific crimes – were viewed as signalling a breakdown in moral, political and racial discipline. German women (whether married or single) who undertook such liaisons were considered (especially if they were younger women) to be weak-willed, or, if married, guilty of betraying their husbands at the front. In either case, 'individualistic' sexual gratification was presented as having overridden loyalty and service to the community, and as such demonstrated a lack of 'national consciousness'. Although many liaisons were 'innocent', there was a fear among the authorities that displays of kindness or tenderness would develop into assistance to a would-be escapee, or that in a sexual relationship 'pillow talk' would reveal sensitive information to the

Reich's enemies. This fear induced prosecutors to invoke the Decree for the Protection of Defensive Capacity of the German People (VO *Schutz der Wehrkraft des deutschen Volkes*) of 25 November 1939 that forbade sexual relations with foreigners, and which was augmented by a further decree in May 1940 and a government circular of July 1941(discussed below) prohibiting *all* relations, especially with Polish workers. But the extent to which a relationship was viewed by the authorities on the ground as a serious breach of 'national trust' determined which court would deal with the matter; and the outcome of the subsequent judicial process often depended very much on the ideological disposition of the court's personnel. An ordinary Lower Court (*Amtsgericht*) was much more likely to pass a mild sentence than was a Special Court, such as that at Königsberg which sentenced one unfortunate woman to ten years' penal servitude for having sex with a Polish PoW.[66]

The courts of the Third Reich operated within a political and social culture that had become heavily overladen with biological–racial overtones.[67] Even during the 1920s, the focus had begun to turn away from the nature of the crime, its context, and the circumstances of the defendant to a 'science' of character[68] in order to determine whether or not the defendant was fit to remain in the 'people's community'. This approach built on a long-standing and pernicious discussion about the nature of criminals and crime that effectively portrayed the 'criminal impulse' in terms of biological and racial determinants. This discourse, propounding the 'racial purification' of the nation of its 'criminal' elements, found its first judicial articulation after 1933 in the Law against the Professional Criminal (1934) and its final expression, exactly a decade later, in the Law against the Community Outsider.[69] As Thierack stated in his report *Criminal Law in the Fifth Year of War* (1943–44), the courts had 'the public hygiene task of continuously purifying the national body so as to ensure that in the end the bad elements do not overgrow the good ones'.[70]

While the implementation of the Law against the Community Outsider was a matter primarily for Himmler's police, the judiciary was still ascribed a role in those cases believed to be 'redeemable' by 'returning to the community the criminally inclined outsider once again as a useful member' by 'rendering [him or her] harmless' (*Unschädlichmachung*) through court orders for sterilisation. If, however, conditioned and guided not only by policy but by the outlook and prejudices of his professional caste, a prosecutor or a judge decided the defendant had no use whatsoever to the community on grounds of social behaviour, race, or medical record, then that person's fate was sealed.[71] At the Oldenburg Special Court, for example, Witte and Hoyer almost unfailingly chose to prosecute defendants under the notoriously inflexible and punitive paragraphs (1, 2, and 4) of the wartime decrees that made a death sentence mandatory, however innocuous the 'crime'. Thus in 1940, they tried twenty-one cases under the war economy decree, but in 1942 they applied the first paragraph of the decree against undermining national defence against 423 defendants, in some cases, for misdemeanours that had previously been tried using a different decree. This judicial 'flexibility' was a practice that appears to have been widespread among their peers, especially where a person had one or more previous convictions, was a foreigner, or a Jew.[72]

An illustration of the racial bias in the application of judicial terror can be found in Hamburg where, by 27 August 1943, the Special Court had passed a total of 16 death sentences, 5 of which were against foreigners, although the latter frequently constituted only a small percentage of the 124 cases. Similarly, in neighbouring Kiel, about one-third of the death sentences passed by the Special Court were against foreigners, who accounted for barely 10 per cent of the region's population.[73] Again with regard to the Oldenburg Special Court, in most of the cases of 'looting under cover of war' the bench appeared to go out of its way to apply the broadest possible meaning to the term in order to justify mandatory death sentences against foreigners, and, increasingly, against Germans.[74] Between June 1942 and November 1944 Hoyer handed down 14 death sentences against foreigners (2 of which Thierack commuted to penal servitude) for 'looting' offences; 6 of the 12 executed were Poles. Even where the prosecution called for prison or penal servitude because of mitigating circumstances, such as the youthful status of the accused, and even where the Reichsgericht (not known for its leniency) was in favour of a lesser punishment, Hoyer insisted on the death sentence. In March 1943, a Ukranian and two Polish youths were sentenced and executed for removing items from a bombsite during clearing work. As the war dragged on and turned against Germany, Hoyer's court gained a reputation for its 'deployment of the state's toughest medicine', now against 'ordinary Germans' as well. As far as Hoyer was concerned, the removal of even the smallest item from a bombsite was evidence of 'parasitical' behaviour, justifying forfeiture of life as set down in a Ministry circular of February 1942 – as a 24-year-old seamstress found to her cost. She had removed some items of household linen, damaged in an air-raid, from an old people's home, and soon found herself brought before the court. Whether or not she had, according to the law, actually 'looted' the items was of little consequence to Hoyer and the prosecutor, who had by now abandoned 'legal paragraphs' for 'healthy popular instinct'. They concluded that the defendant had plundered the goods, and that in doings so she had 'harmed' the national community in its gravest hour, and 'thereby the court had gained an extremely negative impression of her character'. The unfortunate young woman was executed the following day.[75]

Hoyer's final death sentence, in November 1944, was passed against an inmate of Sachsenhausen for taking a woman's cardigan while clearing a bombsite in July of that year. The defendant, a man called Maidow, told the court that he had intended to keep the cardigan for his own use, given that his camp uniform was ragged. Like the seamstress, he was labelled a 'parasite' who 'took advantage of the war to exploit the misfortune of the people in order to enrich himself'. As one who'd had a number of brushes with the law in earlier years, Maidow was taken into preventive custody in 1937; the medical expert witness, Dr Jacobs, described him as a person of inherited low intelligence and a weak-will, but nevertheless criminally responsible. Hoyer described Maidow as an 'asocial' and 'dangerous habitual criminal' who had lost his right to remain part of the community. Maidow too was duly executed. In this, as in similar cases, the language of the court revealed the extent to which its personnel believed themselves to be expunging social and racial impurities from the Führer's 'national community'.[76] From September 1942 certain categories of persons convicted by the courts but whose sentences were considered to be too mild, or who were deemed 'incorrigible', were to be handed over to Himmler's SS. This happened to two burglars sentenced by the court in Hamburg to eight years' penal servitude, and to a further sixty persons convicted by the same court. By the end of the war, around 20,000 prisoners from across the Reich had been handed over to the SS for 'special treatment'.[77]

The situation was worse still for Jews. During the later 1930s they found themselves in court mostly for 'blood crimes' or 'race outrage' (*Rassenschande*), and liable (under paragraphs 2 and 5 of the Law for the Protection of German Blood, i.e. 'Nuremberg Laws', 1935) to sentences of varying length of penal servitude. In 1937, for example, there had been 565 prosecutions under these laws involving 355 Jews. Most cases ended in fines or short prison terms.[78] But the judicial system's contribution to Hitler's war against the Jews, and others considered *Untermenschen*, became more ominous once the racial cleansing of the Reich had been put in full gear during the war. Thus in July 1941 Schlegelberger sent a circular to public prosecutors and judges complaining that the courts were betraying the war effort by sentencing too leniently Poles who had sexual relations with German women, or who had committed other misdemeanours. Because they posed a danger to the security of the Reich, and in order to demonstrate the judiciary's positive role in the war effort, Schlegelberger instructed that *as a general rule* death sentences should be pronounced in cases of 'racial miscegenation'.[79] Other circulars quickly followed the July missive, each with similar content. They stressed how 'each judge and prosecutor had to always keep [such instructions] in mind and so fulfil his duty as demanded by the Führer and the public'.[80] This ministerial advice was extended to Jews. In a striking but not unusual case, 31-year-old Paul Berkheim, a 'half-Jew', was condemned to death in early 1943 by the Special Court in Berlin after a judicial revision (he had originally received a sentence of seven years' penal servitude from a different senate at the court) for having an affair with a Gentile woman. Berkheim's 'crime', according to the prosecutor, Dr Wolfgang Berthold, was that of 'contaminating the race in three instances' at a time when the German nation was in a 'struggle for its . . . future' against world Jewry.[81] In a case of the previous year, 74-year-old Markus Luftgas was handed over to the Gestapo for execution on Schlegelberger's order after having being sentenced by the Special Court in Kattowitz to thirty months' prison for hoarding eggs (and thereby being in breach of the war economy decree).[82] The regime considered that his sentence, like Berkheim's, was too lenient, and so did not reflect the will of the Führer. By 'rectifying' the sentence, the judicial system was brought closer to the Führer's will and thus fulfilled its role as part of the machinery of racial terror.

The decision by a court to try someone under the draconian paragraphs of a wartime decree was taken in the full knowledge that a death sentence would be the most likely outcome. Therefore, while it is possible to agree with Eric Johnson that Jews, and others considered by the regime to be racially inferior, bore the brunt of judicial terror (for instance, about half of all death sentences were passed by courts operating in the annexed territories of the East), increasingly the courts showed little restraint in their ruthless treatment of 'ordinary Gertmans' (Johnson's usage), especially from 1942.[83]

Table 6.3 Death sentences passed (% carried out), 1933–45

	All courts	People's Court
1933	78 (82.0)	—
1934	102 (77.4)	4 (100)
1935	98 (95.9)	9 (88.8)
1936	76 (89.4)	10 (100)
1937	86a	32 (87.5)
1938	85a	17 (94.1)
1939	139a	36a
1940	250 (27.2)	53a
1941	1,292 (9.9)	102a
1942	4,457 (12.7)	1,192a
1943	5,336 (16.7)	1,662a
1944	4,264 (18.3)	2,097a
1945	297 (42.7)	a

Note: a = no data.
Source: Walter Wagner, Der Volksgerichtshof im nationalsozialistischen Staat (Stuttgart, 1974), pp. 943–4.

The data in table 6.3 exclude executions in the wake of the failed attempt on Hitler's life in July 1944 and up to an estimated 30,000 death sentences passed by military tribunals.[84] Under Thierack's presidency the People's Court had passed death sentences 'sparingly' (around 5 per cent of all sentences passed prior to 1941),[85] before Freisler – who was considered by Rothenberger and Thierack as mentally unstable – transformed it into a 'revolutionary tribunal to purify the nation'.[86] The sharp increase from 1941 is explained both by the intensification of racial terror through the courts in the annexed Polish territories after the invasion of the Soviet Union in June and, from 1942, by the intensification of judicial terror within the Reich's pre-1938 borders.[87]

Even allowing for the substantial contribution made by the People's Court, however, it was the Special Courts that passed the majority of death sentences. To give just a few examples: during the war Freiburg Special Court tried around 988 persons in 727 known trials, sentencing approximately 28 to death; the 916 trials in the Special Court at Saarbrücken ended in 36 death sentences; Oldenburg passed 55 death sentences, 50 of them between 1941 and 1944 under Hoyer's chairmanship; the special court in Kiel processed about 10,000 indictments, half of which came to trial, involving 10,000 persons and handed down around 100 death sentences during the war years – a relatively low rate when compared to other courts, such as that at Bremen which tried 918 defendants in 562 trials and sentenced 49 of them to death; the Berlin Special Court held about 8,500 trials involving 12,500 persons and sentenced to death 1,000 of them.[88] When translated into percentages, these death sentences represent a high rate of attrition. In spite of the fact that nearly half of the wartime sentences are accounted for by the roughly two dozen Special Courts created in the annexed territories in the East after 1940, Thierack considered the courts also as 'summary tribunals of the home front', a role that was emphasised by Gauleiter Florian and other speakers addressing the chairmen of the Special Courts during a four-day seminar in June 1944.[89]

Increasingly the courts operated as *ad hoc* hearings at the sites where the crimes were alleged to have taken place. Indeed, even in the final days of the war, the courts continued with their bloodlust. In Regensburg, for example, the Special Court condemned to death the cathedral's deacon and a 70-year-old warehouse worker for urging the citizens of the town at an open-air meeting not to resist the advancing American troops. The chairman, an experienced 50-year-old judge, and the public prosecutor, ten years his junior, showed no hesitation in passing sentence, even though the war was effectively over for the city. The men were executed within a day of sentencing, a pattern that had become all too common in the closing year of the war.[90] Maintaining the political status quo through a swift judicial process had been the *raison d'être* of the Special Courts since their reintroduction in March 1933. But now the swiftness between trial, sentencing and execution created a climate in which the everyday exercise of law degenerated into little more than lynch-mob justice every bit perverse as the 'show trials' of the People's Court.

Already by 1943 increased case loads had led to a much more haphazard, arbitrary and ruthless approach to both court procedure and to the carrying out of sentences as a means to ensure the Special Courts' retention of their terror function. And it was not only the judges and prosecutors who eschewed legal formalism in order to gain results: the judicial administration did the same. Thus in early September 1943, the state secretary himself, impatient at the slackness of a system that had allowed around 300 clemency appeals to build up, and which had become a source of administrative embarrassment that had put him personally under pressure to show results, set about processing the files himself at mid-day on 7 September. Between 7.30 that evening and 8.30 the following morning, Rothenberger sent 186 persons to their deaths by hanging from meat-hooks (the prison guillotine had been damaged during an Allied raid earlier that week) at the notorious Plötzensee prison in Berlin. Over the next five days a further 100 inmates, including a number of prisoners not on the condemned list, were killed in a similar manner. He later justified this and other criminal actions by stating that he had been working according to the Führer's will, and that 'in war the rules are silent' (*inter arma silent leges*).[91]

IV

What drove Germany's legal profession to such murderous lengths? One explanation has been found in the country's subordination to the regime and the party, though, as I suggested earlier in this chapter, that was not as comprehensive as has been assumed.

Nonetheless, it is a fact that the judiciary, and the courts in particular, came under pressure as soon as Hitler came to power and as his regime grew in confidence.[92] Quite apart from the personal and institutional rivalries that pitted the likes of Himmler against Gürtner and Thierack against Schlegelberger, there was deep dissatisfaction with those judges who kept to legal formalism and thus passed sentences that often did not suit Hitler's local paladins, and which was matched by his own anger at the outcome of the Reichstag fire trial in 1934.[93] This led to Himmler's police arrogating to themselves the task of 'correcting' sentences by arresting and murdering defendants thought to have been too mildly treated by the courts – and to Hitler's own interventions in the judicial process, often based on what he had read in the newspapers.[94] According to Lothar Gruchmann, this drove Gürtner (reluctantly) to accommodate himself to what he understood to be Hitler's wishes in order to prevent worse from happening.[95] In spite of initial successes in maintaining a semblance of institutional autonomy (notably, *vis-à-vis* the ambitions of individuals like Kerrl and Frank, and, indeed, scoring a triumph with the incorporation of the Länder Justice Ministries into his Reich Ministry in 1934 (the so-called *Verreichlichung*), the 'Gürtner era' is viewed as a bleak one. Thus from 1933 through to the war decrees, the conservative-led Justice Ministry found itself shifting from the position of willing collaborator in restoring state authority to being locked into a dynamic determined by some vague idea of pursuing the Führer's will.

Following Gürtner's untimely death, in January 1941, Schlegelberger was left to run the Justice Ministry, and did so with calculated ruthlessness until his own fall through intrigue, in August 1942 (and only at that point did the Ministry fall to fanatical Nazis).[96] As acting-minister Schlegelberger also believed that the best way to avoid direct intervention in the daily operations of the Ministry and the courts was to anticipate Hitler's 'will' in order to continue to demonstrate the judiciary's willingness and usefulness in pursuing the aims of the regime, even where this meant sacrificing the lives of others.[97] Almost as soon as he took over the responsibility of the Justice Ministry, he adapted quickly to the extreme policy of racial attrition in the East (especially after the invasion of the Soviet Union in June 1941), also driven partly by a turf rivalry with Himmler's SS over who was to exercise 'criminal law' according to the 'articulated will of the Führer' in the annexed territory of occupied Poland.[98] To that end, also, the acting-minister issued a series of policy directives to the presidents of the High Courts in an attempt to ensure that those courts, too, worked towards the goals of the regime. Until the beginning of 1942, at the very latest, Schlegelberger's behaviour can be put down to a certain personal opportunism. But it also illustrates a general problem for the historian: namely, where to locate the boundary between 'working towards the Führer', pursuing personal ambition and working towards a particular understanding of the law?

There were two factors that hastened the judiciary's slide into the mire. The first had to do with the courts' differing sentencing practices, arising from lack of experience and confusion over policy. The discrepancy in sentencing had serious implications because of the way it affected public morale and attitudes towards the regime. On the one hand, the public was sensitive to overly harsh sentencing for apparently harmless acts, such as listening to foreign radio broadcasts, but approved of tough sentences for theft, especially postal theft.[99] The situation was worse when sentences varied wildly for the same crime. For example, the Rostock Special Court passed a death sentence against a butcher for profiteering, whereas the court in Warnemünde passed a comparatively light custodial sentence against a canteen manager for a similar crime; in Berlin the Special Court applied the death penalty against a worker for taking a shirt from a bombsite, whereas the Oldenburg court (unusually) sentenced to penal servitude a foreign worker for removing a wristwatch that had lain near a corpse after a raid.[100] Such unevenness in sentencing was a direct result of the steady deterioration in the quality of the Special Courts, especially in Poland, due to their increasing case-loads and to their reliance on inexperienced personnel, as Douma has shown.[101]

The second issue was not unrelated, but was more of a hindrance to Schlegelberger's strategy of working towards the Führer in order ostensibly to protect the autonomy of the judiciary, namely, the evident *unwillingness* – or, better, foot dragging – among notable sections of it to follow the exhortation to abandon 'legal paragraphs' and follow instead a fickle 'popular instinct', even when Hitler himself was the conduit.[102] Such judges tended to be older and less willing to depart from legal positivism, even if they shared a loyalty to the regime; if non-party members, they were viewed with suspicion in certain quarters for displaying a 'conservative resistance' to the aims of the regime by 'failing to sacrifice their inner convictions for the good of the nation' (thus Schlegelberger, in a letter to Bormann of 10 July 1942).[103] These judges – including even members of the People's Court – increasingly became reluctant to impose the sorts of sentences favoured by younger colleagues keen to prove themselves or by fanatics like Hoyer, even though they might have shared the hatred for the twin evils of bolshevism and crime.[104]

In an effort to overcome the problems of uneven sentencing and judicial resistance, Schlegelberger (like Gürtner before him) intensified the system of reporting that had been in place since 1934, whereby the presidents of the regional High Courts had regularly to compile dossiers on the case-work of their jurisdictions and report to the ministry. At the same time regular confer-ences held under the aegis of the presidents would allow for discussion and 'guidance'.[105] This way the ministry hoped to keep an eye on sentencing and to 'correct' anomalies in practice, as they arose, and to 'guide' sentences so that they fell into line with the wishes of the Führer. But Schlegelberger had little success.[106] After his departure in August 1942, a 'regeneration' (i.e. nazification) of the Justice Ministry and the presidencies of the High Courts took place through a purge, but essentially left intact the main body of judges and prose-cutors.[107] Thierack and Rothenberger refined the practice, with Rothenberger holding regular conferences, and Thierack initiating a regular commentary on selected cases, the so-called 'Letters to Judges' (*Richterbriefe*). Over the two years that followed, 21 commentaries on 46 cases were published, in an attempt to provide guidance over what the regime interpreted as 'good' and 'bad' case law.[108] But even those attempts to influence the courts remained unsuccessful, as evidenced by the regularity and increasingly vehement tone of the numerous circulars to the presidents of the High Courts and to the 'People's Court', as well as to the Reich's chief public prosecutors.[109] The refusal to bend in the regime's direction finally led Hitler to vent his ire in what was to be his final speech to the Reichstag, on the 20 April 1942, and which contained the threat of dismissal for those not working towards him.[110]

The unevenness of judgments and the apparent unwillingness of some courts to dispense justice according to the 'will of the Führer' were not accounted for exclusively in terms of calculated resistance. An internal report of early September 1942 by Himmler's security police,[111] barely a fortnight after Schlegelberger's departure from the Justice Ministry, sought to identify where the problem lay. Its author stated that not just non-party judges, but even those who were more disposed towards the aims of the regime, were unhappy about the attempts by the Ministry to influence the sentencing practice of individual judges, in particular where this led to instructions regarding the preferred sentence even before the trial had commenced. The report cited the case of a Polish worker who, under cover of darkness, stole items from gardens and sheds until apprehended. The prosecutor, as an obedient soldier of Hitler's judicial 'shock troops',[112] was instructed to demand a sentence of ten years in a 'punishment camp' (verschärftes Straflager); which is what the man got. The case was now being discussed – and the court criticised – because the penalty should have been that of death. Had the 'correct' sentence been applied in the first place, there would have been no need for criticism or for intervention. But the decisive point here was not that the Justice Ministry was actively seeking to 'direct' sentencing, but that some judges were resisting it, though not always with success.[113] Himmler's office concluded that the solution to the problem lay in correcting the political and ideological outlook of the corps of judges, most of whom were ostensibly ignorant of policy and displayed political naivety. Until this happened 'a true rehabilitation of criminal law cannot be expected in the long term'.[114] It was imperative, therefore, to educate judges 'not just in the real or supposed will of the Führer' but in the broad aims of the regime.[115] For 'if the judge is to be a help to the Führer, then he must also know the aims of the leadership'.[116]

Conclusion

Is it really conceivable that in 1942 or 1943 any of the 14,000 judges did not know or understand the aims of the regime? This is doubtful, as the few examples, cited above, of those willing to work – or, better, sentence – towards the Führer, and indeed as the actions of those judges who were unwilling to do so, testify. The concept of 'working towards the Führer' allows us to accommodate the complexity of motives – stemming from ideology, personal opportunity or institutional pressure – that drove jurists to become the executors of Hitler's 'will' and thus participants in the crimes of the Third Reich.

The violent conditions that were created by Hitler's regime, and which in turn fed it, dovetailed with extant social and cultural factors specific to Germany's judiciary in the 1930s and early 1940s. On the one hand, not only did the demographic profile of the judiciary become younger (table 6.1), but its intellectual character suffered. By the beginning of the war, there were many judges and prosecutors who had graduated at the beginning of the 1930s with mediocre law degrees and who were inadequately equipped to handle the cases before them. Klaus Bästlein has shown that 66 per cent of the judges and prosecutors at the Hamburg Special Court during the war years were born after

1900, and that many of them were junior personnel (made up of the *Assessoren*) who could complete their training by a spell at these courts. They were unlikely to risk their careers by dissenting from their more senior colleagues. According to Bästlein, this cohort was responsible for around 240 death sentences.[117] They, like 31 year-old Wolfgang Berthold, introduced earlier, sought a safe refuge in the knowledge that when they brought a charge or pronounced a sentence they did so in Hitler's name. Mobilised to serve on the 'home front' (in some cases on the 'Eastern Front'!), these inexperienced jurists sentenced towards the Führer as 'little Freislers': with a vehemence that bespoke a lack of imagination and a lack of moral responsibility.[118]

On the other hand, there were the older and more experienced jurists who also worked in the direction of the regime. For them, a traditional authoritarianism led them initially to share the same path as Nazism. And even when that path clearly began to follow a course that some of them were unwilling to take, those who remained on it could justify their actions either in much the same way that Gürtner and Schlegelberger did – with the argument that as long as they remained at their posts the integrity of the law was safe – or by reference to the critical and life-threatening conditions facing the nation at war. Members of this older cohort of jurists could remember their earlier youthful *Fronterlebnis* and the breakdown of order in 1918:

> The terrible collapse at the end of the [First] World War is an experience that the *Frontkämpfer*, and also those [who came] after him, must never be allowed to forget. This experience commands the resolute solidarity of all sections of the population. It demands that the soldier knows the rules of life of his people; that he knows what it is he vouchsafes with his entire being and with his life.[119]

The experience of the First World War had taught the judiciary that the role of its courts was to hold the home front firm against the enemy at the door, at any cost.[120]

The sum of all this was a terrible harvest of death. For, in a state where the norms of civil society were absent, judicial terror became the weapon of choice in controlling the population.[121] Thus the courts, the Special Courts in particular, through the examples they made of those individuals deemed on account of their 'crimes' to have placed themselves outside of the 'people's community', not only 'worked towards the Führer' but sought to ensure that the rest of society did the same.

Notes

1 Hans W. Koch, *In the Name of the Volk: Political Justice in Hitler's Germany* (London, 1989); Ingo Müller, *Hitler's Justice: The Courts of the Third Reich* (Cambridge, MA, 1991); Klaus Bästlein, 'Als Recht zu Unrecht wurde: Zur Entwicklung

der Strafjustiz im Nationalsozialismus', *Aus Politik und Zeitgeschichte: Beilage zur Wochenzeitung Das Parlament*, B13–14/89 (24 March 1989), pp. 1–18.

2 Zentral-Justizamt für die Britische Zone (ed.), *Das Nürnberger Juristenurteil, Vollständige Ausgabe* (Hamburg, 1948); Heribert Ortendorf and Hein ter Veen (eds), *Das Nürnberger Juristenurteil: Eine kommentierte Dokumentation* (Frankfurt am Main and New York, 1985); Fritz Bauer, Adelheid L. Rüter-Ehlermann and C. F. Rüter , *Justiz und NS-Verbrecher: Sammlung deutscher Strafurteile wegen Nationalsozialistischer Tötungsverbrechen 1945–1966* (Amsterdam, 1968); Eberhard Kolb, 'Die Maschinerie des Terrors: Zum Funktionieren des Unterdrückungs- und Verfolgungsapparates im NS-System', in Karl-Dietrich Bracher, Manfred Funke, Hans-Adolf Jacobsen (eds), *Nationalsozialistische Diktatur 1933–1945. Eine Bilanz* (Bonn, 1983), pp. 270–84.

3 *Akten der Reichskanzlei, Regierung Hitler*, part 1: *1933/34*, vol. 1: *30. Januar bis 31. August 1933, bearbeitet von Karl-Heinz Minuth* (2 vols, Boppard am Rhein, 1983), p. 165 (hereafter, *Regierung Hitler*, 1:1, 1:2, etc.). For Schlegelberger, see the useful brief study by Eli Nathans, *Franz Schlegelberger*, special issue of *Kritische Justiz: Der Unrechts-Staat*, 3 (1990).

4 *Ursachen und Folgen vom deutschen Zusammenbruch 1918 und 1945 bis zur staatlichen Neuordnung Deutschlands in der Gegenwart: Eine Urkunden- und Dokumentensammlung zur Zeitgeschichte*, ed. and intro. Herbert Michaelis and Ernst Schraepler (26 vols; Berlin, 1958–1970), vol. 19, pp. 430–1, and vol. 24, p. 391; Dietmut Majer, *Fremdvölkishe im Dritten Reich: ein Beitrag zur nationalsozialistischen Rechtssetzung und Rechtspraxis in Verwaltung und Justiz unter besonderer Berücksichtigung der eingegliederten Ostgebiete und des Generalgouvernements* (Boppard am Rhein, 1981).

5 National Council of the National Front of Democratic Germany Documentation Centre of the State Archives Administration of the German Democratic Republic, *Brown Book: War and Nazi Criminals in West Germany: State, Economy, Administration, Army, Justice, Science* (Verlag Zeit im Bild, Dresden, n.d. [1965]), p. 111; Dr Norbert Podewin (ed.), *Braunbuch, Kriegs- und Naziverbrecher in der Bundesrepublik und in Berlin (West)*, 3rd edn reprint (East Berlin, 1968); references are to the German edition.

6 Here one should cite the late Martin Broszat, the late Tim Mason, the late Detlev Peukert, and Hans Mommsen, each of whose path-breaking contributions to the social history of the Third Reich has both influenced and been influenced by Kershaw.

7 Klaus Marxen, 'Strafjustiz im Nationalsozialismus Vorschläge für eine Erweiterung der historischen Perspektive', in Bernhard Diestelkamp and Michael Stolleis (eds), *Justiz im Dritten Reich* (Frankfurt am Main, 1988). On the moral responsibility of individual jurists, Günter Spendel, *Rechtsbeugung durch Rechtsprechung: 6 Strafrechtlichen Studien* (Berlin and New York, 1984).

8 Thus 24 of the 69 presiding judges and senior public prosecutors of the OLGs whose political affiliation under the Republic was known: only 3 could be called liberal (2 Centre Party, one Deutsche Demokratische Partei); 4 belonged to the right-of-centre German People's Party (DVP), and the rest were members of the nationalist right. Lothar Gruchmann, *Justiz im Dritten Reich*

1933–1940: Anpassung und Unterwerfung in der Ära Gürtner (Munich, 1988), p. 288, fn. 114.

9 Hermann Weinkauff, *Die Deutsche Justiz und der Nationalsozialismus: Ein Überblick. Die deutsche Justiz und der Nationalsozialismus* (Stuttgart 1968), part 1, p. 108; Richard Schmid, 'Kräfte – Tendenzen – Strömungen in Justiz und Beamtenschaft', in Oswald Hirschfeld (ed.), *Auf dem Weg ins Dritte Reich: Kräfte – Tendenzen – Strömungen* (Bonn, 1982), p. 115; 'Frühling am Reichsgericht', *Leipziger Volkszeitung*, 14 April 1931, cited in Bundesminister der Justiz (ed.), *Im Namen des Deutschen Volkes: Justiz und Nationalsozialismus* (Cologne, 1989), pp. 57–58; Ralph Angermund, *Deutsche Richterschaft1919–1945: Krisenerfahrung, Illusion, politische Rechtsprechung* (Frankfurt am Main, 1990), pp. 43–4; Hans-Konrad Stein-Stegemann, 'In der "Rechtsabteilung" des "Unrechts-Staates", Richter und Staatsanwälte in Hamburg 1933–1945', in Justizbehörde Hamburg (ed.), '*Für Führer, Volk und Vaterland . . .': Hamburger Justiz im Nationalsozialismus* (Hamburg, 1992), pp. 161, 174.

10 Gruchmann, *Justiz im Dritten Reich*, p. 226; Eva Douma, *Deutsche Anwälte zwischen Demokratie und Diktatur 1930–1955* (Frankfurt am Main, 1998), pp. 49, 116, 226.

11 Stein-Stegemann, 'In der "Rechtsabteilung"', pp. 193, 195–6, 208ff. Gruchmann, *Justiz im Dritten Reich*, pp. 253, 257, gives the example of Klaus von Dohnanyi who was not a member of the NSDAP, but who was nonetheless promoted to *Regierungsrat* (government advisor) at the age of 38; see p. 288, n115, for the reference to the chief prosecutors.

12 Lothar Gruchmann, 'Franz Gürtner – "Justizminister unter Hitler"', in Ronald Smelser, Enrico Syring and Rainer Zitelmann (eds), *Die braune Elite 2. 21 weitere biographische Skizzen* (Darmstadt 1993), p. 134.

13 Gruchmann, *Justiz im Dritten Reich*, pp. 29–48.

14 Otto Thierack was justice minister for Saxony 1933–36, then president of the People's Court until his appointment as Reich justice minister in August 1942. Dr Curt Rothenberger, who became state secretary, had been president of the Hamburg Higher Court since 1933. Roland Freisler had been a state secretary in the Prussian Justice Ministry and then, from 1934, in the Reich Ministry, when the two were incorporated. He was handed the presidency of the People's Court. Thus, for the first time, almost a decade after Hitler came to power, the judicial system was put in the hands of a cohort of fanatical Nazis. See Robert Wistrich, *Wer war Wer im Dritten Reich* (Munich, 1983), pp. 75–7, 272–3; and Klaus Bästlein, 'Vom hanseatischen Richtertum zum nationalsozialistischen Justizverbrechen: Zur Person und Tätigkeit Curt Rothenbergers 1896–1959', in Justizbehörde Hamburg (ed.), '*Für Führer, Volk und Vaterland . . .*', pp. 74–145, for biographical details.

15 Gerhard Pauli, *Die Rechtsprechung des Reichsgerichts in Strafsachen zwischen 1933 und 1945 und ihre Fortwirkung in der Rechtsprechung des Bundesgerichtshofes* (Berlin and New York, 1992), p. 15. The conventional view, however, continues to present the judiciary as 'marginalised' and 'coordinated': see Hans-Ullrich Thamer, *Gewalt und Verführung: Deutschland 1933–1945* (Berlin, 1986), pp. 384–6.

16 Supported in this by Field Marshall von Hindenburg as head of the associations of Frontsoldaten: *Ursachen und Folgen*, vol. 9, p. 393; *Regierung Hitler, 1:1*, pp. 323–4.

In the end, the circular affected those lawyers who had commenced their profession after 1918.

17 Gruchmann, *Justiz im Dritten Reich*, pp. 149–51, 165–7; see also Jane Caplan, *Government without Administration: State and Civil Service in Weimar and Nazi Germany* (Oxford, 1988), pp. 141–9.

18 On the 31 March Hanns Kerrl and Hans Frank, now the justice minister, respectively, of Prussia and Bavaria, ordered the immediate suspension of lawyers, judges and civil servants who were Jews. Thus the new laws merely 'regularised' a situation that already existed: Gruchmann, *Justiz im Dritten Reich*, pp. 127–9, 149ff., 165–7, 1117; Martin Broszat, *The Hitler State: The Foundation and Development of the Internal Structure of the Third Reich* (London and New York, 1987); German original: *Der Staat Hitlers: Grundlegung und Entwicklung seiner inneren Verfassung*, trans. John W. Hiden (Munich, 1969), p. 337; Müller, *Hitler's Justice*, p. 61, gives 1,500 as the number affected by the measures. It is important to make a distinction between lawyers admitted to the bar and legal personnel (prosecutors, judges, etc.) employed by the State: see the brief discussion in Charles E. McClelland, *The German Experience of Professionalization: Modern Learned Professions and Their Organizations from the Early Nineteenth Century to the Hitler Era* (Cambridge and New York, 1991), pp. 222–3.

19 Gruchmann, *Justiz im Dritten Reich*, 150, 221–40. H. Schorn, *Der Richter im Dritten Reich: Geschichte und Dokumente* (Frankfurt am Main 1959), p. 730; Konrad Jarausch, *The Unfree Professions: German Lawyers, Teachers, and Engineers, 1900–1950* (New York and Oxford, 1990), pp. 97, 100–2, 254; Angermund, *Deutsche Richterschaft*, pp. 43–4. Crohne, as vice-president of the Volksgerichtshof, after Freisler's death, was its most senior judge, presiding over the trials of the remaining July 'plotters' in early 1945, notably that of General Fromm, against whom Crohne passed the death sentence for 'failure and cowardice': Walter Wagner, *Der Volksgerichtshof im nationalsozialistischen Staat* (Stuttgart, 1974), pp. 905–7.

20 The sample is compiled from Podewin (ed.), *Braunbuch*, pp. 147–87; for a similar sample of Nazi jurists in Czechoslovakia, see Union of Anti-Fascist Fighters (ed.), *Criminals on the Bench: Documents Concerning Crimes Committed on the Occupied Territory of Czechoslovakia by Two Hundred and Thirty Nazi Judges and Public Prosecutors Who Today Hold Legal Posts in Western Germany* (Prague, 1960), pp. 31–59.

21 Stein-Stegemann, 'In der "Rechtsabteilung"', pp. 152–3, 173, 175.

22 *Deutsche Justiz: Rechtspflege and Rechtspolitik; amtliche Blatt der deutschen Rechtspflege* (1933), pp. 640–3. The following passage, including quotations, is from this source; *Deutsche Justiz* (1934), p. 786.

23 Hanns Kerrl was Prussian justice minister from 22 March to June 1934 (after which Gürtner took over the post). He became a Reich minister without portfolio on 16 June 1934 until his death in 1941: *Regierung Hitler*, 1:2: *12. September bis 27. August 1934, bearbeitet von Karl-Heinz Minuth* (2 vols; Boppard am Rhein, 1983), pp. 1332f.

24 Bästlein, 'Als Recht zu Unrecht wurde', p. 17; and 'Die Akten des ehemaligen Sondergerichts Kiel als zeitgeschichtliche Quelle', *Zeitschrift der Gesellschaft für Schleswig–Holsteinische Geschichte*, 113 (1988), p. 204.

25 Stein-Stegemann, 'In der "Rechtsabteilung"', pp. 191–2. It should be noted, however, that under the Republic there were constant efforts to rejuvenate the judiciary through early retirements, notably in 1923 when Severing announced a cut in the size of the bureaucracy: see Caplan, *Government Without Administration*, pp. 14–101, *passim*.

26 Podewin (ed.), *Braunbuch*, pp. 117, 177 and table 22 (photostat of report of sentence carried out, 12 June 1944).

27 Adelheid L. Rüter-Eckermann and C. F. Rüter (eds), *Justiz und NS-Verbrechen Sammlung Deutscher Strafurteile wegen nationalsozialistischer Tötungsverbrechen 1945–1966* (Amsterdam, 1970), vol. 5, pp. 195–6, 199–200.

28 Podewin (ed.), *Braunbuch*, pp. 139, 178 and table 29 for Schüle's curriculum vitae;

29 Angermund, *Deutsche Richterschaft*; Henry V. Dicks, *Licensed Mass Murder: A Socio-Psychological Study of Some SS Killers* (London, 1972), chapter 2, *passim*; Bästlein, 'Als Recht zu Unrecht wurde', p. 79, n14; Stein-Stegemann, 'In der "Rechtsabteilung"', pp. 163ff., 173ff.

30 Werner Johe, *Die gleichgeschaltete Justiz: Organisation des Rechtswesens und Politisierung der Rechtsprechung 1933–1945 dargestellt am Beispiel des Oberlandesgerichtsbezirks Hamburg* (Hamburg, 1967), p. 85.

31 Jens Luge, *Die Rechtsstaatlichkeit der Strafrechtspflege im Oldenburger Land 1932–1945* (Hanover, 1993), pp. 62–5; Manfred Zeidler, *Das Sondergericht Freiberg: Zu Justiz und Repression in Sachsen 1933–1940* (Dresden, 1998), p. 24. See Douma, *Deutsche Anwälte*, pp. 90–4, for the example of the president of the Higher Court of Hamm, Dr Semmler: born in 1902, he joined the NSDAP in 1922, had become chief public prosecutor by the age of 34 and president of the court at 40; and Hinrich Rüping, *Staatsanwaltschaft und Provinzialjustizverwaltung im Dritten Reich: Aus den Akten der Staatsanwaltschaft bei dem Oberlandesgericht Celle als höherer Reichsjustizbehörde* (Baden-Baden, 1990), pp. 151–4, on the career of Karl Schnoering (born 1886) who was public prosecutor at the courts in Celle between 1937–1945; Bästlein, 'Vom hanseatischen Richtertum', pp. 91, 94f., 107f.

32 Stein-Stegemann, 'In der "Rechtsabteilung"', pp. 199–202.

33 Müller, *Hitler's Justice*, pp. 218, 297; Gruchmann, *Justiz im Dritten Reich*, pp. 70–1.

34 Gotthard Jasper, 'Justiz und Politik in der Weimarer Republik', *Vierteljahrshefte für Zeitgeschichte*, 30 (1982), pp. 167–205; Hinrich Rüping, 'Strafrechtspflege und politische Justiz im Umbruch vom liberalen Rechtstaat zum NS-Regime', in Josef Becker (ed.), *1933 – Fünfzig Jahre danach: Die nationalsozialistische Machtergreifung in historischer Perspektive* (Munich, 1983), pp. 153–68.

35 Gottfried Zarnow (pseud. for Ewald Moritz), *Gefesselte Justiz* (n.p., 1931), and countered by Erich Küttner, 'Gefesselte Justiz? – Entfesselte Lüge', *Die Justiz*, 36:7 (1931) pp. 329–41; Dr Franz Gürtner, *Deutsche Zeitung*, 17 Feb. 1933; cf. Ministerialrat (*Reichsgericht*) Rietzsch, 'Abnahme der Strafen – Zunahme der Verbrechen', *Deutsche Justiz*, 95:40 (1933). Such allegations had been aired long before the general crisis of the early 1930s: *Deutsche Juristenzeitung*, Jan. 1928; 'Zeitspiegel', *Deutsche Richter-Zeitung*, 24:8–9 (1932), pp. 250–4; Angermund, *Deutsche Richterschaft*, p. 40.

36 Georg Dahm and Friedrich Schaffstein, *Liberales oder autoritäres Strafrecht?* (Hamburg, 1933); Georg Dahm, 'Autoritäres Strafrecht', *Monatsschrift für Krimi-*

nalpsychologie und Strafrechtreform, 24 (1933), p. 171; see also: Dr jur. Fabricius, MdR, 'Nationalsozialismus und Juristentum', *Völkischer Beobachter*, 3 Aug. 1932, cited in 'Zeitspiegel' (1932), p. 251; Richard J. Evans, *Rituals of Retribution: Capital Punishment in Germany 1600–1987* (Oxford, 1996), pp. 624–31.

37 For the alleged failure of law and the 'compromise state', see Heintzeler, 'Autoritärer Staat', *Deutsche Justiz*, 96:47 (1934), p. 1438. This aspect is dealt with more fully in my forthcoming book: *Rethinking the Weimar Republic: State, Society and Politics, 1916–1936* (Arnold, 2004).

38 *Regierung Hitler*, 1:1, p. 244.

39 *Ibid.*, pp. 276–7.

40 Schlegelberger, 'Rechtschöpfung', *Deutsche Justiz* (1934), p. 4.

41 International Military Tribunal, *Nuremberg Trials, Major War Criminals*, vol. 20 (London 1948), pp. 264–5, 269ff. (hereafter, *IMT*, vol., etc.); Franz Gürtner, 'Aufruf: Führer und Reichskanzler', *Deutsche Justiz*, 96:33 (1934). For Goering's address to public prosecutors in the wake of the blood purge of 30 June, see *Deutsche Justiz*, 96:28 (1934), p. 881; Gerhard Kramer, 'The Courts of the Third Reich', in Jacques Rueff (intro.), *The Third Reich* (London, 1955), p. 631; Ralf Wallenhaus, *Konservatives Staatsdenken: Eine wissenssoziologische Studie zu Ernst Rudolf Huber* (Berlin, 1997), p. 180f.

42 Dr Wilhelm Gallas, 'Die Krise des Strafrechts und Ihre Überwindung im Staatsgedanken', *Zeitschrift für die gesamte Strafwissenschaft*, 53 (1934), p. 18.

43 *Deutsche Richter-Zeitung*, 25:4 (1933), p. 122. For similar comments from his counterpart in Saxony, see the same journal, 25:7 (1933), p. 161.

44 Lothar Gruchmann, 'Hitler über die Justiz: Das Tischgespräch vom 20 August 1942', *Vierteljahrshefte für Zeitgeschichte*, 12 (1964), p. 98; Werner Jochmann (ed.), *Adolf Hitler Monologe im Führerhauptquartier 1941–1944: Die Aufzeichnungen Heinrich Heims* (Bindlach, 1988), pp. 347–54, here 350; Bästlein, 'Vom hanseatischen Richtertum', p. 118.

45 *Deutsche Richter-Zeitung*, 25:4 (1933), p. 99; Thamer, *Gewalt und Verführung*, p. 384.

46 *Regierung Hitler*, 1:1, p. 164.

47 Heintzeler, 'Autoritärer Staat', p. 1440.

48 *Deutsche Justiz*, 95:50 (1933), pp. 726–7. See Roland Freisler's statement on the 'end of the neutral state, and hence, of neutral law', in *Deutsche Justiz*, 96:10 (1934), p. 303.

49 Quoted in *Deutsche Richter-Zeitung*, 25:8–9 (1933), p. 227; see *Deutsche Richter-Zeitung*, 25:10 (1933), pp. 270–1, for Dr Oegg; Dr Erich Schultze, 'Die Denkschrift des Preussischen Justizministers über "Nationalsozialistisches Strafrecht"', *Deutshe Richter-Zeitung*, 25:12 (1933), pp. 329–31; Dr Lehmberg (vice-president of the Landgericht, Berlin), 'Volksverbundenheit der Richter', *Preussische Justiz: Rechtspflege und Rechtspolitik*, vol. 95A:44 (1933), pp. 541–2; similar views were expressed by another judge, a Dr Flitzer, in a later issue of the same journal, 95:46 (1933), pp. 608–9. For Gürtner's views see 'Richter und Rechtsanwalt im neuen Staat: Rede des Reichsministers der Justiz. Dr Gürtner, gehalten auf der Arbeitstagung der Akademie für Deutsche Recht am 17. März 1934', *Deutsche Justiz*, 96:12 (1934), pp. 369–72

50 Bundesarchiv Berlin-Lichterfelde, R22/1314, Bl. 22; *Deutsche Richter-Zeitung*,

25:10 (1933), p. 281; Johe, *Die gleichgeschaltete Justiz*, p. 103; Müller, *Hitler's Justice*, pp. 68–81.

51 Reinhard Mann, *Protest und Kontrolle im Dritten Reich: Nationalsozialistische Herrschaft im Alltag einer rheinischen Grossstadt* (Frankfurt am Main, 1987); Robert Gellately, *The Gestapo and German Society: Enforcing Racial Policy 1933–1945* (Oxford, 1990); Eric Johnson, *The Nazi Terror: Gestapo, Jews and Ordinary Germans* (London, 2000); Jeremy Noakes and Geoffrey Pridham (eds), *Nazism 1919–1945*, vol. 2: *State, Economy and Society 1933–1939. A Documentary Reader* (Exeter, 1984), pp. 478–81.

52 William Sweet, 'The Volksgerichtshof: 1934–45', *Journal of Modern History*, 46 (June 1974), p. 329.

53 RGBl I (1933), pp. 136–38, 'Verordnung der Reichsregierung über die Bildung von Sondergerichten', 21 March 1933; Gruchmann, *Justiz im Dritten Reich*, pp. 944–56; Müller, *Hitler's Justice*, pp. 153–73; Hans Wüllenweber, *Sondergerichte im Dritten Reich: Vergessene Verbrechen der Justiz* (Frankfurt am Main, 1990).

54 Dr Wilhelm Crohne, 'Bedeutung und Aufgabe der Sondergerichte', *Deutsche Justiz*, vol. 95 (1933), pp. 384–5; Huber, *Verfassungsgeschichte*, vol. 7, p. 1054; Johe, *Die gleichgeschaltete Justiz*, pp. 81–116; Müller, *Hitler's Justice*, pp. 153–4; Anthony McElligott, 'Dangerous Communities and Conservative Authority: The Judiciary, Nazis and Rough People 1932–1933', in Tim Kirk and Anthony McElligott (eds), *Opposing Fascism: Community, Authority and Resistance in Europe* (Cambridge, 1999), pp. 39–42.

55 *Deutsche Justiz*, 97 (1935), p. 1775; Wolfgang Idel, 'Die Sondergerichte für politische Strafsachen' (Diss. Jur., Freiburg, 1935), p. 36, cited in Podewin (ed.), *Braunbuch*, p. 111; *Statistisches Jahrbuch für das Deutsche Reich 1935* (Berlin, 1935), p. 529; Broszat, *Der Staat Hitlers*, pp. 407–9. See the comments of von Papen on the purpose of the courts in his evidence to the International Military Tribunal, *IMT*, vol. 16, p. 281, and those of Schlegelberger, *IMT*, vol. 20, p. 233.

56 Heinz Boberach (ed.), *Meldungen aus dem Reich: Die geheimen Lageberichte des Sicherheitsdienstes 1938–1945* (Herrsching, 1984), vol. 15, report for 2 Dec. 1943, p. 6101 (hereafter, *Meldungen*). The People's Court (*Volksgerichthof*) came into operation in July 1934, and displaced the Reich Court at Leipzig which had been the highest court prior to 1933; the 26 Higher Courts (*Oberlandesgerichte*), and to a lesser extent, the Provincial Courts (*Landgerichte*), continued to play an important role in determining the personnel and supervision of the Special Courts (*Sondergerichte*) which displaced the Jury Courts (*Schwurgerichte*), and eventually the Lower or Stipendiary Courts (*Amtsgerichte*): Bästlein, 'Als Recht zu Unrecht wurde', pp. 15–18.

57 *Deutsche Richter-Zeitung*, 25:7 (1933), pp. 193–4, and 25:12 (1933), pp. 329–31.

58 Peter Hüttenberger, 'Heimtückefälle vor dem Sondergericht München 1933–1939', in Martin Broszat, Elke Fröhlich and Anton Grossmann (eds), *Bayern in der NS-Zeit IV. Herrschaft und Gesellschaft im Konflikt* (Munich and Vienna, 1981), part C; Bästlein, 'Die Akten des ehemaligen Sondergerichts Kiel', p. 177.

59 *Deutsche Justiz*, 97 (1935), p. 1811; Zeidler, *Das Sondergericht Freiberg*, pp. 15–20.

60 Manfred Zeidler, 'Gegen "Volkschädlinge", "Wehrkraftzersetzer" und "Hochverräter": Das Sondergericht Dresden und der Volksgerichtshof am Münchner Platz

1940–1945', in Norbert Haase and Birgit Sack (eds), *Münchner Platz, Dresden: Die Strafjustiz der Diktaturen und der historische Ort* (Leipzig, 2001), p. 47.

61 Jeremy Noakes (ed.), *Nazism 1919–1945*, vol. 4: *The German Home Front in the Second World War: A Documentary Reader* (Exeter, 1998), pp. 124–35; Broszat, *The Hitler State*, pp. 339–40.

62 *Meldungen,* vol. 15, p. 6072; Zeidler, 'Gegen "Volkschädlinge"', pp. 53–5, 57–8.

63 *Ibid.,* vol. 2, report for 20 Oct. 1939, p. 376; Zeidler, 'Gegen "Volkschädlinge"', p. 58.

64 See, in general, Evans, *Rituals of Retribution*, pp. 632f.

65 Noakes (ed.), *Nazism 1919–1945*, vol. 4, p. 136.

66 *Meldungen,*vol. 15, reports for 29 Nov. 1943, pp. 6075–7, 2 Dec. 1943, pp. 6097–101, and 13 Dec. 1943, pp. 6139–47; Luge, *Die Rechtsstaatlichkeit*, pp. 120, 192f.

67 Jeremy Noakes, 'Social Outcasts in the Third Reich', in Richard Bessel (ed.), *Life in the Third Reich* (Oxford, 1987), pp. 83–96; Detlev J. K. Peukert, 'The Genesis of the "Final Solution" from the Spirit of Science', in Thomas Childers and Jane Caplan (eds), *Re-Evaluating the Third Reich* (New York, 1993), pp. 234–52; Volker Roelcke, 'Using Bodies in a Culture of Biologism: Psychiatric Research in Germany, 1933–1945', paper presented at the conference 'Using Bodies: Humans in the Service of Twentieth-Century Medicine', Welcome Institute, London, 3–4 Sept. 1998; Jordan Goodman, Anthony McElligott and Lara Marks (eds), *Useful Bodies: Humans in the Service of Medical Science in the Twentieth Century* (Baltimore, MD, and London, 2003), Editors' introduction.

68 Ernst Kretschmer, *Physique and Character: An Investigation of the Nature of Constitution and of the Theory of Temperament*, 2nd German edn, trans. W. J. H. Sprott (London, 1925).

69 *IMT*, vol. 27, pp. 451–63, 1701–Postscript; see Michael Burleigh and Wolfgang Wippermann, *The Racial State: Germany 1933–1945* (Cambridge, 1991), pp. 136–82.

70 Cited in Bästlein, 'Die Akten des ehemaligen Sondergerichts Kiel', p. 201.

71 *IMT*, vol. 27, p. 459; Leon Poliakov and Joseph Wulf (eds), *Das Dritte Reich und seiner Diener: Auswärtiges Amt, Justiz und Wehrmacht, Dokumente und Berichte* (Wiesbaden, 1989 [1956]), pp. 231ff.; Lothar Gruchmann, 'Euthanasie und Justiz im Dritten Reich', *Vierteljahrshefte für Zeitgeschichte*, 20 (1972), pp. 232–79; Nik Wachsmann, 'From Indefinite Confinement to Extermination: "Habitual Criminals" in the Third Reich', in R. Gellately and N. Stoltzfus (eds), *Social Outsiders in Nazi Germany* (Princeton, NJ, 2001), pp. 165–91.

72 Luge, *Die Rechtsstaatlichkeit*, pp. 121, 197; Bästlein, 'Die Akten des ehemaligen Sondergerichts Kiel', pp. 167, 177; Johnson, *Nazi Terror*, pp. 329–31, 334f. The texts can be found in Noakes (ed.), *Nazism 1919–1945*, vol. 4, pp. 128f. See also Michael P. Hensle, *Die Todesurteile des Sondergerichts Freiburg 1940–1945* (Munich, 1996), p. 166.

73 *Meldungen,* vol. 15, report for 29 Nov. 1943, pp. 6073, 6075, 6077–8 (in the Hamburg example the author of the report is quoting data first presented in the Richterbrief, no. 7 (1 Nov. 1943); Bästlein, 'Die Akten des ehemaligen Sondergerichts Kiel', p. 177; Podewin (ed.), *Braunbuch*, pp. 125–40, *passim*.

74 Luge, *Die Rechtsstaatlichkeit*, pp. 195–7, 200, 207–20, on which the following is based.

75 Johnson, *Nazi Terror*, pp. 312, 322; see Hensle, *Die Todesurteil*, pp. 42–142, for 33 similar cases.

76 Hensle, *Die Todesurteile*, pp. 170–1.

77 Bästlein, 'Die Akten des ehemaligen Sondergerichts Kiel', pp. 168–70, 200–1; and 'Vom hanseatischen Rictertum', p. 121; Nik Wachsmann, '"Annihilation through Labour": The Killing of State Prisoners in the Third Reich', *Journal of Modern History*, 71 (1999), pp. 624–59.

78 *Statistisches Jahrbuch für das Deutsche Reich* (Berlin, 1938), p. 681; see Poliakov and Wulf (eds), *Das Dritte Reich*, pp. 184–228, for discriminatory laws against Jews.

79 Nuremberg Doc. NG-505, quoted in Nathans, *Franz Schlegelberger*, p. 69. On the condition and treatment of Polish and other forced labour in wartime Germany see above all: Majer, *Fremdvölkishe im Dritten Reich*; Ulrich Herbert (ed.), *Europa und der 'Reichseinsatz': Ausländische Zivilarbeiter, Kriegsgefangene und KZ-Häftlinge in Deutschland 1938–1945* (Essen, 1991); and Ulrich Herbert, *A History of Foreign Labour in Germany 1880–1980: Seasonal Workers/Forced Labour/Guest Workers* (Ann Arbor, MI, 1990).

80 Nathans, *Franz Schlegelberger*, p. 70.

81 Podewin (ed.), *Braunbuch*, pp. 126–7.

82 Poliakov and Wulf (eds), *Das Dritte Reich*, pp. 250–2; Martin Broszat, 'Zur Perversion der Strafjustiz im Dritten Reich', *Vierteljahrshefte für Zeitgeschichte*, 6 (1958), pp. 422f.; Johnson, *Nazi Terror*, ch. 10 and *passim*.

83 Johnson, *Nazi Terror*, pp. 315–17; Noakes and Pridham (eds), *Nazism*, vol. 2, pp. 479, 481.

84 For variations in the data, see: Bundesarchiv Berlin-Lichterfelde R3001/alt R22/1314; Bästlein, 'Vom hanseatischen Richtertum', p. 124; and Wüllenweber, *Sondergerichte im Dritten Reich*, p. 42. For a thorough, and devastating, discussion of the military courts, see the excellent study by Manfred Messerschmidt and Fritz Wüllner, *Die Wehrmachtjustiz im Dienste des Nationalsozialismus: Zerstörung einer Legende* (Baden-Baden, 1987), p. 87, and that by Fritz Wüllner, *Die NS-Militärjustiz und das Elend der Geschichtsschreibung: Ein grundlegender Forschungsbericht* (Baden-Baden, 1991).

85 Wagner, *Der Volksgerichtshof*, pp. 876, 945; Helmut Heiber, 'Zur Justiz im Dritten Reich: Der Fall Elias', *Vierteljahrshefte für Zeitgeschichte*, 3:4 (1955), pp. 294–5.

86 Freisler, who was 48 years old when appointed, was – according to Rothenberger in his 1944 autobiographical notes – 'pathologically unstable', a verdict in which Thierack concurred: Bästlein, 'Vom hanseatischen Richtertum', p. 127; Helmut Heiber, 'Zur Justiz', pp. 276–7, 292. In general see: Sweet, 'The Volksgerichtshof', *passim*; Bästlein, 'Als Recht zu Unrecht wurde', pp. 16–17; Klaus Marxen, *Das Volk und seine Gerichtshof* (Frankfurt am Main, 1994).

87 Ian Kershaw, *The 'Hitler Myth': Image and Reality in the Third Reich* (Oxford, 1987), pp. 187, 192. Schlegelberger in a letter to Bormann (15 May 1942) wrote of the need to anticipate the Führer's will by making more use of the death penalty: Klaus Oldenhage, 'Justizverwaltung und Lenkung der Rechtssprechung im

Zweiten Weltkrieg: Die Lageberichte der Oberlandesgerichtspräsidenten und Generalstaatsanwälte (1940–1945)', in Dieter Rebentisch and Karl Teppe (eds), *Verwaltung contra Menschenführung im Staat Hitlers: Studien zum politsch-administrativen System* (Göttingen, 1986), pp. 118–9; Johnson, *Nazi Terror*, pp. 312–15.

88 Figures cited in Hensle, *Die Todesurteile*, pp. 173–4; Bästlein, 'Die Akten des ehemaligen Sondergerichts Kiel', p. 171, n13. Wagner's data do not appear to distinguish between the 6 senates of the People's Court, the 70 or more *Sondergerichte*, the 26 High Courts and the Reich Court (which could order a revision of sentences): Wagner, *Der Volksgerichtshof*, pp. 876–80, 942–3, 945–6. Angermund, *Deutsche Richterschaft*, pp. 216–7; Evans, *Rituals of Retribution*, p. 593.

89 In a letter of 5 July 1943 to the chairmen and chief prosecutors of the Higher Courts, cited in Podewin (ed.), *Braunbuch*, p. 113; Hinrich Rüping, *Staatsanwaltschaft und Provinzialjustizverwaltung*, Anlage 11: *Arbeitstagung für Sondergerichtsvorsitzende auf der Reichsburg Kochem vom 11. Juni bis 14. Juni 1944*, pp. 193–4.

90 *Meldungen*, vol. 15, report for 29 Nov. 1943, p. 6078; Adelheid L. Rüter-Eckermann and C. F. Rüter (eds), *Justiz und NS-Verbrechen Sammlung Deutscher Strafurteile wegen nationalsozialistischer Tötungsverbrechen 1945–1966* (Amsterdam, 1969), vol. 2, pp. 233–346; Johe, *Die gleichgeschaltete Justiz*, p. 97; Bästlein, 'Die Akten des ehemaligen Sondergerichts Kiel', p. 170; Wagner, *Der Volksgerichtshof*, pp. 811–14. Further examples can be found in the studies by Luge (*Die Rechtsstaatlichkeit*), Rüping (*Staatsanwaltschaft und Provinzialjustizverwaltung*) and Johnson (*Nazi Terror*), cited above.

91 Wagner, *Der Volksgerichtshof*, pp. 813, 815; Bästlein, 'Vom hanseatischen Richtertum', p. 124–5. For an account of executions see Bundesarchiv Berlin-Lichterfelde, R3001/alt R22/1314, Bl. 109–11; Hensle, *Die Todesurteile*, pp. 174–5; Johann Dachs, *Tod durch das Fallbeil. Der deutsche Scharfrichter Johann Reichart (1893–1972)* (Munich, 2001 [1996]), pp. 97–110.

92 Broszat, 'Zur Perversion', pp. 390, 397, 403; Dietmut Majer, 'Justiz und NS-Staat. Zum Einfluß der NSDAP auf die Organisation und Personalpolitik der Justiz 1933–1945', *Deutsche Richterzeitung*, 56 (1978).

93 Gruchmann, *Justiz im Dritten Reich*, p. 79; cf. *ibid.*, pp. 571–3, 658–75; Nathans, *Franz Schlegelberger*, pp. 21, 23, n64, 27–9, 34–5; *IMT*, vol. 26, pp. 307–21: 785–PS, 786–PS, 787–PS, 788–PS. A sustained and vicious campaign by the SS magazine *The Black Corps* against the judiciary led even Hans Frank to attack the journal (and, hence, Himmler) in a speech at Munich University for calling members of the legal profession 'sewer rats'. Frank thus earned Himmler's enmity and subsequently found himself outside of Hitler's inner circle: *IMT*, vol. 12, pp. 150–5, vol. 22, p. 541, vol. 28, pp. 130, 162; Bästlein, 'Vom hanseatischen Richtertum', pp. 110–14. On Schlegelberger's relations with Thierack, see Heiber, 'Zur Justiz', pp. 277, 285, 292–3.

94 Broszat, 'Zur Perversion', pp. 408–16, 419, 423; and *The Hitler State*, p. 341.

95 Gruchmann, *Justiz im Dritten Reich*, pp. 1102, 1105f., 1109.

96 *IMT*, vol. 20, pp. 269–71, 274, vol. 22, p. 244; Heiber, 'Zur Justiz', pp. 295–6; Nathans, *Franz Schlegelberger*, pp. 37, 74.

97 Oldenhage, 'Justizverwaltung und Lenkung der Rechtssprechung', p. 117; Broszat, 'Zur Perversion', p. 417.

98 Nathans, *Franz Schlegelberger*, pp. 59–68, *passim*; in general, see Martin Broszat, *Nationalsozialistische Polenpolitik* (Stuttgart, 1961), and Majer, *Fremdvölkishe im Dritten Reich*.

99 *Meldungen*, vol. 2, reports for 23 Oct. 1939, p. 386, and 6 Nov. 1939, p. 425; vol. 3, reports for 12 Feb. 1940, p. 752, and 26 Feb. 1940, pp. 812–13; vol. 15, reports for 29 Nov. 1943, pp. 6071–78, 2 Dec. 1943, pp. 6096–101, 13 Dec. 1943, pp. 6139–47 and 16 Dec. 1943, pp. 6155–9.

100 *Ibid.*, vol. 9, report for 18 Dec. 1941, pp. 3112–15; vol. 10, report for 19 March 1942, p. 3495–6; vol. 13, report for 30 May 1943, pp. 5306, 5309.

101 *Ibid.*, vol. 2, reports for 11 Oct. 1939, p. 342, and 13 Oct. 1939, pp. 352–3; vol. 8, report for 1 Sept. 1941, pp. 2717–20; vol. 11, report for 3 Sept. 1942, pp. 4169–70; vol. 13, reports for 20 May 1943, pp. 5268–72 and 30 May 1943, pp. 5301–7; Douma, *Deutsche Anwälte*, pp. 37–51, 148, 150, 224–7.

102 Müller, *Hitler's Justice*, pp. 192–7; Johnson, *Nazi Terror*, pp. 355–7.

103 *Meldungen*, vol. 15, report for 2 Dec. 1943, p. 6100; Stein-Stegemann, 'In der "Rechtsabteilung"', pp. 209–10; Kramer, 'The Courts of the Third Reich', p. 630; Lothar Gruchmann, 'Ein Unbequemer Amtsrichter im Dritten Reich: Aus dem Personalakten des Dr. Lothar Kreyssig', *Vierteljahrshefte für Zeitgeschichte*, 82 (1984), pp. 463–88; Angermund, *Deutsche Richterschaft*, pp. 206–7, 228–9; Luge, *Die Rechtsstaatlichkeit*, pp. 63, 78, 123–4, 134–7, 163–5, 222, 271; Douma, *Deutsche Anwälte*, pp. 122, 128, 145.

104 *Deutsche Richter-Zeitung*, 25:5 (1933), pp. 155–6; Bästlein, 'Die Akten des ehemaligen Sondergerichts Kiel', p. 206; Hensle, *Die Todesurteile*, p. 28.

105 Hans Michelsberger, *Berichte aus der Justiz des Dritten Reiches: Die Lageberichte der Oberlandesgerichtspräsidenten von 1940–45 unter vergleichender Heranziehung der Lageberichte der Generalstaatsanwälte* (Pfaffenweiler, 1989); Oldenhage, 'Justizverwaltung und Lenkung der Rechtssprechung', *passim*.

106 Gruchmann, *Justiz im Dritten Reich*, pp. 1091–5, 1100–2, 1104, 1106f., 1110–11; Bästlein, 'Vom hanseatischen Richtertum', pp. 116, 119.

107 Bästlein, 'Vom hanseatischen Richtertum', p. 119.

108 Heinz Boberach, *Richterbriefe: Dokumente zur Beeinflüssung der deutschen Rechtsprechung 1942–1944* (Boppard am Rhein, 1975), p. xxiv; *Meldungen*, vol. 13, report for 13 May 1943, pp. 5245–9; Broszat, 'Zur Perversion', pp. 432–7; Johe, *Die gleichgeschaltete Justiz*, pp. 155–196; Bästlein, 'Die Akten des ehemaligen Sondergerichts Kiel', p. 197; and 'Vom hanseatischen Richtertum', p. 122f.

109 *Meldungen*, vol. 11, report for 3 Sept. 1942, p. 4169; vol. 15, report for 2 Dec. 1943, p. 6101; Boberach, *Richterbriefe*, p. 425.

110 *Ursachen und Folgen*, vol. 17, Doc. Nr. 3203a, p. 719; Broszat, *The Hitler State*, p. 341; and 'Zur Perversion', pp. 426–7; Gruchmann, 'Hitler über die Justiz', p. 98; Oldenhage, 'Justizverwaltung und Lenkung der Rechtssprechung', pp. 114–5, 120; Michelsberger, *Berichte aus der Justiz des Dritten Reiches*, p. 20; Bästlein, 'Vom hanseatischen Richtertum', p. 116.

111 *Meldungen*, vol. 11, report for 3 Sept. 1942, pp. 4166–70, on which the following account is based; Broszat, 'Zur Perversion', pp. 439–43.

112 *Deutsche Justiz*, 97 (1935), p. 1776; there were approximately 2,500 prosecutors.

113 Oldenhage, 'Justizverwaltung und Lenkung der Rechtssprechung', pp. 107–8.

114 *Meldungen*, vol. 11, report for 3 Sept. 1942, pp. 4167–9.

115 *Ibid.*, p. 4168.

116 *Meldungen*, vol. 13, report for 30 May 1943, p. 5302.

117 Bästlein, 'Vom hanseatischen Richtertum', p. 107; and 'Die Akten des ehemaligen Sondergerichts Kiel', p. 204; Rüter-Eckermann and Rüter (eds), *Justiz und NS-Verbrechen*, vol. 3, p. 628.

118 *Deutsche Justiz*, 96:21 (1934), p. 631; *Meldungen*, vol. 13, report for 30 May 1943, p. 5305; Douma, *Deutsche Anwälte*, pp. 145–56. Rüping, *Staatsanwaltschaft und Provinzialjustizverwaltung*, pp. 151–4. The complaint about a decline in the intellectual and moral quality of this cohort had already been aired at the time when it would have been graduating its students: *Deutsche Richter-Zeitung*, 23:4 (1931), p. 128.

119 *IMT*, vol. 34, pp. 132–5: 4065–PS.

120 Bästlein, 'Vom hanseatischen Richtertum', pp. 77–9.

121 Franz Neumann, *Behemoth: The Structure and Practice of Nationalism Socialism 1933–1944* (New York, 1983 [1942–44]).

7

Nazi masters and accommodating Dutch bureaucrats: working towards the Führer in the occupied Netherlands, 1940–45

Bob Moore

Although the phrase 'working towards the Führer' has become an integral part of the vocabulary for understanding the mechanics of governance and authority *within* the Third Reich, the same notion can also be seen operating outside of the *Altreich* in many of the territories occupied by German forces during the Second World War. Manifestations of this phenomenon in occupied Poland have been explored by Ian Kershaw himself in a study of the career of Arthur Greiser as *Gauleiter* of the Warthegau. In effect, the independence afforded to the Hitler-appointed satraps of conquered territories, and the limited guidance and direction provided from Berlin, gave Greiser and his counterparts an enormous degree of freedom to pursue broad policy objectives (or even the assumed wishes of the Führer) in any way they saw fit.[1]

Comparing Hitler's statements on what was to happen in Poland and the extreme measures adopted by his subordinates make it possible to see where local initiatives occurred, but some semblances of the same behaviour patterns can be identified in the occupied countries of Western Europe – and at two different levels. While Nazi plans for the governance and administration of Poland precluded any role for an indigenous bureaucracy or the residual Polish social structures, control of Western Europe was predicated on maintaining a high degree of normality in the administrative sphere and making every use of the indigenous structures insofar as they did not actively conflict with German military aims or the principles of National Socialism. Taking the Netherlands as a case study, and concentrating specifically on the persecution of the Jews as a policy issue, it is possible to show how overlapping jurisdictions, polycratic agencies and governmental disorder became increasingly commonplace, and examples of 'working towards the Führer' can be identified in the behaviour patterns of both the German politicians–administrators and the residual indigenous state bureaucracy.

It is perhaps not surprising to find examples of this type of behaviour within the German executive. Its members had grown accustomed to the system that had developed within the Third Reich since the seizure of power and knew that their careers and preferment depended on impressing their bosses in Berlin, often with limited guidance. More surprising is the fact that there were also examples of similar behaviour patterns among many Dutch organisations, agencies and individuals. Even in relation to Nazi policy towards the Jews, something that should have been intellectually and culturally abhorrent within a liberal and democratic society, it is possible to find examples of Dutch organisations and functionaries exceeding even the expectations of their German overseers.

The structures of German rule in the occupied Netherlands reflected the *ad hoc* and provisional nature of much Nazi thinking on the governance of Western Europe. Plans in the autumn of 1939 saw the country purely as a zone for military occupation; but, only two days after the capitulation, Hitler summarily changed his mind and installed a civilian political *Reichskommissar*, Arthur Seyss-Inquart, as 'supreme executive power.[2] The Reichskommissar was directly subordinate to Hitler and was to receive directives and guidelines exclusively from the Reich Chancellery. Seyss-Inquart, four subordinate *Generalkommissare*, and a number of special representatives (*Beauftragte*) effectively oversaw the continued operation of a retained Dutch administrative apparatus, the prime consideration being to maintain security and governance with the minimum expense of military and manpower resources. The fact that little thought had been given to the status or governance of an occupied Netherlands, either by Hitler or by any element of the German bureaucracy inevitably meant that Seyss-Inquart and his men had a good deal of operational latitude. However, the emergent organisational structure effectively imported many of the facets common to Nazi rule elsewhere, namely overlapping jurisdictions, confused chains of command and a spirit of institutional Darwinism. This was not helped by the proliferation of officials that also seemed to beset the system. While it was argued after the war that 200 supervisory officials would have been sufficient to oversee the whole apparatus, by 1941 there were 1,596 German civil servants employed in the Netherlands.[3] This was partly a function of the country being seen as a prime posting – where one could make a career with the possibilities of rapid promotion – while having none of the drawbacks of living in Eastern Europe; but it was also a manifestation of the main appointees bringing their own staffs and placemen into the system.[4]

Even at the highest level, chains of command were far from clear – and in the light of knowledge on Nazi rule elsewhere – perhaps deliberately so. Thus while Seyss-Inquart was able to appoint two long-time Austrian associates, Friedrich Wimmer and Hans Fischböck as Generalkommissare for, respectively, administration and justice, and finance and economy, the posts of Generalkommissar for security and for special affairs were dictated by Himmler and Bormann, who had their chosen nominees appointed to those positions. Thus Hanns Albin Rauter, already a higher SS and police leader, although nominally subordinate to Seyss-Inquart, had enormous power over police and security matters in the Netherlands and took many of his orders directly from Himmler in Berlin. Likewise, Fritz Schmidt (the only non-Austrian of the four) was made Generalkommissar for special affairs at the specific behest of Martin Bormann.[5] In this way, both SS and NSDAP came to have independent influence and access to the governance of the Netherlands.

The structures of Nazi rule undoubtedly had an impact on the tragic fate of the Jews in the Netherlands. With no direct guidance from Berlin, Seyss-Inquart and his subordinates were left to improvise policies and structures based on previous experiences and the general tenets of Nazi racial policy.[6] Although the Dutch people were perceived by Nazi ideologues as fellow-'Aryans' there was no immediate intention to incorporate the country into the Reich proper and there was consequently no question of imposing all the stipulations of the Nuremberg Laws overnight, as had been done in Austria. Whatever the experiences of Seyss-Inquart and his henchmen in that country, the model with which they were most familiar could not be imported wholesale into a new environment.

In his history of the Netherlands in the Second World War, Louis de Jong notes that there is no evidence for how the plans of Seyss-Inquart and his lieutenants developed in the early months of occupation, or for what instructions they received from Berlin.[7] De Jong clearly took the view that such instructions existed but could not be substantiated from the archival record. However, given what is now known about the nature of Nazi rule in both Germany and the occupied territories, it seems just as likely that there was no direct guidance given from the centre in this early period and that many of the steps taken against the Jews were autonomous actions carried out by the Seyss-Inquart and his colleagues. Although not trammelled by the same restrictions as were Nazi Party and SS functionaries in other occupied Western European countries who had to operate under a military government, the Nazis in the Netherlands were nevertheless constrained by wider issues and could not afford to alienate or provoke widespread unrest among the 'Aryan' Dutch.[8]

Their credentials as committed National Socialists and anti-Semites were unimpeachable; but, with no specific guidance from the centre, it is perhaps not surprising that early measures against the Jews tended to follow the same patterns of identification, registration, social isolation and economic exclusion that had been evident in the *Altreich*. Legislation against ritual slaughter was soon followed by the exclusion of Jews from the Air-Raid Protection Service, and then a gradual process of retirement and dismissal from government service and from the teaching professions.[9] This raises the crucial question of whether the German administrators in the Netherlands were working towards specific policy goals in relation to the Jews, or were merely carrying out measures they deemed appropriate for a country populated by fellow-'Aryans' and a future candidate for incorporation within the Reich itself. In the light of what is now known about decision making about Jews inside the Reich, the latter seems far more likely.

In enacting even limited anti-Semitic ordinances against the Jews, the Seyss-Inquart regime was risking provoking civil disobedience and unrest, and thereby undermining its prime function of administration with minimum disruption. Thus any actions of this type had to be driven either by an ideological commitment to anti-Semitism or by a desire to carry out measures that were likely to win approval in Berlin. In spite of the limitations, there is no doubt that several high-ranking German officials were committed to increasing the tempo of anti-Semitic measures as 1940 drew to a close. Up to that point, peace and order had been maintained; but that was to change as Generalkommissar Schmidt gave permission for Dutch Nazis to take action against Jews in cafés, restaurants and on the streets.[10] In Amsterdam, Seyss-Inquart's *Beauftragte* Dr Böhmcker specifically sanctioned notices in shop and restaurant windows saying that Jews were unwelcome,[11] and also advocated the creation of a ghetto in the city. Certainly both Böhmcker and Schmidt seem to have been the most active proponents of anti-Semitic measures in this period. Both men could argue that this was part of their remit: Schmidt as Generalkommissar for special affairs and Böhmcker as representative for Amsterdam, the city with by far the largest concentration of Jews.[12] At the same time Hans Fischböck as Generalkommissar for finance and the economy was active in developing measures to exclude Jews from the economy and seize their assets. His pedigree in such matters was unsurpassed, having been part of the Austrian bureaucracy that had been so successful in expediting the emigration of Jews after the *Anschluss* and confiscating their assets.[13] Although the latter was closely connected with Seyss-Inquart, the other leading functionaries had their own allegiances that superseded their loyalty to the Reichskommissar: Schmidt to Bormann, Hess and the NSDAP; and Rauter to Himmler, Heydrich and the RSHA. This state of affairs was epitomised by Jacob Presser: 'The *Reichskommissariat* was not a cohesive unit but a conglomerate of people posted to the Netherlands by various departments in Germany and hence, by and large, more concerned to carry out the intentions of their own chiefs than to work in the spirit of the *Reichskommissar* himself.'[14]

Whereas this chaotic system of overlapping jurisdictions and split loyalties may have been detrimental in many areas of policy, the fact that all the men involved and the agencies they represented were similarly committed to the idea of dealing with the 'Jewish question' meant that disputes were over *methods* and *leadership* rather than overall aims.[15] Indeed, it could be argued that this level of agreement, as evidenced by the accord and bonhomie shown at the occasional *Judenkonferenze* convened by Seyss-Inquart,[16] actually served to facilitate progress and encouraged the functionaries to outdo each other in attempts to impress both the Reichskommissar and their (un-)official bosses in Berlin. While it may be difficult to disaggregate the motivations of ideological commitment and career advancement at later stages in the occupation, the fact that functionaries in the Netherlands, perhaps relying on the patterns established in Germany and Austria, had introduced many of the measures which were to form the cornerstones of the 'successful' implementation of the final solution before this had been fully planned in Berlin does demonstrate a propensity for 'working towards' the Führer and his presumed ideological objectives. However, with templates for such actions already in existence from other areas under German rule, it begs the question of whether these were truly acts of imagination – second-guessing what would please the Führer – or merely a slavish copying of existing tried and tested models used elsewhere.

To some degree, this autonomy was a temporary phenomenon. Preparations for Operation Barbarossa would not have gone unnoticed, even in the faraway Netherlands, and on 13 August 1941 Seyss-Inquart attended a conference in Berlin chaired by Eichmann which clearly outlined the intention to find a solution for the Jewish question in all occupied territories.[17] Yet even if this set the parameters for what was to follow, there was still space for local initiatives. Wildt notes that, even in the early part of 1942, Himmler was prepared to give his RSHA departmental chiefs a good deal of freedom, and he took tighter control only when the systematic killing of Polish and Western European Jews in the camps began.[18]

In occupied Europe, the idea of autonomous action directed towards carrying out the perceived wishes of the leadership can be taken a stage further by looking at the indigenous bureaucracy. As Queen Wilhelmina and the Dutch Government in May 1940 departed for exile in Britain, they left behind a working governmental apparatus controlled by the secretaries-general of the individual ministries. They were charged with the task of continuing their roles 'in the interests of the state', under a series of instructions issued in May 1937.[19] Although Seyss-Inquart gave them the option of resignation, the overwhelming majority initially chose to stay, and they became an integral part of the new administration. Since 1945, debate has raged about the interpretation to be placed on their behaviour. Was this just crass collaboration with the victorious Germans? Such an interpretation made it easy to condemn all those who took part as being at fault for their wartime behaviour. The idea that there was a clear division between *goed* and *fout* in the conduct of Dutch officials and the population at large was a theme explored at length by Louis de Jong in his history of the wartime Netherlands,[20] but that approach has its dangers in seeing the period and its actors in purely black or white terms.[21] A more useful tool with which to understand bureaucratic behaviour may be the concept of *aan-*

passing: accommodation to a new reality. This was a form of behaviour common to Dutch coalition and consensus politics in the pre-war era, but it can be used also to characterise the reaction of the population at large to German occupation. In the early period of occupation, this can be linked with another concept, that of *attentisme*: a policy of wait-and-see. With Britain on the verge of collapse and the Germans apparently winning on all fronts, this was a sensible and pragmatic response to a situation that showed no signs of changing for the foreseeable future.

Accommodation and *attentisme* became less sustainable for the civil servants, as German ideological and economic demands on the Netherlands increased later in the occupation and an overall Nazi victory seemed less assured. However, the vast majority of the civil servants chose, for primarily pragmatic reasons, to stay in post. Trading a regular income, social status and a guaranteed pension for the uncertainties of unemployment was not done lightly.[22] Civil servants who retired or chose to go were succeeded by more 'reliable' individuals, usually by members of one of the indigenous Dutch national socialist parties. In addition, the Germans also engaged in a policy of dismissing functionaries felt to be obstructing their wishes. Mayors and other, lower ranking, administrators were replaced if their conduct was suspect. In this way, the Dutch administration of 1943 had a character rather different from the one inherited by the Germans in 1940. Moreover, the attitude of the Dutch government-in-exile also changed. On 13 May 1943, Radio Oranje broadcast a message aimed specifically at civil servants that revoked their 1937 instructions. How the civil servants still in post were supposed to react to this change was not made clear.

There were, therefore, plenty of committed Dutch national socialist collaborators doing their best to meet the wishes of the German occupiers and fulfil their own ideological ambitions. More complex are the cases of individuals in key positions who did not share the ideological perspective of the Nazis, but who were nonetheless prepared to carry out their duties over and above the expressed wishes of the Seyss-Inquart regime. Two case studies, each in some way linked to the successful Nazi persecution of the Jews in the Netherlands, again provide an appropriate focus.

The first of these is Sybren Tulp, a former colonial soldier and Dutch National Socialist Party (NSB) member. In the aftermath of the February strike of 1941, the German administration decided on a series of changes to leading administrative personnel in Amsterdam. The long-serving mayor W. de Vlugt was replaced by the Germanophile E. J. Voûte and Tulp was appointed to replace Chief of Police H. J. Versteeg.[23] Both replacements were seen as more 'reliable' and amenable to German policy aims. Thus it should not be surprising that their attitudes were more accommodating; but, in the case of Tulp, it appears that some of his actions in relation to the persecution of Jews exceeded the expectations even of his German masters. Tulp's appointment had been made to counteract what was perceived to be an increasingly anti-German tendency within the Amsterdam police force.[24] To the Germans, he seemed like an ideal appointment. Outgoing and jovial, albeit with a certain distance from his subordinates, he was potentially capable of winning over the police to the National Socialist cause. His career included periods of service in Suriname and as military commander in Batavia. Ill-health forced his retirement in 1938, but by that time he had some clearly formulated socially conservative and anti-democratic ideas that were reinforced by what he found on returning to the Netherlands, and by a six-month visit to Germany and Italy during 1939.[25]

His attitudes were nonetheless something of a mixture. Although he became a Dutch National Socialist Party (NSB) member in The Hague, he did not adopt a high profile and was less than impressed with Anton Mussert as party leader. Conversely, he had unlimited admiration for Hitler, and for Rauter, who had, he felt, a soldier's mentality and preached a form of camaraderie and iron discipline which Tulp found appealing. He also believed in a coming political struggle that would result in major changes across Europe and the creation of a new authoritarian political order.[26]

He was probably surprised, however, to have been recommended to Rauter as a candidate to head the Amsterdam police. As a pensioned army officer he had no need for a second career in spite of being only 50 years of age, but was delighted to be given a post of importance.[27] There is no record of what discussions took place between Rauter and Tulp when the latter was appointed in April 1941 or of what instructions the new appointee was given, but it is clear from subsequent events that he had some clear ideas on what, in organisational terms, he wished to achieve.[28] In line with practice common inside the Third Reich, Tulp's main aim was to establish the parameters of the role that the Amsterdam police would play in the new order. In that respect, the main competition came from the German police, both *Ordnungspolizei* and *Sipo*–SD, stationed in the Netherlands. Thus, from the beginning, Tulp jealously guarded the work done by his men, and was keen to volunteer his organisation and his men for any new tasks which Rauter dictated. In this case, Tulp was effectively in competition with another branch of the security apparatus, also controlled by Rauter, but struggles for competence were to frame many of his later actions.

The first example of Tulp's assiduousness came in September 1941 when Rauter, in an attempt to wrest control of the Jewish question from Seyss-Inquart, used an existing agreement that allowed him to issue decrees in protection of public order to forbid Jews from moving house or from entering public buildings. Although the decree was ill-thought-out and deemed unenforceable by the Justice Ministry, Tulp instructed his officers to apply the decree to the letter,[29] only to have to rescind his orders when his own men did not comply, and the Germans themselves set the measure aside.[30] Although this episode led to Seyss-Inquart seeking and receiving an assurance directly from Hitler that he, as Reichskommissar, was still in charge of measures against the Jews, the struggle for responsibility and for specific roles continued. In this, Tulp continued to support his superior, Rauter, and to do everything possible to involve the *Amsterdamse Politiekorps* in anti-Semitic actions. This was in spite both of the uneasiness of many of his officers about being given this role and of the German leadership's unwillingness to involve him in the decision-making process. This pattern continued into 1942, with Tulp apparently desperate to the win the patronage of his German masters and to convince them of the Politiekorps' trustworthiness and loyalty to the new regime. In the Spring of 1942, when measures against the Jews were stepped up, Tulp was again in the forefront, setting up an Office for Jewish Affairs within his organisation. Yet, in spite of his enthusiasm, he was informed of the deportation programme only in late June 1942, perhaps three weeks before it began.

The development of the deportation process also demonstrated Tulp's commitment to his task. When it became apparent that sending instructions by post to Jews to report for deportation would not produce results, German police were sent to make arrests. A week after this began, the Amsterdam police were given the task of delivering the call-up papers by hand, but it remained the German police who enforced the measures with arrests and raids on selected neighbourhoods. Tulp was clearly unhappy with this turn of events, but his manpower resources had been depleted in the summer of 1942 and he was not in a position to demand more work. As the task of rounding up Jews became more onerous in the late summer, the Germans were ultimately forced to ask for more help, and, from 2 September onwards, Tulp was able to employ his men five nights a week in arresting Jews and handing them over to the holding centre at the *Hollandsche Schouwburg* or taking them directly to the trains waiting at Amsterdam Central Station.[31] His commitment was such that he could be found at the offices of the *Zentralstelle* almost every evening, encouraging his younger officers; and on 2 October he personally led a raid in which several hundred Jews were arrested. A similar raid planned for the following day was cancelled when Tulp fell ill with a cold. His condition worsened with the onset of rheumatic fever, and he died some three weeks later.[32]

Although he was committed to a conservative form of national socialism and was married to a fanatical supporter of the NSB,[33] there was no indication that Tulp was particularly anti-Semitic or had any specific grievance against the Jews. His one recorded statement on the issue was made prior to the war when he had written of opposition to Germany being fomented by 'international Jewry'.[34] Thus his single-minded pursuit of a major role for his police force in measures against the Jews requires another explanation. Respect for authority (*gezagsgetrouw*) has often been cited as an explanation for much

Dutch bureaucratic behaviour during the occupation, and as a reason for the lack of opposition to German measures. As a former infantry soldier, Tulp possessed this attribute to a high degree, and also had a mentality which made him incapable of doubting the purpose of his superiors. Thus when given by Rauter the task of heading the Amsterdam police, he did his best to fulfil the confidence of his masters, even in the power struggles within the regime. He seems to have discovered Rauter's interest in measures against the Jews not through direct negotiation, but via a process of elimination. By submitting requests for involvement in a range of policy issues, Tulp discovered the predilections of his boss by noting those which gained some positive response. Thus he became aware of Rauter's priorities without being told explicitly what they were.[35]

In sum, Tulp could be seen as the classic functionary of the National Socialist State, but his precise motivation is more difficult to discover. In some respects his can be seen as the obvious behaviour of someone imbued with respect for authority, institutional competence and thoroughness – traits not uncommon among the Dutch bureaucratic classes. His ideological commitment to ational socialism, while evident, was less important than his championing of the role of the Amsterdam Politiekorps *vis-à-vis* the German Ordnungspolizei.[36] In identifying the advantages for SS men of 'working towards the Führer', Kershaw has argued that they brought opportunities for institutional expansion, power, prestige and enrichment.[37] Perhaps there were elements of Tulp pursuing power and prestige when it came to second-guessing the wishes of Rauter but it is more likely that his actions were an inversion of the first factor, of resisting the institutional expansion of German agencies by showing that tasks could be better carried out by the Dutch themselves.

While it cannot be claimed with certainty that the involvement of the Amsterdam police in the rounding up of Jews in the city made a material difference to the, ultimately, very high levels of Jewish mortality in the Netherlands during the occupation, their role was certainly seen as central by the less-than-impartial former Sipo–SD chief in Amsterdam, Willi Lages. Writing after the war he noted: 'The main support of the German forces in the police sector and beyond was the Dutch police. Without it, not 10 per cent of the German occupation tasks would have been fulfilled … Also it would have been practically impossible to seize even 10 per cent of Dutch Jewry without them.'[38]

A second example of 'working towards the Führer' can be seen in an individual who had *no* apparent background in the principles of National Ssocialism and did *not* owe his advancement to the occupiers. This was Jacobus Lambertus Lentz who, since 1936, had been the chief inspector for population registration in the Netherlands. Described as 'an exceptionally diligent and exceptionally capable' civil servant,[39] he began his career as a lowly clerk in 1913 and rose through the ranks of the Population Registry.[40] A government decision to improve the nature of population registration in 1928 led to the creation of the post of inspector, to which Lentz was appointed in 1929.[41] In 1932, his department was transferred from the Central Bureau for Statistics to the Ministry of the Interior and this allowed Lentz the freedom to impose new standards on population registration across the country, encapsulated in a decree of 1936. This involved a complete card index for each individual in the entire population, held by the municipality in which he or she resided and containing basic information such as addresse, date of birth, family ties and religious affiliation.

For this work, Lentz was awarded a Knighthood of the Order of Oranje-Nassau, and he could doubtless have afforded to rest on his laurels in spite of being in only his early forties. However, his ambitions went beyond guaranteeing accurate registration, as he developed ideas about identity cards that would carry an individual's details and photograph. These could be used for all manner of purposes: to facilitate commercial or monetary transactions, to assure identification for benefit recipients and to reduce fraud, and, more morbidly, to identify the victims of road-traffic accidents and suicides.[42] Discussed by an interdepartmental commission in March 1939, the scheme was strongly recommended but sidelined by the fourth (conservative-confessional) Colijn cabinet which needed a simpler system to facilitate rationing in the event of war.[43] Discussed again by the de Geer cabinet in March 1940, the introduction of such cards, which perceived every citizen as a potential criminal, was seen by this more liberal administration as contrary to the traditions of Dutch society.[44] Lentz saw the thwarting of his ambitions as a symbol of the bankruptcy of all the country's political parties and of parliamentary democracy. He even turned to politics himself and founded his own party, the *Nederlands Volksgemeenschap*, but this attracted no more than 200 members.

Lentz's background and pre-war career demonstrate that his subsequent cooperation with the Germans was driven not by ideological persuasion or by loyalty to those who had promoted him, but by a desire for technocratic perfection. That this could be achieved only by rejecting parliamentary democracy was merely a side issue. He saw the German victory in the west as an opportunity to put into practice ideas that had been rejected by pre-war Dutch governments. His opportunity came when the SD 'requested' that the Dutch instigate a system of identity cards.[45] The secretaries-general of the Justice and Interior Ministries decided that although the measure had been rejected only a few months before, it would now be of benefit in ensuring their prime consideration: the maintenance of law and public order. In a book published to explain the structure and workings of his system, Lentz made quite clear his view that the introduction of identity papers (*persoonsbewijzen*), which he said had been actively discussed in the Netherlands since 1927, was a natural extension of the need for order in modern society.[46]

In August 1940, he was sent to Berlin for five days, taking with him examples of documents to discuss with the Germans, who had themselves

introduced a system of *Kennkarte* in 1939.[47] The Germans were impressed
by what they saw, and thought Lentz's scheme better than their own. In the
first instance, however, his system had to use existing passports or ration cards
with photographs affixed, as it was estimated that a complete reform would
take more than a year to introduce.[48] In the meantime, Lentz set to work to
create a sophisticated identity card using watermarked paper, and containing
a photograph and fingerprint. His apparent obsession with fraud ensured
that the cards were made as forgery-proof and as difficult to alter as possible.
In addition, he established a control system which involved having all the
information on the identity documents replicated on cards held at a central
location.

During the post-war investigation of his conduct, Lentz claimed that the
information his system made available to the Germans could be found in other
lists and registers, but the comprehensive nature and centralised accessibility
of his card index undoubtedly made it far more useful. Indeed, he is on record
as having argued against moving the central card index to the east of the country specifically because of its importance to the Sipo–SD, the Ordnungspolizei
and the administration.[49] Although theoretically remaining under the control
of Karel Frederiks, the secretary-general of the Interior Ministry, it seems likely
that this chain of command was by-passed as German instructions to Lentz
were increasingly sent direct and no longer received formal approval from the
secretary-general, although it is clear that he knew of their contents.[50]

There is no doubting the impact of Lentz's system on everyday life in the
occupied Netherlands. The identity cards were used to control the issue of
ration cards; they also limited movement, as individuals were subject to spot-
checks by the security forces. Jews had their cards marked with a capital 'J'.
Early forgeries and fraud, even if superficially convincing, could be detected by
reference to the central records, making it difficult for Jews to avoid the authorities and to maintain a day-to-day existence. More organised resistance networks against forced labour ran into similar problems, as thousands of people
tried to go into hiding from late 1942 onwards. As a former civil servant who
escaped to London during the war described it, the central collection of 5.5
million cards for all the Dutch men and women above the age of 15 was an
eldorado for the Gestapo–SD and the police, containing all manner of information, photographs and fingerprints.[51] Realising that forged cards would
never be entirely effective, the resistance ultimately concentrated its efforts on
stealing blank cards – often with the connivance of local officials – and destroy-
ing local population records. The most famous examples of such actions were
the resistance attack on the Amsterdam Population Registry in March 1943
and the RAF bombing raid on Lentz's headquarters in The Hague on 11 April
1944.[52] Neither was entirely successful, but both inflicted severe material
damage to some records. Increasingly, Lentz found it difficult to control the

staff in the provincial population registration offices as they adopted a less-and-less cooperative attitude towards the occupying power,[53] and he himself became a target for the resistance. From early 1943 onwards, he was repeatedly denounced in the underground press and received a series of death-threats. He undoubtedly knew of the dangers his system carried, as its potential for promoting schemes on racial hygiene had been pointed out at the International Demographic Congress in 1937, which Lentz attended.[54] However, he remained incapable of seeing beyond the perfection of his system to the detrimental effects it was having on 'Dutch' (resistance) interests, and reacted with horror to any idea that it might be better if the records were destroyed.[55]

He also seems to have possessed a political naivety when it came to showing what his system could do. This naivety extended to using data from the card indexes to compile a list of all the surnames in the Netherlands that might be 'Jewish' and then presenting this work of scholarship to Generalkommissar Wimmer – a perfectly rational thing for a proud and ambitious civil servant to do, save for the fact that Wimmer's own family name appeared in the list. He survived this potentially dangerous *faux-pas*, but the threats from the resistance led him to submit his resignation. Rauter refused to accept Lentz's request but gave him a bodyguard. By August 1944, Lentz was a mental wreck. Still technically in post, he had long since ceased to be effectual. In de Jong's words: 'There Lentz stayed, broken and trembling, chained to a system which he had created with so much devotion, satisfaction and bureaucratic obtuseness some four years earlier.'[56]

Under other circumstances, his single-minded pursuit of the perfect system might have been seen as the hallmark of the first-rate civil servant; but in the context of the occupation, Lentz effectively handed a potent weapon to the occupiers. De Jong portrays him as a 'martinet *in optima forma*',[57] a man who was undoubtedly pro-German but not a National Socialist, a dry perfectionist, driven by his work, who was largely estranged from the world around him. His work was in effect his life, and he could often be found working half the night.[58] After his death, family and some former-colleagues painted a different picture, one of a man who was both intelligent and charming, and who threw himself into his work as his marriage foundered.[59] However, the image of one retreating into perfection at work when his social life is imperfect may be a case of reversing cause and effect.

For Lentz, the German occupation was of importance only insofar as it allowed him to realise his bureaucratic ambitions free from the structures and strictures of democratic government. There is also no indication that he was particularly anti-Semitic, and he seems to have railed against Jews only insofar as they attempted to avoid or undermine his system, by not registering or by using stolen or forged identity papers in attempts to go underground and avoid deportation.[60] His compilation of 'Jewish' surnames can therefore be seen as a demonstration of what could be done with his system rather than the act of a convinced anti-Semite.

Arrested on 20 May 1945, Lentz was brought to trial in March 1947.[61] The charges laid were very specific ones: allowing the Germans access to the population registries; assisting the process of finding workers for labour service in Germany by using the ration-card system; and colluding with the infamous 'second' ration-card issue in 1943. The specificity of the charges may have been to protect his superiors, especially former Secretary-General Frederiks, who should also have been in the dock according to the press.[62] The trial itself shed little further light on Lentz's motivation, and all the statements made both by Lentz and by witnesses have to be seen as coloured by the nature of the post-war purging process (*zuivering*) carried out by the Dutch State. Former Secretary-General Frederiks described Lenz as a 'very capable, but single minded (*eenzijdig*) civil servant' who had one great fault,[63] that he was 'wedded to his work'.[64] One of his subordinates noted the frequency with which Lenz was told in meetings that he was going too far, but he chose to ignore the advice.[65] In his own writings, Lentz portrays himself as one who was given tasks to perform rather than as an active and willing participant.[66] In a statement to the police he claimed simply: 'In my job, I repeatedly came in contact with German authorities. I admit that I co-operated (*samengewerkt*) with the Germans in the course of my job ... I was never pro-German, I have never been interested in politics. As a civil servant I felt it my duty to carry out my assigned tasks properly (*naar behoren*).'[67] He also claimed that his categorising of certain '*mischlinge*', on his own initiative, had saved them from anti-Semitic measures, and that he fought German attempts to coordinate his office with their operations.[68] Moreover, he was keen to point out where his actions had (supposedly) saved people, for example in restricting the extension of compulsory labour service for women and girls.[69] He even claimed to have received three separate envelopes containing letters from the Dutch government-in-exile that in 'flattering' terms condoned his work and his actions (*beleid*).[70] No trace of these testimonials was found after the war. At his trial, in a long summation, his defence lawyer's main claim was that Lentz had been used by his superiors.[71] In spite of all this, on 1 April 1947, he was found guilty and sentenced to three years, although the prosecutor had asked for twelve. The leniency of the court was explained by his former good conduct and the fact that he had not been given adequate or proper direction, a clear statement that the judges did think others equally culpable.[72] Certainly, even some of those who gave evidence against him thought that he was something of a scapegoat, and while others had been able to cloak their activities under the aegis of superiors, Lentz had operated under his own name in and in the clear light of day.[73]

How useful is the notion of 'working towards the Führer' in understanding the nature of German rule in the occupied Netherlands? Certainly, it seems that the *coterie* of Austrian and German functionaries sent to govern the country brought with them their experiences of working in the Hitler State. Creating practical programmes on the basis of outline policies, often with no specific order or guidance from the centre, was not a novelty. Competition between agencies, overlapping jurisdictions and rivalries between individuals were also nothing new, and these same attributes of the regime inside Germany were imported wholesale by the Netherlands. Thus it is hardly surprising to find Seyss-Inquart and his four Generalkommissare generally working towards what they perceived to be the objectives of Hitler's National Socialism, but at the same time trying to impress and obey the instructions of their immediate superiors in Berlin; thus furthering their careers and protecting their own positions from being undermined by their colleagues. This is certainly sustainable in relation to the persecution of the Jews where, within the limits imposed by the need for stability and order in Western Europe, a process of cumulative radicalisation can be identified as operating between various leading German functionaries and agencies – each attempting to outdo the others in their assiduous pursuit of the Jewish 'enemy'.

In the case of the Dutch it could be argued that the conduct of both Tulp and Lentz represented a continuation of existing behaviour – of deference to authority and unthinking execution of orders – adapted to changed circumstances. While there are elements in Tulp's previous career and ideological predilections which go some way to explaining his enthusiasm for facilitating the persecution of the Jews in the Netherlands, the same cannot be said of Lentz. For him, none of the categories of career, power, prestige, or institutional expansion have much meaning. Politically naive, devoted to his work and seemingly unaware of the consequences of a perfect population registration and identity-card system, his unquestioning devotion to the pursuit of technocratic perfection made him an ideal collaborator – working towards the ideals of the Nazis and their Führer – but in pursuit of a bureaucratic rather than an ideological or personal goal. In that respect, he represents a more sinister trait: a civil servant who has an unquestioning belief in hierarchy and deference to authority, a man who believes that 'orders are orders',[74] and a technocrat uncommitted politically or ideologically but who was apparently able to abandon any moral or ethical consideration in order to perfect the system for which he was responsible. In his statement about his wartime activities, he begins with a reflection on the terrible bombing of his headquarters in 1944, in which he holds the Allies responsible for the deaths of 60 innocent civilians,[75] rather than any comments on the way identity cards had affected Dutch society during the occupation. Even in his cell, after his arrest, Lentz wrote about his wartime career in terms of what he had done '*in het Nederlandsch belang*' (in the interests of the Netherlands),[76] apparently unwilling or unable to see the dividing line between the responsibilities of the conscientious civil servant and the wider interests of the society he was meant to serve.[77]

Notes

The author would like to thank Dick van Galen Last for his hospitality and comments on this chapter, and also the staff of the Nederlands Instituut voor Oorlogsdocumentatie (NIOD) and Café de Zwart for their kind co-operation.

1 Ian Kershaw, '"Working towards the Führer": Reflections on the Nature of the Hitler Dictatorship', *Contemporary European History*, 2:2 (1993), pp. 103–18; reprinted in Ian Kershaw and Moshe Lewin (eds), *Stalinism and Nazism: Dictatorships in Comparison* (Cambridge, 1997), pp. 88–106, and in Christian Leitz (ed.), *The Third Reich* (Oxford, 1999). See also Ian Kershaw, 'Improvised Genocide? The Emergence of the "Final Solution" in the "Warthegau"', *Transactions of the Royal Historical Society*, 6th series, 2 (1992), pp. 51–78.

2 Gerhard Hirschfeld, *Nazi Rule and Dutch Collaboration: The Netherlands under German Occupation, 1940–1945* (Oxford, 1988), pp. 16–19.

3 Hirschfeld, *ibid.*, p. 23, cites statement by Dr H. Piesbergen, head of the Reichskommissar's Chancellery, 12 April 1949, NIOD, Doc. I-1318, a-2.

4 This was not limited to the Generalkommissare, as many other agencies, such as the Foreign Office, Four Year Plan, Economics Ministry and Labour Procurement, also attempted to place within the bureaucracy officials who were mandated to take instruction from their superiors in Berlin rather than from Seyss-Inquart or his subordinates.

5 At this stage, Bormann was chief of staff in the office of Deputy-Führer Rudolf Hess: Hirschfeld, *Nazi Rule*, pp. 24–5.

6 *Ibid.*, p. 29.

7 Louis de Jong, *Het Koninkrijk der Nederlanden in de Tweede Wereldoorlog*, vol. 4: *Mei '40–Mei '41* ('s-Gravenhage, 1972), pp. 694–5; all references to page numbers of this and other volumes of the work come from the popular rather than the academic editions.

8 Peter Romijn, 'De Oorlog, 1940–1945', in J. C. H. Blom, R. G. Fuks-Mansfeld and I. Schöffer (eds), *Geschiedenis van de Joden in Nederland* (Amsterdam, 1995), p. 316; see also Michael Wildt, *Generation des Unbedingten: Das Führungskorps des Reichssicherheitshauptamtes* (Hamburg, 2002), pp. 511–13.

9 Romijn, 'De Oorlog, 1940–1945', p. 317.

10 De Jong, *Het Koninkrijk*, vol. 4, pp. 814–15.

11 Bob Moore, *Victims and Survivors: The Nazi Persecution of the Jews in the Netherlands, 1940–1945* (London, 1997), p. 66.

12 Approximately half the Jews in the Netherands were resident in the City of Amsterdam (*c.*70,000 out of *c.*140,000): see Jos Scheren and Friso Roest, *Oorlog in de Stad: Amsterdam 1939–1941* (Amsterdam, 1998); and Jos Scheren, 'Aryanisation, Market Vendors and Peddlers in Amsterdam', *Journal of Holocaust and Genocide Studies*, 14:3 (2000), pp. 415–29.

13   Joseph Michman, 'Planning for the Final Solution Against the Background of Developments in Holland in 1941', *Yad Vashem Studies*, 17 (1986), p. 148.

14   Jacob Presser, *Ondergang: De Vervolging en Verdelging van het Nederlandse Jodendom, 1940–1945* ('s-Gravenhage, 1977), vol. 2, p. 151.

15   Presser, *ibid.*, p. 151, argues that this harmony extended to the extermination (*uitroeiing*) of the Jews.

16   *Ibid.*, pp. 157–8. For the minutes of one such meeting, see, e.g., NIOD, HSSpF, Archief 114/85a.

17   Wildt, *Generation des Unbedingten*, pp. 610–11.

18   *Ibid.*, p. 693.

19   Hirschfeld, *Nazi Rule*, p. 133: 'Aanwijzingen betreffende de houding aan te nemen doorde bestuursorganen van het rijk … in geval van een vijandelijke inval'.

20   Louis de Jong, *Het Koninkrijk der Nederlanden in de Tweede Wereldoorlog* (13 vols; 's-Gravenhage, 1969–88).

21   For the critics of De Jong's approach see J. C. H. Blom, 'In de ban van goed en fout. Wetenschappelijk geschiedschrijving over de bezettingstijd in Nederland', in G. Abma, Y. Kuiper and J. Rypkema (eds), *Tussen Goed en Fout* (Franeker, 1986), pp. 30–52; Chris van der Heijden, *Grijs Verleden: Nederland en de Tweede Wereldoorlog* (Amsterdam, 2001), and the review of the latter by Ido de Haan, 'Een wereldbeeld in grijstinten', *Vrij Nederland*, 10 March 2001, pp. 62–3. For two recent studies of other senior civil servants during the occupation see: Meindert Fennema, 'Hans Max Hirschfeld, Secretaris-Generaal van een Onthoofd Ministerie', in M. de Keizer, M. Heijmans-van Bruggen and E. Somers (eds), *Onrecht: Oorlog en rechtvaardighei in de twintigste eeuw* (Zutphen, 2001), pp. 152–76; and Peter Romijn, 'Frederiks' "Op de bres": een ambtelijke apologie', in N. J. D. Barnouw *et al.* (eds), *Oorlogsdocumentatie '40–'45 Tiende jaarboek van het NIOD* (Zutphen, 1999), pp. 140–64.

22   J. H. Sikkes, … *In geval van een vijandelijken inval: Ambtelijke verdrag in bezettingstijd en de daarvoor geldende aanwijzingen* (Deventer, 1985), p. 55.

23   *Het Vaderland*, 7 May 1941; Moore, *Victims and Survivors*, p. 201.

24   Guus Meershoek, *Dienaren van het Gezag: De Amsterdamse politie tijdens de bezetting* (Amsterdam, 1999), p. 147.

25   NIOD, Doc. I-1716, Sybren Tulp, 'Levensloop S. Tulp', NSB Persdienst, 23 April 1941.

26   Guus Meershoek, 'De Amsterdamse hoofdcommissaris en de deportatie van de joden', in: N. J. D. Barnouw *et al.* (eds), *Oorlogsdocumentatie '40–'45 Derde jaarboek van het Rijksinstituut voor Oorlogsdocumentatie* (Zutphen, 1992), p. 13. The one complication to Tulp's worldview was his continuing loyalty to Queen Wilhelmina and the Dutch monarchy. For an English version of this article, see Guus Meershoek, 'The Amsterdam Police and the Persecution of the Jews', in Michael Berenbaum and Abraham J. Peck (eds), *The Holocaust and History: The Known, the Unknown, the Disrupted and the Re-Examined* (Bloomington, IN, 1998), pp. 284–300.

27   Meershoek, 'De Amsterdamse hoofdcommissaris', p. 13.

28   Meershoek, *Dienaren*, pp. 150–1.

29   *Ibid.*, pp. 182–3.

30   *Ibid.*, p. 183.

31   Meershoek, 'De Amsterdamse hoofdcommissaris', p. 33.

32   *Ibid.*, p. 35.

33   Meershoek, *Dienaren*, p. 149.

34   Meershoek, 'De Amsterdamse hoofdcommissaris', p. 31; and *Dienaren*, p. 150.

35   Meershoek, 'De Amsterdamse hoofdcommissaris', p. 32.

36   Even colleagues who regarded his collaboration as deserving the death penalty thought that the sentence should be carried out with a golden bullet, in recognition of the leadership and purpose Tulp had given to the Amsterdam police during his period as chief: *Leeuwarder Courant*, 22 February 1992.

37   Kershaw and Lewin, *Stalinism and Nazism*, p. 106.

38   Hirschfeld, *Nazi Rule*, p. 173, cites W. Lages, 'Tweede commentaar op Abel Herzberg's Kroniek der Jodenvervolging', pp. 30f., NIOD, Doc. I-998, O-3; Moore, *Victims and Survivors*, p. 203.

39   De Jong, *Het Koninkrijk*, vol. 5, p. 423.

40   G. H. J. Seegers and M. C. C. Wens, *Persoonlijk gegeven: Grepen uit de geschiedenis van bevolkingsregistratie in Nederland* (Amersfoort, 1993), pp. 83–5.

41   *Ibid.*; see also NIOD, Doc. I-1045, Lentz Map A, Proces-Verbaal, Statement by Lentz to Rechercheur A. de Wever, 22 May 1945.

42   De Jong, *Het Koninkrijk*, vol. 5, p. 424.

43   De Jong, *ibid.*, p. 425, points out that the absence of cabinet minutes makes it impossible to decide if the Colijn Government had any objections of a more principled kind to the scheme; see also J. L. Lentz, *Persoonsbewijzen: Handleiding voor de uitvoering van het besluit persoonsbewijzen* (Arnhem, 1941), p. 7.

44   De Jong, *Het Koninkrijk*, vol. 5, p. 425; Moore, *Victims and Survivors*, p. 196.

45   De Jong, *Het Koninkrijk*, vol. 5, pp. 425–6. The Germans were surprised that, while the Dutch had a sophisticated system of registration, they had not instituted identity cards.

46   Lentz, *Persoonsbewijzen*, pp. 1–2, 6.

47   NIOD, Doc. I-1045, Lentz Map A, J. L. Lentz, 'Ambtelijke Herinneringen', 29 April 1945, pp. 8–9. It is notable that this was written at the end of the occupation but before his arrest, suggesting that he was preparing for an inquiry at which he would have to answer charges about his conduct. In fact, the process had been planned in London in a document dated 24 April 1944: see NIOD, Doc. I-1045, Lentz Map B, Zuivering Bevolkingsregisters GB/5193/44.

48   De Jong, *Het Koninkrijk*, vol. 5, p. 426.

49   *Ibid.*, p. 431.

50   NIOD, Doc. I-1045, Lentz Map A, Proces-Verbaal, Statement by Johannes Kan to Opsporingsambtenaar Putter, 26 September 1945, pp. 1–1a; De Jong, *Het Koninkrijk*, vol. 5, p. 433.

51   NIOD, Doc. I-1045, Lentz Map B, P. J. Koene to Hoofd Bureau Inlichtingen, London, 6 January 1944.

52   De Jong, *Het Koninkrijk*, vol. 6, pp. 714–36, and vol. 7, pp. 797–804; Moore, *Victims and Survivors*, p. 198.

53   De Jong, *Het Koninkrijk*, vol. 7, p. 618.

54   Seegers en Wens, *Persoonlijk gegeven*, p. 91.

55 De Jong, *Het Koninkrijk*, vol. 5, p. 432; Moore, *Victims and Survivors*, p. 198.

56 De Jong, *Het Koninkrijk*, vol. 5, p. 432; see also NIOD, Doc. I-1045, Lentz Map A, Proces-Verbaal, Statement by Adrianus Wilkeshuis to Opsporingsambtenaar Putter, 28 September 1945, p. 6.

57 De Jong, *Het Koninkrijk*, vol. 5, p. 432.

58 *Ibid.* See also NIOD, Doc. I-1045, Proces-Verbaal, Statement by Johannes Kan to Opsporingsambtenaar Putter, 26 September 1945.

59 *Het Parool*, 2 April 1947.

60 Lentz had been brought up in The Hague, close to the Jewish quarter of that city. There is some evidence that he acted as a Sabbath *goy* in his youth: *Het Vrije Volk*, 20 April 1974. NIOD, Doc. I-1045, Lentz Map A, Proces-Verbaal, Statement by Johannes Roelin to Opsporingsambtenaar Putter, 12 October 1945, p. 28, in which Roelin claimed that Lentz did have a hatred for the Jews, but then quotes an example of the Jews trying to undermine the bureaucratic principles of his system.

61 Seegers en Wens, *Persoonlijk gegeven*, p. 100.

62 Frederiks had been allowed to retire without a blemish on his character or his record as a civil servant, something which many press commentators found abhorrent, especially when Frederiks appeared as a witness in Lentz' trial: see, e.g., *Het Ochtendpost*, 8 March 1947.

63 NIOD, Doc. I-1045, Lentz Map A, Proces-Verbaal, Statement by Karel Johannes Frederiks to Opsporingsambtenaar Putter, 1 October 1945, p. 7.

64 *Trouw*, 19 March 1947.

65 *Ibid.*

66 NIOD, Doc. I-1045, Lentz Map A, J. L. Lentz, 'Wat ik in de oorlogsjaren 1940–1945 deed in het Nederlandsch belang' (undated MS), pp. 3–6.

67 NIOD, Doc. I-1045, Lentz Map A, Proces-Verbaal, Statement Lentz to Rechercheur A. de Wever, 22 May 1945.

68 NIOD, Doc. I-1045, Lentz Map A, J. L. Lentz, 'Wat ik in oorlogsjaren 1940–1945 deed', p. 8.

69 *Ibid.*, p. 10.

70 NIOD, Doc. I-1045, Lentz Map A, J. L. Lentz, 'Ambtelijke Herinneringen', 29 April 1945, p. 55.

71 *Trouw*, 19 March 1947. For the full text of the defence summation see NIOD, Doc, I-1045, Lentz Map C, Strafzaak tegen J. L. Lentz, 18 March 1947, pp. 157–90, especially p. 166.

72 NIOD, Doc. I-1045, Lentz Map A, Na-Oorlogsche Rechtspraak 1947, no. 835 Zaak Lentz, 1 April 1947, p. 273. *Het Parool*, 2 April 1947. The editors also took the view that although the sentence was just, Lentz had been something of a scapegoat, and the trial left a 'sour and bitter after-taste'.

73 NIOD, Doc. I-1045, Lentz Map A, Proces-Verbaal, Statement by JosephReuser, 18 December 1945, p. 54.

74 NIOD, Doc. I-1045, Lentz Map A, Proces-Verbaal, Statement by Johannes Kan to Opsporingsambtenaar Putter, 26 September 1945, p. 1a; Statement by Karel Johannes Frederiks, 1 October 1945, p. 7.

75 NIOD, Doc. I-1045, Lentz Map A, J. L. Lentz, 'Ambtelijke Herinneringen', 29 April

1945, p. 1. An unknown commentator, possibly Louis de Jong himself, has written '100,000 Jews!' next to Lentz's statement about the victims of the bombing.

76 NIOD, Doc. I-1045, Lentz Map A, J. L. Lentz, 'Wat ik in oorlogsjaren 1940–1945 deed', p. 1.

77 NIOD, Doc. I-1045, Lentz Map A, Proces-Verbaal, 26 September 1945, pp. 16, 24. See, e.g., statements by Jan Minkhorst (12 October 1945), and Jacob de Goede (19 October 1945), to Opsporingsambtenaar Putter.

8

Working towards the Reich: the reception of German cultural politics in South-Eastern Europe

Tim Kirk

I have dreamed of man's estate, of his courteous and enlightened social state; behind which in the temple, the horrible blood sacrifice was consummated. Were they, those children of the sun, so sweetly courteous to each other, in silent recognition of that horror? It would be a fine and right conclusion they drew. (Hans Castorp in Thomas Mann, *The Magic Mountain*)

The German 'new order' in Europe during the Second World War was enforced by brutal occupation policies. It was characterised chiefly by plunder, the exploitation of slave labour recruited from the populations of occupied countries and, above all, by the consequences of the Nazis' racial agenda: the mass-murder of the Jews and the forced displacement of native populations to make room for German settlement. Hitler and the Nazi leadership scarcely thought it worthwhile trying to disguise the nature or intentions of the new continental regime. Yet, as in the Reich, the occupation regimes represented a broader coalition of forces – state, party, military, business, and not least local collaborators – each with distinct and often conflicting or contradictory interests. As often as not, those who 'worked towards the Führer' in occupied Europe, no less than in Germany itself, worked against each other. The misery of a repressive occupation or the brutalities of 'resettlement' were compounded by what Ian Kershaw has described as the 'systemlessness' of the governance and administration that characterised the Nazi dictatorship, and was now exported from the Reich to occupied Europe.[1]

There were nevertheless those, both in Berlin and abroad, who had a longer term perspective and planned for a permanent post-liberal authoritarian order. Those who believed – or at least affected to believe – in the reality of a stable post-war Europe under the domination of Nazi Germany now, during the war itself, set about establishing new relationships with the local elites in capital cities across the Continent. These were people for whom the 'horrible blood sacrifice' of the war was in the service of a new civilisation, whose role it was to create and maintain a climate of opinion sympathetic to the Reich and its objectives. For, like other imperial powers, Germany wanted to reinforce its military presence, political authority and economic clout with a broader cultural influence, and was sensitive, moreover, to how that cultural influence was received. More than any of the other belligerents, Germans, whether employed by the State or by private associations and companies, were engaged in a wide range of cultural and educational activities both in the occupied countries and in the nominally independent, or neutral, states. These activities encompassed several broad spheres of interest: firstly, educational and academic work through newly established institutes and exchanges, but also directly through local schools and universities; secondly, the promotion of German achievements in the arts through concert tours, art exhibitions, book fairs, theatre performances and film – the sort of routine activity which had begun in peacetime and continued after the war; and, thirdly, the more determined promotion of Nazi political values in the cultural milieu and institutions of the host country. German observers monitored and commented on the reception of the Reich's efforts in education, culture and propaganda, and also reported on a range of other areas, such as religion, youth movements, sport and leisure activities, and 'racial hygiene' (*Volksgesundheit*). A number of agencies and organisations, ranging from the armed forces, the SD and the Nazi Party to private companies and individuals, reported back to the Reich from the Balkans. Among the most detailed reports are those filed with the *Gaugrenzlandamt Niederdonau* in Vienna. They comprised a regular digest of the region's press, along with analyses of political developments, public opinion, economic trends and cultural events in the Balkans between 1941 and 1944, and reflected the changing relationship between German 'protectors' and local elites, as local perspectives shifted from enthusiasm for the 'new Europe' to evasion and rejection as the tide of the war turned.[2]

The focus of this chapter is the assessment by German observers of local responses to German cultural activity in one part of the Continent: South-Eastern Europe. The Balkans, from Slovakia and Hungary in Central Europe to Turkey in the 'Near-East', was a region composed largely of nominally independent states allied to the Axis, and was to play a significant role in the construction of the Nazi 'new order'. It had long been seen as a region for potential German economic penetration and political domination. A century earlier Friedrich List and the 'historical school' of German economists had decried the loss to Germany of human resources and expertise represented by emigration to North America, and recommended instead a migration of Germans into the Balkans, such as had taken place during the eighteenth century. (His ideas were selectively revived and given a contemporary resonance by the ideologues of the Nazi 'new order'.[3]) The goal of a German-led *Mitteleuropa*, extending into the Balkans and dominating the Middle-East, had been revived prior to and during the First World War, and had been a concomitant of German proposals for an economic union with Austria–Hungary.[4] The defeat of the Central Powers in 1918 put an end for the time being to German ambitions in South-Eastern Europe, but both Italy and Germany were able to exploit revisionism in the region both among those who had lost territory (Hungary and Bulgaria) and among those who aspired to independent nationhood (Croatia and Slovakia). Moreover, the authoritarian right-wing politicians of the region looked on Italian Fascism and Nazism with some admiration.

During the mid 1930s German trade with South-Eastern Europe increased as the Reich attempted to lay the practical foundations of a 'greater economic area' (*Großraumwirtschaft*) by developing bilateral trade agreements with the region's ailing economies, and thereby seeking to absorb them into a German-dominated sub-continental economic system. Germany's strategy was to import the region's surplus primary products in return for German goods, but the Balkan states became impatient with Berlin's unwillingness to pay in hard currency or even deliver the goods they promised, and by 1938 the trade had started to contract. Moreover, the Balkan states had, to some extent, managed to circumvent dependence on Germany by maintaining trading links with Western Europe.[5] After the *Anschluss*, however, German economic – and political – influence was reinforced. Border areas with German-speaking populations were annexed directly – in western Czechoslovakia in 1938, Poland in 1939, and northern Yugoslavia in 1941, each time amid the political rhetoric of revisionism and self-determination. When the territories of 'Lower Styria', 'South Carinthia' and 'Upper Carniola' were incorporated directly into the existing *Gaue* of Styria and Carinthia in 1941, the occasion was celebrated as a homecoming. Marburg an der Drau (the Slovene Maribor) was a jewel in the crown of the Reich, according to the *Westdeutscher Beobachter*, while the *Danziger Neueste Nachrichten* reported from the 'liberated' district that the Mieß (Meža) valley was once again part of Carinthia. It remained, the *Kärntner Grenzruf* reported, only for the inhabitants of the 'liberated' Mießtal to learn German.[6]

Beyond these directly incorporated areas the Balkans experienced the whole range of political arrangements deployed by Germany in wartime Europe. Italy annexed southern Slovenia and much of Dalmatia directly. Puppet states were set up in Slovakia and Croatia (including most of Bosnia and Hercegovina), part of the latter also falling within Italy's nominal sphere of influence, as – *de facto* – did the territories acquired by Albania and Montenegro (which became an Italian protectorate) in Kosovo and Metohija. Hungary acquired territory in the western Vojvodina, along with territory from Slovenia and Croatia. Bulgaria annexed much of Macedonia and a strip of eastern Serbia. The rest of Serbia ('*Altserbien*') was declared an exclusively German sphere of influence and placed under military rule, along with the eastern part of Vojvodina (the Banat).[7] Three Axis powers (Germany, Italy and Bulgaria) and local collaborators shared responsibility for the government of Greece.[8] These were not the only boundary changes: under the terms of the two Vienna awards Hungary acquired southern Ruthenia from Slovakia and northern Transylvania from Romania. This was a partial restoration to Hungary of the territory lost after the First World War, just as the territory lost to Germany and Austria had been restored to the Reich.[9] The occupying powers sought to match ethnic boundaries with the new national frontiers. Germany planned, for example, to remove over 250,000 Slovenes, one-third of the entire Slovene population of the incorporated areas, in order to make room for 80,000 German settlers, while those remaining would be 'Germanised'. The upheavals of war prevented the full implementation of the plans, and in practice only 80,000 were expelled and only 14,000 Germans settled. The Hungarians pursued a similar policy, and it was only in the Italian-occupied Ljubljana province that a more restrained policy was applied.[10] Many of the displaced inhabitants of South-Eastern Europe were recruited, with a greater or lesser degree of compulsion, to work in the fields and factories in Germany, although fewer were enlisted from the Balkans than from Poland and the Soviet Union.[11] The most brutal displacement was the deportation and mass-murder of the Jewish population, first and most completely in those areas where the Germans were in more or less direct control, such as Yugoslavia. Jews in Slovakia survived longer, and the Hungarians resisted German pressure until 1944.[12]

'Racial policy' and 'resettlement' underlined the Nazis' determination to establish a formal empire rather than merely to gain political influence and economic advantage, although the discussion of those imperial objectives was couched in pseudo-constitutional terms. A new kind of international relations was posited to replace existing international law, with its supposedly outmoded liberal notions of nominal equality between sovereign nations. The nation state (*Volksraum*) would give way to a *Großraum* encompassing a number of related nations (*Völkerfamilie*) under the leadership of a '*Führungsvolk*'.[13] The Nazis were the heirs to the annexationists of the First World War, and many of the middle-class Germans who had supported Germany's war aims now saw the new expansion as something of a career opportunity: whether in business or administration, it meant 'jobs and influence, pomp and circumstance'.[14]

The *Südosteuropa-Gesellschaft* (SOEG), established in Vienna on 8 February 1940, sought to co-ordinate German interests in the Balkans. An early instance of the decentralised administration of an anticipated post-war German-dominated Großraum, it was a state agency masquerading as a private society, under the auspices of Walther Funk and the Reich Economics Ministry, by which it was funded. Its first president, Josef Bürckel, Reich commissioner for the unification of Austria with the German Reich, was replaced by Baldur von Schirach in August 1940. August Heinrichsbauer was its executive secretary. The society represented the ambitions of the Economics Ministry in territory properly still within the remit of the Reich Foreign Ministry, and it also had ambitions in the sphere of cultural politics. It was an embodiment of the institutional proliferation and factional rivalry that characterised the politics of the Nazi dictatorship. Relations with Ribbentrop very quickly became tense. In particular the Foreign Ministry managed to thwart the society's plans to establish a cultural association, the Prince Eugene Society (after the Austrian military leader of the 'reconquest' of the Balkans following the failed Turkish siege of Vienna in the late seventeenth century). It was only later that a less controversial working group on cultural policy (*Kulturpolitischer Arbeitskreis*) was established, ostensibly to deal with matters relating to German minorities in the Balkans. From 1942, when the group began to meet regularly as a committee, it became directly involved in organising cultural activity in the region, such as travelling exhibitions, tours by the companies of the Burgtheater and the Theater in der Josefstadt, and performances by the Vienna Philharmonic. The society also launched a number of publications, including a regular journal of cultural affairs that was published in the various languages of the Balkan states.[15]

The cultural activities undertaken in the Balkans under the auspices of the Südosteuropagesellschaft were only a part of the Reich's cultural diplomacy in the region. The role of culture in the construction of the 'new order' was a subsidiary one, but was important nevertheless, in that German cultural authority both underpinned the Reich's political presence and made sense of it too. Cultural anxiety had been fundamental to the common project which united the political right since the turn of the century. For conservatives the political threat from the 'masses' was associated with a broader cultural crisis represented by popular culture, on the one hand (pulp fiction, the mass-circulation press, cinema, and the music hall), and the 'cultural bolshevism' of 'degenerate' avant-garde modernism, on the other. The perceived triumph of commercial culture and American values during the 1920s constituted a cultural defeat for German values, and was seen by many on the Right as a metaphor for the political disaster of the revolutions that followed the First World War.[16] These anxieties were by no means restricted to Germany: they were shared by cultural conservatives across Europe. Cultural envoys from the Reich found that their own views on culture were shared by the local establishment in most of the many authoritarian right-wing states of the Balkans.[17] The defence of a 'traditional' or 'healthy' European culture, or cultures – the classical canon of the humanist gymnasium for the educated middle classes, and folk-culture for the people – was a basis on which an understanding could be built between Germany and its client states; and German scholars were as keen to map the cultures of the Balkans as they were to chart its terrain.[18]

Culture was also a forum for international competition, and in this respect the Nazis in the Balkans were both anticipating their Cold War successors and building on the experience of earlier ventures. Cultural diplomacy was still a relatively recent phenomenon in the second quarter of the twentieth century, but the feeling that military might alone would not suffice to sustain a claim to international greatness was not new. Friedrich von Bernhardi devoted a chapter of his book on Germany and the coming war to Germany's historical cultural mission. In the chapter immediately preceding his famous essay on 'world power or downfall', Bernhardi cited Treitschke to support his argument that Germany had made a unique and unparalleled contribution to Western civilisation and had a unique historical mission to fulfil. As a precedent, he referred admiringly to the example of the British empire and its 'supreme national self-confidence', and quoted approvingly Lord Rosebery, speaking at the Royal Colonial Institute in 1893: 'We have to remember that it is part of our responsibility and heritage to take care that the world, so far as it can be moulded by us, should receive the Anglo-Saxon and not another character.'[19] The assertion by Germany and the West of rival claims to cultural superiority was an important part of the international antagonism that culminated in the First World War. Prior to 1914 there had been a wider discussion about the need to match Germany's bid for world power with a cultural claim to international greatness.[20] Both before and during the First World War official German propaganda and conservative intellectuals made much of the superiority of German *Kultur* over Western *Zivilisation*. The democracies had responded in kind, and during the war had portrayed Germany as the very antithesis of a cultured nation. After that war it was felt in Berlin that Germany had been unable to prevent the charges of barbarism from sticking, and that there was a need to promote German culture in a positive light. Moreover, relations with France were then still strained, if not openly hostile, and there was a great deal of pressure to compete with the French, who were leaders in the new field of cultural diplomacy. To that end a cultural section was established in the German Foreign Office in 1919.

From the outset international cultural contacts were conceived as a matter for national cultural elites, and were initially a matter of educational and academic exchanges, on the one hand, and the promotion of classical German culture, on the other, through concert and theatre tours, art exhibitions, and so on. This organisational framework was broadly comparable with the efforts of other leading powers in the field of cultural diplomacy. Arnold Bergsträsser, a pioneer of student exchanges with America during the 1920s and an important influence in establishing the German Academic Exchange Service (*Deutscher Akademischer Austauschdienst*, DAAD), set out some of the principles and benefits of cultural contact in a theoretical work of 1926: *Sinn und Grenzen der Verständigung zwischen Nationen*. His outlook reflected a conservative perspective: nationalist in the sense of Moeller van der Bruck and elitist in the spirit of Stefan George and Ernst Jünger. The nation was seen as a *Wertungsge-*

meinschaft in which the masses could experience the substance of culture only in so far as it was articulated by an educated elite. Adolf Morsbach, director of the DAAD from 1927, made the acceptance of Bergsträsser's ideas more or less compulsory at briefing sessions for German university students taking up exchanges abroad, and Bergsträsser himself was frequently invited to address them.[21]

After 1933 domestic cultural policy was strengthened and centralised, with the establishment of Goebbels's Ministry of Popular Enlightenment and Propaganda, and the Foreign Office fought a rearguard action against the new ministry, which in 1933 took over responsibility for art exhibitions abroad, along with film and sport;[22] and against the new Reich Education Ministry established under Bernhard Rust in 1934, which took over responsibility for academic contacts abroad. Civil servants also had to contend with Nazi appointees and careerists who saw themselves as modernisers and reformers in institutions they believed to be too stuffy, conservative and ineffectual. Traditionalists in the Foreign Office establishment resented the creeping politicisation of cultural diplomacy. They thought of their own approach as apolitical and sought to preserve a notional distinction between culture and propaganda. In practice their hostility was founded as much on straightforward snobbery as on principle, and was directed as much against the *populism* of the Nazis as against the blurring of a distinctions between politics and culture. According to a leading German official in occupied France, the difference between the type of propaganda favoured by the Nazis and cultural diplomacy proper was to be understood in terms of class: propaganda should be primitive, and aimed at the mass of people, not at a few intellectuals; whereas external cultural policy (*auswärtige Kulturpolitik*) should be so aimed at the intellectual leaders of a foreign country as to avoid giving the impression that they were underestimated, or frightening them off by pitching the level too low.[23] Mentalities had to be changed and the local elites of occupied Europe educated in new ways of thinking and appropriate aesthetic tastes, but not by a direct propaganda assault that insulted the intelligence.

To that end, cultural agreements (*Kulturabkommen*) were established with those countries where the Reich was already pursuing political, economic or strategic interests, as it was in the Balkans from the mid-1930s. The first of these cultural accords was struck with Hungary in 1936, and more were agreed after the outbreak of war – with Bulgaria in 1940, Romania in 1941 and Slovakia in 1942. Such agreements were meant to bolster Germany's presence in the region, by ensuring the promotion of German language teaching in schools and universities, the expansion of cultural contacts, such as exchanges of academics, writers and artists, and the organisation of lecture tours, and concert and theatre performances. Such schemes were not without difficulties. While the German Government was interested in promoting exchanges, German intellectuals were not necessarily particularly interested in all of the partner countries: Hungary, for example, quite apart from the language difficulties, was not seen as having a culture with an intellectual tradition equal to that of Germany.[24] Moreover, Germany was always in competition with other powers. Hungary signed similar agreements with Poland, Italy and Austria. Britain stepped up its cultural diplomacy during the late 1930s, and the British Council established a British Institute in Budapest just after the outbreak of war. A German diplomat reporting on the cultural politics of Bulgaria to the Foreign Office in Berlin in 1938 recommended action to counter the influence of France and Italy in an anti-Communist authoritarian state which was also economically dependent on the Reich, but reluctant to embrace Nazi values. The same envoy also reported from Bucharest, where he found a similar cultural domination by France and Italy: if Romania were to be 'saved' for Germany, a revolution in the methods of cultural policy was needed, bringing to the region institutions comparable with the *Institut Français*.[25] In Berlin the director of the cultural section of the German Foreign Office argued that for Germany to do nothing in this field, while Britain, France and Italy intensified their own activities, was in reality a step backwards, and with the appointment of Ribbentrop as foreign minister in 1938 this line of argument was broadly accepted. In fact, in so far as the neutral countries were concerned, the war raised the stakes of cultural competition and led to an increase in cultural diplomacy on all sides. German academic and cultural institutes – *Deutsche Wissenschaftliche Institute* and *Deutsche Institute* – were set up in Scandinavia, the Balkans and the Iberian peninsula to compete with British and French cultural influence.[26]

In the wake of the German victories of 1940 and 1941 the scope for direct Anglo-German cultural competition was very limited, but was still present in the neutral states. In this respect Turkey is an interesting case. On the periphery of South-Eastern Europe, and a German ally during the First World War, Turkey had been among the earliest testing grounds for cultural diplomacy. German–Turkish associations had been established on the eve of the war, and German university lecturers were appointed to posts in Constantinople in 1916 and 1917.[27] A report from Turkey of December 1943 noted the increase in British cultural influence in Ankara, and commented that the essentially political and propagandistic nature of British cultural diplomacy was particularly striking in the Turkish case. The SD filed an exhaustive report, detailing the pro-British activities of Halide Edip, professor of English at Istanbul University, who – it was claimed – had made the English department there a 'centre of British cultural propaganda' and appointed British staff (including Ronald Syne and Stephen Runcieman, the latter having come to Istanbul as a cultural adviser to the general consul). Moreover, the British Council in Ankara had paid an enormous rent for the interior minister's house, showered the seminar libraries at the university with offers of British and American books, and appeared to have a limitless supply of funds. Its activities, which also included free language lessons and public lectures, the publication of periodicals in English and French, and the promise of an exhibition of Turkish art in London, were held to constitute 'a serious danger' to German influence in Turkey, and a series of thirteen detailed proposals was put forward to remedy the situation, involving not so much direct competition as a strengthening of influence in those areas where Germany was considered still strong. There should be more exhibitions of German engineering, medicine and technology, and closer links with scientists, doctors and engineers. Turkey should be included more often in the lecture tours of the Balkans undertaken by German academics. There should also be more support for the German book trade: subventions for translations into Turkish; lower prices for German magazines; and the commissioning of a German–Turkish dictionary (to match the existing Turkish–German volume). German *Kulturfilme* (documentaries) should be sent to Turkey, where the medium was scarcely known, and Turkish artists should be invited to exhibit in the Reich.[28]

In the Balkans proper, British and French influence were more or less excluded during the war, but a German institute was set up in Bucharest in April 1940, in Belgrade in October of the same year and in Sofia in November.[29] The Balkan states themselves were encouraged to follow the Reich's example by forging their own cultural links. In the spring of 1942, for example, the Romanian press celebrated a cultural agreement with Spain 'with enthusiastic articles about the two nations' common Latin origins', while the presence of a Bulgarian orchestra in Sofia prompted reports that a similar agreement with Bulgaria was in the offing.[30] Similarly, a few days later, Slovakia signed cultural agreements with Japan, Italy, Hungary and Bulgaria, an occasion of great significance for the Slovaks, it was reported, who now felt they had joined the 'first rank of European cultural nations'.[31]

The gushing newspaper commentaries that accompanied such agreements, and the polite reviews that attended the cultural events they generated, concealed enormous political tensions. Much of the region was a war zone, characterised by savage inter-communal violence and partisan warfare; and even where political conditions were less turbulent the path to the new cultural order was far from smooth. German observers were irritated by socialist activity in Hungary, and by the Slovaks' censoring, on religious grounds, of German plays and films. And while they looked approvingly on closer cultural relations between the client states of the region, they were less comfortable with the continuing efforts to secure cultural influence of more serious rivals – above all the Americans (even after the German declaration of war on the USA), but also Fascist Italy and Vichy France. Typically, the flourishing cultural activity of Germany's allies was reported back in neutral tones, but with more than a hint of suppressed anxiety, and the Reich authorities were quick to act if they thought they were losing the advantage. The establishing of the German Institute in Slovakia, for example, followed concern expressed in January 1942 about the intensification there of Italian cultural influence, and the setting up of the Italian Institute in Bratislava (Pressburg). Much of this 'influence' was in fact routine activity, and very similar in nature to some of the things the Germans themselves were doing. Italian academics were seconded as guest-professors in Hungary along with language teachers at university and secondary-school levels. Italian film specialists were also invited to Bratislava following the première of the *The Iron Crown*, which had won the prize for best Italian film in Venice the previous year.[32] Cultural relations between Italy and Hungary were also lively, building as they did on a long-established political relationship. Shortly afterwards a Hungarian cultural institute was opened in Milan, a Hungarian ballet was performed in Rome, talented Hungarian film-actors were sent to Italy and Italian conductors came to Budapest.[33] All this activity was reported back to the Reich in the lengthy '*Kulturberichte Südosteuropa*' – with some concern and an increasing pique: in April 1942, for example, it was reported that despite the recent show in Budapest of Viennese fashions, some Hungarian newspapers had responded to a subsequent Italian show by hailing Turin (*sic*!) as the capital of European fashion.[34]

Worse was to follow. The following year the Hungarian Government made the Italian cultural delegation a gift of the old parliament building, and *Pester Lloyd* (Budapest's German-language newspaper) commented:

We Hungarians are never afraid to say that the greatest treasures of our western Christian culture have come to us directly from Italy . . . We Hungarians understand the present development of Italian intellectual endeavour better than most other nations.[35]

The Italians were, however, less successful elsewhere. In Croatia, despite the much stronger Italian political and military presence, and the efforts of the Italians to make their cultural presence felt, the Germans appeared satisfied that the Croats' 'stronger cultural links with Germany' were prevailing. Similarly, the Italians appeared to have made little headway in the east of the Balkans. They were undertaking very little cultural activity in Sofia, while in Bucharest Italian efforts were 'overshadowed' by the much more active cultural exchanges between the Romanians and the Germans. The German film company UFA, for example, had been cooperating closely with the Romanians.[36] The overthrow of Mussolini in July 1943 dramatically curtailed their activity, but in terms of cultural influence the main beneficiaries of the collapse of Italy, at least in Hungary and Romania, appeared to be the French rather than the Germans.[37]

Much of Germany's cultural influence in South-Eastern Europe came through the promotion of international scholarly and scientific conferences, under the auspices of the agreements described above. Such cooperation encouraged perspectives that were consonant with the nazified scholarship of the Reich, and these were then disseminated into the popular consciousness by means of press reports. For example, the Hungarian newspaper Ujság (a liberal-democratic daily) reported in April 1941 on the broader racial family to which the Magyars belonged. Hungarians usually resisted the suggestion of their racial affinities with Finns and Estonians, but were now located within a non-Aryan *Völkerfamilie*, more than half of whose population consisted of Asiatic nomads.[38] Similar – more speculative – racial research preoccupied south-Slav scholars. Most German influence was much less overtly ideological, however, and rested on the routine work carried out in the schools and universities of the region, reinforced by exchanges between teachers, students and school pupils. In November 1941 the *Donauzeitung* reported in some detail on the range of cultural exchange activities between the Balkan countries and Germany or Italy, and among the South-East European states themselves. German-language publications in the Balkan capitals, the article concluded, had much to contribute to the building of new cultural networks in the region, and referred to *Neue Ordnung* (Zagreb), *Slowakische Rundschau* (Bratislava) *Das schaffende Ungarn* (Budapest) and *Bulgarische Wochenschau* (Sofia).[39]

Alongside this essentially educational activity there was a range of more directly cultural events, which made a greater impact on local public opinion. In the context of the Nazis' wholesale plunder of works of art from occupied Europe, and of wrangles over the *national* identity of cultural and intellectual figures from the Middle Ages and the Renaissance, travelling art exhibitions were organised to take the best of German art to neighbouring countries.[40] Since German art was not widely known abroad, it was argued in 1940, Germany should endeavour – as unobtrusively as possible – to raise its international artistic profile. This could be achieved by exhibiting works in international exhibitions such as the Venice Biennale, and encouraging art associations to exhibit abroad. Such exhibitions were to be accompanied by lecture tours. Of course, as the cost of sending works to foreign exhibitions could often be prohibitive, 'excellent reproductions' were often substituted, and this was especially the case in South-Eastern Europe (Greece, Yugoslavia and Bulgaria). The 'neutral' Balkan states were clearly a favoured destination for German exhibitions, and an architecture exhibition prepared by Albert Speer was planned for the region in 1940, starting in Belgrade in the autumn, before moving on to Sofia (in December) and Athens, Budapest and Bucharest the following year. In the event, the intention of exhibiting in neutral states was overtaken by the German invasion of Yugoslavia and Greece, and the exhibition was forced to look for new hosts elsewhere in Europe.[41] In 1941 an exhibition of German war artists toured Southern Europe, starting in Rome and Madrid, and continuing in a number of Balkan capitals; and the only signifi-

cant exhibition of German sculpture outside of the Reich was in Croatia and
Slovakia in 1942, accompanied by previews in the local press and a discursive
general article on Germany's new monumental sculpture in the *Deutsche
Zeitung in Kroatien.*

Of all the arts, music was the Reich's most successful cultural export, and
there were regular concert tours abroad by leading German orchestras and
conductors. Almost immediately after the outbreak of the war, for example, as
Germany sought to consolidate its political hold on the still neutral states of
South-Eastern Europe, a series of concerts was held there. It started with
Furtwängler in Budapest in November 1939, and continued throughout the
winter, with regular performances planned for the following year by the
Vienna Philharmonic and the Dresden String Quartet, among others. According to the reports from the SD the tour was an extraordinary success in terms
of cultural policy. Accompanying social events had permitted the German per-
formers and local artists to meet, and the tours had bolstered the position of
both ethnic German minorities and Reich citizens in the Balkan states.[42] There
was also a great deal of encouragement and assistance for local events, such as
those which took place across Europe in 1941 to mark the 150th anniversary of
Mozart's death. Indications of interest in, or enthusiasm for, Germany's contribution to Europe's musical heritage were always welcome, but especially if a
Wagner performance was involved, such as the first production of *Das Rheingold* in Sofia in 1943, in Bulgarian. Wagner had always been popular in Sofia,
apparently, but that was the first time his work had been performed in Bulgarian, and it was an enormous success.[43] Even among the local social elites which
furnished the Nazis with their collaborators, however, classical music was not
to everyone's taste, and there was some concern in the spring of 1942 at reports
from Bucharest of 'signs of decadence' (*Verfallserscheinungen*) among well-to-
do young men, which found expression in a dissipated and indolent way of life.
The Romanian '*Malagambisten*', named after a fashionable jazz musician, were
not unlike the 'swing youth' in Germany. They listened with great enthusiasm
to jazz music and cultivated 'an exaggerated fashion cult' by parading up and
down the Calea Victorei in Bucharest in clown costumes, much to the fury of
the local press.[44]

Although there was disapproval of jazz on racial grounds, the Nazis had
always been ambivalent about modern culture – after all, radio, film and the
mass-circulation press were the chief vehicles of their propaganda. Of these
new media, radio was perhaps the most straightforward. It was a more recent
development, generally state-controlled, and much was made of its importance in bringing the nation's cultural heritage (*nationales Kulturgut*) to the
people. In Bulgaria, for example, the radio served to strengthen the indigenous
national community with dedicated programming aimed at workers, peasants,
soldiers and children, and had arranged thousands of folk-songs for broadcast

across the country.[45] At the same time radio broadcasts were a way of ensuring a wider audience abroad for German culture. While Hungarian radio also transmitted folk-music, and 50 per cent of its output in 1943 consisted of Hungarian works, the broadcasters were keen to raise the level of music broadcasts. Every major classical concert in Budapest was broadcast by the national radio network, which meant that listeners in the provinces could also enjoy performances 'of a European standard' from Karajan, Furtwängler and the Vienna Philharmonic.[46]

Film was a more problematic medium. It had established itself as an element of popular culture prior to the First World War, before the development of state cultural policies, and was largely in private hands. Although the German film industry was the largest on the Continent, it had to compete not only with American, French and Italian imports, but with the indigenous film industries. In Hungary there was a long-established film-production industry. Elsewhere in the Balkans local film production was modest, being restricted to newsreel and short films with a folk-culture content. German film imports gradually displaced those from America and elsewhere after the outbreak of the war. In Romania 560 (62 per cent) of the 899 films shown (feature films, documentaries and newsreel) were American, and only 108 (12 per cent) German (34 were Romanian, none of them feature films, and only 2 were Italian). In the first eleven months of 1942 about half (52 per cent) of all films were German, and a quarter Italian. But although the number of German films had increased (to 172), the real difference was that there were altogether now only 328 films shown, and 7 of those were still American, despite the entry of the USA into the war in December 1941.[47] American films also continued to be shown in Hungary, despite the fact that their import had been banned, and there was some irritation on the part of German commentators that the 'stars and stripes' could be seen, and the American national anthem heard in European cinemas while the Reich was at war with the USA. This state of affairs was, not unexpectedly, attributed to Jewish influence in the Hungarian film industry, both in film production (where Jews were said to have held back the development of the industry's true potential), and in the distribution branch, where Jewish representatives promoted films that were written produced and financed by their 'racial comrades' (*Volksgenossen*) in the USA. A representative of the British Council, on the other hand, reported that the Hungarians themselves were so anti-Semitic that it was difficult to promote British films in Budapest because local people were suspicious of Jews working in the Ministry of Information and the British film distribution industry.[48] American films were condemned for their 'inner hollowness', a trait that was attributed to the influence of Jews in Hollywood.[49] This reinforced the propaganda image of a decadent American culture, a 'transatlantic lifestyle' which was trivial and superficial, a matter of 'a daily bath, an automatically regulated refrigerator, air conditioning, a car for father, a car for daughter, bigger houses, thicker Sunday papers. Luxury, waste, imitation, buying up everything that's expensive and famous – none of that creates a culture'.[50]

There were grounds for optimism, however. After all, German films were more intellectually demanding than American films, and dealt with important political issues. Their intellectual sophistication, and not the decreasing competition, was the reason they were becoming relatively more popular. The film *Jud Süss*, it was argued, was a good example because it dealt with Jewish machinations, and the Jewish problem was the most pressing issue facing South-Eastern Europe. There was more than a little wishful thinking in the notion that audiences were drawn to more demanding material. Similar reasons had been advanced in Germany itself, equally unconvincingly, for the perceived unpopularity of American films.[51] Although the local press in most of the region's capitals printed favourable reviews of German films, and they were generally assured an outwardly appreciative audience, albeit one drawn from the among the collaborationist *apparatchiki* of the local elites, it soon became clear that the appeal of the German film and its elevated theme was not unlimited, while there seemed to be a steady audience for the more 'trivial' genres. In an uncharacteristic but telling outburst in the summer of 1943, a cultural commentator noted that a Swedish film dealing with the problem of childlessness (but otherwise without 'artistic values') had received a very sympathetic review in *Pester Lloyd*, while audiences routinely had difficulties with German films because of their subject matter. Italian films, on the other hand, were regularly praised for their cinematography and production values (despite their lack of 'content').[52] The most ironic blow of all was that a Catholic newspaper in Slovakia, a clerical fascist puppet state created by Germany, had itself condemned a number of German films, on grounds of immorality, because they featured divorce, adultery and similar themes.[53]

The problem was that cultural consumption had become a means of expressing political commitment, just as German cultural diplomacy had intended; but the audiences of occupied Europe had never fully committed themselves to the specific ideological agenda, and were now openly turning away from it. Despite censorship, legal prohibitions and the purging of libraries, a preference for jazz, Hollywood films, and English and French literature became a means of distancing oneself from the Axis as the tide of war turned. Less than a week after the Battle of Stalingrad the Hungarian newspaper *Magyar Nemzet*, now clearly aligned with a broad, if indistinct, anti-Nazi coalition of political forces, published a report entitled 'What does Budapest read?' This revealed that English and French literature were particularly sought after, that Voltaire was increasingly popular, and banned German works, such as those of Thomas Mann and even of Jewish writers, were available in Swiss editions.[54] Stalingrad seemed to embolden the opposition to German occupation across Europe. From the other end of the Continent the SD reported that there was an increasing rejection of German propaganda and German political intentions in the field of culture – a rejection not only of German culture, but of any cultural event that was suspected of German influence. Almost the entire Dutch intelligentsia, it was reported, was resolute in boycotting all German cultural events, and the resistance was urging people to stay away from theatre performances altogether. Here too jazz and swing groups were a focus for the young.[55]

German commentators were increasingly aware of this shift and responded by reinforcing the message that all of 'civilised', or sometimes 'Christian', Europe was involved in a struggle to the death with bolshevism. As Soviet troops drew nearer to the Balkan states, persuasion and propaganda and cultural diplomacy were insufficient, and Hungary, whose wavering solidarity had caused concern for some time, was directly occupied by German troops on 19 March 1944, with tragic consequences for its Jewish population.[56] Life in Budapest was transformed by the political repression that followed. Meetings were banned and all cultural institutions were closed down indefinitely by decree following the German occupation.[57] The events were accompanied by outspoken protest from some Hungarian intellectuals, and there was little sense, other than in the increasingly surreal reports by German commentators, that the pretence of a cultural new order could be maintained against the background of the approaching Red Army, and the Allied invasion of Western Europe. German music and art 'continued to enjoy significant success'; Professor Schneider's lectures on the 'Ring Cycle' were, apparently, well received in Bucharest; while in Bulgaria cultural institutions had made a virtue of necessity by decentralising, following attacks on Sofia. Since the greater part of the capital's population had been evacuated anyway, the National Theatre had undertaken a tour of the provinces.[58]

In the weeks and months that followed, Bulgaria fell to Soviet forces, and the new dominant power, no less than its predecessor, immediately addressed cultural issues, as well as military and political questions. Literature, film, radio and the press were all swiftly subjected to a new censorship; and, setting a pattern for the whole of the future Soviet *bloc* in Eastern Europe, the Nazi cultural project was put into reverse as the new government instigated a 'cleansing' of public life of all traces of fascism. Collaborators were dismissed from the civil service, and the education system was to be purged, as the country was subjected to a 'progressive Bolshevisation'. Further north, in Zagreb, rallies were still being held in March 1945 by the Croatian fascist leadership, which continued to swear the country's undiminished allegiance to its German ally in the present decisive struggle against the bolshevik hordes storming Europe from the Arctic to Constantinople.[59]

The Cold War and the uses of cultural diplomacy by the Soviet Union and the West alike were to demonstrate the significance of cultural diplomacy and propaganda victories in the calculations of politicians. Moreover, despite the otherwise implacably opposed value systems of the two antagonists, there was a shared anti-fascist rhetoric that persisted for much of the rest of the century: to that extent both East and West defined themselves in conscious opposition to fascism – and, above all, to Nazism. Political leaders in both halves of the divided Continent knew that there had been a receptive political constituency for fascism in much of Europe during the 1930s and the Second World War, and that after the fall of France in 1940 many more Europeans had been willing to accept that the most probable political future was under the leadership of Nazi Germany.

The possibility of a fascist or *'fascisant'* new order in Europe had been a future that had appealed to a much wider constituency than the Nazi Party and its supporters. There was a far-reaching consensus about German war aims between Nazis and conservatives at home, as was revealed by the plans of the 1944 conspirators (discussed by Hans Mommsen in chapter 10), and at least a part of the political leadership in most European countries was prepared to collaborate. If political leaders in Berlin were able to work towards the Führer all the more easily when they shared (some of) his aims, collaborators abroad were prepared to 'work towards the Reich' because they had something to gain from such a collaboration. To that extent, the European 'new order', and the new fascist culture it sought to build, were more than a Nazi project.

Notes

1   Ian Kershaw, '"Working towards the Führer": Reflections on the Nature of the Hitler Dictatorship', *Contemporary European History*, vol. 2 (1993), no. 2, pp. 103–18, here 109.

2   Österreichisches Staatsarchiv, Archiv der Republik, Reichsstatthalterei Wien 41a/VI.

3   See List, 'Die Ackerverfassung, die Zwergwirtschaft und die Auswanderung' first published (in 4 parts) in *Deutsche Vierteljahresschrift* (1842), and Wilhelm Roscher, 'Nationalökonomische Ansichten über die deutsche Auswanderung', *Deutsche Vierteljahrs Schrift*, vol. 3, part 1: *Abteilung* (Stuttgart and Tübingen, 1848), both excerpted in Reinhard Opitz (ed.), *Europastrategien des deutschen Kapitals*, 2nd edn (Bonn, 1994), pp. 61 and 75. For the perspective from the 1940s, see Gerhard Knoll, 'Die Mitteleuropa-Ideen von Friedrich List, in Gesellschaft für Europäische Wirtschaftsplanung und Grossraumwirtschaft e. V., *Nationale Wirtschaftsordnung und Grossraumwirtschaft: Jahrbuch 1941* (Berlin, 1941).

4   Friedrich Naumann, *Mitteleuropa*, (Berlin, 1915), published in English in London (1916); Henry Cord Neyer, *Mitteleuropa in German Thought and Action* (The Hague, 1955), especially pp. 137–250; Georges Henri-Soutou, *L'or et le sang: les buts de guerre économiques de la première guerre mondiale* (Paris, 1989).

5   E. A. Radice, 'The German Economic Programme in Eastern Europe', in M. C. Kaser and E. A. Radice, *The Economic History of Eastern Europe 1919–1975*

(3 vols; Oxford, 1985), vol. 2: *Interwar Policy, the War and Reconstruction*, pp. 299–308.

6   R57/893: *Westdeutscher Beobachter*, 16 April 1941, 'Marburg an der Drau'; *Danziger Neueste Nachrichten*, 6 May 1941, 'Das Mießtal wieder bei Kärnten!; *Kärntner Grenzruf*, 17–18 May 1941, 'Aus dem befreiten Mießtal'.

7   Martin Seckendorf (ed.), *Die Okkupationspolitik des deutschen Faschismus in Jugoslawien, Griechenland, Albanien, Italien und Ungarn (1941–1945)* (Berlin and Heidelberg, 1992).

8   See, for example, Mark Mazower, *Inside Hitler's Greece: The Experience of Occupation 1941–44* (New Haven, CT, and London, 1993).

9   E.A. Radice 'Territorial Changes, Population Movements and Labour Supplies', in Kaser and Radice, *Economic History*, pp. 309–28.

10 Tone Ferenc, 'Die Kollaboration in Slowenien', in Werner Röhr (ed.), *Okkupation und Kolaboration in der deutschen Okkupationspolitik* (Berlin and Heidelberg, 1994), pp. 337–48, here 338.

11 See Ulrich Herbert (ed.), *Europa und der 'Reichseinsatz': Ausländische Zivilarbeiter, Kriegsgefangeneund KZ-Häftlinge in Deutschland 1938–1945* (Essen, 1991).

12 See, *inter alia*, Walter Manoschek, '*Serbien ist Judenfrei': Militärische Besatzungspolitik und Judenvernichtung in Serbien 1941/42* (Munich, 1993); David Cesarani (ed.), *Genocide and Rescue: The Holocaust in Hungary 1944* (Oxford, 1997).

13 Clifton J. Child, 'The Concept of the New Order', in Arnold Toynbee and Veronica M Toynbee (eds), *Hitler's Europe* (London, New York and Toronto, 1954), pp. 41–72, here 51–3.

14 Richard Overy, *Goering: The 'Iron Man'* (London, 1984), p. 109.

15 Dietrich Orlow, *The Nazis in the Balkans: A Case Study of Totalitarian Politics* (Pittsburgh, PA, 1968), pp. 22–7, 44, 84–8.

16 Adelheid von Saldern, 'Massenfreizeitkultur im Visier. Ein Beitrag zu den Deutungs-und Einwirkungsversuchen während der Weimarer Republik', *Archiv für Sozialgeschichte*, 33 (1993), pp. 21–58; Elizabeth Harvey, 'Culture and Society in Weimar Germany', in Mary Fulbrook (ed.), *Twentieth-Century Germany: Politics, Culture and Society 1918–1990* (London, 2001), pp. 58–76.

17 On the political character of the regimes of the region during this period see Ewin Oberländer (ed.), *Autoritäre Regime in Ostmittel- und Südosteuropa* (Paderborn, 2001).

18 R57/894 Deutscher Feuilleton Dienst, 'Neue Aufgaben der historischen Landeskunde. Deutsche Wissenschaft erforschst den Südostraum Europas'. On *Kulturbodenforschung* and the suggestive uses of geography see Guntram Henrik Herb, *Under the Map of Germany. Nationalism and Propaganda 1918–1945* (London, 1997).

19 Friedrich von Bernhardi, *Germany and the Next War* (London, 1914), p. 79.

20 Rüdiger vom Bruch, *Weltpolitik als Kulturmission: Auswärtige Kulturpolitik und Bildungsbürgertum in Deutschland am Vorabend des ersten Weltkrieges* (Paderborn, 1982).

21 Volkhard Laitenberger, 'Theorie und Praxis der "kulturellen Begegnung zwischen den Nationen" in der deutschen auswärtigen Kulturpolitik der 30er Jahre', in

Friedrich H. Kochwasser (ed.), *Interne Faktoren auswärtiger Kulturpolitik im 19. und 20. Jahrhundert* (Stuttgart, 1981), part 1, pp. 196–206.

22 Jan-Pieter Barbian, '"Kulturwerte im Zeitkampf": Die Kulturabkommen des "Dritten Reiches" als Instrumente nationalsozialistischer Außenpolitik', *Archiv für Kulturgeschichte*, 74 (1992), pp. 415–59, here 417.

23 Michels, *Das deutsche Institut*, pp. 47–8.

24 Barbian, 'Kulturwerte', pp. 419–25.

25 *Ibid.*, pp. 429, 435.

26 Michels, 'Die deutschen Kulturinstitute im besetzten Europa', pp. 14–15.

27 Vom Bruch, *Weltpolitik*, pp. 29–30.

28 Heinz Boberach (ed.), *Meldungen aus dem Reich: Die geheimen Lageberichte des Sicherheitsdienstes der SS 1938-1945* (17 vols; Herrsching, 1984), vol. 15, report for 27 December 1943, pp. 6190–4.

29 Michels, 'Die deutschen Kulturinstitute', p. 16.

30 Österreichisches Staatsarchiv, Archiv der Republik, Reichsstatthalterei Wien 41a/VI, Kulturberichte Südosteuropa: Kulturbericht (ereafter, Kb) 34, 21–7 April 1942.

31 Kb 35, 28 April–5 May 1942.

32 Kb 21–2, 13–26 January 1942.

33 Kb 25, 6–21 February 1941.

34 Kb 32, 21–7 April, 1942.

35 Kb 93–4, 7–20 June 1943.

36 Kb 25, 6–21 February 1942.

37 Kb 109, 26 September–3 October 1943.

38 R57/894 *Madjarische Presseauszüge* 79/41, Vienna 12 April 1941; *Kroatische Presseauszüge*, 18 January 1941.

39 R57/894, *Donauzeitung*, 14 November 194, 'Kulturaustausch im Südosten'.

40 See Jonathan Petropoulos, *Art as Politics in the Third Reich* (Chapel Hill, NC, and London, 1996), pp. 100–50; Otto Thomae, *Die Propaganda-Maschinerie. Bildende Kunst und Öffentlichkeitsarbeit im Dritten Reich* (Berlin, 1978), pp. 77–94.

41 *Ibid.*, pp. 87–8.

42 *Meldungen*, vol. 3, report for 22 January 1940, pp. 671–2.

43 Kb 115, 8–14 November 1943.

44 Kb 34, 21–7 April 1942.

45 Kb 24, no date.

46 Kb 131, 20–6 March 1944.

47 Kb 80, 8–14 March 1943.

48 Kb 23, 27 January–2 February 1942.

49 Kb 20, 6–12 January 1942.

50 'Amerikanische Lebensart', Stiftung Archiv der Parteien und Massenorganisationen, Bundesarchiv Berlin, NSD 41/32.

51 'Above all, American films are increasingly unpopular because they are felt to be culturally inferior to German films': *Meldungen*, vol. 4, report for 23 May 1940, p. 1168.

52 Kb 93–4, 7-20 June, 1943.

53 *Katolicke Noviny*, 23 January 1942, cited in Kb 25, no date.

54 Kb 77, 15–21 February 1943.

55 *Meldungen,* vol. 12, report for 1 February 1943, p. 4736.

56 See Igor-Philip Mati_, *Edmund Veesenmayer: Agent und Diplomat der deutschen Expansionspolitik* (Munich, 2002), pp. 189–284.

57 Reichsstatthalterei Wien, 40, 256 Südosteuropa Wochenbericht.

58 Kb 131, 20–6 March 1944.

59 Reichsstatthalterei Wien, 40, 287 Südosteuropa Wochenbericht, 22–9 October 1944; *ibid.,* 306 Südosteuropa Wochenbericht, 11–18 March 1945.

9

Assessing the 'other Germany': the Political Warfare Executive on public opinion and resistance in Germany, 1943–45

Pauline Elkes

I

With the fall of France in June 1940, Whitehall and the Chiefs of Staff recognised that Britain's strategic situation was so desperate that all avenues of warfare, from aerial bombardment and economic blockade to 'irregular' operations, should be pursued.[1] A month later, the Special Operations Executive (SOE) was created as a 'Fourth Arm' of the armed forces, charged with the specific task of 'setting Europe ablaze', using sabotage, subversion and 'black' propaganda.[2] But the continuing advance of German military forces in Europe led to a reappraisal of Allied strategy and the role of the SOE, and to its replacement in September 1941 with the Political Warfare Executive (PWE).[3]

This new department was established to conduct all forms of political warfare 'against enemy, satellite and occupied countries'.[4] Its specific remit was 'to undermine and destroy the morale of the enemy, and sustain and foster the spirit of resistance in enemy-occupied countries'.[5] Until the PWE's creation, official thinking in Whitehall had been guided by a recognition of the potential for resistance in Germany and the view that this should be monitored and if possible encouraged. Thus policy privileged the use of propaganda as a means to split public opinion in Germany in order to destroy the consensus thought to underpin Hitler's power. The message to Germans was that the British Government would support efforts to challenge, reject or overthrow the Nazi regime. But the changing scenario on the Continent led to an altered perception of German public opinion, thought now to be very much behind Hitler in the euphoria of military successes.[6] This official view, also shared more broadly within British society, increasingly lost sight of the distinction between supporters of the regime and opponents loosely termed the 'other Germany'. Over the course of the next year there was a struggle for recognition of this 'other Germany', but one which ultimately failed with the announcement, at the Casablanca Conference in January 1943, of Roosevelt's demand for Germany's 'unconditional surrender'. This ultimatum in many respects abrogated the need to foster resistance in Germany through propaganda since the Allies no longer considered internal dissent to be part of their overall strategy.

This did not mean, however, that monitoring internal developments in Germany, particularly the nature of public opinion and acts of resistance to the regime, was of no importance. On the contrary, such information became more important as the PWE began to anticipate the social and political conditions with which the Allies would be confronted at the end of the war. Since the Allied objective was to ensure the total defeat of Germany and the establishing of a liberal, Western-style, democracy, the PWE intensified its interest in the political conditions in Germany, and increasingly intelligence was used to inform officials in Whitehall who were involved in other areas of policy making towards Germany. The intelligence gathered by the PWE, however, consistently stood in contradiction to Allied policy throughout this period. In fact, in almost every weekly report for the last two-and-a-half years of the war, officers working in the PWE provided information illustrating that, despite all its shortcomings, the 'other Germany' was a reality, as Willy Brandt was to assert many years later.[7]

My intention is to consider the 'other Germany' as filtered through the reports of the PWE between 1943 and early 1945 when the Allies pursued their policy of 'unconditional surrender'. An examination of the weekly intelligence reports of the German Section of the PWE allows us to gauge how much information was available to the British Government about the nature of public opinion, and the potential for and existence of resistance, in Germany during this period, when increasingly harsh policies, coercion and terror became the order of the day of the Nazi regime.

The chapter thus presents the perspective of British intelligence on German resistance to the Nazi regime. Historians have largely ignored the reports of the PWE. Yet, as I show, those reports throw considerable light on the extent to which British intelligence was aware of conditions within Germany and of the potential for resistance to the regime. Under Bruce Lockhart, a career intelligence officer who was the Director-General of the PWE, intelligence analysis was based on a combination of official propaganda, secret reports and letters smuggled out of Germany which were then interpreted 'against the grain' by officers of the PWE, young men in their early twenties and drawn mainly from Oxbridge.[8] It outlines the many varieties of resistance, distinguishing between opposition, mere dissent, protests and non-conformity, that existed at all levels in German society – and the response of the Nazi regime to such behaviour – and which until only recently have been little acknowledged in the literature.[9] In many respects they parallel the secret reports compiled by Himmler's security service, the SD (*Sicherheitsdienst*), and, together with the detailed reports of the exiled SPD (*Sopade*), utilised to great effect by historians, notably Marlis Steinert and Jeremy Noakes, and not least by Ian Kershaw in his path-breaking

Hitler Myth and in his earlier study of public opinion and dissent in Bavaria.[10] In similar fashion, the PWE reports, based as they were upon 'human intelligence' and presented by 'amateur' officers who believed they were 'telling it as it is', provide a fairly accurate picture of conditions and opinions in Germany during the war, and especially during its latter phase, as will be seen.[11] The reports reveal clearly that Whitehall was aware of the nuances in civilian responses to the war and the regime's policies that belie the influential postwar description of the Third Reich as a 'totalitarian' state.[12] And yet the reports remained limited in their impact on the shaping of Allied and notably, British, policy, though that need not reduce their value to the historian. In short, the information and conclusions contained in the weekly reports of 1943–45 are reflected in the historiography of the Third Reich which illustrates the complex, paradoxical and sometimes contradictory behaviour of German society in relation to the Nazi regime.

II

It was already clear to officers in the German Section of the PWE that the adverse turn of events in Germany's war, especially after Stalingrad, was having a detrimental effect on the resolve of the 'home front'. The intelligence officers identified five indicators of the change of mood and attitude in Germany: people had lost belief in victory; they were tired of fighting; they were no longer in the mood to submit to increasing war work; they were now actively resisting total war measures; and they had lost confidence in the Führer. Ordinary Germans, they concluded, already had a 'tendency not towards consolidation under adversity but towards disintegration' as the strains of war deepened, and the evidence for this weakening community was provided by the growing list of executions (and, indeed, the regime's willingness to publish lists of those executed as a means of intimidation).[13] Moreover, disaffection was being observed among those sections of the population in which, apparently, Nazism had traditionally found greatest appeal.

The officers noted, for example, the increase in resistance among peasants to new regulations concerning food production and delivery. Farmers were refusing to bring in the harvest and to maintain extra cattle stock as dictated by the Government; instead, they either hoarded foodstuffs or engaged in alleged acts of sabotage; prosecutions for unjustified abandonment of farm work by labourers were reported; and, for the first time, publicly aired complaints about deteriorating living conditions, the adverse progress of the war and the role of government were registered. The refusal to obey the authorities was due to a combination of factors, including the feeling among farmers that the newly acquired eastern territories would or should supply all the necessary food for the Reich, and the problems created by the shortage of everyday consumption goods. The sense of growing dissatisfaction with the regime was given apparent credence by the Führer's threat that farmers should 'take the opportunity to collaborate politically . . . or remain outside [the *Volksgemein-schaft*]'.[14]

The report concluded that the failure of the peasants to meet the higher standards of production set by the authorities had produced sufficient concern within the regime to warrant a fairly threatening response, but nevertheless emphasised that this particular form of dissent should not be seen as anything more than localised reaction against the increased demands of the Reich Food Estate.[15] In spite of this prognosis, the information was considered important by the PWE, for it provided grounds for believing that it would be possible to slow down the Nazi war economy by using propaganda to encourage the sabotage of the production of food.

Similarly, the reports and assessments of the German Section cast an interesting light on the attitudes and behaviour of women to the Nazi regime, especially in the sphere of labour mobilisation. Because labour shortages were putting a serious strain on the war economy, the regime decided to mobilise for industrial work all men aged 16–65 and also all women aged 17–45. The response was desultory, to say the least.[16] Indeed, attempts to evade the call-up resulted in the creation of a range of bizarre excuses and 'illnesses'. In the city of Posen (present-day Poznan), *Gauleiter* Greiser identified 'certain groups of idle Germans . . . who sit in cafés and discuss ways of evading the recently published labour duty regulations'.[17] Women evaders gave reasons from 'studying Japanese and Chinese' or being otherwise busy as a secretary 'to a friend' to having heavy family responsibilities. Women trying to get an exemption certificate besieged doctors' waiting-rooms, leading the authorities to swiftly announce that the Labour Office would disregard those certificates unless a doctor attached officially to the Labour Office signed them.[18]

At the beginning of 1943, the military commentator for the Army High Command (OKH) at Radio Berlin, Lieutenant-General Kurt Dittmar, warned women over the airwaves that it was their duty to work in the factories.[19] In July the PWE had noted: 'men and women still take up an attitude of passive resistance . . . and seem only to submit to compulsion and do not conceal their feelings towards the new work'.[20] With the recruitment crisis continuing into the autumn, the Reich women's leader Gertrud Scholtz-Klink is said to have declared: 'The Führer has mapped out for us the only possible path. It is of no importance where the Führer's path leads: our duty is to follow him.'[21] This attempt to convince the women of the Reich that they had no choice but to involve themselves in the war also failed, and at the beginning of November the intelligence officers noted that passive resistance by women was creating 'a very difficult problem for the German authorities . . . Here Himmler's methods cannot be applied, at least [not] on the grand scale, if only on account of the inevitable repercussions on morale at the front'.[22] Inevitably, there was recourse to police methods to force women into the factories, though women continued to defy the call-up.[23] But these women (and their male counterparts) remained defiant of the regime's calls for a general mobilisation of the home front, even in the face of the threat of sterner measures against them under the punitive wartime regulations.[24]

Of course, the refusal to register and work in the factories cannot be assumed to have been politically motivated action against the regime, just as it cannot be assumed that it was not. One of the many complaints made by ordinary women at this time was that they did not see why they should work in industry when the wives of influential men in the Nazi Party were exempt.[25] But the problem went deeper, resting on a fundamental contradiction between Nazi ideological claims about the role of women in the Reich and the requirements of the nation during total war. An article in the Swiss newspaper *St. Gallen Tageblatt* of 31 January 1943 illustrates the conflict faced by the German authorities with regard to mobilising women for the war effort:

> A significant fact which has *not escaped widespread notice and popular comment* is that only a year ago even Hitler declared himself opposed to the employment of women on a larger scale, because the future stamina of the German race depended upon girls and young women being shielded from the rigours of war for the function of marriage and motherhood. To-day Sauckel mobilises all women from 17 to 45 without exception, including all women who are married but not yet mothers.[26]

Some women used this contradiction between the Führer's ideas on women and the nation's needs as more than just a ruse to avoid industrial work: they used it to register their unhappiness about other issues. Many questioned the regime over the very essence of Nazi ideology, which had identified their roles in the Reich as mothers, home-makers and carers, that was now being contradicted by the demands of war which propelled them into the male sphere of the Third Reich. They registered their objection to this by their refusal to move into industry, protesting in a variety of ways. The disillusionment and horror at the huge loss of life at the front, and increasingly at home, brought a fierce reaction from some women: 'Why should we have children if they are to be killed in 20 years time?' One young mother bitterly complained: 'In Europe one does nothing but build for 20 years and then destroy – we mothers educate children for this, and when we have brought them up, from 14 years [of age] they no longer belong to us but to the state.'[27]

By making such comments, these women fundamentally questioned the purpose of war – and thus ran the very real risk of falling foul of the regime – while not necessarily being motivated by anti-nationalist sentiment. Thus, as Adelheid von Saldern argues, the evidence militates against casting women simply as either 'perpetrators' or 'victims'.[28] The weekly reports show that women did not always choose the 'safe haven' of home life merely to avoid conscription, but rather exploited the 'space' bestowed by the 'hallowed' position accorded to mothers in Nazi Germany to voice their particular concerns.

The PWE reports are mostly silent on the question of German youth. Nevertheless, what intelligence was gathered certainly challenges the Nazi (and popular post-1945) picture of a massive army of young people enthusiastically supporting Hitler and the Nazi regime (though of course many youths were enthusiastic about the war, at least initially).[29] Partly to discipline German youth as part of the Nazi machine and partly to counteract the emergence of what was deemed subversive behaviour, greater pressure was applied to incorporate boys and girls into one or other of the Nazi youth organisations. By March 1943 it was estimated that an additional million boys aged 14–18 had been sworn into the Hitler Youth.[30] But this effort to marshal youth via social discipline was never complete and had to be augmented by more negative measures of policing. Marlis Steinert, in her study of public opinion and everyday life during the war, shows how the Gestapo and the courts increasingly came to play a role in this, applying more draconian measures in their attempts to get to grips with the problem of 'wild' youths, now labelled 'asocials', and their allegedly 'subversive behaviour'.[31] A PWE report of May 1943 noted that a 'serious problem' had arisen in Oberhausen, an industrial town in the Ruhr, because the juvenile workers whose parents had been evacuated were not 'taking advantage' of the hostels provided for them by the authorities. The Nazi authorities had announced on 12 May that juveniles living in these hostels would 'be brought up physically, ideologically and morally according to the regulations which apply to the Hitler Youth, by specially selected hostel leaders and for educational reasons must wear the regulation uniform of the Hitler Youth'.[32] Recognising that these hostels were actually Hitler Youth training centres, the youths in question had baulked at the prospect of being subjected to a relentless party discipline, preferring to find homes with others living in the area.[33]

The Nazi leadership was wary of any alternative organisation that challenged its purchase on youth, especially where it was self-organised as in the case of the mainly working-class 'Edelweiss Pirates', or the more middle-class 'swing' movement.[34] At the end of June PWE intelligence officers quoted a Nazi Party source in the *Hannoversche Zeitung* dated 8 September 1942 that revealed the extent of the concern over 'swing' youth:

> [W]e owe it to the honour of German youth ruthlessly to make a clean sweep of these adolescents and conspicuous types who . . . draw attention to themselves by their physical neglect, their defective deportment, their dirty appearance and *their provoking hairstyles* and who already in peacetime refused to undertake any tasks whatsoever for the benefit of the community . . . complaints of provoking

and brazen behaviour, these people have met in the shelter huts and at seats and have annoyed passers by, insulting them in a vulgar manner.[35]

On the personal instruction of Hanover's Gauleiter, the police rounded up a large number of these mostly middle-class boys and girls aged 14–18. The usual punishment for 'swing' youth was fairly mild: they had to present themselves to the police president for labour service, dressed in working clothes and with their hair cut short according to regulations. Failure to observe this order could lead to arrest and even imprisonment. PWE intelligence officers commented: 'Doubts concerning the political attitude of the rising generation, as well as the need to employ every available labour unit, is suggested by the drastic measures adopted to round up those who have escaped mobilisation.' In Kreis-Salzburg-Land compulsory meetings for youths were announced, and those who did not attend were warned that they would be fined up to RM 150. In some areas, in order to make them conform to the ideals of the Hitler Youth, the local food office was instructed to issue ration cards only on the production by youths of completed Hitler Youth membership application forms.[36]

The PWE – uncannily using much the same turn of phrase as adopted by the Nazi authorities in Germany – reported on the 'destruction' of the family that resulted from the mobilisation of fathers to the front and mothers to the factory, thus leaving adolescents to allegedly 'grow up wild'. Those absent parents also created a space for the leaders of the Hitler Youth who had 'taken the matter into their own hands' and subsequently sought to enforce a curfew on youngsters under the age of 18, which meant that they could not attend cinemas where performances extended beyond 9.00 p.m.[37] Other measures, such as the directive in early 1944 from the Justice Ministry allowing local Hitler Youth leaders to participate in the administration of juvenile courts, greatly extended the extent of the party's control over German youth.[38]

The increasingly draconian response by the Nazi regime to the youth question was the subject of a PWE supplement dated 10 July 1944. The report, entitled *Youth Protection Camps in Germany*, included details of two camps set up to deal with those young people alleged to be 'running wild'.[39] Its authors commented that it would be 'fanciful' to describe them as concentration camps, but that there were certain common traits between the two establishments: the anonymity of camp administration as far as the public was concerned; the stress laid on harsh discipline; the possibility of adding an indefinite term of detention to any legal sentence; the imposition of police supervision on released camp inmates without the necessity of any legal process; and, finally, the possibility of imposing detention without legal process and without warning. These shared characteristics led the report's authors to conclude that it was safe to describe these camps as the first stage towards 'concentration camps for the young'.[40]

The PWE appeared reluctant to consider the potential of youth as a source of resistance to the regime. This was not the case with other groups. When the

North Africa Campaign turned against Germany in May 1943, provoking popular fear that this could turn into a 'second Stalingrad',[41] allegedly 'thousands of
women and elderly men gathered to obtain news about their relatives in the
Afrika-Korps' in front of the headquarters of the OKW Information Office in
Berlin. The PWE, perhaps over-optimistically, described this and similar
demonstrations in other parts of Germany as 'riots'.[42] The event revealed to the
PWE a willingness to openly challenge the authorities, moving from 'grumbling' to open dissent (which to the Nazi authorities must have brought back
memories of the similar protests by women that had taken place during the
First World War and did so much to undermine the imperial wartime Government).[43]

At the beginning of October the PWE reported that many Germans, even
those who were ardent Nazis a year before, were openly telling foreigners that
they desired nothing but an end to the war, and were prepared to draw the conclusion that the regime must go, 'though there was still no evidence that they
considered the possibility of themselves in assisting its departure'.[44] The reasons for this apparent passivity were clear. As the tide of war turned against
Germany, propaganda was intensified and, following Himmler's appointment
as Reich interior minister in August 1943,[45] the use of terror increased with
harsh sentences being invoked for bagatelle 'crimes'. The death penalty for
those accused of sabotaging wartime morale, such as distributing 'a political
poem of an inciting and disruptive nature', became common.[46] Germans and
foreigners alike were warned that 'high treason leads like lightning to the scaf-
fold'; traitors were defined by the regime as 'those who commit treachery ver-
bally or in their thoughts', who as 'weaklings and traitors will be seized and
annihilated'.[47] Himmler's 'mailed fist against defeatism' was aimed at both the
well to do, particularly businessmen who were labelled 'profit-patriots', and at
ordinary working people. Thus by purging from the home front all those
deemed undesirable, regardless of gender, generation or race, the regime
believed it could achieve the purest distillation of the *völkisch* community that
would hold steadfast against the enemy.

A major source of anxiety for the regime had always been the possibility of
a repeat of 1918 were morale and public opinion to go against the regime.[48] The
PWE documented the wave of strikes in Austria, Hamburg, Essen, Duisburg
and Oberhausen, in which some workers had been arrested, while others were
induced to return to work only after the threat of being shot. Many of the
strikes, such as those in Austria, were triggered by the food shortages, but anti-
war demonstrations were also reported, particularly from towns subjected to
heavy Allied air-raids where workers deserted their workplaces for safer areas.[49]
The potential for such activity to become politicised, especially as the situation
grew desperate and with defeat looming, was clearly recognised by the PWE –
and by the Nazi authorities, too. Endless reassurances from the leadership con-

firmed that collapse 'was not possible': '*This time Germany has the Führer*. Like a rock in a stormy ocean, never wavering, never doubting, [he is] an example to all in strength and tenacity, in unshakeable determination and supreme concentration.'[50]

The fear of social disorder in Posen resulted in the regime establishing 'an invisible auxiliary band of *men trained in the use of arms* who are ready to . . . *crush relentlessly any attempt by asocial elements of the population* who endanger the property or security of other people'.[51] This special force, known as the *Stadtwacht*, had been created to aid local police forces, the Gestapo and the SS in containing any disorder that could escalate into an uprising. The reports recognised, in particular, how the Nazi regime was growing increasingly paranoid about the presence of millions of foreign workers in the Reich.[52] By the middle of July 1943 there was growing evidence of a deep and widespread anxiety that, in the event of defeat, foreign workers would rise up against the Germans.[53]

This *angst* was justified in part by the fact that large numbers of foreign workers were actually billeted in civilian homes. In the industrial cities of Essen and Oberhausen in the Ruhr, for instance, about 25 per cent of all foreign workers had private lodgings; but in Berlin, with nearly 250,000 foreign workers, at least half were billeted in private homes.[54] Such propinquity allowed for intimate relationships to develop. There was plenty of evidence of such liaisons, and to intelligence officers in London this suggested the possibility of collaboration against the regime, something the Nazi authorities themselves had already considered. In a supplementary report of April 1943 containing a breakdown of the nature of crimes committed by foreigners, officers within the PWE recognised the important role foreign workers might play if such a front were to crystallise, specifically in terms of their potential for taking part in an internal uprising, sabotage and other subversive activities.[55] By categorising foreign workers into nationalities and the kinds of crimes they were assumed to be prone to commit, the German Section of the PWE was trying to devise a scheme for identifying the tasks to be given to the various groups in any prospective campaign launched by the PWE in the hope that foreign workers would *do* rather than merely *feel* something. For example, French foreign workers would utilise their relatively good standing among the population to 'persuade' German civilians to help in any action, while Poles and Czechs could be relied on to take part in subversion and sabotage.

By the middle of November it had become clear to the PWE that, since 'no German appeared to have any rational grounds for expecting any end to the war except defeat, it seems profitable to consider not so much the moral factors tending towards national collapse but rather those inhibiting immediate capitulation'. Importantly the German Section thought capitulation could be brought about either by the leadership *or* by the German people, an important distinction being made between them. As far as PWE intelligence was concerned, the 'so-called leaders', referring to German army officers and industrialists,

> must be regarded for the present purpose only as outstanding representatives of the general mass of the people . . . [who,] despite their important status and position, cannot act. They are inhibited from acting by much the same factors as inhibit the general mass – difficulty of discussion, fear of denunciation, lack of organisation, lack of agreed aims, uncertainty as to the consequences of action, conflict of loyalties, etc.

But, realistically, the officers confirmed that this was most unlikely, unless it was as a result of dissension between the leaders, with 'some thinking that they see a way out for themselves by sacrificing others'.[56] But these intelligence officers also believed that 'the mass of people can, however, produce a situation which forces the leadership to capitulate'. Underlining the recognition of the existence of 'the other Germany', intelligence officers in the German Section considered the possibility that 'the mass of people might act directly by revolution'. But in the final analysis this, too, was dismissed with the recognition that 'a revolution arising spontaneously out of the German people is very unlikely, since the most powerful factor inhibiting any revolution from below is still undoubtedly the Gestapo and all that it stands for'. Finally, the report considered one more avenue open to the German people to force the leadership out of power. This was the effect on the regime of the failure of the people to produce the goods necessary to carry on the war. But the report's authors concluded on the downbeat note that, even were this to happen, it would be achieved 'not so much by voluntary sabotage as by involuntary failure owing to the lack of will to make the necessary effort'.[57] The assessment was not wholly accurate – as the 'July plot' itself demonstrates. But it highlights the crucial problem at the heart of generating a resistance movement in Germany during the war, namely the nature of the relationship between elites and the mass of society. There was indeed a resistance in wartime Nazi Germany, but one 'without the people', as Ian Kershaw has noted.[58]

As 1943 drew to a close it was clear that the mass of people could not be relied on to bring down the regime, any more than the regime could rely on the support of the people. The increased pessimism among ordinary people regarding the outcome of the war had resulted in their withdrawal into the private sphere and a reluctance to become concerned or involved in political issues. Instead, the civilian population was retreating into 'simple, unpolitical [sic] ideals of domesticity and purely personal relations, and whilst accepting that the ideals of National-Socialism were an 'illusion' they appeared to have no conception of any alternative for which they are prepared to work'. This rather gloomy, yet accurate, perspective is corroborated by the internal reports of Himmler's security police who used terms such as 'Gleichgültigkeit' or 'Rat-losigkeit' to describe the widespread mood of popular resignation to the flow of events since the spring of 1943.[59]

From the end of May 1943, the PWE had started to receive information that there were problems within the Nazi Party and between the party and the German Army. The officers in the German Section, however, initially displayed little serious interest in the potential resisters, commenting acidly that they were 'rats on a sinking ship' who had no chance of doing anything to form a political movement against the regime.[60] The possibility of a direct challenge to the Nazi regime began to take shape only in August 1943 when an article in a Swiss newspaper on the previous month's events in Italy asked 'whether a similar fate may not be in store for Hitler and National Socialism', naming Keitel, Doenitz and Goering as possible leaders.[61] Brauchitsch was seen as an 'obvious analogy for Badoglio [who took over power on 25 July 1943 after Mussolini's removal] – a professional soldier, former Commander-in-Chief, latterly in retirement on account of his disagreement with the political Leader'.[62]

In order to assess the probability of an internal coup the intelligence officers observed the reaction of the Nazi leadership to the situation, and noted that Goebbels was obviously taking the threat very seriously when, in his speech of 3 October, he repeatedly stated that there was no soldier to be found of any rank who would put 'cowardly subjection above honour' since the German nation was too politically mature to be taken in by the hypocritical lies of its enemies and the 'bitter lessons of November 1918'.[63] Read against the grain, the speech was seen by PWE officers as more or less an admission by some quarters of the Nazi leadership that the German people would be willing to surrender on the basis of a negotiated peace, a situation that the regime could not contemplate. This was confirmed in October when a report came to London that rumours were circulating in elite circles alleging that Himmler would soon be cooperating with the Wehrmacht to oppose Hitler. This seemed to corroborate good evidence previously obtained by British intelligence that a military coup would be impossible without Himmler's cooperation, even if it meant that he would have to be eliminated later. The report also suggested that Himmler was preparing to negotiate peace with Russia, an idea corroborated by other reports received by the German Section informing its officers that there was a degree of admiration for the totalitarian Soviet system among 'the young men destined to be Germany's future leaders'.[64] This sneaking admiration for Stalinist Russia – also evident in later reports –explains in part the ambivalence of Churchill towards those individual Germans who had put out peace feelers to Britain, and his lukewarm response to the resisters.[65] But in mid-October 1943, intelligence officers also concluded that those who had hoped for a 'German Badoglio' in July had now lost heart due to the passage of time and also as a result of Himmler's increased campaign of terror against all dissenters. The main reason, however, according to the intelligence available, was that those generals who might have been considered as potential leaders of a revolt had been 'paralysed by the occupation of key positions by other generals irrevocably committed to the regime'.[66]

Over the next four months discussion concerning an internal coup receded, but in mid-February 1944, intelligence officers began to receive information on rumours circulating the Reich that Field Marshall Rundstedt was involved in negotiations with the Allies. Meanwhile, Himmler, having already made contact with the Allies, was also being considered as a possible leader to replace Hitler.[67] The rumours persisted into mid-March, with an alleged 'neutral source' informing the PWE that leading German officials were still talking of the desirability of a 'German Badoglio'.[68] But as the military situation worsened, British intelligence officers recognised a sense of hopelessness among the German people and, given the 'German propensity for self-pity', added the barb that the people would now cling to Hitler as a 'scapegoat . . . somebody on whom the whole blame could be laid when the victorious Allies came to allot punishment for war-guilt'.[69]

This scepticism diverted the PWE's attention to the 7 million foreign workers inside the Reich as a potential catalyst in any attempt to overthrow the regime. A plan had been put forward by Hugh Dalton in 1940, but had been shelved; it was now revived by Ritchie Calder (charged with liasing between PWE and the Foreign Office) in April 1944. Calder's operational plan was codenamed 'Trojan Horse' and was designed specifically to coincide with 'Operation Overlord' – the planned Allied invasion of Europe scheduled to take place in Normandy. The plan drew on the situation reports of the PWE and its assessment of the potential of foreign workers in the Reich as a sort of 'fifth column'. Already ensconced within the enemy camp, these workers were 'expected to develop certain explosive or revolutionary forces as the war enters its final critical period'. In what was clearly a domino-effect scenario, the PWE thought it possible that German workers would join the revolt in widespread strikes, thus precipitating civil war.[70] Calder hoped that such a revolt, combined with 'Overlord', would result in the breakdown of the home and fighting fronts. But there were disadvantages to the plan – first, should the revolt fail, then reprisals would be too terrible to contemplate; and, second, were it to succeed, the chaos inside Germany would seriously hamper Allied military operations. These considerations ultimately led to the plan being shelved for a second time.

As Allied forces approached the frontiers of the Reich, reports began to filter through indicating a changed attitude among the soldiers expected to fight for Hitler 'to the bitter end'. Whilst not openly resisting orders, some troops were reportedly making an important distinction in their interpretation of the Soldiers' Oath, insisting (technically wrongly, of course) that it was sworn to the

Fatherland and not to Hitler. In particular, the declining morale of soldiers on the Eastern Front absorbed the attentions of both Hitler's regime and the PWE. A batch of captured letters written by German soldiers in Russia showed the degree to which disaffection had set in, with British intelligence quoting one officer who had stated that every one of his soldiers was claiming 'I did not start the war, we were better off when we were unemployed, we were much better off before the National Socialist government set in.' This letter contained information about the breakdown of discipline on the Eastern Front, with the officer 'praying' that there would not be an unprecedented retreat homewards, and warning: 'I am deeply convinced that these hordes would behave in a worse manner than the Bolsheviks themselves, if only in order to establish some sort of political 'alibi' for themselves. One can sense a change in outlook among the majority of men – especially among the NCOs [sic].'[71]

Thus barely a few months before the attempt upon Hitler's life, the PWE was hopeful that, were such dissent to become widespread among the-rank-and-file of the army, the possibility of a coup in Germany led by the generals could not be ruled out. Nevertheless, when the resisters finally struck against Hitler in July 1944, they did so not only without the people, but also without external support. Officers at the PWE could merely document the plot's failure and the terrible retribution meted out to those involved or thought to be involved.[72]

During the last months of the war the German people were subjected to a toxic mix of terror and propaganda as the regime resolved to hold the home front. The PWE reports spoke of Himmler's 'mailed fist without the velvet glove' delivering 'brutal hardness' to anyone who disobeyed the regime's *diktat* to the people to remain in their towns and villages, and to fight the advancing Allies to the bitter end. A decree of 16 February, publicised by the German News Agency (*Deutsche Nachrichten Büro*), allowed for special courts-martial to mete out instant (death) penalties against offenders. Himmler, who issued the decree on the Führer's orders, now shared with Otto Thierack, the Reich minister of justice, the right to 'issue the regulations necessary to supplement, alter and execute it'. The decree strengthened the position of the Gauleiter, who now had the authority to appoint the members of the court and the prosecutor. These courts-martial represented a radical innovation to curb 'all criminal actions endangering German fighting strength or fighting determinism'. All those who displayed even the slightest lack of resolve were made subject to this draconian measure, including those runaway party officials and even the mayor of Breslau or the runaway mayor of Königsberg.

Meanwhile Goebbels bombarded the German people with propaganda. The policy of 'unconditional surrender' allowed Hitler's war now to truly become the 'People's War', and victory was inevitable, they were assured, simply because they had managed to survive 1944. As the position in Germany rapidly deteriorated, the Propaganda Ministry attempted to keep secret the news of the military advance of the Allies and intensified the 'People's Sacrifice' campaign. The contradictions between propaganda and reality, however, could not be hidden from the PWE. For instance, on the one hand Goebbels's Propaganda Ministry trumpeted the success of the textile and equipment collections, and yet, on the other hand, announced that in order to avoid 'inconveniencing' the people by having to make trips to the collection centres, party members would visit each household with lists of requisitioned goods. But usually the signs of defeatism were more overt. Officials in the Reichsgau Danzig–West Prussia urged the people 'not to weaken, not to lose their nerve', while in the Saar region it became clear that Hitler Youth were being called up for service for fear that they might leave and seek safety with their families in the interior. All juveniles born in 1928, 1929 and 1930 (13-, 14- and 15-year-olds) were thus kept back.[73] As the British forces crossed the Rhine the civilian population was ordered to 'stick it out and, if need be, to face death bravely'. Now, in the final stage of the war, even children as young as 12 were mobilised and made to swear unconditional obedience to the men left behind in charge of the defence of German soil. The PWE noted that the 'unheroic slinking away of the fighting men leaving defenceless non-combatants' caused even greater resentment and fear to spread among what it termed 'ordinary' Germans.[74]

Even at this late stage, in weighing up the potential for an internal challenge to the regime, the German Section of the PWE turned its attention to the German Army. Officers in the German Section had received some indication that the Nazi leadership was still paranoid about the army's reliability. Indeed, the PWE, ignoring the setback suffered after July 1944 by those elements within the army that might have considered abandoning Hitler, concluded that

nothing but a move by the Wehrmacht could overthrow the present regime and provide an alternative capable of executing an orderly capitulation. Present circumstances are such as might easily convince a rapidly increasing number of conscientious officers that it was now their duty to save at all costs whatever could still be saved out of Germany's ruin rather than allow the whole future, as the present, to be sacrificed to political intransigence.[75]

The final reports of the PWE cover the final moments of the Third Reich and document for British eyes the extent of the disintegration in progress in the Reich. Thus Hitler's Order of the Day on 16 April, during the Battle of Berlin, included desperate measures to ensure that civilians remained behind to defend the Reich and that the army held firm. Soldiers were ordered to kill any officer unknown to them, irrespective of his rank, should he order a retreat. Berliners were instructed to arrest *agent provocateurs* and rebellious foreigners. Women were urged to fight, using the guns taken from the dead or, failing that, to arm themselves with the 'scissors from the home'. Children as young as 10 were mobilised for the defence of the city in a last sacrificial offering to the Reich. Yet Hitler's birthday was to be celebrated in an effort to revive what the intelligence officer compiling the report called the people's 'blind and mystical faith' in him. These instructions not only indicated to the German Section that Hitler had little understanding of the situation, but that he had indeed lost his hold on reality.[76]

And, in its final report of the war, the PWE turned its attention to the problems that would face the occupying powers, warning against the disappearance of major Nazi leaders; the existence of the 'Werewolf' organisation that was sworn to fight a guerrilla war against the Allies; and the potential problem of the long-term effects on young Germans of the ideological training of the Hitler Youth.[77]

III

It is clear from the reports of the PWE's German Section, from its inception in September 1941 until the end of the war, that Churchill's cabinet was supplied with detailed, fairly accurate and up-to-date intelligence on German public opinion and the potential for resistance. Information on the plans, the potential leaders and the people likely to be involved in a German resistance to Hitler was made available long before the 'July Plot'. The reports also show that intelligence officers understood the practical problems facing the plot's conspirators, their inability to take decisive action because of the relatively small number of generals and civil servants willing to become involved, and the power structure of the Nazi State in which the key positions were held by people loyal to the Nazi regime. In relation to ordinary Germans the PWE's weekly reports contain a wealth of evidence of a disillusioned and fragmented society existing under extreme stress which increasingly registered its dissatisfaction with the regime in a variety of ways, ranging from non-conformance, passive resistance and, occasionally, public protest. Especially after the fall of Stalingrad the refusal to submit to the regime in 'blind faith and loyalty' was, for the intelligence officers, confirmation of the failure of the totalitarian aims of the Nazi regime and the myth of the *Volksgemeinschaft*, and revealed to them the existence of the 'other Germany'.[78] Its reality was manifested also in the deployment of increasingly brutal terror by Himmler's police apparatus, aided and abetted by a corrupted judicial system, as a means of holding together the home front when propaganda and the Hitler myth began to fail.

Yet the PWE and its masters in Whitehall never really managed to exploit the popular disaffection they were observing, nor to take seriously the emergent resistance movement. There are a number of explanations for this, not least the social conditioning of the intelligence officers themselves, who in the main came from upper-class and Oxbridge backgrounds. Their interpretation of

developments in Germany were thus coloured by the way they perceived workers, youths and women *per se*. On the one hand, strikes by industrial workers
and the behaviour of young people were seen not as manifestations of political dissent or ideological resistance to the regime, but as localised unrest over
the regime's economic or social policies, though today that behaviour is seen
by some historians as significantly more important than the contemporary
account would suggest.[79] On the other hand, women's refusal to register for
industrial work and their evasion of their duty to involve themselves in the
'total war' campaign were, for intelligence officers who believed them to have
been staunch supporters of Hitler, indicators of their contrary nature. But, in
the final analysis, the intelligence officers were looking for signs of a mass
resistance movement capable of successfully overthrowing the regime, and
concluded that no such potential existed in Germany.

Nevertheless, the existence of the 'other Germany' was acknowledged, and in
February 1944 was used in an attempt to get the Allied leaders to issue a declaration of positive intent to the German people. Throughout the latter years of
the war, the PWE's recognition of the 'other Germany' had resulted in various
notes and memoranda being exchanged between itself and the Foreign Office
concerning the possibility of a declaration to the German people concerning
Allied intentions in the post-war settlement. At the beginning of December
1943 a note was sent from Tom Harrison, a personal private secretary at the
Foreign Office, to Sir Peter Scarlett, one of the directors of the PWE , about the
imminent announcement of a joint declaration of intention towards the
German people. Harrison asked whether the PWE could 'dress them up' in
terms palatable to the German people.[80] Officers in the PWE then suggested
that the Allies might wish to avoid any reference to the intention to impose a
constitution on Germany or to the re-education of the German people once
hostilities had ceased.[81]

Clearly, reactions in the PWE were shaped by concern over the emergence of
a pro-Russian tendency in Germany, and this led the PWE to make representations to the Foreign Office in February 1944. Talks took place between the
PWE, the Joint Intelligence Committee and the Political Intelligence Depart-
ment/War Cabinet and Foreign Office concerning the policy of 'unconditional
surrender', and whether or not the term should be replaced by 'prompt surrender', as suggested by Charles Peake, the political liaison officer at Supreme
Headquarters of the Allied Expeditionary Force.[82] On 10 February Scarlett
wrote to Sir Orme Sargent at the Foreign Office, pointing out why a declaration was desirable, including the advice that it would go some way to refuting
Goebbels's 'devil's plans' propaganda which alleged Allied intentions to totally
annihilate the German people. Scarlett argued that as the situation grew
steadily worse, the Germans would be likely to accept any alternative to the
continuation of the war.[83] Eventually, after further discussion, Sir Alexander

Cadogan put the proposal before Churchill on 25 April. Churchill gave a lengthy reply in which he refused flatly to get involved, stating instead:

> The matter is on [*sic*] the President. He announced it at Casablanca without any consultation. I backed him up in general terms. I have pointed out to the Cabinet that the actual terms contemplated for Germany are not of a character to reassure them at all, if stated in detail. Both President Roosevelt and Marshall Stalin at Tehran wished to cut Germany into smaller pieces than I had in mind. Stalin spoke of very large mass executions of over 50,000 of the Staffs and military experts. Whether he was joking or not could not be ascertained. He certainly said that he would require 4,000,000 German males to work for an indefinite period to rebuild Russia.
>
> By all means circulate [a] historical summary of events. Personally, I am not going to address the President on the subject. For good or ill, the Americans took the lead, and it is for them to make the first move.
>
> It is primarily a United States affair.[84]

Churchill's response, with its implied refusal to recognise the 'other Germany', illustrates the problem faced by policy makers whose decisions appeared to disregard the information of the intelligence officers who, as Sir Michael Balfour contends, sought merely to portray the situation 'as it was' rather than presenting a picture of life in wartime Germany that Whitehall preferred to see.[85] Clearly for much of its existence, the PWE was reporting 'against the grain' of existing policy.

Nevertheless, as I stated at the outset, the reports themselves are a fascinating source for the social historian. What is most striking about the reports is the accuracy of their detail and their confirmation of the existence of a non-fascist tradition in the shape of the 'other Germany' made *at the time*, a confirmation that was suppressed by the policy of 'unconditional surrender' and was subsequently disregarded by a post-war literature harnessed to the mantra of 'totalitarianism' which accompanied the Cold War.[86] It is only recently that the 'varieties of resistance' in the everyday life of German society have once more been recognised. As David Crew put it, 'the realities of everyday life in Nazi Germany will simply not submit to black and white descriptions'.[87] The history of consent/dissent, conformance/non-conformity and collaboration/resistance has been extensively researched over the past thirty years, its list of contributors to the debate growing almost by the day.[88] What is perhaps striking about this historiography is that the best of it draws on the internal reports of the Reich. The weekly reports compiled by the PWE must also count as a worthy source for the historian interested in getting inside the Third Reich.

Notes

1   See J. M. A. Gwyer and J. R. M. Butler, *Grand Strategy*, vol. 3, part 1: *July 1941–August 1942*. (London, 1964, 1966), p. 9.

2   This was Churchill's legendary instruction to Hugh Dalton, then minister of economic warfare.

3   *Hansard*, 11 Sept. 1941, col. 294. It has taken sixty years for an official history of the PWE to appear: David Garnett, *The Secret History of PWE: The Political Warfare Executive, 1939–1945* (London, 2002); see also M. R. D. Foot, *SOE in France* (London, 1966); Michael Balfour, *Propaganda in War, 1939–1945: Organisations, Policies and Publics in Britain and Germany* (London, 1979); Michael Stenton, 'British Propaganda and Political Warfare 1940–1944: A Study of British Views on How to Address Occupied Europe', unpublished PhD thesis, Cambridge University, 1980.

4   Balfour, *Propaganda in War*, p. 91.

5   R. H. B. Lockhart, *Comes the Reckoning* (London, 1947), p. 125.

6   Ian Kershaw, *The 'Hitler Myth': Image and Reality in the Third Reich* (Oxford, 1987), pp. 121–48.

7   Willy Brandt, Address to conference at Goethe House, New York, April 1988, reproduced in David Clay Large (ed.), *Contending with Hitler: Varieties of Resistance in the Third Reich* (Washington, DC, and Cambridge, 1991), p. 9.

8   Pauline Elkes, 'The Political Warfare Executive: A Re-Evaluation Based on the Intelligence Work of the German Section', PhD thesis, University of Sheffield, 1996; chapter 3 gives information on the organisational structure and personnel of the PWE.

9   Some of this more recent scholarship is summarised in English in Ian Kershaw, *The Nazi Dictatorship: Problems and Perspectives of Interpretation*, 4th edn (London, 2000), chapter 4; as well as Clay Large (ed.), *Contending with Hitler*, see Francis R. Nicosia and Lawrence D. Stokes (eds), *Germans Against Nazism: Nonconformity, Opposition and Resistance in the Third Reich: Essays in Honour of Peter Hoffmann* (New York and Oxford, 1990); and, with documents, Jeremy Noakes (ed.), *Nazism 1919–1945: A Documentary Reader*, vol. 4: *The German Home Front 1939–1945*, 2nd edn (4 vols; Exeter, 1998), and Martyn Housden, *Resistance and Conformity in the Third Reich* (London and New York, 1997).

10 Ian Kershaw, *Popular Opinion and Political Dissent in the Third Reich: Bavaria 1933–1945* (Oxford, 1983). Marlis G. Steinert, *Hitler's War and the Germans: Public Mood and Attitude during the Second World War*, trans. Thomas E. J. De Witt (Athens, OH, 1977); Noakes (ed.), *Nazism 1919–1945*, vol. 4; *Meldungen aus dem Reich 1938–1945: Die geheimen Lageberichte des Sicherheitsdienstes der SS*, ed. Heinz Boberach (17 vols; Herrsching, 1984).

11 Michael Handel, 'The Politics of Intelligence', *Intelligence and National Security*, 2 (October 1987), pp. 5–46; Lesley K. Wark (ed.), *Espionage: Past, Present, Future?* (Essex, 1994). On the issue of 'telling it as it is', see, Elkes, 'The Political Warfare Executive'.

12 Kershaw, *The Nazi Dictatorship*, pp. 20–46; David Schoenbaum, *Hitler's Social Revolution* (New York, 1967).

13 Foreign Office (hereafter, FO), 898/185 WR, 28 Dec. 1942–3 Jan. 1943.

14 FO, 898/185, 10 Jan. 1943, supplement: 'Growth of Peasant Troubles in Germany'.

15 Kershaw, *Popular Opinion*, pp. 282–96; J. E. Farquharson, *The Plough and the Swastika: The NSDAP and Agriculture in Germany, 1928–45* (London, 1976), pp. 221–48.

16 'Verordnung über die Meldung von Männern und Frauen für Aufgabe der Reichsverteidigung', 27 January 1943, *Meldungen*, vol. 13, report for 20 May 1943, p. 5276.

17 FO, 898/185, 15–21 Feb. 1943.

18 *Ibid.*, 8–14 Feb. 1943.

19 *Ibid.*, 10–17 Jan. 1943. On Dittmar, see Robert Wistrich, *Wer war wer im Dritten Reich: Ein biographisches Lexikon: Anhänger, Mitläufer, Gegner aus Politik, Wirtschaft, Militär, Kunst und Wissenschaft* (Munich, 1983), pp. 54–6.

20 FO, 898/185, 19–26 July 1943.

21 *Ibid.*, 20–6 Sept. 1943. On Scholtz-Klink, see Claudia Koonz, *Mothers in the Fatherland: Women, the Family and Nazi Politics* (London, 1988), pp. 387ff.

22 FO, 898/185, 8–14 Nov. 1943.

23 *Ibid.*, 6 Dec. 1943, supplement: 'German Women Defy Orders to Register'.

24 Noakes (ed.), *Nazism 1919–1945*, vol. 4, pp. 124–35.

25 FO, 898/185, 15–23 March 1943.

26 *Ibid.*, 1–7 Feb. 1943.

27 *Ibid.*, 24–30 May 1943.

28 As argued by Claudia Koonz in the final chapter of *Mothers in the Fatherland*, though vigorously countered by Gisela Bock in a review of the book. English readers can follow the arguments in Adelheid von Saldern, 'Victims or Perpetrators? Controversies about the Role of Women in the Nazi State', in David F. Crew (ed.), *Nazism and German Society 1933–1945* (London and New York, 1994), pp. 141–65.

29 *Meldungen*, vol. 13, report for 4 March 1943, p. 4889; Peter Stachura, *The German Youth Movement 1900–1945: An Interpretative and Documentary History* (London, 1981).

30 FO, 898/185 22–28 March 1943. The Hitler Youth had a membership of 1.7 million in 1939: Jeremy Noakes and Geoffrey Pridham (eds), *Nazism 1919–1945: A Documentary Reader* (Exeter, 1984), vol. 2: *State, Economy and Society 1933–1939*, p. 420; Hans W. Koch, *Hitler Youth: Origins and Development, 1922–1945* (London, 1976). Stachura, *The German Youth Movement*, p. 135, makes no distinction between the different organisations for boys and girls, and hence gives the total number as *c.*7.2 million.

31 Steinert, *Hitler's War*, pp. 219–; Jeremy Noakes, 'Social Outcasts in Third Reich', in Richard Bessel (ed.), *Life in the Third Reich* (Oxford, 1987), pp. 83–96.

32 FO, 898/185, 31 May–6 June 1943.

33 Noakes (ed.), *Nazism 1919–1945*, vol. 4, pp. 421–40, for excellent sources and discussion of this problem.

34 Detlev J. K. Peukert, *Inside Nazi Germany: Conformity, Opposition and Racism in Everyday Life*, trans. from the German by Richard Deveson (Harmondsworth, 1989); and *Die Edelweißpiraten. Protestbewegungen jugendlicher Arbeiter im 'Dritten Reich': Eine Dokumentation*, 3rd edn (Cologne, 1988).

35   FO, 898/185, 21–27 June 1943; Housden, *Resistance and Conformity*, p. 88, has images of 'swing' youth.

36   FO, 898/186, 18–24 Oct. 1943, supplement: 'The Condition of the Young People'.

37   *Ibid.*, 25–31 Oct. 1943.

38   *Ibid.*, 3–9 Jan. 1944.

39   *Ibid.*, supplement to report from 10 July 1944.

40   *Ibid.*

41   *Meldungen*, vol. 13, reports for 3 May 1943, p. 5203, and 30 May 1943, p. 5285; Kershaw, *The 'Hitler Myth'*, p. 172. On the early part of the campaign in North Africa, see Gerhard Schreiber, *Germany and the Second World War*, vol.3: *The Mediterranean, South-East Europe and North Africa, 1939–1941: From Italy's Declaration of Non-Belligerence to the Entry of the United States into the War*, trans. Dean S. McMurray, Ewald Osers, Louise Willmot (Oxford, 1995).

42   FO, 898/185, 10–16 May 1943.

43   Ute Daniel, *The War from Within: German Working-Class Women in the First World War* (Oxford, 1997); Alison Owings, *Frauen: German Women Recall the Third Reich* (Harmondsworth, 1995), has some very revealing accounts by women of their wartime experiences.

44   FO, 898/186, 27 Sept.–3 Oct. 1943.

45   Peter Padfield, *Himmler Reichsführer SS* (London, 1990), p. 426.

46   FO, 898/186 11–17 Oct. 1943.

47   *Ibid.*, 20–6 Sept. 1943.

48   Tim Mason, 'The Legacy of 1918 for National Socialism', in A. J. Nicholls and Erich Matthias (eds), *German Democracy and the Triumph of Hitler: Essays in Recent German History* (London, 1971), pp. 215–39.

49   FO, 898/186, supplement to report of 22 Nov. 1943; see Kershaw, *Popular Opinion*, pp. 296–315, and Timothy Kirk, *Nazism and the Working Class in Austria* (Cambridge, 1996), pp. 93–108, for examples of workers strikes, absenteeism, sabotage, unrest and dissent in the workplace.

50   FO, 898/186, 25–31 Oct. 1943; see Timothy Mason, 'The Workers' Opposition in Nazi Germany', *History Workshop*, 11 (spring 1981), pp. 120–37; Kershaw, *Popular Opinion*, pp. 296–315; Ronald Smelser, *Robert Ley. Hitler's Labour Front Leader* (Oxford, New York and Hamburg, 1988), pp. 261–97; Kirk, *Nazism*, pp. 86–108.

51   This little-known force deserves further investigation.

52   Their number, including PoWs working in the economy, had risen from 1.2 million at the end of May 1940 to 6.3 million at the end of May 1943, and peaked at 7.5 million by the end of September 1944: Fritz Blaich, *Wirtschaft und Rustung im 'Dritten Reich'* (Düsseldorf, 1987), p. 105.

53   FO, 898/185, 5–11 July 1943.

54   *Meldungen*, vol. 13, report for 15 March 1943, p. 4953.

55   FO 898/185, supplement to report of 12 April 1943. It concluded: 'Poles are the only large category of foreign workers who provide a percentage of reported crimes higher than the proportion of the total foreign worker population they rpresent. Whilst the Poles are represented as specialising in crimes of violence, the Russians appear to specialise in truancy, which accounts for over 60% of Russian crimes. The French, who represent 17% of both crimes and foreign worker popu-

lation (including working prisoners of war), owe three-quarters of their convictions to their friendly relations with the civil population, almost entirely to relations with women.' The report commented that there was clearly a brake on the reporting of crimes committed by Italians (only one crime was reported), who constituted 4.5 per cent of foreign workers, while Poles and Czechs accounted for the vast majority of crimes classed as 'treason'.

56 FO, 898/186, 15–21 Nov. 1943.

57 *Ibid.*

58 Kershaw, *The Nazi Dictatorship*, pp. 183–217; cf. Anton Gill, *An Honourable Defeat: A History of The German Resistance to Hitler* (London, 1994), pp. 1, 23; Hans Rothfels, *The German Opposition to Hitler: An Assessment*, trans. from the German by Lawrence Wilson (London, 1961), and Peter Hoffmann, *The History of the German Resistance 1933–1945*, trans. from the German by Richard Barry (Cambridge, MA, 1977), typify the older approach, while Detlev J. K. Peukert, *Inside Nazi German: Conformity, Opposition and Racism in Everyday Life*, trans. from the German by Richard Deveson, Penguin edn (Harmondsworth, 1989), is the classic study representative of more recent approaches.

59 *Meldungen*, vol. 13, report for 30 May 1943, p. 5285.

60 FO, 898/185, 31 May– 6 June 1943.

61 *Ibid.*, 16–22 Aug. 1943.

62 *Ibid.*

63 FO, 898/186, 27 Sept.–3 Oct. 1943.

64 *Ibid.*, 4–11 Oct. 1943.

65 Indeed, it was this instinctual mistrust about their aims that had lain behind Churchill's policy of 'absolute silence' in January 1941: see Patricia Meehan, *The Unnecessary War: Whitehall and the German Resistance to Hitler* (London, 1992).

66 FO, 898/186, 11–17 Oct. 1943.

67 *Ibid.*, 7–13 Feb. 1944.

68 *Ibid.*, 6–12 March 1944.

69 *Ibid.*, 3–9 April 1944.

70 FO, 898/370, 22 Apil 1944.

71 FO, 898/186, 13–19 March 1944.

72 *Ibid.* 17–21 July 1944, and 31 July–8 Aug. 1944; Kershaw, *The Nazi Dictatorship*; Hans Rothfels, *The German Opposition to Hitler: An Assessment*, trans. from the German by Lawrence Wilson (London, 1961); and *The Political Legacy of the German Resistance Movement* (Bad Godesberg, 1969); Peter Hoffmann, *Stauffenberg: A Family History, 1905–1944* (Cambridge, 1995).

73 FO, 898/187, 15–21 Jan. 1945.

74 *Ibid.*, 19–25 March 1945.

75 *Ibid.*, 5–11 Feb. 1945.

76 *Ibid.*, 16–22 April 1945.

77 *Ibid.*, 30 April–7 May 1945.

78 See Peukert, *Inside Nazi Germany*, pp. 21–5, for a number of perceptive questions that would allow one to pursue the history of the 'other Germany' in an everyday-life context.

79 *Ibid.*, pp. 118–19.

80   FO, 371/39076, 7 Dec. 1943.

81   *Ibid.*, 9 Dec. 1943; this file also contains Roberts's response to this in a Foreign Office Minute entitled 'Propaganda to Germany'.

82   FO, 371/39024, 31 Jan. 1944.

83   *Ibid.*, 10 Feb. 1944.

84   *Ibid.*, 25 April 1944.

85   Interview with Michael Balfour, St Antony's College, Oxford, 3 Feb. 1992.

86   Peukert, *Inside Nazi Germany*, p. 247.

87   Editor's introduction to Crew (ed.), *Nazism and German Society*, p. 1.

88   In addition to the already cited literature see: Rüdiger von Voss and Günther Neske (eds), *Der 20. Juli 1944: Annäherung an den geschichtlichen Augenblick* (Pfüllingen, 1984); Jürgen Schmädeke and Peter Steinbach (eds), *Der Widerstand gegen den Nationalsozialismus: Die deutsche Gesellschaft und der Widerstand gegen Hitler*, Foreword by Wolfgang Treue (Munich, 1985); Peter Hoffmann, *German Resistance to Hitler* (Cambridge, MA, 1988); Klemens von Klemperer, *German Resistance Against Hitler: The Search for Allies Abroad 1938–1945* (New York, 1992); Fabian von Schlabrendorff, *The Secret War Against Hitler*, trans. from the German by Hilda Simon (Colorado and Oxford, 1994).

10

Beyond the nation state: the German resistance against Hitler, and the future of Europe

Hans Mommsen

Despite the continuing public interest in the history of the German resistance movement against Hitler any synthesis of its concepts regarding foreign affairs is still missing.[1] This is especially true concerning the European idea and the extent to which the German resisters against Hitler found their way to support a future unified Europe. From the angle of a critical evaluation of their general political views, the attitude taken by the divergent groups among the German opposition to the idea of European unification seems to be more than a marginal problem. It indicates their determination to oppose on principle Hitler's policy of aggression and not only because they would prefer more cautious or indirect strategies by which to retain Germany's supremacy over the European continent. Moreover, their ideas relating to the structure of post-war Europe enable us to assess the degree to which the resisters were ready to overcome their inherited nationalistic motivations which partly explains their active participation in the attempt to overthrow and replace the Nazi dictatorship. This, however, is less the case with respect to the socialist Left which had been in favour of European integration from the start.

As far as the national conservative resisters were concerned, most of them had to go rather a long way to get rid of their strongly nationalistic vision of Germany's future role within Europe. Obviously, the great many contact feelers to the British and then the US government that had been put out since the autumn of 1938, and which were continued even after Germany's triumph over France, were destined to achieve the acceptance by the Western powers of a moderate revision of the German border with Poland and to secure the *Anschluss* of Austria, as well as to find acceptance of the outcomes of the Munich agreement.

These efforts still remained in the context of the bilateral diplomacy of the Western powers and did not raise the issue of any restoration of the League of Nations, or of including Germany in an international alliance. Hence, the foreign policy ideas of the national conservative resisters up to 1940 followed the path of bilateral relations, following the example set by Hitler himself, when he left the League of Nations in October 1933 and signed the British–German Naval Agreement in 1935 and the ensuing non-aggression treaties.

The obvious failure of the direct contacts with the Anglo-Saxon powers, however, strengthened the efforts of Helmut von Moltke for the Kreisau Circle, on the one hand, and of Carl Goerdeler for his group consisting mainly of notables and pensioned officers, on the other hand, to pin their hopes on the non-belligerent European states. According to Moltke's vision they might serve as mediators, because they had a common cause with Germany with respect to preserving the European identity against the obnoxious influence of either the United States or the Soviet Union.

These rather vague ideas were taken up by Father Alfred Delp, who opposed any interventions by what he called '*raumfremde Mächte*' (extra-regional powers), that did not belong to the specific Western tradition – and he defined that tradition as a symbiosis between Christianity, the Germanic heritage and classical antiquity.[2] Similar ideas were promoted by those groups who hoped to engender the ecumenical dialogue and who entertained rather intensive contacts with several groups of the resistance after 1941. Thus, Willems Visser't Hooft, an important Dutch liaison partner between the German resistance and the foreign evangelical churches, wrote in a memorandum that one of the foremost targets of the resistance was 'to safeguard the integrity of European life'.[3] This ambivalent position, which sought to establish an independent stance as between the East and the West, was reflected in Moltke's vision of how to establish the Europe of the future as well.

The majority of those comprising the national conservative opposition, however, embraced various notions of *Großraumpolitik* based on the creation of extended political units roughly identical with geographical zones. The idea of forming greater spheres of influence, a proposal which had been favoured both by the National Socialist leadership and by other major powers, such as Japan, the USA and the Soviet Union, also left its imprint on the foreign policy views of the national conservative resisters. After the German–Soviet Non-Aggression Treaty, in particular, prominent members of the opposition, such as Ludwig Beck, Ulrich von Hassell and even Hans Oster, complained that Hitler had frivolously disregarded German interests in Eastern and South-Eastern Europe, and threatened her continental supremacy.[4]

Hitler's temporary support of the nation state and the cessation of Germany's claims for further expansion in the East were reflected in the Reichstag speech of 6 October 1939, in which he proposed to establish ethnically homogenous zones in Eastern Europe. This stance bitterly disappointed many of his conservative opponents.[5] Actually, Hitler's opportunistic assurance that he would be able to reduce nationality tensions in Eastern Europe led to the dislocation of hundreds of thousands of ethnic Germans, who left the Baltic states, Volhynia and, later on, also Bessarabia, and gave rise to a mass migration from which the infamous resettlement programme of Heinrich Himmler, known as *Generalplan Ost*, emerged.[6]

This policy seemed to run counter to the schemes which were discussed in Berlin among the members of the semi-oppositional 'Wednesday Society' (*Mittwochsgesellschaft*) by Johannes Popitz, Ludwig Beck and Carl Schmitt (who still had not lost all of his influence), creating a system of rival power *blocs* transcending national boundaries.[7] Deliberations of this kind did not remain isolated. In particular, after the German victory over France a veritable planning euphoria set in, especially among the industrial management, dealing with a European '*Grossraum*' economy.[8]

After his resignation from the advisory positions he had held with Schacht and Goering (originally designed to block the influence of Walter Darré, the chief of the *Reichsnährstand*), Carl Goerdeler, the former mayor of Leipzig, showed much sympathy with these plans to establish a European *Grossraum* economy, since they seemed to coincide with his endlessly repeated demands for the Continent to return to a free-trade economy based on transnational cooperation. It was only a small step from this position to his proposal of a European confederation based on close economic relations between the major powers, an idea which found expression in the never-ending flow of memoranda he directed to sympathisers and government agencies alike.[9]

At an early stage, however, Goerdeler still believed that economic cooperation could be achieved without giving up anything meaningful of Germany's national sovereignty. Together with close supporters Beck, von Hassell and Popitz, he believed that German supremacy could still be preserved in a future Europe. Above all, Ulrich von Hassell, who came from the right wing of the German Nationalist People's Party and had been a member of the Middle Europe Economic Conference (*Mitteleuropäischer Wirtschaftstag*), still hoped that a 'West under German leadership' (*Abendland unter deutscher Führung*) was possible. Hassell hoped to achieve the overdue unity of the European peoples on the basis of their common front against bolshevism.[10] Even Father Alfred Delp, who belonged to the intellectual heart of the Kreisau Circle, supported this view. With his roots in the Roman Catholic youth organisation New Germany (*Neudeutschland*), he argued that he could not conceive of any future Europe without Germany taking a leading role therein.[11]

Ideas of this kind did not depart too far from the dreams of the Nazi regime's few foreign policy experts, and especially those of Heinrich Himmler. As late as 1943, for example, a memorandum by Fritz Dietlof von der Schulenburg expressed continued support of the idea of a system of '*Städteringe*', a network for cooperation between major European cities including Prague, St Petersburg and Brussels.[12] Hence, until 1942 the views of the national conservative resisters regarding the European question continued to be somewhat ambivalent and contradictory. That they engaged themselves in the issue of the future of the European peoples at all was due in part to the fact that the Nazi regime as such did not officially develop realistic and credible ideas in this respect, but it also reflected the general trend of thinking in European terms that became dominant after the tide of war turned against Germany.

Conversely, Hitler prevented any clear-cut proposition of what the future role of the occupied or satellite countries should be, and what those countries might expect after the end of the war. With the exception of some semi-official publications such as Karl Richard Ganzer's 1941 *Das Reich als europäische Führungsmacht* ('The Reich as a Leading European Power'), there were no serious directives concerning German territorial demands either in the west or in the east. Having launched the German offensive against the Soviet Union, Hitler rejected the attempts by Alfred Rosenberg and others to determine German war aims. Even in 1943–44, when there was an urgent need to set out German proposals for the future integration of the Continent in order to counter the increasingly effective Allied propaganda on behalf of a democratic Europe, Hitler expressly prohibited an initiative by Rosenberg to press into service a group of pro-Nazi foreign journalists who would make the German case.[13]

The German opposition's attempts to come up with a viable vision for the future of Europe, then, served to fill the effective vacuum left by the Reich's lofty official 'continental *bloc*' propaganda, in practice little more than a barrage of vitriolic attacks against Great Britain, the USA and, above all, the Soviet Union. The complexity of the positions taken up by the members of the national conservative opposition is typically reflected in Adam von Trott zu Solz's statement that it was not too late to achieve a 'fraternisation of the common people of Europe against the capitalistic powers and the Soviet threat'.[14] This somewhat disillusioned assessment was directed not only against the Nazi dictatorship but against Western capitalism, which he believed had to be replaced by a new social order that would abolish mass society as well as social injustice. In that respect, von Trott was opposed also to the political conditions in Britain, as his correspondence with Shiela Grant Duff shows.[15] Hence, the critical reactions of most of his former English friends were not completely unjustified.

While any vision of the future structure of Europe developed by the Kreisau Circle was inseparably bound up with a desire for the fundamental reform of society, the ideas of the more conservative group around Goerdeler were guided by a rather more traditional notion of foreign policy. In his famous memorandum 'The Goal' (*Das Ziel*), a text which was intended for the German generals and which, since the autumn of 1941 had played something of the r ole of a *vademecum* for the national conservative resisters, Goerdeler pleaded for a cautious approach to the European question. He recommended that

Germany should not violate the interests of the smaller nations but should instead leave to the European nation states the freedom of action necessary 'to develop their domestic issues according to their needs and their peculiar conditions'.[16]

Goerdeler regarded concessions of this kind as a precondition of establishing a European *bloc* under Germany's leadership, something that in his view was 'overdue'. In conjunction with this, he emphasised his conviction that 'the union of the European states led by Germany' would become a reality within twenty years, provided that the war could be ended in time. Goerdeler ascertained that this could be achieved if Germany granted acceptable conditions to the other European nations.[17] This rather vague programme shows that at this stage Goerdeler still adhered to the principle of the nation state. This was underlined by his unwillingness at that time to dispense with an independent national army, which he regarded as the 'school of the nation'.[18]

While Goerdeler and his closer followers supported a rather traditional form of German nationalism, thinking still in terms of German hegemony, the group around von Moltke and Yorck von Wartenburg pursued a somewhat different line, which was strongly influenced by Roman Catholic political and social ideas, and which was committed to the so-called *Reichsgedanke* and to federative principles. These ideas were deeply imbedded in the corporatist ideology of the Austrian social philosopher Othmar Spann.[19] In particular, the Jesuit members of the Kreisau Circle, who enjoyed close connections with the Committee for Matters Related to Religious Orders (*Ordensangelegenheiten*), founded by the Catholic hierarchy in order to defend its monasteries against increasing attacks by the SS and the Gestapo, had a formative influence on its thinking. The issue promoted above all others by the Kreisau Circle's Jesuit members was their demand for the revival of a specifically Christian Europe, and of course recourse to Christian universalism implied the abrogation of the idea of the *nation*. Hence, Georg Angermeier, who was among the advisers of Rösch and Delp, concluded that the 'European nation' could be the 'only possible realisation of Europe's future order'.[20] Angermeier hoped in particular that the end of the war would result in the elimination of inherited nationalism and the restoration of the 'universalist' unity of the West.

From the standpoint of their Christian universalist position, the Kreisau spokesmen were opposed to the traditional idea of the sovereignty of the nation and the state and wanted instead to establish a European political system founded on a network of autonomous regional units relying on the principle of self-government. The political order they envisaged entrusted not only local and regional bodies but even professional estates (*Berufsstände*) with political prerogatives. By promoting ideas of this kind, Moltke had Anglo-Saxon conditions in mind, and above all the high degree to which private initiatives replaced the tasks of central administrative bodies. The functions hitherto filled by the nation state would either be divided according to the principle of subsidiarity or else be transferred to an all-encompassing confederation straddling the boundaries of the former nations and possibly extending across the entire Continent.

Ideas of this kind were articulated assertively by the Catholic journal *Highland* (*Hochland*) edited by Hans Muth, and they influenced the aims of the 'White Rose', the well-known students' resistance group which originated in Munich and had spread to other German universities, until it was suppressed by the Gestapo. In their fifth leaflet, written in 1942, the group asserted that only through intensive cooperation between the European peoples could the foundations for a new start (*Aufbau*) be laid.[21] At the same time, Moltke and Yorck regarded the defeat of National Socialism as a challenge for Europe as a whole, and both men claimed the necessity of a European confederation which would have the political function of delivering orders and instructions to the self-governing units that would replace the nation states after the war, above all Germany and France.[22]

Hence, some, at least, of the resisters held the conviction that the unification of Europe was just a question of time and asserted the necessity of supranational cooperation. The notion of a federal union of European nations was, in Moltke's judgement, already predetermined by the fascist war economy, because with the continuation of war the regime felt compelled to modify the campaign of plunder it had originally introduced. Apart from Himmler's ruthless exploitation of Eastern Europe, the Nazi regime out of sheer necessity reorientated the war economy in the direction of an integrated economic system.[23]

Relying on information provided by Peter Yorck von Wartenburg at the Economics Ministry, Moltke may well have overestimated the success of Albert Speer's reliance on the national economies of the occupied countries to sustain the war economy, rather than directly exploiting their resources for German industry. Nevertheless, Moltke perceived in the war economy the basis for a future integrated European economy. He had already expressed the expectation, in a key memorandum of 1941 entitled 'The Situation, the Aims and the Tasks' (*'Ausgangslage, Ziele und Aufgaben'*), that a comprehensive common economy (*Gemeinwirtschaft*) would emerge out of a general European demobilisation coordinated by an inter-European economic bureaucracy.[24] This expectation, however, never became reality, not least because following the Third Reich's collapse even the West European nations proved unable to restore their economies without the assistance of the USA. In fact, in some ways, Europe's economy appeared to relapse into the fundamentally fragmentary condition that had characterised the 1930s.

Moltke's vision consisted in establishing Europe as a federation of self-governing units of comparable size. These regional units would be based on historical foundations, but would not be identical with the nation state. They would, however, be entrusted with the ordinary administrative functions formerly belonging to central state agencies. Moltke anticipated that although they would have divergent democratic constitutions, the new regional units would be established and controlled by those elite circles which had assumed the moral leadership in Europe amid a landscape of decay. They would take over the responsibility for the emergence and establishment of the self-governing units after the general breakdown of fascist dictatorship and the ousting of the various governments of collaboration.

Moltke's scenario reckoned with the complete destruction of inherited political institutions and the emergence of a fundamentally new political order that was to grow from the bottom upwards, leaving behind the burnt-out concept of the sovereign state. He believed strongly that such a fundamentally new structure and mentality would emerge from the ruins, ridding the Continent of the historical burden of more than three centuries of erroneous development, of a course of history that had replaced individual persons with mass-consumers and had alienated them from their religious roots, that is from their Christian heritage.

These ideas must be interpreted in the context of the Kreisau Circle's philosophy, according to which National Socialism embodied the culmination of a continuous deterioration of the human condition that had set in with the emergence of the absolutist state: it had initiated the loss of the universalist community of Christendom and the religious ties of the individual. This had led necessarily to the uncertainties of mass society, of capitalist materialism and extremist nationalism. This philosophy of European decay, a process that had begun with the Reformation, had strong affinities with contemporary Roman Catholic social doctrine. At the same time, however, it reflected the deep psychological repercussions of the alleged cultural crisis since the end of the nineteenth century, and it was closely related to the fundamentalist conviction that this crisis would be overcome by an occidental renaissance as promulgated by Catholic authors throughout the 1920s.

At the end of this regeneration of Europe envisaged by Moltke stood a new society based on the responsibility of its individuals and signified by the absence of any coercive structures. The political process relied primarily on the activities of what Moltke called the '*kleine Gemeinschaften*' ('small communities'), consisting of voluntary organisations and *ad hoc* associations, which would emerge at the local level, and whose members would embrace common Christian values and the duty of public responsibility. These spontaneously formed small communities, the natural cells of society, were expected to pursue public interests within the community, the universities, the professional groups and through an assortment of public activities ranging from fire-fighting to healthcare. Moltke no doubt had in mind the role of the 'Friendly

Societies' as well as the high level of private sponsorship he had become acquainted with, especially in England and South Africa.[25]

In some respects Moltke's vision was a conservative variation on the role of the Soviets in the Communist tradition. Small communities would counteract the shortcomings of mass society, being designed as quasi-natural elected bodies based on a system of indirect voting, a system that would supply the personnel for their social and representative institutions. New forms of political organisation would be introduced that would avoid the drawbacks of the modern centralist state.

The organisational principles of the Kreisau Circle, atavistic as they were, corresponded with the expectation that there would emerge a new public mentality no longer driven by divergent and competing social interests but one subscribed instead to universal Christian values. Moltke's famous dictum to Lionel Curtis must be put into this context: 'For us post-war Europe is less a question of borderlines and soldiers, of hydrocephalous organisations and big schemes, than of restoring the picture of man within the hearts of our fellow-citizens.'[26]

The resisters were convinced that the unification of Europe was just a question of time and thus believed in the necessity of supranational cooperation. The Kreisau Circle especially put a great deal of energy into conceptualising the future political and economic structure of a European federation, as is demonstrated impressively by Theodor Steltzer's memorandum 'The Problem of a European Constitution' ('Das europäische Verfassungsproblem'), written in 1942 (which has survived to this day in Stockholm). The memorandum concluded with a plea for the 'formation of a European federation' which would be provided with a responsible (*handlungsfähige*) government, and which should exclude any possibility of a hegemonic solution. It left open the question of whether Great Britain would belong to this federation or to a USA-led *bloc*.[27]

The scheme elaborated by the Kreisau Circle, therefore, was not a national but a European programme, and Moltke and his followers put much energy into establishing contacts with West European resistance groups that were to form the core of the new moral elite envisaged by the group. He found support for this vision from the general secretary of the Ecumenical Council of the Protestant churches in Geneva, Visser't Hooft, who believed in the possibility even of achieving a merger of the different groups within the European resistance to form a leadership that would agree on the target of building a renewed Europe according to the Christian tradition.[28]

Within the Kreisau Circle such ideas were shared by von Trott, who believed that it would be possible to achieve a synthesis between what he called 'the democratic pre-mass Europe' and the 'democratic post-mass Europe', combining the virtues of pre-democratic social structures with those which might re-emerge after the fall of the Nazi regime had introduced the end of the mass society which he regarded as the main source of the European catastrophe.[29] The common formula was the principle of 'personal socialism' bridging Western individualism and Communist collectivism, and guaranteeing a new identity and a new kind of citizenship.

In addition to this, Adam von Trott expected that European federalisation would mean the 'definitive triumph over European nationalism, at least where its militarist version was concerned'. In his view, this would necessarily result 'from the practical application of the Christian-European tradition'. Thus von Trott consistently supported the establishment of common European institutions. Already during the winter of 1939–40 he had demanded the establishment of a European customs and monetary union, the installation of a European supreme court and the introduction of pan-European citizenship. These steps would merely be the starting-point for the administrative coordination of Europe that was then expected to ensue.[30] Like von Trott, Moltke proposed to establish a 'supreme legislature' – that is, a European parliament – and he was daring enough to demand that it was to be elected not by the regional administrative units that would replace the inherited nation states, but by individual citizens. Thus, he anticipated the direct vote to the European parliament, enacted five decades later.[31]

The third Kreisau meeting, in June 1943, dealt with the details of a future European economy, including a European economic division of labour, the resolution of the tensions within a common agricultural market and the problems of surplus production. It also demanded common policies for taxation, finance and traffic as a precondition for the gradual amalgamation of the national economies.[32] Meanwhile both the Kreisau Circle and Goerdeler's group had come around to the idea that a European currency union and even a common currency should be established. This, however, reflects the extent to which the independence of non-German currencies in wartime Europe had become fictitious.

Originally, Goerdeler and his followers were reluctant to follow the path of the rather more radical Kreisau Circle's proposals for a future Europe. But after 1942 they continually adapted their position step-by-step to that of the Kreisau Circle. This could also be seen with respect to the envisaged domestic reforms, where something like a convergence of opinions of the initially rival opposition groups took place. From the start Goerdeler rejected the autarkic position of the German Government and was opposed to its excessive armament expenditures. He demanded instead the return to international economic cooperation and the establishment of a negotiated system of currency relations.[33] By demanding close European economic cooperation Goerdeler became totally isolated as a political adviser to Hitler's cabinet, but he still believed nevertheless in the possibility of convincing the leading circles of the

Third Reich of the soundness of his ideas. Thus early in 1939 he proposed establishing a European union comprising France, Great Britain and Germany as the nucleus which would eventually bring about a reform of the currency systems, a free market economy and a coordination of the legislation of the respective states.

More or less contemporaneous with the Kreisau Circle's third meeting, Goerdeler urgently supported the elimination of European customs' barriers and called for a common economic law, coordinated traffic systems and the establishment of a common Ministry for Economy and Foreign Affairs. He even accepted that the future confederation of European states, relying as it would on the voluntary alignment of sovereign nation states, should possess real power and, in complete contrast to his earlier position, that members would have to transfer to the European authority essential prerogatives, such as the maintenance of independent armed forces.[34]

There was some dispute among the resisters about where the boundaries of the future European state should be drawn, and whether Russia should belong to it. At the start Moltke – and this was true also of Goerdeler and Hassell – expected a global subdivision consisting of an Anglo-Saxon union with the centre of gravity in the USA and a united continental Europe including parts of Africa, while Russia's future remained open, with the expectation that it would be something of a protégé (*Schutzbefohlener*) of the European zone, as it was described in 'The Situation, the Goals and the Tasks' (1941).[35] Only later did the inclusion of Great Britain and Russia became a commonly held conviction among the resisters.

Significant for the gradual retreat of the national conservative resisters from the traditional concept of the nation state was the impact of Christian ideas, and this development was related to the increasing public influence of the churches in Germany during the later years of the war. In this respect, the contribution of the ecumenical movement to the conceptualisation of a future European community cannot be overestimated.[36] Simultaneously, a strong ideological undercurrent, particularly in Roman Catholic circles but also in the Protestant camp, came out in favour of the rather vague idea of the '*Abendland*' (the west), an idea that signified a regeneration of the common occidental Christian heritage of Europe.[37] Theodor Steltzer, a leading member of the Kreisau Circle, gave expression to those ideas when he conceived of the future of the Continent under the formula 'Europe under the Cross'.[38]

It is misleading to regard the plea for a common Europe by the national conservative opposition as simply the result of the prospect of the imminent defeat of Germany and the obvious fact that there was not the slightest chance of restoring Germany's past hegemony. While deliberations of this kind had some impact, the principal weight of the resisters' decision to overcome nationalist mentalities and to pave the way for supranational cooperation should not be dismissed out of hand. Goerdeler's memorandum, written early in 1944 under the title 'Praktische Massnahmen zur Umgestaltung Europas' ('Practical Steps to Re-Order Europe'), argued correctly that the regeneration of the inner and living unity of Europe had remained the only possible perspective for meaningful political action.[39] The Kreisau Circle in particular dropped the idea that there existed a peculiarly 'German way' with respect to national institutions, and embraced a pan-European concept, although its philosophy remained deeply embedded in the German idealist heritage.

The liberal resistance group established by Hans Robinsohn and Ernst Strassmann promulgated similar ideas. When Strassman was taken into custody by the Gestapo in 1942, Robinsohn, who was of Jewish descent, fled to Denmark and joined with the national conservative opposition. In the autumn of 1941 Robinsohn had already predicted that after the war a confederation of the European states would come into being, and he pointed to the erosion in practice of the principle of nation state sovereignty under the impact of the war.[40]

Originally Moltke and his friends had hoped that at the end of the war the opponents of war would gain the political lead in all the countries of Europe and that they would effectively call for a truly European peace agreement. This perspective appeared rather bleak after the declaration on unconditional surrender at Casablanca, which deliberately excluded any German initiative, even after the defeat of the Nazi regime. Despite this changed situation, the Kreisau Circle clung to the hope that the victors would be attracted to the common European impetus to achieve a fundamentally new order and, therefore, would not deny its necessity. Moltke, realised, however, that the German contribution to the establishment of the new European order he envisaged would have to be made within the framework of the 'tension zone of the American–English–Russian triangle' (*Spannungsfeld des amerikanisch–englisch–russischen Dreiecks*). In conjunction with this, Moltke was able to argue that 'Germany's European right for co-determination' appeared as an indisputable precondition for any peace in Europe.[41]

The instructions to the regional administrator (*Landesverweser*), which had been laid down in the spring of 1943, included the continuation of the work of the small and middle-sized communities even under Allied occupation. Moltke and his fellow resisters were truly convinced that an actual and ongoing domestic reform within Germany would have positive effects on the process of regenerating confidence at the European level. In particular, the principle of 'personal socialism in conjunction with the creation of an overall self-government' was perceived as a way of solving the European social and economic crisis and would serve as Germany's 'constructive contribution' to achieving the reconstruction of a renewed Europe.[42]

In the immediate war situation the utopian element of all these ideas is obvious, but their visionary strength deserves serious attention. The unrestricted call for a pan-European solution preceded the almost complete erosion of nationalist sentiments in post-war Germany, and thus constituted a mentality marked by a high degree of national indifference, which prevails still today. (There was, of course, no direct connection between the views of the German resistance movement and post-war developments in this respect.) Yet, in so far as the history and ideology of the resistance can be studied from the viewpoint of potential alternatives to fascist politics in Germany, it indicates that the process of effective denationalisation had already begun under the conditions of the regime, and that it emerged as a consequence of the ruthless and criminal exploitation of national values by the Nazi regime. Secondly, although the attempts of the German resistance to develop their idea of the new Europe of the future contained illusory and utopian elements, they nevertheless reflect the conviction that there could be something like a common European identity, and with it the potential for a solidarity that exceeded mere market relations and material interests. The challenge of the Nazi assault on Europe brought this into the foreground, and there are some indications that similar developments could occur again in our time.

Notes

1 See Hermann Graml, 'Die außenpolitischen Vorstellungen des deutschen Widerstands', in Hermann Graml (ed.), *Widerstand am Dritten Reich: Probleme, Ereignisse, Gestalten* (Frankfurt and Main, 1994), pp. 92–139, who dates from 1966. The rather sketchy survey by Rainer Blasius is no substitute for a comprehensive analysis: Rainer Blasius, 'Deutschland und Europa im Denken des Widerstandes', in Michael Kissener, Harm-Hinrich Brandt and Wolfgang Altgeld (eds), *Widerstand in Europa: Zeitgeschichtliche Erinnerungen und Studien* (Konstanz, 1995), pp. 39–65.

2 Cf. Alfred Delp, 'Betrachtungen über Europa in der Neujahrsnacht, 1.1.1945', in Delp, *Gesammelte Schriften*, ed. Roman Bleistein (Frankfurt and Main, 1984), vol. 3, pp. 78 ff.; cf. Roman Bleistein, *Alfred Delp: Geschichte eines Zeugen* (Frankfurt am Main, 1989), pp. 362f.

3 Dietrich Bonhoeffer, *Gesammelte Schriften*, ed. Eberhard Bethge (Munich, 1965), vol. 1, pp. 362f.; see Klemens von Klemperer, *German Resistance Against Hitler: The Search for the Allies Abroad 1938–1945* (Oxford, 1992), pp. 272f.

4 Graml, 'Außenpolitische Vorstellungen', p. 111.

5 *Hitler: Reden und Proklamationen 1932–1945*, ed. Max Domarus (Munich, 1965), vol. 2, part 1, p. 1383.

6 Cf. Karl Heinz Roth, '"Generalplan Ost" – "Gesamtplan Ost": Forschungsstand, Quellenprobleme, Neue Ergebnisse', in Cordula Tollmien, Mechthild Rössler and Sabine Schleiermacher (eds), *Der 'Generalplan Ost': Hauptlinien der nationalsozialistischen Planungs- und Vernichtungspolitik* (Berlin, 1993), pp. 25ff.

7 Klaus Scholder (ed.), *Die Mittwochsgesellschaft: Protokolle aus dem geistigen Deutschland* (Berlin, 1982), 1005th session, 11 December 1940, pp. 261f.; and see

Lothar Gruchmann, *Nationalsozialistische Großraumordnung: Die Konstruktion einer deutschen Monroe-Doktrin* (Stuttgart, 1962).

8   Hans W. Neulen, *Europa und das Dritte Reich: Einigungsbestrebungen im deutschen Machtbereich 1939–1945* (Munich, 1987), pp. 25f.; Ludolf Herbst, *Der totale Krieg und die Ordnung der Wirtschaft: Die Kriegswirtschaft im Spannungsfeld von Politik, Ideologie und Propaganda 1939–1945* (Stuttgart, 1982), pp. 127ff.; see Gerhard Hass and Wolfgang Schumann (eds), *Anatomie der Aggression* (East Berlin, l972).

9   See chapter 3 in Sabine Gillmann (ed.), *Politische Briefe und Schriften Carl Friedrich Goerdelers* (Munich, 2003).

10 Statement by Ulrich von Hassell, 23 February 1940, in *Europa-Föderationspläne der Widerstandsbewegung 1940–45: Eine Dokumentation*, ed. Walter Lipgens (Munich, 1968), p. 107; see Graml, 'Außenpolitische Vorstellungen', p. 281.

11 Delp, 'Betrachtungen über Europa', p. 78.

12 Fritz Dietlof von der Schulenburg, Memoir, titled 'Städte-Ringe' (summer 1943), BA Koblenz, Nachlass von der Schulenburg; see Hans Mommsen, 'Fritz-Dietlof Graf von der Schulenburg und die preußische Tradition', in Mommsen, *Alternative zu Hitler: Studien zur Geschichte des deutschen Widerstandes* (Munich, 2000), p. 255.

13 See Neulen, *Europa und das Dritte Reich*, pp. 29f.

14 Trott to Percy E. Corbett, June 16, 1941, quoted in Klemperer, *German Resistance*, p. 281.

15 See Sheila Grant Duff, *Fünf Jahre bis zum Krieg (1934–1939)* (Munich, 1978), pp. 54f., 66.

16 Wilhelm Ritte von Schramm (ed.), *Beck und Goerdeler: Gemeinschaftsdokumente für den Frieden, 1941–1944* (Munich, 1965), pp. 98f.; see Hans Mommsen, 'Gesellschaftsbild und Verfassungspläne des deutschen Widerstandes', in Mommsen, *Alternative zu Hitler*, pp. 154f.

17 *Ibid.*, pp. 99f.

18 *Ibid.*, p. 88.

19 *Ibid.*, pp. 96ff.; Wilhelm Ernst Winterhager, 'Politischer Weitblick und moralische Konsequenz: Der Kreisauer Kreis in seiner Bedeutung für die deutsche Zeitgeschichte', *Geschichte in Wissenschaft und Unterricht*, 38 (1987), pp. 402–17.

20 Antonia Leugers, *Georg Angermaier 1913–1945: Katholischer Jurist zwischen nationalsozialistischem Regime und Kirche* (Mainz, 1994), pp. 108ff.

21 The leaflet is reprinted in *Europa-Föderationspläne*, p. 189; see Hans Mommsen, 'Der deutsche Widerstand gegen Hitler und die Wiederherstellung der Grundlagen der Politik', in *Die Weiße Rose und das Erbe des deutschen Widerstandes* (Munich, 1993), pp. 211f.

22 Helmuth James von Moltke, 'Ausgangslage, Ziele und Aufgaben, April 24, 194', in Ger van Roon (ed.), *Neuordnung im Widerstand: Der Kreisauer Kreis innerhalb der deutschen Widerstandsbewegung* (Munich, 1967), pp. 412f.

23 See Neulen, *Europa und das Dritte Reich*, pp. 26f.

24 Van Roon (ed.), *Neuordnung im Widerstand*, pp. 512f., 515; see memorandum 'Gedanken zur europäischen Ordnung' (presumably 1941), in *Dossier: Kreisauer Kreis. Dokumente aus dem Widerstand gegen den Nationalsozialismus*, ed. Roman Bleistein (Frankfurt, 1987), p. 129.

25 For the biographical background see van Roon (ed.), *Neuordnung im Widerstand*, pp. 61ff.

26 Letter to Lionel Curtis, in Michael Balfour, Julian Frisby and Freya von Moltke (eds), *Helmuth James von Moltke 1907–1945: Anwalt der Zukunft* (Stuttgart, 1975), p. 185.

27 Ernst Wilhelm Winterhager, *Der Kreisauer Kreis: Porträt einer Widerstandsgruppe* (Berlin, 1985), pp. 223–8.

28 Klemperer, *German Resistance*, pp. 231ff.

29 Adam von Trott zu Solz, 'Memorandum für die britische Regierung, April 1942', in van Roon, *Neuordnung im Widerstand*, p. 573; see Trott, 'Bemerkungen zum Friedensprogramm der amerikanischen Kirchen, November 1943', *ibid.*, pp. 580ff.

30 Hans Rothfels, 'Trott und die Außenpolitik des Widerstandes', *Vierteljahrshefte für Zeitgeschichte*, vol. 12 (1964), pp. 315f.; these were notes by Trott made during the winter of 1939–40; see 'Memorandum for Sir Stafford Cripps', *Vierteljahrshefte für Zeitgeschichte*, 7 (1959), pp. 318ff.

31 Cf. Hans Mommsen, 'Der Kreisauer Kreis und die künftige Neuordnung Europas', in Mommsen, *Alternative zu Hitler*, pp. 214f.

32 Moltke, 'Fragestellung zur Wirtschaftspolitik, June 14, 1943', in van Roon (ed.), *Neuordnung im Widerstand*, pp. 552f.

33 See his memorandum sent to Hitler on October 26, 1935, in Bundesarchiv Berlin-Lichterfelde, R 43 II/318a.

34 Carl Goerdeler, 'Friedensplan (August 1943)', in Gerhard Ritter, *Carl Goerdeler und die deutsche Widerstandsbewegung* (Munich, 1964), p. 556; see Goerdeler, 'Die Aufgaben der deutschen Zukunft', in *Europa-Föderationspläne*, pp. 171f.

35 Cf. van Roon (ed.), *Neuordnung im Widerstand*, pp. 227, 512.

36 Klemperer, *German Resistance*, pp. 226ff.

37 See the brillant analysis by Dagmar Poepping, *Abendländisches Denken in der Zwischenkriegszeit* (Hamburg, 2003).

38 *Dossier: Kreisauer Kreis*, p. 261.

39 *Europa-Föderationspläne*, pp. 166f.

40 See Horst R. Sassin, *Liberale—m Widerstand. Die Robinsohn–Strassmann-Gruppe 1934–1942* (Hamburg, 1993), pp. 228, 241f.

41 *Dossier: Kreisauer Kreis*, p. 252.

42 'Erste Weisung an die Landesverweser, August 9, 1943', in van Roon (ed.), *Neuordnung im Widerstand*, pp. 56f.; 'Denkschrift zur Befriedung Europas (spring 1943)', in *Dossier: Kreisauer Kreis*, p. 255.

Personal reflections on Ian Kershaw

John Breuilly

I was appointed lecturer in history at the University of Manchester in October 1972. Those were times of expansion: I was one of three appointments made at the same time. We joined a department with many colleagues just a few years older than myself and with only a thin layer of established senior people. Ian Kershaw was one of those colleagues.

The department was divided into four sections: ancient, medieval, economic and modern. I was in the modern section. Ian had been appointed in 1968 to the medieval section, though with a foot in the economic section as he taught medieval economic history. In 1974 a new post for the modern section was created. Ian, whose research interests had been moving from medieval England to the Third Reich, applied. I was on the appointing panel. There was a strong field of candidates. Ian's position was a strange one, the reverse of other candidates who had doctoral research in modern European history but few publications and little teaching and administrative experience. Ian had impressive publications, teaching and administrative experience but had only just started research on the Third Reich. However, Ian's research idea was fascinating and important. To investigate *public* or *popular* opinion in the Third Reich implied that this was a subject in its own right, not merely the manipulated product of the regime or an aggregate of atomised, private views held by individuals. It offered a way of connecting everyday life to the politics of the regime, history from below and above. Coupled with what we knew of Ian's record of achieving the tasks he set himself, this was decisive. So Ian moved from being lecturer in History at Manchester University to become . . . lecturer in History at Manchester University. That decision proved far more successful than any of us could have dreamt at the time.

Thus Ian and I became close colleagues, sharing responsibility for teaching of modern German history as well as cooperating in many other ways. In retrospect the 1970s appear as a time of innocence. Research was not formally assessed as part of an elaborate game with financial rewards and penalties but was an activity pursued purely for its own sake. Whether one could nowadays make the kind of switch Ian did in 1972 is debatable; there would be questions of lost research output to consider as one prematurely liquidated one invest-ment and speculated in another. Postgraduates were not eagerly sought-after sources of revenue but enthusiastic and talented individuals who attached themselves to an academic supervisor. We taught courses to undergraduates; we did not deliver modules to 'customers'. With little professorial intervention and apparent indifference on the part of the university administration, we could teach pretty much whatever we wanted, provided our colleagues agreed. My first book *Nationalism and the State* arose out of such teaching. Ian read the whole work in draft and we discussed it many times.

We taught across a wide range and did not regard this as a distraction from narrowly focused research. I taught European history from 1500 and national-ism in modern world history. Chronologically that was very narrow compared to Ian who went from the decline of Rome to the 1970s. One book he should write might be entitled *Inflation from Emperor Diocletian to Harold Wilson*. Ian's research training cultivated the meticulous source criticism central to medieval history but also the use of powerful concepts needed to handle the massive documentation and historiography of the Third Reich. To rejig the old maxim: 'Who knows the Third Reich who only the Third Reich knows?' Ian is not one of those 'experts' who lack that necessary perspective. When he writes of charismatic authority in relation to Hitler he also knows about how princely power worked in medieval Europe. When he expresses scepticism about the fashionable idea of national socialism as 'political religion' he does so as some-one who has closely studied religious institutions (especially Bolton Priory) and deeply Christian societies.

Friends as well as colleagues, we discussed with passion our common inter-ests. Some of the best discussions took place in the pub after a game of foot-ball. We were among the founding figures of the History All-Stars Five-a-Side squad. (The two editors of this volume were later acquisitions.) I was brought up in the belief that football was the only worthwhile winter sport. I knew rugby only as an alien middle-class sport imposed by grammar school. When I met Ian I learnt there was a popular northern English variant to this, a strange game where men appeared to lay eggs as they back-heeled the oval ball. I never did convert to this creed and never joined Ian and other believers in their pil-grimages to that sacred site, the Hotel George in Huddersfield where, on 29 August 1895, rugby league formally originated as a breakaway from rugby union or their regular visits to Watersheddings, the Oldham Rugby League Club stadium until Good Friday 1995. Nevertheless, I understood the deep and knowledgeable enthusiasm for a game played when young, when great sports-men rather than intellectuals were the heroes to emulate. Short of a playing career Ian fancied the job of rugby correspondent for the *Oldham Evening*

News. His classic essay 'Ellery Hanley's haircut', published in a distinguished but alas ephemeral Manchester journal glorying in the title *Debris*, shows what success he could have made of such a career.

We took our game seriously, the only way to play. I vividly recall the two of us sitting slumped in the changing room, grieving after defeat. I also remember pick-up games where Ian selected the thugs and I chose the creative players. Ian's team always won. Maybe it reflects on why I chose nineteenth- and Ian twentieth-century Germany to research.

After the game conversation would turn from sport to history. We didn't talk about students, university affairs, or colleagues. But equally we did not just discuss research. That always was important but placed within more far-ranging conversations which comes back, I think, to the ethos of broad as well as specialised undergraduate teaching. Once we experimented with a series of joint seminars with the Department of Government as a way of providing intellectual support to the undergraduate degree in Politics and Modern History and to bring colleagues together across departmental and discipline divisions. It was decided we would discuss the recent books of Perry Anderson, *Passages from Antiquity to Feudalism* and *Lineages of the Absolute State*. There were three seminars. At each a political theorist (Mike Evans) placed Anderson's arguments within the framework of Marxist theory. At the first meeting an ancient historian, Alan Bowman, examined Anderson's arguments about the demise of Rome. At the second, Ian put on his medieval hat and analysed Anderson on feudalism. At the third, with Anderson present, I critiqued the *Lineages* volume. Discussion ranged across Marxist theory, state formation and change, and some two thousand years of European history. There was a proposal that a special volume of *Past and Present* publish the critiques, other contributions and a response from Anderson. It fell through which was a shame because those papers constituted a more sustained critical analysis than any published reviews of what remains the most ambitious attempt at an interpretative Marxist history of Europe up to the era of bourgeois revolutions. This project arose not out of specific research interests but as an aspect of trying to teach and understand history in a much broader way. Another example of this is the way for a good number of years Ian and I alternated in organising a series of talks on German history in cooperation with the Goethe Institute in Manchester.

There was a price to pay for this ethos. In what was essentially a culture of trust, some academics did little research or, even if they did, failed to publish. Their knowledge and ideas extended no further than their best students and most attentive colleagues. Some academics taught badly and were never brought to account. Too much time was devoted to undergraduates. As Ian has caustically observed, being an academic is easy if you don't do the job properly. But for those academics who did 'do it properly', as well as for committed postgraduates who needed little more than penetrating and intelligent conversations with older and more experienced historians, those were good times.

They ended abruptly in 1981 when the Thatcher Government made the first deep cuts in university funding. It did not impact immediately in History at Manchester because the university relied on early retirements as the principal way of reducing staff. Given that the Department of History had exported many senior people to chairs elsewhere and replaced them with young lecturers, there was little scope for such a policy. It was slow-growing departments with older age profiles which bore the brunt. However, the Department of History would be badly affected in the medium-term as it continued to export senior people but took a back seat when new appointments began to be made.

In 1987 Ian, another Manchester colleague, and myself were all on a shortlist of four for the chair of modern history at the University of Nottingham. By then Ian had published books based on his research into popular opinion in the Third Reich. He was offered and accepted the post, and our time as colleagues came to an end. However, Ian and Betty continue to live in Manchester. He has been a staunch Lancastrian all his life, with just postgraduate time in Oxford and various spells of research and teaching in Germany. There were various pubs just five minutes walk from our houses. We met regularly for an evening's intense discussion, mainly about German history. We continued to swap plans and drafts of our work. To this day Ian remains the first person I turn to for a penetrating opinion of my ideas. In 2002, when I was working on a book project in Berlin, the first critical opinions I looked at again were those Ian had given.

Very often such opinion takes the form of a bucket of cold water. Ian's down-to-earth realism, dry sense of humour and phlegmatic temperament seem to me to be essential qualities for his chosen field of research in the Third Reich. It is a subject which so often induces either a hectoring, moralising style or a depressing, monotonic recital. Too much idealism leads either to dismissing a whole society as pathological or seizing upon examples of non-conformity so as to detach the regime from at least some groups within German society. Ian's approach negates such moralism or polarising, seeking instead to grapple with the complexities of a history which appeared to most of its participants as a cage in which they had to live rather than something to affirm or reject. Yet this realist is also an emotional man, an avid fan of Wagner (along with rugby league, an enthusiasm I do not share) who avoids a soulless, dutiful bearing of witness.

Such an approach can run the danger of turning into an antiquarian narrative of the 'ordinary' and 'everyday'. What makes Ian's work special is that, coupled with scholarly empiricism, the explicit use of concepts enables him to place massive amounts of evidence within a meaningful framework. The concept of charisma is used – as Weber meant it to be used – to analyse a mode of power. However, in Weber's hands it remained a residual category exemplified through impressionistic sketches, subject to some brilliant speculations (e.g. about the problems of routinisation and succession) and confined to the perspective from above, part of a sociology of domination. Ian took the concept, related it in detail to one case and explored the perspective from below, turning it into part of a sociology of compliance. This brilliant and sustained deployment of a few powerful concepts later enabled Ian to write an 'anti-biographical' biography of Hitler. To return to the personal, I think the capacity to do this kind of work was fostered by the culture of broad but demanding undergraduate teaching and an atmosphere of warm collegiality, a term I once heard aptly defined as 'trust and the expectation of generosity'. At the same time, Ian is not seduced by concepts; they are intellectual devices designed to do jobs of work.

They have done very considerable work. I think only fellow professional historians can fully appreciate just how much research and conceptualising goes into the books Ian has published. The learning is worn lightly, as learning should be. Footnotes do the humble job of enabling the reader to check the evidence; they aren't occasions for digressions or displays of erudition. Furthermore, this is work that involved long periods of research in Germany. The field is one in which many historians as well as others take an intense interest, in Germany, Britain and many other parts of the world. (I once heard the claim that there are more US historians studying the Third Reich than there are German academic historians – period.) The sources involved, the rapidly expanding secondary literature, the many controversies: all this ensures that such work is read in a close and detailed way. To produce as much original and significant work on the Third Reich as Ian has done, culminating in what will long be the best study of Hitler, is extraordinary.

I left Manchester for Birmingham in 1995. I try as often as possible to get up to Manchester to meet with Ian and other colleagues. It says much about the collegiality generated in those days that a few times a year a dozen or so of us still gather together. In the last few years Ian has become a celebrity with the immense success of his Hitler biography, as consultant to the rightly acclaimed television series *The Nazis: A Warning from History*, and recognition in the form of a knighthood. Yet he remains the same man I have always known: undemonstrative, shrewd, realistic, a good friend who listens as well as he talks, and whose work demonstrates that in significant historical writing brilliance and originality must be allied to hard work and plain truthfulness.

Ian Kershaw bibliography

Nadine Rossol

'Antisemitismus und Volksmeinung: Reaktionen auf die Judenverfolgung', in Martin Broszat and Elke Fröhlich (eds), *Bayern in der NS Zeit*, vol. 2: *Herrschaft und Gesellschaft im Konflikt* (Munich, 1979), pp. 281–348.

Der Hitler-Mythos: Volksmeinung und Propaganda im Dritten Reich (Stuttgart, 1980).

'Popular Opinion in the Third Reich', in Jeremy Noakes (ed.), *Government, Party and People in Nazi Germany* (Exeter, 1980), pp. 57–75.

'Alltägliches und Außeralltägliches: ihre Bedeutung für die Volksmeinung 1933–1939', in Detlev J. K. Peukert and Jürgen Reulecke (eds), *Die Reihen fast geschlossen: Beiträge zur Geschichte des Alltags unterm Nationalsozialismus* (Wuppertal, 1981), pp. 273–92.

'The Führer image and Political Integration: The Popular Conception of Hitler in Bavaria during the Third Reich', in Gerhard Hirschfeld and Lothar Kettenacker (eds), *Der Führerstaat: Mythos und Realität, Studien zur Struktur und Politik des Dritten Reiches* (Stuttgart, 1981), pp. 98–132.

'The Persecution of the Jews and German Popular Opinion in the Third Reich', *Yearbook of the Leo Baeck Institute*, 26 (1981), pp. 261–89.

'How Effective Was Nazi Propaganda?' in David Welch (ed.), *Nazi Propaganda: The Power and the Limitations* (Kent, 1983), pp. 180–205.

'1933: Continuity or Break in German History', *History Today*, 33:1 (1983), pp. 13ff.

'Ideology, Propaganda and the Rise of the Nazi Party', in Peter D. Stachura (ed.), *The Nazi Machtergreifung* (London, 1983), pp. 162–81.

Popular Opinion and Political Dissent in the Third Reich: Bavaria 1933–1945 (Oxford, 1983).

'Life in the Third Reich: The Hitler Myth', *History Today*, 35 (November 1985), pp. 23–9.

The Nazi Dictatorship: Problems and Perspectives of Interpretation, 4th edn (London, 2000 [1985]); German edn: *Der NS Staat: Geschichtsinterpretation und Kontroversen im Überblick* (Reinbeck, 1988).

'Widerstand ohne Volk? Dissens und Widerstand im Dritten Reich', in Jürgen Schmädeke and Peter Steinbach (eds), *Der Widerstand gegen den Nationalsozialismus: Die deutsche Gesellschaft und der Widerstand gegen Hitler*, 2nd edn (Munich and Zürich, 1986), pp. 779–98.

The Hitler Myth. Image and Reality in the Third Reich (Oxford and New York, 1987); German edn: *Der Hitler-Mythos: Führerkult und Volksmeinung* (Stuttgart, 1999).

'Hitler and the Germans', in Richard Bessel (ed.), *Life in the Third Reich* (Oxford, 1987), pp. 41–56.

'German Public Opinion during the Final Solution: Information, Comprehension, Reaction', in Asher Cohen, Joav Gelber and Charlotte Wardi (eds), *Comprehending the Holocaust: Historical and Literary Research* (Frankfurt, 1988), pp. 145–58.

'Hitlers Popularität: Mythos und Realität im Dritten Reich', in Hans Mommsen and Susanne Willems (eds), *Herrschaftsalltag im Dritten Reich, Studien und Texte* (Düsseldorf, 1988), pp. 24–96.

'Indifferenz des Gewissens: Die deutsche Bevölkerung und die "Reichskristallnacht"', *Blätter für deutsche und internationale Politik*, 11 (1988), pp. 1319–30.

'Le mythe du Führer et la dynamique de l'etat nazi', *Annales: Economies, Sociétés, Civilization. Melanges d'Historie sociale*, 43:3 (1988), pp. 583–614.

'The Churches and the Nazi Persecution of the Jews: A Review', *Yad Vashem Studies*, 19 (1988), pp. 427–37.

'How Necessary Is a Historicization of the Third Reich? A Survey of Some Recent Publications on Nazism', *European History Quarterly*, 19:3 (1989), pp. 395–406.

'The Nazi State: An Exceptional State?' *New Left Review*, 176 (1989), pp. 47–67.

'Social Unrest and the Response of the Nazi Regime', in Francis R. Nicosia and Lawrence D. Stokes (eds), *Germans Against Nazism: Nonconformity, Opposition and Resistance in the Third Reich: Essays in Honor of Peter Hoffmann* (New York and Oxford, 1990), pp. 157–74.

(Ed.), *Weimar: Why Did German Democracy Fail?* (London, 1990).

'Die Erforschung des Hitler Staates: Der Beitrag Martin Broszats', in Klaus-Dietmar Henke and Claudio Natoli (eds), *Mit dem Pathos der Nüchternheit: Martin Broszat, das Institut für Zeitgeschichte und die Erforschung der NS Zeit* (Frankfurt and New York, 1991), pp. 771–836.

Hitler: A Profile in Power (London, 1991; new rev. edn 2001); German edn: *Hitlers Macht: Das Profil der NS Herrschaft* (Munich, 1992).

'Der 30. Januar 1933: Ausweg aus der Staatskrise und Anfang des Staatsverfalls', in Heinrich August Winkler (ed.), *Die deutsche Staatskrise 1930–1933: Handlungsspielräume und Alternativen* (Munich, 1992), pp. 277–84.

Germany's Present, Germany's Past (London, 1992).

'Improvised Genocide? The Emergence of the "Final Solution" in the Warthegau', *Transactions of the Royal Historical Society*, 6th series, 2 (1992), pp. 51–78.

'Ideologe und Propagandist: Hitler im Lichte seiner Reden, Schriften, Anordnungen, 1925–1928', *Vierteljahreshefte für Zeitgeschichte*, 40 (1992), pp. 263–71; reprinted in English as: 'Ideologue and Propagandist: Hitler in the Light of His Speeches, 1925–1928', *Yad Vashem Studies*, 28 (1993), pp. 321–34.

'German Popular Opinion and the "Jewish Question", 1939–1943: Some Further Reflections', in Arnold Paucker, Silvia Gilchrist and Barbara Suchy (eds), *Die Juden im nationalsozialistischen Deutschland* (Tübingen, 1986), pp. 356–88; shortened in Herbert A. Strauss (ed.), *Hostages of Modernization: Studies on Modern Anti-Semitism, 1870–1933/39* (Berlin and New York, 1993), vol. 1, pp. 69–79.

'Arthur Greiser – Ein Motor der "Endlösung"', in Ronald Smelser, Enrico Syring and Rainer Zitelmann (eds), *Die braune Elite 2. 21 weitere biographische Skizzen* (Darmstadt 1993), pp. 116–27.

'"Normality" and Genocide: The Problem of "Historization"', in Thomas Childers and Jane Caplan (eds), *Re-Evaluating the Third Reich* (New York and London, 1993), pp. 20–41.

'"Working towards the Führer": Reflections on the Nature of the Hitler Dictatorship', *Journal of Contemporary European History,* 2 (1993), pp. 103–18; reprinted in Ian Kershaw and Moshe Lewin (eds), *Stalinism and Nazism: Dictatorships in Comparison* (Cambridge, 1997), pp. 88–106, and in Christian Leitz (ed.), *The Third Reich* (Oxford, 1999), pp. 153–78.

'Nationalsozialistische und stalinistische Herrschaft: Möglichkeiten und Grenzen des Vergleichs', *Bulletin d. Hamburger Instituts für Sozialforschung,* 16:5 (1994), pp. 55–64; reprinted in Eckhard Jesse (ed.), *Totalitarismus im 20. Jahrhundert: Eine Bilanz der internationalen Forschung* (Bonn, 1996), pp. 213–22.

'The Hitler Myth', in David F. Crew (ed.), *Nazism and German Society, 1933–1945* (London and New York, 1994), pp. 197–215.

'Totalitarianism Revisited: Nazism and Stalinism in Comparative Perspective', *Tel Aviver Jahrbuch für deutsche Geschichte,* 23 (1994), pp. 23–40.

'Der Überfall auf Polen und die öffentliche Meinung in Deutschland', in Ernst Willi Hansen, Gerhard Schreiber and Bernd Wenger (eds), *Politischer Wandel, organisierte Gewalt und nationale Sicherheit: Beiträge zur neueren Geschichte Deutschlands und Frankreichs. Festschrift für Klaus-Jürgen Müller* (Munich, 1995), pp. 237–50.

'The Extinction of Human Rights in Nazi Germany', in Olwen H. Hufton (ed.), *Historical Change and Human Rights,* Oxford Amnesty Lectures, 1994 (New York, 1995), pp. 217–46.

'"Cumulative Radicalisation" and the Uniqueness of National Socialism', in Christian Jansen, Lutz Niethammer and Bern Weisbrod (eds), *Von der Aufgabe der Freiheit: Politische Verantwortung und bürgerliche Gesellschaft im 19. und 20. Jahrhundert. Festschrift für Hans Mommsen zum 5. November 1995* (Berlin, 1995), pp. 323–36.

'Taking Stock of Totalitarianism: A Comparative View of Nazism and Stalinism', *Esprit,* 1–2 (Jan.–Feb. 1996), pp. 101–21.

'Führer und Hitlerkult', in Wolfgang Benz, Hermann Graml and Hermann Weiß (eds), *Enzyklopädie des Nationalsozialismus* (Stuttgart, 1997), pp. 22–33.

'Hitler and the Nazi Dictatorship', in Mary Fulbrook (ed.), *German History since 1800* (London, 1997), pp. 318–38.

(Ian Kershaw and Moshe Lewin) 'The Regimes and Their Dictators: Perspectives of Comparison', in Ian Kershaw and Moshe Lewin (eds), *Stalinism and Nazism: Dictatorships in Comparison* (Cambridge, 1997), pp. 1–25.

'Adolf Hitler: Das Wesen seiner Macht', *Damals,* 30:9 (1998), pp. 68ff.

Hitler 1889–1936: Hubris (London, 1998); German edn: *Hitler 1889–1936,* part 1 (Stuttgart, 1998).

'Bayern in der NS-Zeit: Grundlegung eines neuen Widerstandskonzeptes', in Horst Möller and Udo Wengst (eds), *50 Jahre Institut für Zeitgeschichte: Eine Bilanz,* edited for the Institut für Zeitgeschichte (Munich, 1999), pp. 315–29.

'Der Nationalsozialismus als Herrschaftssystem', in Dittmar Dahlmann and Gerhard

Hirschfeld (eds), *Lager, Zwangsarbeit, Vertreibung und Deportation: Dimension der Massenverbrechen in der Sowjetunion und in Deutschland 1933 bis 1945* (Essen, 1999), pp. 111–32.

Hitler 1936–1945: Nemesis (London, 2000); German edn: *Hitler 1936–1945*, part 2 (Stuttgart, 2000).

'Trauma der Deutschen', *Der Spiegel*, 19 (2001), pp. 62–75.

Index